D0638055

CORPORATE
COMMUNICATION

SUNY Series, Human Communication Processes
Donald P. Cushman and Ted J. Smith III, editors

CORPORATE COMMUNICATION

Theory
and
Practice

EDITED BY

Michael B. Goodman

WITHDRAWN

State University of New York Press

Published by
State University of New York Press, Albany

© 1994 State University of New York

All rights reserved

Printed in the United States of America

No part of this book may be used or reproduced
in any manner whatsoever without written permission
except in the case of brief quotations embodied in
critical articles and reviews.

For information, address State University of New York
Press, State University Plaza, Albany, N.Y. 12246

Production by Diane Ganeles
Marketing by Nancy Farrell

Library of Congress Cataloging-in-Publication Data

Corporate communication : theory and practice / edited by Michael B.
    Goodman.
        p. cm. — (SUNY series, human communication processes)
    Includes bibliographical references and index.
    ISBN 0-7914-2055-8 (acid-free). — ISBN 0-7914-2056-6 (pbk. : acid
-free)
    1. Communication in management.   2. Communication in
organizations.   3. Corporate culture.   I. Goodman, Michael B.
II. Series: SUNY series in human communication processes.
HD30.3.C67   1994
658.4'5—dc20   93-39171
                                                                    CIP

10 9 8 7 6 5 4 3 2 1

HD
30.3
.C67
1994

*FOR MY STUDENTS
AND COLLEAGUES*

Contents

Figures and Tables

Preface

During the last decade, companies expanded, restructured, downsized, right-sized, merged, and divested. In this complex and changing environment, the need for an organization to communicate its message efficiently, effectively, and coherently with its internal and external audiences continued to remain. Some might argue, and I think rightly so, that the need to communicate in times of major change is critical to the very survival of the organization.

In making sweeping organizational change, many corporations consolidated traditional disciplines such as public relations, employee communications, advertising, training, and press relations under one management function called corporate communications. This effort to centralize communication seemed to contradict a trend for decentralizing management functions. However, having a central group responsible for developing, projecting, and maintaining the corporation's image and culture makes management sense to many companies throughout the world.

The creation of a corporate communication group consolidates numerous disciplines to meet the strategic goal of developing and perpetuating a corporate image and culture through consistent and coherent messages throughout various media from print to television.

Communication has become more complex as businesses compete more in a global environment. And the complexity brought on by an explosion in the number of tools for communication—computers, corporate television, faxes, E-mail—has fueled the need for a corporation to consider its communications as central to its strategic plans. More coordination and integration of advertising and public relations programs, as well as coordination with internal and marketing programs, is a trend underscored by the results of The Association of National Advertisers 1992 survey of corporate advertising practices (26).

Corporate Communication offers a close look at the growing professional practice of corporate communication. It provides a discussion of critical functions and collects essays and case studies under nine categories arranged as chapters in this book.

Each category or chapter begins with an overview and is followed by essays and cases drawn from papers presented at the annual Conference on Corporate Communication at Fairleigh Dickinson University and printed in the refereed *Proceedings,* as well as a short list of readings for further study. The essays and case studies provide numerous perspectives on topics such as diversity, sexual harassment, global corporate communications, and communicating corporate culture. These essays are also meant to stimulate thought, provoke discussion, and encourage additional research into these topics.

As a discipline, corporate communication is more art than science; but its body of knowledge is as old as rhetoric itself. Its theoretical foundation is interdisciplinary, drawing from language and linguistics, anthropology, sociology, psychology, management and marketing. Its practice within contemporary corporations is seen as a strategic tool to lead, motivate, persuade, and inform numerous audiences inside and outside the organization. This book, and its companion, *Corporate Communication for Managers,* also published by SUNY Press, is intended to explore further corporate communication as a professional practice and an academic discipline.

I would like to thank my colleagues at Fairleigh Dickinson University for their active support and participation in our annual Conference on Corporate Communication: Dr. Martin Green, Communications Department Chair; Drs. Mary Cross and Walter Cummins, who have served as editors of the conference *Proceedings* every year since its beginning in 1988; Professors Harry Keyishian, Walter Savage (Emeritus), Don Jugenheimer, and Jack Colldeweih; Dr. Kenneth Greene, Social Science Department Chair; Dr. Richard Ottaway, Department of Management; Dr. Robert Chell, Psychology Department Chair; Dr. Peter Falley, Dean of the College of Arts and Sciences; Dr. Geoffrey Weinman, Vice President for Academic Affairs; and Francis Mertz, University President.

Also, thanks to the members of our board of corporate advisors for our graduate program in Corporate and Organizational Communication: Linn Weiss of Schering-Plough; David

Powell and Dennis Signorovitch of Allied Signal; Gus Merkel of AT&T Company; Robert Muilenberg of Jersey Central Power & Light; Hank Sandbach of Nabisco Brands; Dr. Craig Burrell of Sandoz; and Ronald Zier of Warner-Lambert Company.

Thanks to our Schering-Plough Distinguished Professors: Tom Garbett, Corporate Consultant and Former Executive at Doyle Dane Bernbach; Professor John Ryans of Kent State University; Sandy Sulcer, Vice Chairman and Cleve Langton, Executive Vice President of DDB Needham Worldwide.

I am grateful to the hundreds of professionals and academics who have presented papers at our annual conference and published their work in the *Proceedings*. It is the active support of these people and those professionals and academics who attended the conferences that encouraged me to write this book and collect in it essays from the conference.

Credit also goes to my fine graduate research assistants at Fairleigh Dickinson University: Laura Hagen, Jill Reed, Karen Glover, Jane Schlesser, Adam Yates, Priyanka Kapoor, Pat Siccone, and Natalie Vuksan; as well as our department secretary Chris Napolitano.

A special thanks to the graduate students I have had the pleasure of teaching in my graduate corporate communication seminars. I would also like to thank Dr. Don Cushman of SUNY at Albany.

And finally, thanks to my wife, Karen Goodman, my best critic, editor, and friend; and to my sons, David Goodman and Craig Cook.

Acknowledgments

"Technical Innovation for Revitalizing Corporate Culture: The Case of Desktop Publishing," Terri Toles-Patkin, Eastern Connecticut State University (1989). Dr. Toles-Patkin's article appeared in the *Proceedings of the Second Converence on Corporate Communication,* May 1989. It appears here with her permission.

"Groupware—One Experience," Steve Lang, Til Dallavalle, Alicia Esposito, Bellcore (1992). Steve Lang, Til Dallavalle, and Alicia Esposito's article was presented at the *Fifth Conference on Corporate Communication,* May 1992. It appears here with their permission.

"Communicating Sudden Change in Tasks and Culture: The Inglis Montmagny Story," Randall Capps, Western Kentucky University (1992). Dr. Capps's article appeared in the *Proceedings of the Fifth Conference on Corporate Communication,* May 1992. It appears here with his permission.

"Truth and Taste: High Ethical Standards for Communicators," William Buchholz, Bentley College (1992). Dr. Buchholz's article appeared in the *Proceedings of the Fifth Conference on Corporate Communication,* May 1992. It appears here with his permission.

"Corporate Language and the Law: Avoiding Liability in Corporate Communications," Kristen Woolever, Northeastern University (1989). Dr. Woolever's article appeared in the *Proceedings of the Second Conference on Corporate Communication,* May 1989; a slightly different version appeared in *IEEE Transactions on Professional Communication* 33:2, June 1990. It appears here with her permission.

"NIMBY: Defining and Dealing with the Not-in-My-Back-yard Syndrome," Nancy Blethen, Blethen Associates (1989). Nancy Blethen's article appeared in the *Proceedings of the Second Conference on Corporate Communication,* May 1989. It appears here with her permission.

"Using CEO's and Other Amateurs in Corporate Video," Richard Doetkott, Chapman University (1990). Professor Doetkott's article appeared in the *Proceedings of the Third Conference on Corporate Communication,* May 1990. It appears here with his permission.

"High-speed Management: A Revolution in Organizational Communication in the 1990s," Donald P. Cushman, SUNY at Albany (1992). Dr. Cushman's article appeared in the *Proceedings of the Fifth Conference on Corporate Communication,* May 1992. It appears here with his permission.

"Perspectives on Communicating Corporate Culture to Employee-Owners: The Weirton Steel Corporation Case," Jay Morris, Ohio University (1990). Jay Morris's article appeared in the *Proceedings of the Third Conference on Corporate Communication,* May 1990. It appears here with his permission.

"Analyzing Corporate Communications Policy Using Ethnographic Methods," Margaret Whitney, The Albany Company (1988). Dr. Whitney's article appeared in the *Proceedings of the First Conference on Corporate Communication,* May 1988. It appeared in different form in *IEEE Transactions on Professional Communication* 32:2 (June 1989). The article presented at the conference appears here with her permission.

"Perceptions of Communicative Competence in Organizational Settings: The Influence of Styles and Stereotypes," Ann Bohara and Patrick McLaurin, The Wharton School, University of Pennsylvania (1990). Dr. Bohara and Mr. McLaurin's article was presented at the *Third Converence on Corporate Communication,* May 1990 as "Styles and Stereotypes: The Relationships Between Corporate and Ethnic Communication." They have revised and updated their text for this book. The article appears here with their permission.

"Sexual Harassment and Immediacy Behaviors in the Multicultural Workplace: A Communication Paradox," Loretta

Harper and Lawrence Rifkind, Georgia State University (1992). Drs. Harper and Rifkind's article appeared in the *Proceedings of the Fifth Conference on Corporate Communication,* May 1992. It appeared in different form in *IEEE Transactions on Professional Communication* 35:4 (December 1992). The article presented at the conference appears here with their permission.

"Carnival, Resistance and Transgression in the Workplace," Jeanne Rogge Steele, The University of North Carolina at Chapel Hill (1992). Jeanne Steele's article appeared in the *Proceedings of the Fifth Conference on Corporate Communication,* May 1992. She has revised it for this book. The revised article appears here with her permission.

"Public Relations and Commercial Speech at the Crossroads: Impact on the Pharmaceutical Industry," Dulcie Murdock Straughan, University of North Carolina at Chapel Hill (1991). Dr. Straughan's article appeared in the *Proceedings of the Fourth Conference on Corporate Communication,* May 1991. It appears here with her permission.

"Case Study of a Public Affairs Program: *Time Magazine*'s Environmental Challenge," Nancy VanArsdale, East Stroudsburg University (1991). Dr. VanArsdale's article appeared in the *Proceedings of the Fourth Conference on Corporate Communication,* May 1991. It appears here with her permission.

"Using Corporate Video to Communicate Advanced Technology," Julie Longo, Martin Marietta Aerospace (1989). Julie Longo's article appeared in the *Proceedings of the Second Conference on Corporate Communication,* May 1989. It appears here with her permission.

"Using New Video Technology in External Organizational Communication: A Case Study of the Government Information Channel," Ronnie Bankston and Laura Terlip, University of Northern Iowa (1992). Drs. Bankston and Terlip's article appeared in the *Proceedings of the Fifth Conference on Corporate Communication,* May 1992. It appears here with their permission.

"Crisis Communication: Knowing How is Good; Knowing Why is Essential," David L. Sturges, et al., University of Texas

(1990). Drs. Sturges, Carrell, Newsom, and Marcus Barrera's article appeared in the *Proceedings of the Third Conference on Corporate Communication,* May 1990. This essay has appeared in different form in *SAM Advanced Management Journal* 56:3 (Summer 1991). The article as it appeared in the conference *Proceedings* appears here with their permission.

"They Speak English But ... : The United Kingdom as a Foreign Country," Nicholas D. J. Baldwin, Director, Wroxton College of FDU, England (1992). This essay is derived from Dr. Baldwin's graduate seminar lectures on international business and international corporate communication and culture at Wroxton College of Fairleigh Dickinson University. The essay appears here with his permission.

"The Politics of Broadcasting in the European Community: The Television Without Frontiers Directive," Mitch Baranowski, Up with People—Europe (1992). Mitch Baranowski's article appeared in the *Proceedings of the Fifth Conference on Corporate Communication,* May 1992. This essay has appeared in different form in *IEEE Transactions on Professional Communication* 36:1 (March 1993). The article as it appeared in the conference *Proceedings* appears here with his permission.

1

Overview: Corporate Communication

❖

Michael B. Goodman

What is Corporate Communication, and who does it?

Corporate communication, put simply, is the total of a corporation's efforts to communicate effectively and profitably. Obviously the actions any particular corporation takes to achieve that goal depends in large part on the character of the organization and its relationship with its suppliers, its community, its employees, and its customers. In practice, corporate communication is a strategic tool for the contemporary corporation to gain a competitive advantage over its competitors. Managers use it to lead, motivate, persuade, and inform employees and the public as well.

Corporate communication is more art than science. Its intellectual foundations and body of knowledge began with the Greeks and Romans—with rhetoric. Its theoretical foundation is interdisciplinary, using the methods and findings of:

- anthropology
- communications
- language and linguistics
- sociology
- psychology
- management and marketing

As a focus of academic study, corporate communication can be considered in the large context presented here, or it can be seen as a part of public relations. Given the business environment, the more encompassing definition works well in both the applied context of the workplace, as well as within the context of academic study.

Corporate communication is the term used to describe a wide variety of management functions related to an organization's internal and external communications. Depending on the organization, corporate communications can include such traditional disciplines as public relations, investor relations, employee relations, community relations, advertising, media relations, labor relations, government relations, technical communications, training and employee development, marketing communications, and management communications. Many organizations also include philanthropic activity, crisis and emergency communications, and advertising as part of corporate communications functions.

The people who perform these functions may have a variety of technical and professional backgrounds. Most have a firm grasp of the communication process, both written and oral, in a variety of contexts ranging from press releases to videotaped instructions; from a speech at a professional conference to a meeting of the local PTA; from a letter to a disgruntled customer to a letter to the editor of the *Wall Street Journal*. The messages and actions put in motion by these professionals, like any in a successful business, are part of the company's strategic plan, and are intended to achieve clear goals and objectives for the corporation.

What is the strategic importance of corporate communication?

In a management environment that extols the virtues of decentralization to meet the customer's needs quickly, many corporations consolidate their communications. A central group is responsible for communications. It develops, projects, and maintains the corporation's image and culture. For many organizations which operate globally, as well as local and regional ones, the value of a central management structure for communication makes sense.

The elements of communication continue to exert substantial influence in all transactions from simple customer questions of front-line sales and retail personnel, to the pressure negotiations involved in a multinational merger or restructuring. Corporations communicate through people, and the following communication forces need to be considered by individuals and by the organizations:

- language and linguistics
- technology and the environment
- social organization
- contexting and face-saving
- concepts of authority
- body-language and non-verbal communication
- concepts of time

These elements make up the core of communication skills for business on a national and international basis. A group within an organization can set policy and guidelines for written and oral communication. It can also develop training for the entire organization so that its decentralized operating and functional elements at a minimum can create communication expertise for its own autonomous activities and still maintain the larger corporate image. Corporations centralize communications to meet the strategic goal of developing and perpetuating a corporate image and culture through consistent and coherent messages through various media from face-to-face contact to print to video.

Corporations also use a corporate communications structure to manage the considerable complexity in the tools and the media for communications within the corporation itself:

- computer networks, Local Area Networks (LAN)
- interactive video on computers
- corporate TV
- FAX
- E-mail

Corporations also require a central corporate communications capability to communicate with the media on a routine basis, as well as in emergency and crisis situations.

Communication with various publics both local and global are more consistent and effective when the corporation delivers such messages with one clear voice. A central capability is useful for that, and it is essential for global operation. The need to translate a corporate message into another language and into another culture brings communication into the strategy for any transnational activity no matter how small.

Increased concerns among corporations for such issues as diversity and sexual harassment can be the responsibility of the corporate communications group. Corporate mission statements and company philosophies are, in ideal situations, the products of executives who recognize the strategic value of a clear statement of what the corporation stands for, its goals, and its practices. Clear understanding and articulation of the company mission is the cornerstone for building an image in the mind of employees as well as the general public.

The clear statement of the company mission builds the organizational culture among employees. Since the early 1980s, much has been written about corporate culture and its influence on the behavior of employees. How often do we hear of a company described in cultural terms; that is, by its shared values and beliefs? These same beliefs are often the center of advertising campaigns and motivational programs for employees.

A strong corporate culture also creates a recognizable and positive perception of the company among its suppliers, vendors, and customers. The "equity" a company image and culture amasses is then part of its value as a brand name product, stimulating customer loyalty.

A strong organizational identity is the result of a strong culture, as well as the other way around. It has become commonplace in the minds of company employees and the members of the community that the perception of strength and its reality are one and the same.

A strong image and culture cannot be imposed on a group of people, but it can be nurtured. Numerous corporations from American Airlines to Microsoft demonstrate this strength everyday and communicate it through their newsletters and releases, annual and quarterly reports, advertisements, videos, speeches, and interpersonal contacts with internal and external customers.

What is Corporate Communication Philosophy?

Speaking of business and philosophy often evokes jokes about other such oxymorons: *business ethics, military intelligence, political integrity.* Nevertheless, organizations large and small that have a strong commitment to communication with employees and the community have a definite philosophy of communication. Though many companies would not call it a philosophy, they may refer to it as their communication policy or their mission statement.

In both cases the philosophy may be articulated with statements of commitment to employees, customers, and other stakeholders, such as this statement from Levi Strauss & Co. of its aspirations:

ASPIRATIONS STATEMENT: LEVI'S

We all want a company that our people are proud of and committed to, where all employees have an opportunity to contribute, learn, grow and advance on merit, not politics or background. We want our people to feel respected, treated fairly, listened to, and involved. Above all, we want satisfaction from accomplishments and friendships, balanced personal and professional lives, and to have fun in our endeavors.

When we describe the kind of Levi Strauss & Co. we want in the future, what we are talking about is building on the foundation we have inherited: affirming the best of our company's traditions, closing gaps that may exist between principles and practices, and updating some of our values to reflect contemporary circumstances.

What type of leadership is necessary to make our Aspirations a Reality?

. . .

Communications: Leadership that is clear about company, unit, and individual goals and performance. People must know what is expected of them and receive timely, honest feedback on their performance and career aspirations.

Empowerment: Leadership that increases the authority and responsibility of those closest to our products and customers. By actively pushing responsibility, trust, and recognition into the organization, we can harness and release the capabilities of all our people. (Quoted in *Harvard Business Review,* September–October 1990, 135.)

The communications philosophy may also be implied in a company pledge, usually found in an annual report. This appeared in the 1990 annual report of Bristol-Myers Squibb Company after the two pharmaceutical giants merged:

To those who use our products ...
We affirm Bristol-Myers Squibb's commitment to the highest standards of excellence, safety and reliability in everything we make. We pledge to offer products of the highest quality and to work to keep improving them.

To our employees and those who may join us ...
We pledge personal respect, fair compensation, and equal treatment. We acknowledge our obligation to provide able and humane leadership throughout the organization, within a clean and safe working environment. To all who qualify for advancement, we will make every effort to provide opportunity.

To our suppliers and customers ...
We pledge an open door, courteous, efficient and ethical dealing, and appreciation of their right to a fair profit.

To our shareholders ...
We pledge a company-wide dedication to continued profitable growth, sustained by strong finances, a high level of research and development, and facilities second to none.

To the communities where we have plants and offices ...
We pledge conscientious citizenship, a helping hand for worthwhile causes, and constructive action in support of civic and environmental progress.

To the countries where we do business ...
We pledge ourselves to be a good citizen and to show full consideration for the rights of others while reserving the right to stand up for our own.

Above all, to the world we live in ...
We pledge Bristol-Myers Squibb to policies and practices which fully embody the responsibility, integrity and decency required of free enterprise it is to merit and maintain the confidence of our society.

(Annual Report, Bristol-Myers Squibb Company, ii.)

The written statement of corporate commitment to goals and values such as the statements of aspirations and pledges are often the external manifestation of the communication philosophy. It is not necessary for the written statement to exist to have a philosophy, but if the written statement does not represent some corporate behavior and belief and value system, its hollowness will be grossly apparent to everyone in and out of the organization.

In the late 1980s into the 1990s, Total Quality Management programs swept organizations in this country; from government, to defense; from pharmaceuticals to computers, almost every organization of any size has some form of Quality program. Such efforts are change agents intended to make the organization more efficient and productive, and as a result more profitable. Such programs emphasize teamwork and empowerment, and strive to create and perpetuate a humane environment in the workplace.

Communication is at the center of successful Quality programs. Newsletters, pamphlets, magazines, in-house television networks, videotapes, and questionnaires are some of the ways companies use to communicate the company values and beliefs. In addition to these "one-way" communications, organizations are now training their employees in methods of communication, problem-solving, interpersonal and small group participation, and the management skills that support the company culture. In practice we see the philosophy at work in how an organization communicates with its employees, its external audiences, the press, and foreign customers. We see how the corporation presents itself to the world at large. Some signs—the company buildings, vehicles, employee appearance—are easy non-verbal communications to observe. Others are harder to recognize at a glance—attitudes such as an innovative spirit, a commitment to community, and understanding of the coexistence of fair play and competition. These forces are there shaping the corporation, and they are manifested in the organization's communications.

Corporate communication, from the perspective of an anthropologist, encodes the corporate culture. Corporations that do not value communication highly are doomed to wither. George Bush lost the 1992 presidential election, according to Peggy Noonan, Ronald Reagan's speech writer, because the Bush administration failed to see the connection between words and deeds. ("Why Bush Failed," *New York Times,* November 5, 1992: A35 & "As Bush's Loss Sinks In, Finger Pointing Begins," *New York Times,* November 5, 1992: B5.)

Elements of corporate communication guide the development of a strong corporate identity, a reasonable corporate philosophy, a genuine sense of corporate citizenship, a strong relationship with the media, an appropriate and professional way of dealing with the press, a quick and responsible way of communicating in a crisis or emergency situation, and a sophisticated approach to global communications. Each of these is treated in the chapters that follow.

Further Reading

Browdy, E. W. *The Business of Public Relations*. New York: Praeger, 1987.

Conducting Research in Business Communication. Edited by Patty Cambell, et al. Urbana, IL: Association for Business Communication, 1988.

Falsey, Thomas. *Corporate Philosophies and Mission Statements: A Survey and Guide for Corporate Communicators and Management*. Westport, CT: Quorum Books, 1989.

Hayakawa, S. I. *Language in Thought and Action*. NY: Harcourt Brace, 1978.

Jackson, Peter. *Corporate Communications for Managers*. United Kingdom: Pitman Publishers, 1987.

Kinneavy, James L. *A Theory of Discourse*. Englewood Cliffs, NJ: Prentice-Hall, 1971; Norton (paper), 1980.

Lavin, Michael. *Business Information: How to Find It; How to Use It*. 2nd ed. Phoenix, AZ: Oryx Press, 1987, 1992.

Lewis, Philip. *Organizational Communication*. 3rd ed. NY: Wiley, 1987.

Robinson, Judith. *Tapping the Government Grapevine: The User-Friendly Guide to U.S. Government Information Sources*. Phoenix, AZ: Oryx Press, 1988.

Ruch, William V. *Corporate Communication*. Westport, CT: Quorum Books, 1984.

Schramm, Wilbur. *The Process and Effects of Mass Communication*. Urbana, IL: University of Illinois Press, 1954.

Shannon, Claude, and Warren Weaver. *The Mathematical Theory of Communication*. Urbana, IL: University of Illinois Press, 1949.

Swindle, Robert, and Elizabeth Swindle. *The Business Communicator*. Englewood Cliffs, NJ: Prentice-Hall, 1985.

Thayer, Lee. *Communication and Communication Systems*. Homewood, IL: Irwin, 1968.

Organizations Related to Corporate Communication

American Association of Advertising Agencies, 666 Third Ave., New York, NY 10017.

American Marketing Association, 310 Madison Ave., New York, NY 10017.

Center for the Advancement of Applied Ethics, Carnegie Mellon University, Pittsburgh, PA 15213.

International Association of Business Communicators, 870 Market Street, San Francisco, CA 94102.

International Communication Association, P.O. Box 9589, Austin, TX 78766.

Public Relations Society of America, 33 Irving Place, New York, NY 10003.

Society of Professional Journalists, 53 West Jackson Blvd., Suite 731, Chicago, IL 60604.

Speech Communication Association, 5105-E Backlick Rd., Annandale, VA 22003.

Women in Communications Inc., 2 Colonial Place, 2101 Wilson Boulevard, 4th Floor, Arlington, VA 22001.

2

Corporate Communication Practice

❖

Michael B. Goodman

Overview

As you might expect, the enormous changes in the work-place have had an impact on the communication practices of corporations and organizations. A terse "no comment" to an intrepid young newspaper or TV reporter no longer suffices as adequate communication policy or even effective corporate communication. Instead, a policy of developing strong channels of communication both internally and externally has become a standard for most organizations.

Not only has the nature of corporate communication changed over the last few decades, the type of people who create the company messages has changed as well. The typical corporate communication professional is college educated with a degree in the humanities. A major in journalism, English, marketing, public relations, or psychology is also common. Generally the practitioners are loyal company people with a long record in the organization. This reflects the importance of the strategic nature of the organization's communications.

Often the professional has had a minor in economics or business, or depending on the company's core business, some related technical discipline such as engineering or computer science. This may be in stark contrast to a previous generation of business professionals with a background in law or accounting who have handled the company communications.

Using a communication professional underscored another shift in corporate communications emphasis from a total focus on the investment community, to a broader interpretation of community which now includes all "stakeholders" as well as shareholders. A stakeholder is anyone who has a stake in the organization's success—vendors, customers, employees, executives, the local barber, police and the kid on the paper route.

The explosion in the number and type of media available for communications has also had an impact on the communication professional. In the past, mastery of the written word was more than enough. Writing is still the core skill on which all others are built, but a mastery of broadcast media is now essential to the creation of corporate messages for TV, radio, E-mail, cable news programs devoted to business topics, and public speeches.

Skills and Talents for Individuals

Many organizations use personality profile instruments in human resource management, such as Meyers Briggs, to find the right person for the job. A corporate communicator should have: written and verbal skills; face-to-face and telephone interpersonal skills; media savvy; curiosity; active listening skills; and an understanding of advocacy communications. In addition, corporate communications demands an ability to solve problems in groups, to understand media and communication technology, to work ethically, and to feel comfortable in an international, transnational, or global business environment.

However, writing remains the central talent to create any communication in a corporate context. Even though we have experienced great changes in the number of ways we can now communicate with one another, we are still human. Understanding the writing process (see figure 2.1) is fundamental to all types of communication and all types of media applications.

The writing process, which can also serve as a model for the communication process, emphasizes three main areas of analysis: audience, environment or context, and message. Corporations routinely target a message for a particular audience, meeting their needs while achieving the company goals. All successful communication, corporate or otherwise, must put human interaction at its center. Successful communication in a collaborative corporate environment seeks to win both for the organization and for its customers.

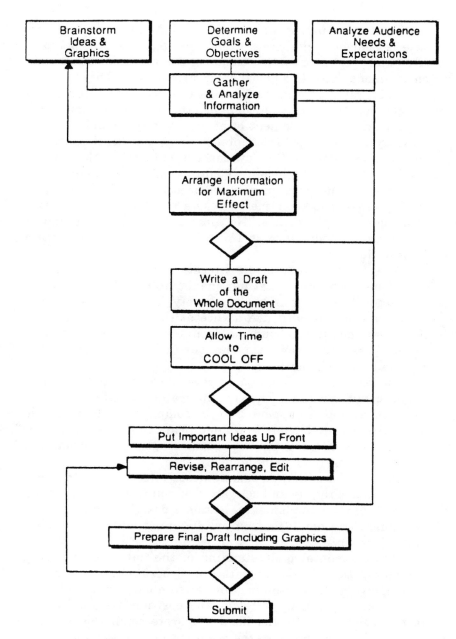

Figure 2.1. The Writing Process is Dynamic,
Incorporating Opportunities to Improve Text and Graphics

The type of person who has the skill and talent to collaborate is someone who can see an issue from several perspectives and create a message based on the analysis rather than on a personal bias. In a global environment, sensitivity to issues from several perspectives is critical since the culture, language, customs, and traditions of others have a tremendous impact on the development of an appropriate communication strategy. As discussed in chapter 9, using the direct approach, common practice in the low-context culture of the United States, used in a high-context culture such as Japan or the United Kingdom can be disastrous, or at least rude or "cheeky."

The ability to see a message as a graphic image or series of images is also essential. No American can deny the impact of our visual media such as TV on how we gather and process information.

America is a very media literate society. Several media critics have observed that our media literacy has turned us into an oral rather than a print society. That is certainly true for mass communication. A glance at the proliferation of TV networks and stations and the decline in the number of daily newspapers underscores the changes in how most Americans receive their information.

Curiosity is also a valuable personal attribute for professional communicators. The communicator must first have an interest in what is happening in the company and to its people and customers to be able to communicate that interest to others. Without interest, the writer's message is at best flat and bland, at worst phony and hollow.

Part of the ability to communicate effectively is the ability to listen carefully and actively. Communicators understand the need for this fundamental business practice: listen to your customers and employees. Active listening builds a relationship of trust.

A fundamental understanding of the nature of advocacy communications is also essential to corporate communicators. A company spokesperson may be called upon to put aside personal opinion in favor of a company position. Because of this fact of corporate life, the ideal corporate communicator is a person who has been with the organization for a long time.

I hesitate to use the word integrity, but any corporate spokesperson should instill trust in the audience. Without trust, the message is not likely to have the desired impact or much positive impact at all for that matter.

Small and Large Group Requirements

Corporations and organizations function as a group, and as groups of groups. Listen to the language used to describe a company: management team, quality circle, quality action team, management committee, board of directors, product management group, crisis committee; and even some older terms from the military influence—management, task force, strategic planning committee, tactical mission task force.

Whether your organization emphasizes old-style hierarchical leadership techniques, what have been called Theory X and Theory Y styles, or more contemporary consensus management styles, the ability to work effectively in and with groups is an essential element in a broader definition of corporate communication.

The Quality revolution that has swept the world in the last decade is built upon a foundation of shared commitment to corporate goals. Communication is a fundamental element in successful quality initiatives. Most communication at work occurs in small groups. The gatherings can be formal or informal, in twos and threes or more. Most of us learned the etiquette of small group behavior in a business setting. And each corporation has its own way of handling such group encounters. When we discuss corporate culture we will have more on this dimension of small group behavior.

Presentations: Meetings and Speeches

Most often we give few formal speeches, but we do give numerous presentations related to company actions and projects. Company and industries each have their own particular way of doing presentations. For example, in engineering or high tech firms, the presentation or briefing is straightforward and factual. Any visuals used tend to be overhead projections, or slides for a formal presentation. Management presentations tend to be brief and direct with the use of slides and video. More effort is spent on the glitz of the presentation than would be for an audience of technical experts.

The corporate communications professionals generally are involved in company-wide meetings, and are called upon to write the speeches of the corporate executives. Meetings now are generally face-to-face. Increasingly, future meetings will be on interactive video networks, computer networks, and by electronic mail. Such new technologies will change both the nature and the style of business meetings.

Selecting Media

The practice of corporate communications demands the professional to be able to determine the best media for both the message and the audience. High technology E-mail to low technology posters in the company lobby, a new company logo to a "dress-down" Friday for employees are possible media for corporate messages.

Selecting the appropriate medium for the message plays a central role in the success of the communication. It also can result in a cost-effective effort.

Selected Essays and Comment

The essay and case studies selected for this chapter are from the presentations at the annual Conference on Corporate Communication at Fairleigh Dickinson University. Each of the authors focuses on a part of communications practice in the context of some technological or cultural change in the organization and the business environment. Dr. Toles-Patkin discusses the way a new communication technology and set of tools such as desktop publishing can have an impact on a company's culture. In the first sample case, Steve Lang introduces a new technology for meetings, Groupware, and presents the findings of the research on this field. Dr. Capps's case shows how a company can change its style of management to embrace a self-directed team approach, and how the change is communicated.

Table 2.1

Selecting Appropriate Media

Medium	Application	Impact	Cost
T.V. Network Video	Company Annual Meetings; Motivational Messages; News conferences; Announcements; Training	High	High
Radio	Company Annual Meetings; Motivational Messages; Announcements; Training	Moderate	Moderate
Film	Company Annual Meetings; Motivational Messages; Company History; Training	Moderate	High
Print	Company Annual Reports; Newsletters; Magazines; Announcements; Policies; Reference Documents	Low	Low
Computer Network E-Mail	Time-Critical Messages; Proprietary Technical Information; Routine Memos and Action Items; Reference Material Policies	Moderate	High
Posters Displays	Motivational Messages Seasonal Announcements Safety and Quality Messages	Low	Low

Technological Innovation for Revitalizing Corporate Culture: The Case of Desktop Publishing

❖

Terri Toles-Patkin

This essay examines the mythic framework created by manufacturers of desktop publishing systems in advertisements that link the technology with the revitalization of organizational culture. A content analysis of advertisements published in 1986 and 1988 indicates a dual focus on the technological capabilities of desktop publishing systems and the increased creativity and efficiency to be enjoyed by employees.

The challenges faced by American business—declining productivity, foreign competition, and the like—have led to a recognition of the importance of the value system that provides the foundation for corporate cultures. Organizational cultures are based on a series of communication behaviors that establish, develop and maintain this system of shared beliefs and values. Ceremonies and heroes join together with mythic elements to create a symbolic framework that translates the central beliefs of the organization into measurable everyday actions.

Values, the basic beliefs of the organization, form the core of the culture and define the fundamental character of the organization. Values help employees define success in concrete terms. Heroes, particularly company founders or contemporary top management, provide role models and personify the values. Rites and rituals lend ceremony to the attainment of certain values, and the participants in the organization's communications network maintain the culture through symbolic

19

interpretations of cultural events. Finally, an organization's culture is influenced by its external environment, and the culture must respond to that environment (Deal and Kennedy; Harris; Peters and Austin).

Case studies have indicated that the emergence of a strong corporate culture is fundamental to organizational success. This culture provides cohesion among the social actors and the complex social relations that create the organization. The "fit" between an organization's culture and its day-to-day activities allows for the emergence of excellence (Ernest; Peters and Waterman).

Large-scale social trends, such as the shift to an information economy, have encouraged an interest in fostering individual growth within the organization while simultaneously meeting institutional goals. Empirical studies have shown that clearly articulated organizational values do in fact make a significant difference in the personal lives of employees as well as in the organization's performance overall (Naisbett and Aburdene; Posner et al.).

The stronger an organization's culture, the more difficult it is to change. Innovation typically occurs when the external environment is undergoing rapid change (such as technological development), when the organization is growing quickly, or when adherence to a new value structure is necessary for the survival of the organization (Deal and Kennedy).

The institutionalization of innovation, be it technological, managerial or economic, involves a constant revision of reality-constructs within the corporation. In addition to responding to pressures in the external environment, organizations create new environments by enacting new strategies for existence, defining new versions of reality (Kanter).

The daily culture of a corporation may diverge considerably from the stated organizational goals or guiding beliefs, creating a credibility gap. In order for corporate culture to transform a company, a solid connection must be made between core values and the everyday behavior of the firm (Davis). One method for accomplishing this is the use of particular technologies that lend support to the organization's goals and values. Desktop publishing is but one of several technologies that facilitate organizational change in response to alterations in corporate culture.

Desktop Publishing Technology

Desktop publishing (DTP) is a small, self-contained computer publishing system consisting of a personal computer, page composition software, and a laser printer. DTP systems are capable of producing near-typeset-quality text and graphics at relatively low cost. Desktop publishing permits the compilation and publication of a variety of documents ranging from brochures and newsletters to training manuals and annual reports.

Desktop publishing has become one of the fastest growing personal computer applications largely because it allows professional-looking documents to be created with information generated from commonly used word processing, database manager and spreadsheet packages. Some figures indicate that today's desktop publishing industry sales top $4 billion annually, and that market continues to increase (Brown and Gralla).

One proven application for desktop publishing has been in the corporate setting, where electronic publishing can reduce costs, allow publications to be produced more quickly, and enhance internal control over quality (Ambrosio). Desktop publishing permits cost saving and cost control in document production because the final editing and composing is done in-house, frequently by the author. The time and expense of sending the report out to be printed is eliminated, and control over the final product can belong to the writer. Reduced labor costs are an inevitable result, because of the reduction in both time and personnel required to cut and paste and layout documents. Desktop publishing can produce documents at a cost of $1–$3 per page, compared with $10–$15 for traditional publishing (Anonymous; Bove et al.; David et al.; Grout et al.).

Evolution of Desktop Publishing

In one sense, the evolution of desktop publishing has been gradual. Desktop publishing builds on the foundations laid by the historical growth of printing, incorporating technological advances from Gutenberg's time through today. Hot-type, cold-type, and lithography have all led to today's most common method of printing, phototypesetting (Smith). Desktop publishing differs from phototypesetting in the use of laser printers based on electrostatic printing technology, the printing method that drives copy machines. Computer control and memory are added, but the fundamental technology remains essentially identical.

In another sense, desktop publishing is entirely new. It could not exist without using low-cost microcomputer technology. There are three fundamental components in a DTP system: input devices, software packages, and laser printers. Each interacts with the other components to allow the user to create documents.

Input devices—computers, keyboards, the mouse—enter information into the DTP system for processing. This technology is not as critical for the success of desktop publishing as the other two components, but has contributed to the user-friendly nature of the technology, and thus influences its rate of adoption. Both the Apple Macintosh and IBM PCs and compatibles hold substantial portions of the market, and the Macintosh II and IBM PS/2 offer high-powered graphics and imaging that extend desktop publishing capabilities.

Page composition software is key to the emergence of DTP as a popular new microcomputer application, since it allows the user to merge graphics, word processing and other application programs and tie them all together. Page composition software differs from much other software currently on the market in that it is WYSIWYG, or "what you see is what you get." Essentially, the screen display reflects the appearance of the final output. In addition to the capability to merge application programs, WYSIWYG systems permit the user to view what the page will look like before a hard copy is made (Allen). Aldus Pagemaker and Ventura Publisher together comprise nearly all of this market.

Desktop publishing technology additionally relies on laser printers, which have more than twice the resolution of the best dot matrix printer, and which are capable of producing graphics, a task that daisy wheel printers cannot perform. Laser printers can produce high-quality text and graphics at a much higher speed than conventional printers, and their plummeting cost has encouraged a more widespread usage (Rogers). Laser printers print an entire page at one time, rather than entering each character individually as do conventional printers, and they are quiet, reliable and easy to maintain. A laser printer can produce upwards of eight pages per minute, and the quality closely resembles that from a typesetting machine. Despite criticisms from professional typesetters, the average reader rarely notices the difference in quality between typeset material and documents produced from a laser printer.

As today's desktop publishing market increases in size, the number of equipment manufacturers is decreasing. Vendors today are making more of an effort to respond to user needs, and standards (including screen resolution, screen size, grey scaling and price) are being discussed. Database publishing, image processing and networking capability appear to be on the horizon (Brown and Gralla; Lyons; Stromer).

The research explores the mythology of desktop publishing as communicated in advertisements presented by manufacturers. The symbolic processes embodied by this technology can be used to build organizational commitment, motivate personnel and convey a sense of corporate identity. Corporate culture is a device through which management can direct the course of their organizations over time.

Methodology

A content analysis of all desktop publishing advertising appearing in 1986 and 1988 in eight magazines aimed at consumer, business, computer and technology-oriented audiences was completed. The consumer market was represented by *Newsweek* and *Life,* the business market by *Business Week* and *Inc.,* the computer market by *Byte* and *Personal Computing,* and the technology-oriented market by *High Technology* and *Discover.* Only advertising that specifically referred to desktop publishing was included. Related ads (computer systems, copiers, electronic typewriters, software) were disregarded. Sentence level statements, captions and slogans were included in a formal content analysis, and an examination of the metaphors embedded in the visual images of the advertisements was also completed.

This research focuses on the contribution of the mythic framework communicated in the advertisements to the development and revitalization of organizational cultures. Due in part to the small sample size and in part to the necessity of uncovering the social meaning of linguistic features in context, a qualitative analysis proved to offer greater insight into the social and symbolic significance of desktop publishing in the corporate environment than did the more statistical portion of the content analysis. Accordingly, measures of contextual meaning are given priority over measures of recurrence.

As preliminary research, this effort concentrates on the flow of communication from desktop publishing manufacturers to their corporate clients. It is hoped that a companion study will examine this topic from the viewpoint of individual organizations, and will examine the implementation of desktop publishing in a variety of organizational settings.

Results

The verbal statements in the ads fell along seven dimensions: flexibility, technological capability, creativity, efficiency, low cost, professional image, and the futuristic nature of desktop publishing as a technology. It is important to note that most ads incorporated two or more of these themes simultaneously.

There was little difference between ads appearing in 1986 and 1988 other than that the 1988 advertising assumed that the reader possessed a greater familiarity with the concept and technology of desktop publishing. These ads tended to stress the technological capabilities of the advertisements more than did the earlier ads. Due to the small sample size, and similarities between the ads, both years are combined for this analysis. Unless otherwise stated, all statistics are based on a total sample of 675 statements.

Technology

The technological capability of desktop publishing equipment was emphasized in 27.3% of the cases examined. Many of the ads functioned to legitimate the technology, utilizing complex computer jargon to underline the power inherent in the system. High-resolution graphics, high-quality output and sophisticated software were all mentioned as results of this achievement. "Industry-acclaimed" desktop publishing systems that are "better than the competition" are held up to be admired. Characteristics of specific machines (such as quietness, durability or reliability) were also discussed, both in general terms and with technical specifications. Statements such as "a serious tool for serious needs" were characteristic of this dimension.

Efficiency

The potential of desktop publishing to enhance an organization's efficiency was emphasized in 22.5% of the statements in the sample. The technology's speed, ease of adoption and upgrading, and the capability to utilize software already owned were all mentioned. Saving time was another important factor discussed in this area.

Desktop publishing as a user-friendly, or simple-to-master technology was also stressed, with statements that emphasized the ability of an ordinary person to use a desktop publishing system. All this is done, of course, in a "friendly, intuitive way."

Flexibility

This approach represented 18.2% of the statements sampled. The versatility of desktop publishing systems and their ability to use many types of hardware and software were stressed. DTP as "good for all types of users," not just the data processing department, was a frequent reference, as was the "freedom of choice" offered by desktop publishing.

Creativity

Several ads included statements emphasizing the potential of desktop publishing technology to unlock or enhance the creativity of the individual user. Such references were found in 11.4% of the cases. These statements tended to focus on the "magic" of desktop publishing, indicating that the technology serves as the missing link that many people need in order to fully develop and express their ideas. DTP can remove artificially created boundaries to the individual's personal aggrandizement or success, according to the myths of the ads.

Apple Computer's ads made particular use of this theme, with slogans such as "make yourself look like a star" and "the power to be your best." Xerox joins in by offering the consumer a DTP system that promises to "bring out the genius in you." Visually, many 1986 ads stressed this theme as well, with images of famous thinkers using desktop publishing

(Leonardo Da Vinci figures prominently). Ordinary people were also shown enjoying the fruits of their labors after successfully working with DTP technology. In 1988, the ads promised that the use of desktop publishing would "make your machine more sensitive and intuitive" and help you "create captivating documents" that would "instantly make your data say more."

Professional Image

The use of desktop publishing technology to present impressive-looking documents was discussed in 8.1% of the statements. The focus here centers on the improved professional image that may be presented by taking advantage of desktop publishing. Beating the competition via technology is praised, as is enhancing one's own status. Cordata's slogan—"You may not be an industry leader but you can look like one"—typifies this category. The "eye catching" technology of desktop publishing permits one to make "show-stopping presentation materials" and thus "make the best presentation of your career." It is interesting to note that this theme was stronger in 1986. By 1988, the mystique of technology for augmenting a business image had shifted to facsimile machines.

Futuristic

Desktop publishing was hailed as a futuristic technology in 6.7% of the statements studied. Desktop publishing as "only the beginning" of the "dawn of a new era" in which people may explore the "frontiers of technology" were found.

Some fear appeals were found in this category, implying that the businessperson who does not adopt this technology will be left in the dust. Xerox DTP systems make conventional paper, scissors and glue obsolete, for instance. Obsolescence of earlier technologies was stressed in many ads. Choosing desktop publishing is presented as the safe alternative. "The warm feeling of security that comes standard" is not to be underestimated, particularly when the accompanying visual image features a rock-climber perched precariously alongside a sheer cliff.

Low Cost

The relatively low cost of desktop publishing systems, or of particular components, was stated 5.8% of the time.

Affordability and value for money were emphasized most often in advertisements of smaller manufacturers or as secondary themes in more complex advertisements.

Conclusions

Desktop publishing advertisements are not viewed here as causal agents for the revitalization of corporate culture, but rather as providing a mythos which correlates with the changes that many organizations are currently experiencing. When an organization faces threats, its culture must change. A new leader can often provide a needed role model, transitional rituals may structure interactions, and training programs may aid employees coping strategies. In any case, a tangible symbol of the new policies and procedures must be provided. In many cases, that function is fulfilled by the installation of desktop publishing equipment.

Desktop publishing places control over the publishing process in the hands of individuals who have not previously enjoyed such access. Since DTP is primarily a do-it-yourself kit for nonpublishers, the amateur can replace a pantheon of publishing personnel. That person can now wear many hats— publisher, writer, editor, copy editor, art director, production manager, pasteup artist, printer, and salesperson (Grout et al.). Desktop publishing gives new meaning to A. J. Liebling's now-famous statement that "freedom of the press belongs to those who own one." Desktop publishing eliminates the middleman in the production of documents. Fancy typefaces, interesting layouts and professional-looking work can be churned out easily by hooking up a microcomputer with page composition software and a laser printer.

These capabilities permit desktop publishing to extend the populist notions that first fueled the development of personal computers. In the same way that personal computers were first hailed as the means for ordinary people to break away from the near-mystical control exerted by the "programmer/ priests" of an earlier generation, desktop publishing has been held aloft as the salvation of the ordinary person.

Some figures indicate that corporations spend as much as 10% of their annual revenues on publishing-related activities. However, while a large company may indeed produce a greater quantity of documents than a traditional publishing house in a year, the corporate viewpoint on publishing differs immensely. The in-house publishing function is typically decentralized, with each department covering its own needs, and participants may not define their activities as publishing at all. Of Fortune 1000 companies, 25% of those surveyed reported plans to purchase desktop publishing software, and there were more plans for purchases of desktop publishing programs than any other two software categories combined (Stromer).

There is a correlation between the technological capabilities of desktop publishing systems and the values that are currently being emphasized in the effort to revitalize the corporate cultures of various organizations. Desktop publishing appears to offer a means of meeting institutional goals (productivity, efficiency) while at the same time supporting the personal goals of employees (the entrepreneurial spirit, creativity). Using technology to improve a corporation's competitive stance fits well with the organizational values of the era.

References

Allen, Robert. "In-House Publishing: From Concept to Print." *Modern Office Technology* (1985): 56–62.

Ambrosio, Johanna. "Publishing in-house can sharpen DP image." *Computer World* 2 Dec. 1985: 55–60.

Anonymous. "Electronic Publishing on Rise." *New York Times* 2 Sept. 1985.

Bove, Tony, et al. *The Art of Desktop Publishing.* New York: Bantam, 1985.

Brown, Lauren, and Preston Gralla. "Sales figures show growing market." *PC Week* 10 May 1988: S12.

Davis, Frederic E., et al. *Desktop Publishing.* Homewood, IL: Dow Jones-Irwin, 1986.

Davis, Stanley M. *Managing Corporate Culture.* Cambridge, MA: Ballinger Publishing Company, 1984.

Deal, Terrence E., and Allan A. Kennedy. *Corporate Cultures: The Rites and Rituals of Corporate Life.* Reading: Addison-Wesley, 1982.

Ernest, Robert C. "Corporate Cultures and Effective Planning." *Personnel Administrator* 30.3 (1985): 49–62.

Grout, Bill, et al. *Desktop Publishing from A to Z.* Berkeley, CA: Osborne McGraw-Hill, 1986.

Harris, Thomas E. "Organizational Cultures: An Examination of the Role of Communication." Paper presented at the Sixth International Conference on Culture and Communication, 1986.

Kanter, Rosabeth Moss. *The Change Masters: Innovation for Productivity in the American Corporation.* New York: Simon, 1983.

Lyons, Daniel J. "Business is tough for some makers of publishing tools." *PC Week* 25 July 1988: 111–113.

Naisbett, John, and Patricia Aburdene. *Reinventing the Corporation.* New York: Warner, 1985.

Peters, Thomas J., and Robert H. Waterman, Jr. *In Search of Excellence.* New York: Warner, 1982.

Peters, Tom, and Nancy Austin. *A Passion for Excellence.* New York: Random, 1985.

Posner, Barry Z., et al. "Shared Values Make a Difference: An Empirical Test of Corporate Culture." *Human Resources Management* 24.3 (1985): 293–310.

Rogers, Michael. "The PC Printing Press." *Newsweek* 14 July 1986: 50–51.

Smith, Anthony. *Goodbye Gutenberg: The Newspaper Revolution of the 1980s.* New York: Oxford UP, 1980.

Stromer, Richard. "Proof of desktop packages success is in the figures." *PC Week* 5 Jan. 1988: 112.

Groupware—One Experience

❖

Til Dallavalle
Alicia Esposito
Steve Lang

What Is It?

What is this thing called Groupware? Perhaps an under-standing of what it is not will hasten an understanding of what it is. It is not a new technology nor is it a new manage-ment or process technique. Groupware is a set of tools which uses Computers and Communications to increase productivity and effectiveness of team and group related work or processes. Many names and titles have been applied to this *thing* called Groupware. It has been generically referred to as; Computer Assisted Communications, Interpersonal Computing, Group Decision Support Systems, and Work group Computing to men-tion a few.

Some of the most common communications tools such as: electronic mail, voice mail, overhead projectors, electronic blackboards, meeting rooms, audio/video teleconferencing and of course the "ubiquitous" telephone are also fundamental tools for groupware applications. The magic is in the synergy of these tools when they are integrated for groupware applications.

Within Bellcore the term Teamware has evolved as a de-scriptor for our implementation of groupware. As stated ear-lier, groupware is not new a technology; however, it is a more effective and efficient use of existing computer and communi-cations technologies to support team and work group collabo-rative efforts. During the mid to late 1980s, Bellcore installed

31

thousands of personal computers some of which were connected to Local Area Networks. The productivity improvements as a result of this embedded technology were primarily related to individual gains rather than the synergistic increases which derive from collaborative efforts.

The notion of integrating traditional stand-alone applications using Computers and Communications is not new to Bellcore. Robert Kraut, working in Bellcore's Applied Research Lab, and his team developed a computer-based tool, *"Quilt,"* for collaborative writing several years ago to promote rapid production of documents which required the input and review of many individuals. In 1989 Bellcore's Corporate Telecommunications Department began an investigation of groupware's potential by becoming a member of the Groupware User's Exchange Project which provided research funding to the IFTF (Institute For The Future). The Institute is a non-profit future oriented research group in Menlo Park, CA that researches and documents current groupware applications and the potential for future ones.

As a spinoff from what was learned from the IFTF research, the Corporate Telecommunications Department teamed with Bellcore's Quality Advisors to test the potential benefits of groupware in support of Quality Team meetings. Groupware appeared to offer some immediate benefits to the quality process by accelerating the idea generation activity for the development of possible solutions to reengineering and work flow problems. In addition to the involvement of Quality Advisors, members of other departments were brought into the early planning stages to assess the potential benefits of groupware when applied to planning activities and work group communications processes.

Why Use It?

Exactly what was it that motivated us to explore the use of a combination of tools and technology? First, consider some of the problems associated with traditional meetings. For example, the problem of lost ideas that do not surface in a meeting. This may be due to dominating extroverts in the meeting, an individual's fear of sounding "silly," or some individuals' hesitation to challenge authority. Ideas also have a hard time surfacing when meetings focus on personalities and not on content.

Some other problems experienced in traditional meetings include time wasted on *"political"* posturing, and the serial nature of communications (e.g., one person discussing one topic at one time). In addition, documenting the meeting may be time consuming, long in coming and lose something in the translation.

So why use groupware to address problems like these? In today's global economy we all face an increasingly competitive business environment. As a result we are consistently expected to shorten our business cycles to compete. Our teams must do more than just communicate effectively. The contribution of each employee must be focused and integrated with the whole. In short, we must achieve collaboration.

Expected Benefits

By introducing groupware in Bellcore we anticipated that teams through the use of this technology would reach agreement more quickly on sensitive issues and be more productive than those teams that do not use groupware tools. The teams will use electronic groupware tools which will jump-start team activities such as: electronic brainstorming, consensus testing, voting, idea categorization, evaluation of alternatives, and team document preparation to name a few. Our expectation is that this groupware facilitated collaboration will promote team ownership and support for group decisions. Specifically, the tools will facilitate team functions by:

1. Supporting group decision making and consensus building
2. Improving communications
3. Promoting greater innovation and creativity
4. Enhancing the ability to focus on the task
5. Increasing the number of ideas generated
6. Improving team productivity, team building and ownership

While improved communications among participants may occur, the bigger payoff will come from the expected increase in ideas and input which supports innovation and creativity as the result of greater participation by individual team members.

What Is Required?

Groupware as stated previously is not a new technology nor is it a replacement for team/group dynamics. More importantly it is not the "end all solution." Rather it is an approach to using technology, communications and computers, as an effective and efficient tool to support true collaboration. Five essential ingredients were needed to successfully employ the groupware meeting support tools within Bellcore:

1. A meeting room
2. A meeting facilitator/team guide
3. A set of computer workstations (PCs) on a Local Area Network
4. A set of groupware software tools
5. A disciplined process

The process includes three major steps. To begin the process, there is a preplanning session where the facilitator

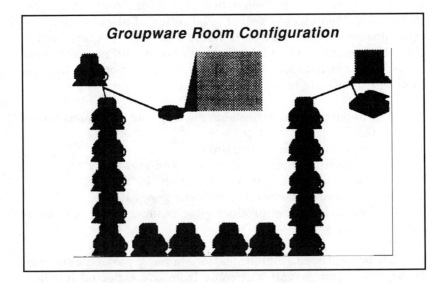

Figure 2.2. Groupware Room

reviews the objectives of the meeting and designs an agenda to achieve the objectives. The second step is conducting the actual meeting with the facilitator using the groupware tools. And finally, there is follow-up by the facilitator to evaluate the meeting's effectiveness and plan the next steps when appropriate. This three step process will support several different types of meeting activities including:

- strategic planning sessions
- idea generation/brain-storming
- resolution of sensitive ideas
- problem solving
- requirements gathering
- negotiations
- systems analysis and design
- team building
- policy development

Some specific characteristics that make groupware meetings productive are:

1. Anonymity—the use of the electronic tools prevents the specific identification of the participants
2. Ability to focus on content, not personality
3. Equality of participation—ideas are not inhibited by dominant personalities, all participants have equal access to the tools
4. Parallel and simultaneous communications—accomplished through a Local Area Network
5. Provides a complete written record of the meeting— each participant can leave the meeting with a record of the meeting accomplishments in the form of a paper copy, a computer floppy diskette, or both
6. Efficiency—participants have fewer meetings
7. Enjoyability—participants appreciate the creative and innovative environment it promotes

Armed with the introductory experience, Bellcore's Corporate Telecommunications Department implemented a groupware lab to gain more experience with specific applications and understand how they might support Bellcore's business processes.

Bellcore's Experience

Our experience with groupware tools developed in today's marketplace began with an exploratory visit to a vendor's location to use their groupware facility. Members of a Quality Improvement organization in Bellcore were so impressed with the potential of these tools that quality improvement teams were invited to explore this approach. Between February and March 1991, four quality improvement teams used this facility. These teams were working on ways to improve their products, services, and basic business planning processes within the company as well as improving teamwork across diverse work groups.

In follow-up surveys participants indicated how they felt about the sessions as compared to traditional meetings (figures 2.3 and 2.4):

- 40% felt that the groupware supported meetings were more than three times as productive.
- 40% felt that the groupware supported meetings were three times as productive.
- 20% felt that the groupware supported meetings were twice as productive.

Additionally:
- 40% felt that their task was accomplished in less than 1/3 the amount of time
- 60% felt that their task was accomplished in 1/3 the amount of time

Productivity & Time Comparisons

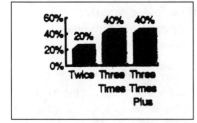 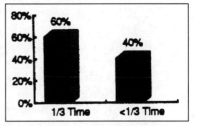

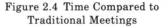

Figure 2.3 Productivity Compared   Figure 2.4 Time Compared to
to Traditional Meetings   Traditional Meetings

Some of the participant verbatim comments were:

"I would recommend this tool to all levels of management."
" . . . it's a time saver, it saves ideas, and analysis is rapid."
"This helps to get everyone's input, regardless of level or personality."
"Without a doubt, groupware could be used to augment the quality process . . . "

One of the Quality Teams that participated had come to the session expecting to complete their assignment (i.e., making recommendations on how to improve team effectiveness in their organization) sometime in July 1991; however, as a result of the productivity from using the groupware tools for one day, they revised their expected completion date to April 1991 and met the revised date.

Coming on Board

Bellcore's experience with the groupware trial provided support for the development of a "lab" site to continue to test the feasibility of using this new tool in our business environment. Our objective was to begin to trial the use of groupware with selected teams in January 1992.

In order to meet that objective, the "lab" site was developed and constructed during November and December 1991. Facilitators were given six days of formal training by the vendor. A one-day application training session was also conducted by a consultant experienced in the use of groupware with actual teams.

We learned that the formal training needed to be supplemented with "hands on" experience in using the tools. Prior to using the groupware tools for the first time with teams, our facilitators received about ten days of informal practice using the equipment. The facilitators also developed a peer group support network. In addition to jointly designing meetings, the members of this network informally certified each other in the use of the tools. This collaborative teaming maximized the group's knowledge and ideas about the application of the groupware tools and helped to reduce what otherwise might have been steep learning curves during the start-up process.

Initial Applications: "Same Time, Same Place"

"Same time, same place" meetings occur when the participants are face-to-face in the same room at the same time. It is the most frequent format for meetings in Bellcore.

With the "lab" site implemented and facilitators trained, we were able to begin using groupware with teams. During January and February 1992, we used groupware with 12 teams or roughly 120 people.

Thus far, our groupware applications have focused primarily on business-planning and quality-improvement activities. We have used groupware to: design organizational vision and mission statements, develop business objectives, explore customer product and service needs, analyze the strengths and weaknesses of our products and services, and to improve team effectiveness.

Managing the Meeting Process Using Groupware

Through these applications, our facilitators have developed insights into the use of groupware as a tool to enhance the process of holding meetings. These insights fall into the following categories:

1. pre-meeting preparation
2. meeting facilitation
3. post-meeting follow-up

Pre-meeting Preparation

Facilitors learned that they need to follow the same pre-meeting process steps, with or without groupware. These steps include such activities as consulting with the person who is originating the meeting to define the purpose and objectives of the meeting. A meeting must then be designed, including the use of tools and techniques, to meet the desired objectives. Our facilitators have found that it usually takes about the same amount of time for pre-meeting activities, with or without groupware.

Additionally, the facilitators found that it is very helpful during pre-meeting consultation with the meeting originator to manage the meeting originator's and participants' perceptions and expectations regarding groupware. Sometimes, facilitators discovered that the meeting originator and participants had totally unrealistic expectations about groupware; facilitators had to provide information to participants prior to the meeting to help them develop a more realistic picture of how groupware would be used.

In the initial applications, facilitators found that meeting objectives could usually be met by using a basic set of groupware tools for generating, organizing, evaluating, and selecting ideas, as well as building implementation plans. This meant that the facilitators really only had to master a manageable set of tools in order to meet the objectives of the meetings. This was extremely helpful during the learning curve.

Meeting Facilitation

The facilitators found that they needed the same basic facilitation skills, with or without, groupware. These skills focus on managing group dynamics, the needs of the individuals, and the task itself. Overall, however, the facilitators discovered that the use of groupware tools requires increased sensitivity to group dynamics. This sensitivity focuses on the following areas:

- Communication and sharing
- Anonymity
- The management of data
- The environment

During the 1991 trial, feedback from the participants indicated the need for ensuring the careful balance of "live talk time" with "electronic talk time." In our initial applications, therefore, the facilitators designed discussion periods into the meeting. This also addressed the tendency for groups to become mesmerized or lured into simply using tools because they were there, at the expense of the meeting purpose or objective. Simply put, the facilitators tried to use groupware as a tool to facilitate a given task, rather than designing a groupware session to use as many tools as possible.

Another communication challenge for groupware facilitators is the need to deal with group members who are used to being in control of meetings. With groupware, some participants may have to share perceived power and control with other members of the group. This loss of control may manifest itself through a lack of interest and participation in the meeting. Facilitators have developed ground rules that they share with meeting participants at the beginning of the meeting to sensitize participants to the need for equal sharing and participation in the meeting.

Another ground rule developed by facilitators and discussed with meeting participants involves creating a sensitivity to anonymity in the groupware environment. The facilitators found that the anonymity feature of groupware requires a heightened awareness by the facilitators and the meeting participants about the impact of anonymity on the group. For example, because the groupware tools may allow group members to remain anonymous as they input ideas and comments, the group may become insensitive to individual perspectives on an issue. Further, if a conflict emerges as a result, and if the group does not get the opportunity to "socially enact" and resolve the conflict, participants may become frustrated, and team dynamics may suffer.

The facilitators also discovered that because some of the groupware tools enhance a group's ability to generate a large volume of ideas, the group may be unable to process such a large number of ideas. In the pre-meeting design, the facilitator must plan for managing the potential volume. Some techniques facilitators have found helpful include cutting down on the time associated with the idea-generation tools, having the group work in pairs or small groups to generate and prioritize ideas, and limiting the time spent during a meeting to edit the group's ideas.

Finally, facilitators found that because groupware enables a group to work more intensely and quickly, the group sometimes tires more easily. Thus, facilitators offer more frequent breaks and are extremely cognizant of environmental factors such as proper heating, lighting, and air flow during the meeting.

Post Meeting Follow-Up

Facilitators found that quantitative data-collection tools such as questionnaires, along with qualitative feedback from the meeting originator and participants, are important to improving the effectiveness of using groupware. Further, the facilitators now hold debriefing sessions with other facilitators after each application to share information and to constantly improve the process of applying groupware to meet our customers' needs. The data collected during these initial applications will also be used in a business case to support the implementation of groupware in Bellcore.

Implementation: July–December 1992

Implementation activities for the July through December 1992 time frame include building a business case for the potential implementation of groupware in the Bellcore environment. As previously mentioned, part of the business case will be built on customer feedback collected during the initial applications.

Another key implementation activity for this time frame will be the expansion of the initial applications to include senior-management applications, cross-organizational teaming applications, and the integration of the tools in the normal day-to-day business environment; e.g., to improve staff meetings. Other activities will include work with distributed-access applications initially focused on *"same time, different place"* meetings where participants are collaborating using groupware at the same time but from different locations.

"Any Time, Any Place"

Although most of our efforts from late 1990 through early 1992 have focused on identifying applications and preparing plans for implementing groupware in the *"same time, same place"* environment. The ultimate objective is to achieve *"any time, any place"* meetings where participant collaborations occur at any time, day or night, and from any location. It has become very clear that to achieve the maximum benefits of groupware technology the *"any time, any place"* mode must become part of the future implementation. The ubiquitous availability of communication networks has prompted groupware meeting participants to request that groupware applications in addition to being in a meeting room should be accessible from their office or home computer/workstations to expand opportunities for collaboration.

Physical and logical connectivity to groupware applications in the *"any time, any place"* collaborative environment will be through personal computers/workstations using public telecommunication networks including integrated Services Digital Network (ISDN) and other architectures such as Local and Wide Area Networks.

Future Applications: 1994...

As groupware applications become widely deployed in Bellcore, we anticipate these applications will supplement the face-to-face meetings between project teams and their customers. This is especially true in those cases where geographical separation precludes frequent face-to-face meetings for project reviews. Other applications will facilitate meetings between Bellcore and industry representatives in the generic requirements development process. These are only a few of the many possible ways where groupware can be used in addition to its present uses in Bellcore.

Literally, with each passing day, we are discovering additional applications where groupware enhances the processes by increasing productivity and customer focus in teams and work groups. Groupware is helping us become a **"best managed"** company which translates to reduced operating costs and increased value to our customers.

In our trial we have only brushed the tip of this productivity improvement iceberg.

Communicating Sudden Change in Tasks and Culture: The Inglis Montmagny Story

❖

Randall Capps

Research conducted at the Tavistock Institute of Human Relations (UK) in the 1950s formed the foundation of what later came to be called the socio technical system. This system views production systems as being comprised of both technological and social parts. Production systems will include such things as equipment and methods of operation used to transform raw materials into products and social systems will include the work structure that relates people to technology and to each other. Socio technical systems theory became the foundation of what came to be called self directed work teams. This way of working has been referred to as "autonomous," "composite" and "self managing."

Most literature on the subject suggests using a process approach to this change and implementing the process over a period of from two to five years.

This study shows how a 125-year-old plant, 600 miles from most of its suppliers and customers, changed from using traditional management to using self-directed work teams. That change was accomplished during a month long close to allow for changes to be made in production equipment. When the plant closed, it was using the traditional production system. When it reopened, it was using self-directed teams.

In the 1950s researchers at the Tavistock Institute of Human Relations (UK) began to study productivity in terms of the relationship between the social system and the technology operating within the organization. The impetus for the research was a change in the technology of coal mining. Changes in this technology resulted in miners being placed in small groups where they were given supervisory responsibility for their own work. This reorganization created a high level of interdependence between workers, a rotation of job responsibilities and the sharing of a common pay rate. The results of these experiments were surprising. Workers in this experiment had reduced absenteeism, fewer accidents, lower turnover rates, fewer stress related illnesses and higher productivity (Pearce, Ravlin 1987).

Since its appearance, socio technical systems theory has revolved as a significant means for redesigning organizations. This approach to working has concentrated on the way people and technology and the work environment relate. A major outcome of the theory has been the development of self-regulating work groups. These self-regulating work groups have spun off several names: "autonomous," "composite" and "self-managing" (Cummings 1977).

While the socio technical concept started in Great Britain, it soon spread to the industrialized world. It has been argued that a rationale for self-directed work teams can be constructed from six basic propositions concerning people at work (Pearce, Ravlin 1987):

1. One of the most psychologically relevant reference groups for most individuals is the work group.
2. Most people wish to be accepted by and to interact cooperatively with at least one small reference group, and usually with more than one group.
3. In order to optimize group effectiveness, group members must assist the group's leader with effective leadership and maintenance functions.
4. Suppressed feelings and unresolved conflicts adversely affect problem solving, personal growth, and job satisfaction.
5. The level of interpersonal trust, support, and cooperation in most groups and organizations is much lower than is either necessary or desirable.
6. The solution to many attitudinal and motivational problems in organizations involves interpersonal dynamics.

One problem in implementing socio technical systems in many organizations has been that individuals involved in redesigning the workplaces have placed more emphasis on the technical systems, the tools, techniques, procedures and devices used by members of the work force and have tended to overlook opportunities to redesign technologies to meet the needs of people (Pasmore, Francis, Haldeman and Shani 1982). Carnall (1982) has argued that the increased challenge and autonomy can lead to several benefits to the organization. Often conflict is reduced and when individuals are provided with opportunities for learning and participating in problem solving, that creates conditions for mutual trust and respect. However, a major benefit to the economics of the organization is that often a considerable reduction of overhead and management costs will result.

Self-regulating work groups are a direct outgrowth of socio technical systems theory and design. According to Cummings (1977), three conditions are necessary if the self-regulating work groups are to flourish: (1) task differentiation, (2) boundary control and (3) task control. Task differentiation refers to the extent to which the group's task is itself autonomous. Boundary control involves the extent to which employees can influence transactions with the task environment. Task control relates to the control employees have in regulating their behavior to convert raw materials into finished products. This last factor is enhanced when employees are empowered to select work methods and to adjust work activities to match task and environmental demands.

If the self-regulating work teams are to be effective, it is important to find a culture which will be conducive to the redesign. It has been suggested by Akin and Hopelain (1986) that culture does not cause productivity but rather the culture is the employee's view of the fundamental structures and processes that constitute culture in a particular setting. Akin and Hopelain suggest that high productivity operations have five elements which contribute to developing this culture: (1) Types of people, (2) teamwork, (3) work structure, (4) the person in charge and (5) the management.

Two characteristics are very important in the people. First they must be willing to work hard and second they must identify closely with the job they are performing.

Several factors relate to teamwork. It is important for employees to have a strong identity about what the team does, what the team stands for and who is on the team. Trust and support is another important element. This element relates to knowing what other team members are doing, how they work, and knowing that they could be counted on to do their part. Akin and Hopelain found that for some workers, status is an important part of teamwork. Status differences in productive groups seem to be determined by the amount of knowledge each member has of the job and by his/her actual performance. Also, part of teamwork is the knowledge each team member has about every other team member.

The work structure includes defining the actual activities required to get the job done and the outcomes or results of those activities. The activities are described in terms of skills required to perform them. Two types of knowledge are important: the skills needed to perform the job and information about how to use those skills.

The person in charge is one key to the productivity of the organization. That person, whatever the title may be, must not boss but rather must allow the work to get done and support employees in accomplishing their jobs. Support often means protecting the team from outside interference.

Management is the term used by employees to refer to that part of the organization that is above them and out of their reach. Akin and Hopelain (1986) found that in cultures of productivity management communicates two basic messages: a desire for productivity and a willingness to support the accomplishment of employees.

Other experts in the field of socio technical design have examined principles which contribute to successful redesign. Cherns (1987) compiled a list of ten principles gathered from a variety of sources which he believed organizations should use in redesigning their workplaces.

Principle 1: Compatibility. The way in which a design is done should be compatible with the design's objectives. Redesign is an arena for conflict because it must satisfy an array of objectives each represented by an organizational element. The way in which this conflict is managed and used to achieve positive results sets the pattern for the handling of later conflicts in the newly designed organization. It is important for the design teams to work on its own process and principles of operation, principles no different from those which guide its design.

The principle of compatibility is critical because it, to a great extent, determines how well the other principles will be followed.

Principle 2: Minimal Critical Specification. This principle relates to identifying what is essential. It may be necessary to specify what is to be done but seldom is it necessary to specify how it is to be done.

Principle 3: Variance of Control. This principle is most closely related to the process of socio technical analysis. The variance control table brings into immediate prominence inefficiencies in the organization's mode of controlling key variances and encourages suggestions for improving those inefficiencies.

Principle 4: Boundary Location. It is crucial in the socio technical system that boundaries not be drawn that will impede the sharing of information, knowledge and learning.

Principle 5: Information Flow. It is critical that information be available for those who need it when they need it. Information serves three functions: control, record, and action.

Principle 6: Power and Authority. Those who need equipment, materials, and other resources to carry out their responsibilities should have access to them and the necessary authority to command them. In return, employees accept the responsibility for them and for their judicious and economical use.

Principle 7: The Multifunctional Principle. Organizations need to adapt to their environments and elements of the organizations need to adapt to their environments of which the most important are usually other organizational elements. This may be accomplished by adding new roles or by modifying old ones.

Principle 8: Support Congruence. Most implications of socio technical analyses and design are usually accepted for production, maintenance and quality control. However, support of production teams requires important and far-reaching changes in reward and information systems, in financial control, in marketing, sales, purchasing, and planning.

Principle 9: Transitional Organization. Since organizations are engaged in change from a traditional to a new organization which implies a change to a new philosophy of management and to a new system of values, the design team and the process it creates must be viewed as a vehicle of transition.

Principle 10: Incompletion as the Fourth Bridge Principle. Implementation should begin with the start of the design and with implementation comes evaluation. Redesign is the function of self-regulating operating teams provided with the techniques of analysis and with sound principles of design. It is important to give operating teams the necessary training and they must also learn the necessary skills and they must learn to operate as a team.

The next decade will hold tremendous challenges and opportunities for organizations. Global competition, deregulation in key industries, and rapid technological change will provide a state of turmoil for many industries. These factors will contribute an atmosphere where organizations will need to do everything possible to remain viable and productive. There will be opportunities for many organizations to redesign their workplace and utilize concepts developed by socio technical theorists. Donovan (1987) characterizes work redesign as a process employees participate in rethinking the organization. It is necessary to look at the whole system—the technical, the social, and the total administrative subsystems.

Clearly the self-directing workteam concept is spreading throughout industrialized countries. It has been suggested that work redesign efforts are a trend likely to shape industry well into the twenty-first century.

Following is a narrative of how Inglis Limited used concepts from socio technical systems theory in a different way from many organizations. They followed many of the implementation concepts suggested by experts. However, the difference with Inglis was that instead of implementing the concept through a process approach, they implemented the process suddenly. The manufacturing facility closed for some renovations at the beginning of January 1992. Some four weeks later the plant reopened with the renovations completed and with a new way of working.

Inglis Limited

Inglis Limited of Montmagny, Quebec, which produces 24" and 30" electric ranges, dates to 1867 when it was opened to produce farm equipment and wood cookstoves. In the intervening hundred and twenty-five years the plant has had several owners. In the early 1960s several plants were consolidated into the Montmagny facility. In the 1970s the plant produced several kinds of appliances including refrigerators, washers, and both wood and electric stoves. By 1981 the factory was facing bankruptcy. This development brought management and mid-management together as they worked to find a buyer. Inglis Limited was producing only electric ranges at the time and saw an opportunity to expand its product line when it took over the facility in 1982.

When Inglis took over the hundred employee factory, it gave them one year to become profitable or be shut down. With the determination of all employees, the plant turned a profit within six months. Within a year the Montmagny plant proved to be the most profitable of the five plants within the Inglis system.

Part of the factors contributing to the plant's poor performance in the 1970s and early 1980s related to poor labor relations. Employees worked on a system where they were paid for piece work. Relations between production workers and management had deteriorated to the extent that production workers simply did not trust management. The situation became so bad during the 1970s that at one time there was a six month strike.

Jean Francois Boulet, Manager of Human Resources, had come to Montmagny in 1982. Boulet met with the production workers and suggested that the lawyers be dismissed and that workers and managers sit down together and work out a contract. During this time he spent many hours on the plant floor talking with the workers in an effort to obtain their trust. He spent many hours in one on one communication to achieve that trust which was so important if the plant was to remain viable.

Inglis, Montmagny was in a unique position. It was the most important employer in Montmagny, a city on the St. Lawrence Waterway with a population of 12,800. Yet, Montmagny is isolated. It is 600 miles from most of its suppliers and equally removed from most of its customers. In the words of one employee, "The plant is close to nowhere."

The three hundred fifty employees are loyal. The average seniority in the plant is slightly in excess of twenty-five years. One unusual fact about these employees is that many of them are the third generation in their family to be employed at this facility.

When the plant became profitable after its acquisition by Inglis, negotiations were started with Whirlpool, the parent company of Inglis, to allow the Montmagny division to develop a stove unit to export to the United States. Finally, agreement was reached and several commitments were made during these negotiations.

Part of the agreement related to Inglis agreeing to spend fifteen million dollars for renovation of the ancient factory. Another part of the agreement related to workers and management moving to a "high commitment" type of work.

This high commitment or socio technical system was used to enable workers to keep their jobs. According to Jean Francois Boulet, "We all succeed together or we fail together."

The effort to move toward high commitment or work teams began with a planning team. The team faced initial resistance from both union and management. The union feared its loss of power and management feared its loss of control.

This factory has been planning for more than two years for February 1992. At that time the renovated factory reopened with new manufacturing requirements and with employees reporting to a totally new system of working.

The Inglis Plan

The High Commitment Design Team was composed of sixteen representatives including the following positions: a management representative, a quality representative, an industrial engineer, a process engineer, three individuals from mid management, two plant union representatives, four hourly representatives, an office union representative and two from the C.S.D. union.

The committee had the mission of contributing to the achievement of company objectives and at the same time fulfilling the needs of the employees. The following problems were presented to the steering committee representing the condition of the company in 1991.

Lost production time
Increased production costs
Employee revenue losses
Poor communication leading to frustration
Poor decision making

Looking at a two year plan, the committee set the following goals for 1993:

Better decision making
Easier planning
Empowered team members
Increased quality
Less lost material
Better motivation of employees

The transition structure was implemented with a High Commitment Review Board charged with the overall responsibility for the change. See chart one.

One of the first responsibilities the Design Team undertook was the establishment of a vision for the Division. This vision, which was adopted in 1990, contained some basic principles and orientations for the division. Following are these principles:

1. Mission of Inglis Montmagny Division

Be the cooking products manufacturer of choice in Canada by empowering our people to continually improve quality and provide best cost products that exceed customer expectations.

We are dedicated to the high commitment philosophy which demands mutual respect, flexibility and accountability in a safe, challenging and changing environment.

2. Values and objectives

The people of the Montmagny Division are proud to be working with Inglis and they want to be winners, to be the best.

Sharing the same vision and agreement between the various partners is the basis for Inglis' success.

The Division's success is associated with the will to continuously improve quality and productivity in every action taken by every individual, with great respect for each person and the quality of working life.

In order to develop initiative and continuous improvement, we will foster mutual support and teamwork. Searching for solutions at the source (of the problem) will prevail over trying to find someone to blame.

Maintaining good union management relationships will allow the level of trust needed in an organizational change and evolution process.

A healthy, safe and involving work environment where access to information at all levels is possible will contribute to make the Division a management reference in the industry.

3. Environmental factors

A. EXTERNAL ENVIRONMENT

Listening to the customer and a careful monitoring of the market is essential to maintain our competitive edge in terms of quality and cost.

Our wish is to keep a level of autonomy in the Montmagny Division consistent with established policies.

In order to keep adequate visibility in our regional area, the Division must maintain its social involvement.

The Montmagny Division is determined to work toward protecting the environment in its operations.

B. INTERNAL ENVIRONMENT

Montmagny Division is embarking in the production of new product designs, with new processes and a renewing organization.

Investments in facilities and equipment are made in order to improve material and manpower costs to maintain and develop job security. A quality purchasing policy for raw materials and equipment is designed to complete them.

In order to maintain a competitive edge, we will need to continue investment in research and development (methods, material, equipment) within the framework of established policies.

4. A management system where. . . .

A. DECISION MAKING

Decision making is decentralized to be as close as possible to employees and at the same time well integrated into the whole company. Once agreed upon, the decision process is maintained as long as no revision is needed.

B. WORK ORGANIZATION

1. Reward system
Reward is designed to give employees incentives to develop and utilize his or her potential, competence and flexibility. It can be upgraded in relation to Division results.

2. Training

Training is useful to eliminate prejudice between people, particularly through listening and feedback.

Training is flexible and tailor made in order to allow manpower to cope with changes, develop responsible ownership, to work in multiskilled teams, to allow for job rotation with proper training. It gives new employees an orientation to help their inclusion in the Division in order to have all the knowledge and the abilities necessary to perform their duties efficiently and safely.

3. Job design

Work systems and organization: It is structured in such a way as to optimize the operations in agreement with established policies.

It is designed to give individuals the skills, information and necessary authority to efficiently function with minimum dependency toward the other.

It applies methods, tools and equipment consistent with new technologies and facilitates the elimination of useless handling.

It is designed economically in order to perform work in a healthy and safe environment.

Work teams are trained and have the authority to allow as much autonomy as possible.

The quality responsibility is built in the task.

The planning of work is done from the beginning, following the production schedule in coordination with involved departments.

During the last quarter of 1991 teams were formed and given training concerning changes which would be made following the closing of the plant at the end of the quarter. The production schedule was heavy during the last half of 1991 to allow for products to be stock piled to accommodate the factory's closure to install new equipment and prepare for the new manufacturing system.

Inherent in the new system was the fact that all employees be trained to perform all of the tasks on their team. Abilities were ranked as "Basic," "Intermediate" and "Advanced." Team responsibilities were developed for each of the production teams.

While Inglis Montmagny made a sudden change from the traditional method of manufacturing to one which used socio technical theory, the first year, 1992, was viewed as a transitional period. Much progress was anticipated in the transitional year to take the Division to where the Design Team planned for it to be by the last half of 1993. The Design Team established the vision for the Division by taking into consideration a long enough period of time for major decisions regarding the redesign and the new stove to be implemented and applied.

The Design Team began with the assumption that all the proposed changes on the equipment, the new stove design and the organization of the work teams be made according to the plan which allowed for any necessary adjustments to be made during the transition period. When the transition period ends, it is the plan of the Design Team that by 1993 work teams in the Division will meet the following criteria:

1. Each team is responsible and autonomous in fulfilling received orders. They can organize their work to satisfy their clients' requirements and to produce quality. They manage their equipment, obtaining the necessary expertise if needed, in order to improve operations. They identify their needs and plan training activities. Rotation is part of the normal operation of the work team. It lets each one accomplish different tasks in his/her team.
2. The teams meet regularly, and when needed, for different purposes. Day to day they coordinate their production schedule. They consistently work to improve the work methods to solve production problems, to apply learned techniques in quality control or improvement of the product. Some members meet representatives of the other teams to coordinate production plans, equipment changes, new policies, etc. Some suppliers are met on occasion to help solve some problems or to learn new things.
3. Teams are responsible for the budgets assigned to their department by the management team who, for its part, follows the company's budget.
4. Training is accessible to everyone and adapted to each one. It permits each member to acquire skills and/or abilities useful to his/her department and allows the polyvalence necessary to a certain rotation in the work team. This polyvalency helps the access to different posts in the office or in the factory.
5. The work team takes care of the new employees' integration and gives them the information and training

required to become a member of the team.

6. When needed, the team meets with the management to communicate its way of doing things, to explain what problems are to be resolved together or to talk about future investments.

7. Individual salary is based upon the sum of responsibilities taken on, the length of service with the company and the conditions established upon hiring or by the negotiating process. For the whole Division, a supplementary remuneration factor corresponds to the quality of the production, the productivity which leaves the factory and the meeting of customer requirements.

8. The supervisors are responsible leaders who are charged to coordinate, train, motivate and help in the team functioning—for example; elaborate an interdepartmental production plan and long term projects, prepare budgets, etc.

It was further agreed that certain goals would be communicated as criteria for production employees and teams for the last half of 1993:

a) Individuals

Individuals feel proud and share a feeling of belonging with their unit and with the Division.

Training is perceived as necessary to assist employees in doing a better job. The work background encourages and stimulates enrichment of knowledge.

It is possible for each one to acquire abilities useful to the organization and personally accessible and desirable. It is possible for each one to identify what abilities are to be acquired in order to follow their own career path.

Information is distributed by well established, efficient and flexible communication networks.

A collaboration and mutual aid spirit exists in and between teams.

b) The teams

Each team is responsible for its "product" which is identifiable.

Each one in the team understands the whole of what there is to do and sees its impacts on others.

Each team develops and integrates the necessary abilities to plan its work, do the routine maintenance (which does not include the specialized maintenance), and proceed with its quality control.

Summary

The Inglis, Montmagny factory was closed on January 3, 1992, to allow for the installation of new equipment and for some remodeling of the factory to accommodate the new team approach to manufacturing. During the period from January 3 to February 24 some employees were involved in training. Others were involved in maintenance activities. According to John Francois Boulet, excitement was high as employees awaited the opening of the factory on February 24 with new production lines and with motivation to move this Division into the twenty-first century.

Notes

The author gratefully acknowledges the Quebec Ministry of International Affairs for a Faculty Enrichment Grant for the summer of 1991.

He also expresses appreciation to John Francois Boulet and the staff at the Inglis Montmagny Division for their cooperation in providing material for this study.

References

Akin, Gib, and Hopelain, David. "Finding the Culture of Productivity, *Organizational Dynamics,* Winter 1986, 19–32.

Barrett, F. D. Teamwork—How to Expand Its Power and Punch. *Business Quarterly,* 52, Winter 1987, 132–139.

Carnall, C. A. Semi-Autonomous Work Groups and the Social Structure of the Organization. *Journal of Management Studies,* 19, 1982, 277–294.

Cherns, Albert. Principles of Sociotechnical Change Revisited. *Human Relations,* 1987, v. 40 no. 3, 153–161.

Cummings, Thomas G. Self-Regulating Work Groups: A Socio-Technical Synthesis. *Management Review,* July 1978, 625–634.

Donovan, Michael. Redesigning the Workplace. *The Journal for Quality and Participation* (Special Supplement) December 1988, 6–9.

Elden, Max. Sociotechnical Systems Ideas as Public Policy in Norway: Empowering Participation Through Worker-managed Change. *The Journal of Applied Behavioral Sciences,* 1986, 22, 239–255.

Emery, F. New Perspectives on the World of Work: Sociotechnical Foundations for a New Social Order. *Human Relations,* 1982, v. 35 no. 12, 1095–1122.

Orsburn, Jack D.; Moran, Linda; Musselwhite, Ed and Zinger, John H. *Self-Directed Work Teams: The New American Challenge.* Homewood, Illinois: Business One Irwin, 1990.

Pasmore, William; Francis, Carole; Haldeman, Jeffrey and Shani, Abraham. Sociotechnical Systems: A North American Reflection on Empirical Studies of the Seventies. *Human Relations,* 1982, v. 35 no. 12, 1179–1204.

Pearce, John A., and Ravlin, Elizabeth C. The Design and Activation of Self-Regulating Work Groups. *Human Relations,* 1987, v. 40 no. 11, 751–782.

Further Reading

Cutlip, Scott, Allen Center, and Glen Broom. *Effective Public Relations.* 6th ed. Englewood Cliffs, NJ: Prentice-Hall, 1985.

Dilenschneider, Robert, and Dan Forrestal. *Public Relations Handbook.* 3rd ed. Englewood Cliffs, NJ: Prentice-Hall.

Fast, Julian. *Subtext: Making Body Language Work.* NY: Viking, 1991.

Goodman, Michael B. *Write to the Point: Effective Communication in the Workplace.* Englewood Cliffs, NJ: Prentice-Hall, 1984.

The Handbook of Executive Communication. Edited by John Louis DiGaetani. Homewood, IL: Dow Jones-Irwin, 1986.

Kahane, Howard. *Logic and Contemporary Rhetoric: The Use of Reason in Everyday Life.* 6th ed. Belmont, CA: Wadsworth, 1992.

Lesley's Handbook of Public Relations and Communications. 4th ed. Philip Lesley, ed. Chicago: Probus, 1991.

Pocket Pal. 13th ed. International Paper Company, 1988.

Pratkanis, Anthony, and Elliott Aronson. *Age of Propaganda: The Everyday Use and Abuse of Persuasion.* New York: W. H. Freeman, 1992.

"PRSA Task Force: Public Relations Body of Knowledge Task Force Report," *PR Review,* 41:1 (Spring 1988): 3–40. An update of the PR Body of Knowledge is scheduled for November 1993 publication.

Tufte, Edward P. *The Visual Display of Quantitative Information.* Cheshire, Connecticut: Graphics Press, 1983.

Van Gundy, Arthur. *Techniques of Structured Problem-Solving.* 2nd ed. NY: Van Nostrand Reinhold, 1988.

Weiner, Richard. *Webster's New World Dictionary of Media and Communication.*

On Communication Research

Anderson, J. A. *Communication Research: Issues and Methods.* NY: McGraw Hill, 1987.

Frey, L., R. Botan, and C. H. Friedman. *Investigating Communication: An Introduction to Research Methods.* Englewood Cliffs, NJ: Prentice-Hall, 1991.

Rubin, R. B., A. M. Rubin, and L. J. Piele. *Communication Research: Strategies and Sources.* Belmont, CA: Wadsworth, 1993.

3

Corporate Citizenship

❖

Michael B. Goodman

Overview

The concept of corporate citizenship might seem relatively new in American business, but it has been an element of the philosophy and culture of successful organizations for as long as those organizations have existed. Put simply, corporate citizenship is the acceptance of the corporation's role as a responsible and significant member of the community in which it is located. The community can be the local towns in which the corporation has its plants and offices, or the nations in which it does business.

Corporate citizenship can also be demonstrated through a traditional relationship with various publics. But in recent times, more often than not, the corporation's citizenship role has been expanded to include philanthropic programs and policy, outreach programs, and government relations: local, state, federal regulators and agencies. For organizations with retail and consumer goods activities, customer relations can take on the visible role of corporate citizenship.

With the change in the American economy and way of life from rural to urban during and after the industrial revolution, the role of the organization in a community changed. No longer was it sufficient for a business to pay taxes only and stay out of the affairs of the community. By the beginning of the twentieth century, the company was an integral part of the community. And its presence there had a strong impact on the lives of the people, whether or not they took home a company paycheck.

Modern corporations either provided social services such as health care or funded public facilities such as parks, playgrounds, recreation buildings, or entered a partnership with the community to maintain the infrastructure of highways and bridges.

Some companies actively encourage their employees to participate in the local United Way campaigns, the Red Cross, Volunteer Fire Department, the National Guard, the Little League, scouting, and scores of other volunteer organizations.

For corporations with research and development ties, the corporation often demonstrates its citizenship through the support of its employee membership and participation in professional, scientific, and scholarly societies and organizations. Such support includes attendance at conferences and encouragement to take leadership roles in the organizations.

For over twenty-two years General Motors has published an "annual accounting of its programs and progress in areas of public concern and its efforts to provide its customers with superior products and services that meet or exceed both private and public demand." *(1992 General Motors Public Interest Report, 1)*. Their *1992 General Motors Public Interest Report* focused on issues of concern not only to the corporation, but to the public as well. It discussed industrial leadership and its importance to the fiscal and social health of the country. It also focused on market issues—the U.S. motor vehicle industry, customer satisfaction, and technology leadership; and social issues—safety, the environment, and energy. Their report contained a discussion on the corporation's role in meeting the needs of people—employees, minorities, and communities. Such an annual accounting of the human side of corporate activity demonstrates corporate citizenship in its best manifestation.

Relations with various publics

Traditionally the public relations function in an organization was concerned with the interaction of the company with local, state, national, or international communities.

To that end public relations may have included a factory tour open to the public or the sponsorship of various sporting events and charitable causes. It may have written and distributed press releases on company products, people, and activities of interest outside the organization. It may have published the company newsletter for its "internal public."

The practice of public relations began early in this century after the industrial revolution with people like Ivy Ledbetter Lee, one of the fathers of modern public relations. He counseled Standard Oil and the Rockefellers to cultivate the favor of the general public as a positive way of counteracting the ill will that often existed between owners and their workers and by extension the community in which the workers lived.

Public relations has come a long enlightened way since the days of handing out nickels to the crowds. The role of public relations is now a strategic element in the business plans of most corporations. The public relations plans contain clearly articulated goals, methods, and measurements which coincide with larger corporate goals.

Philanthropy programs and policy

Corporate philanthropy programs remain a low-profile affair in most large organizations. By far the largest share of corporate giving, according to several annual surveys by the Conference Board, goes to education in the form of the company's matching gifts program. Employees give a donation to selected universities and schools, and the corporation in turn "matches" the donation, effectively magnifying the individual's contribution by up to one-hundred percent.

Most corporations use a foundation or trust to distribute its contributions and donations. The policy of the body is written clearly to conform with the tax laws on charitable gifts and to inform various groups and organizations that receive such funds which ones the corporation supports and which ones it does not. Generally American corporations do not grant charity directly to individuals, nor to they support any single religious group.

Beyond that, the type of activities the corporation supports tends to be closely allied with its line of business. For example, a pharmaceutical company might contribute funds to build a research wing of a local hospital. A chemical company may fund basic research in chemistry at a university close to its headquarters. The organization might encourage its employees to collect money for a community Red Cross drive, or even donate an ambulance to a rural community that does not have one.

National, transnational, and international corporations can also participate in foundation work through granting funds for scientific research, or providing operating and supporting grants to art museums to organize special exhibitions and performances of plays, opera, dance, films.

Corporate philanthropic projects during the 1980s and 1990s have been involved in everything from the centennial celebrations of the Statue of Liberty and Ellis Island to the sponsorship of the U.S. Olympic teams.

Outreach programs

Corporate outreach programs again are closely allied to the core business. For instance, the public utility may sponsor and run a series of seminars at retirement homes and villages on coping with power outages due to a thunderstorm or hurricane. The same utility may offer courses for home owners in how to handle and repair electrical appliances safely.

Restaurants may participate in such urban harvest type programs which take surplus, day-old, unused food from restaurants and distribute them to shelters for the homeless. Other companies may donate services like a telephone bank or computers to help with fund-raising.

Outreach programs also include corporate education programs in communities, schools, and universities. Sometimes this may include adult courses in first-aid, water-safety, crime prevention, or recycling. Company representatives often speak at the high school or college about a career in an industry and one at the company in particular.

Such programs like other corporate citizenship activities are often done with little or no fanfare depending on the corporate attitude toward volunteerism.

Government relations: local, state, federal regulators and agencies

Government relations, what some refer to with a smirk or a sneer as lobbying, is the meeting with local, state, federal, and in some cases international agencies to advocate for the corporation on matters in its interest. Some corporations will provide legislators and agency professionals with position papers and information designed to inform and persuade the agency. In the marketplace of ideas such advocacy efforts often make the decision clear.

Individual corporations have in recent years avoided direct lobbying efforts in favor of joining an industry advocacy association or group that does that work for all companies in a given industry. A quick scan of the telephone directory in New York or Washington, D.C. under "Association of . . . " will give you a snapshot of the tens of thousands of groups formed to represent a particular point of view on an issue or industry.

Because of abuses in the past in trying to influence the government decision-making process, this area of corporate communications demands the highest ethical standards. Each company develops its own Code of Business Conduct which often includes standards and procedures for ethical practices with fellow employees and subordinates, customers, vendors, the community, and the government. Professional organizations and societies, such as the Public Relations Society of America, also issue standards of ethical practice for their members, and for the profession or industry as a whole.

The American consumer has become highly skeptical of business practices and intolerant of companies that operate unethically. No contemporary corporation seeks an investigative reporter's exposé or a spot on the *60 Minutes* hot seat. Maintaining the highest standards for propriety and ethical behavior is the best approach to developing a reputation for honesty and integrity.

Customer relations

Customer relations is often considered the front porch of the corporation. How a corporation routinely treats customers and vendors, as well as how it handles an angry customer's telephone call about a product or service that does not live up to expectations, form the foundation on which the corporation's image is built in the minds of individuals. It can be inviting and cooperative, or cold and impersonal.

Successful companies make every effort to meet customer's needs. The old cliché, "the customer is always right," is not a cliché for most companies. It is an informing philosophy. It is also a central principle in the Quality movements that have infatuated American businesses through the 1980s and 1990s. Satisfied customers come back again. Disgruntled customers do not; and they also tell at least ten others about their bad experience. Good customer relations depends on positive word-of-mouth communications.

The service industry has made customer relations not only central to the company business strategy, but an art form. You might think of junk food and fast food together, but when you visit an American fast food restaurant almost anywhere in the U.S. and around the world, you can count on quick, congenial service. Go into almost any retail store with a problem concerning a purchase, and they will repair or replace the item with no questions asked.

In a market driven economy, companies with close relationships with their customers have a better chance of surviving difficult periods than companies that do not listen to their customers. Solid, positive relations with customers is a fundamental part of the quality revolution in America.

Selected Essays and Comment

The essays selected for this chapter are from the presentations at the annual Conference on Corporate Communication at Fairleigh Dickinson University. Each of the authors focuses on a part of communication theory and practice in the context of corporate citizenship.

Dr. Buchholz examines the classical theory behind the professional communications code of ethics and provides historical perspective and philosophical insight. The discussion also applies these ideas to a contemporary problem in ethical behavior.

Dr. Woolever demonstrates the power of language and the legal implications of those words in the marketplace. The essay reveals the essential function of language in writing about investment information, goods and services marketing, safety information and employee handbooks.

Ms. Nancy Blethen explains the impact of NIMBY—Not-In-My-Backyard syndrome—on the communication between a corporation and the community it is in. She explores the reality of NIMBY groups in planning and implementing any communication effort.

Truth and Taste: Revisiting High Ethical Standards for Communicators

❖

William James Buchholz

In all professional codes, the duty to adhere to the "highest standards" of truth is the central ethical charge from which all other precepts emanate. This essay examines the notion of such standards, focusing in particular upon the manner in which we communicate truth and the consequent standards of "behavioral" taste or aesthetics. Knowledge of the relationship of "truth" and "taste," philosophically linked since classical antiquity, offers insight into the high ethical standards mandated by communication codes of ethics. Because the moral engine of these codes is driven by "enlightened" humanistic philosophy, the works of those writers who have explored the notions of "taste" and "truth," as these affect conduct, provide historical perspective and philosophical insight into the highest standards of truth. Some of these notions and their ramifications are then applied to a twentieth-century problem of truth-telling and ethical behavior.

"Great is Truth, and mighty above all things."

——Book III, *The Bulgate Bible*

"How dreadful knowledge of the truth can be
When there's no help in truth!"

——Sophocles, *Oedipus Rex*

In our culture, truth-telling is highly regarded. As children, we learn that good people tell the truth; bad people lie. Most of our lives, we pay homage to the secular trinity of truth, justice, and the American way, diligently striving as best we can to tell the truth, the whole truth, and nothing but the truth. The highest good, we feel, is truth, "the secret of eloquence and of virtue, the basis of moral authority; it is the highest summit of art and of life" (Henri-Frederic Amiel, *Journal Intime*). Our belief that truth is sacred explains why, after all, so many men and women have been willing to die for it.

But there is a darker side to truth. In facing the truth about ourselves, for example, we often feel like St. Ambrose, lamenting that "truth is always bitter" (Letter 40). In spreading the truth to others, in being a simple teller of truth, a whistle-blower, we can expect to earn the world's contempt: "Truth . . . never comes into the world but like a bastard, to the ignominy of him that brought her forth" (John Milton, *The Doctrine and Discipline of Divorce*).

Truth is sublime and abysmal, its own highest reward and worst punishment. This duality, this schizophrenic aspects of truth and truth-telling, makes living a life devoted to truth extraordinarily difficult—at times nearly impossible. On the one hand, truth attracts us because it is a sacred gift; on the other hand, truth repels us because its dreadful knowledge is a curse. We live our lives straining between truth's poles of solace and distress. Daily we wrestle with truth, half-truth, lies, and white lies. We look for ways to give friends, family, co-workers, and clients the truth so as not to harm them or our relationships with them. Bereft of guidance, except for the iron phrases of the law, we guess at what to say and how to say it. In our personal lives, we look to philosophy and religion as a moral guide; in our professional lives, we look to codes of ethics and professional standards.

This chapter explores some of the difficulties that communication professionals face in searching for guidelines to handle truth. As professionals, we are fortunate to have officially sanctioned standards of conduct that, if they have any value, are able to throw some light on the moral uncertainties involved in handling truth. I should like to concentrate on three of the most widely used of these published standards as ethical touchstones in this inquiry: the Public Relations Society of America (PRSA) *Code of Professional Standards for the Practice of Public Relations,* the International Association of Business Communicators (IABC) *Code of Ethics,* and the Business/Professional Advertising Association (B/PAA) *Code of Ethics.*

The PRSA *Code of Professional Standards for the Practice of Public Relations,* divided into a "Declaration of Principles" and seventeen articles, functions both philosophically and ethically. The "Declaration," a philosophical preamble to the code, forms the value matrix that gives rise to the ethical directives in the articles. Typical of many professional codes, the PRSA preamble espouses "the fundamental value and dignity of the individual." Further, the PRSA declaration emphasizes "the free exercise of human rights, especially freedom of speech, freedom of assembly, and freedom of the press." These first-amendment freedoms guarantee the very practice of public relations, and set all the value bounds for the seventeen articles. Some of these articles are very straightforward; others contain ambiguous terms or phrases badly in need of interpretation. The ambiguous phrasings unfortunately tend to diminish the authority of the code and divorce its *ideal* possibilities from *real* attainment.

In any profession—and most certainly in communication— the core responsibility for the practitioner is to tell the truth (to not deceive, dissemble, lie, manipulate data, create false impressions, and the like). I should therefore like to keep before us the main pledge of the PRSA code: "To conduct ourselves professionally, with truth, accuracy, fairness, and responsibility to the public." This pledge overtly links communication professionalism with the basic moral virtues that lay the foundation for articles one through six:

1. A member shall conduct his or her professional life in accord with the *public interest.*
2. A member shall exemplify *high standards of honesty and integrity* while carrying out dual obligations to a client or employer and to the *democratic process.*
3. A member shall *deal fairly* with the public, with past or present clients or employers, and with fellow practitioners, giving due respect to the ideal of *free inquiry* and to the *opinions* of others.
4. A member shall adhere to the *highest standards of accuracy and truth,* avoiding *extravagant claims or unfair comparisons* and giving credit for *ideas and words borrowed* from others.
5. A member shall not knowingly disseminate *false or misleading information* and shall act promptly to correct erroneous communications for which he or she is responsible.

6. A member shall not engage in any practice which has the purpose of *corrupting the integrity of channels of communications* or the processes of government. (italics mine)

The italicized terms and phrases in these articles, specifically derived from the preamble's general notions of "truth, accuracy, fairness, and responsibility to the public," demand careful interpretation if they are to have any value whatsoever as an ethical guide for professional conduct.

Similar general concepts in need of interpretation appear in the IABC *Code of Ethics,* especially in article 1:

1. Communication professionals will uphold the credibility and dignity of their profession by *encouraging the practice of honest, candid and timely communication.* The highest standards of professionalism will be upheld in all communication. Communicators should encourage frequent communication and messages that are *honest* in their content, *candid, accurate* and *appropriate* to the needs of the organization and its audiences. (italics mine)

"Honest, candid," and "accurate," synonyms for "truth," are never explained except circularly; the code simply directs practitioners to adhere to "the highest standards" in attempting to achieve honesty, candor, and accuracy. In a similar vein, the B/PAA Code forbids lying, deception, exaggeration, and bad taste:

1. No form of business communications shall be prepared or knowingly accepted that contains *untruthful, misleading, or deceptive statements, claims or implications.*
2. No claims shall be made in business communications whose *truth and accuracy are incapable of substantiation through reasonable supporting documentation.*
4. No form of business communications shall be prepared or knowingly accepted that contains *inaccurate or misleading claims* or prices. . . .
6. No form of business communications shall be prepared or knowingly accepted that is *offensive or in bad taste.* (italics mine)

Perhaps one of the most ambiguous concepts in the B/PAA Code is the introduction in article six of communication that is "offensive" or in "bad taste."

This introduction of "taste" in a code of ethics is by no means original with the B/PAA. For years, the PRSA Code directly linked taste with truth in article three:

> 3. A member shall adhere to truth and accuracy and to generally accepted standards of good taste.

The latest PRSA Code has deleted the phrase "generally accepted standards of good taste," no doubt because of the extreme difficulty of interpretation. Instead, the notion of taste has been reduced in the new code to the idea of "extravagant claims or unfair comparisons." Thus eliminated are the difficult questions of taste: What is taste? What are good taste and bad taste? What are generally accepted standards of taste? Why link truth and taste in the same article? The questions linger, but are only hinted at in the new phrasing. Volumes, after all, could be written in trying to answer these questions about taste. Yet, the idea of taste and its relationship to truth offers an entrée—one possible among many, of course—into the central difficulty of the professional codes: *the lack of a standard by which to judge the ethical communication of truth.* In other words, to know the truth is one thing. To know *how* to communicate it ethically, quite another.

In all professional codes, the duty to adhere to a high standard of truth is the central ethical charge from which all other precepts emanate. Yet, ethical strategies to communicate truth demand at minimum some knowledge of the sender's and receiver's values, beliefs, attitudes, and taste as well as their senses of decorum, tact, diplomacy, and protocol. Thus, the question in communicating truth often becomes: what constitutes verbal, visual, or behavioral extravagance (generally unacceptable or "bad" taste) for certain people in any given culture at any given time? In answering this difficult question, my analysis will turn chiefly upon the ways in which high standards of taste can ethically inform the communication of truth.

Toward the highest standard: the relationship of truth and taste

Philosophically, truth and taste have been viewed as coincident since classical antiquity. An understanding of the one term very often leads to an understanding of the other, especially for thinkers whose humanistic ideas of liberty, human rights, and individuality have lain the foundation for all professional codes. To better understand the ramifications of the advice in our communication codes, the key term "truth," its concomitants ("honest, candid, honesty, reasonable, integrity, accuracy") and its opposites ("untruthful, false, unfair, inaccurate, misleading, deceptive") as well as "taste" ("good, offensive, corrupting, extravagant, bad") must be carefully interpreted. Further, we must understand the fundamental role that "reason" plays in determining *both* taste and truth. Classicism (from Plato on) and Renaissance humanism, Walter Jackson Bate notes, both recognize that human reason is "the only means of estimating the simultaneously real, beautiful, and good, and of evaluating the material reflection of these universals in both human ethics and art" (22). Thus, the question of the relationship of truth and taste, as determined through reason, has assumed central importance down through the ages, as philosophers have inquired into the nature of both art and morality.

Some of the most informative inquiries into the nature of taste and truth date from the eighteenth century. In that century, often seen as a philosophical and historical watershed of sorts, western civilization dramatically wrestled with classical and romantic notions of the nature of man. It was an age wherein the basic tenets of modern democracy (large-scale and republican) were first laid out and actually put into effect in America, and for a short time in France. Writing in this enlightened century of rationalism and burgeoning romanticism—the Age of Reason and, in its last decades, the Age of Feeling—many philosophers, artists, and divines passionately explored the issues of morality and aesthetics. They hoped to discover the truths in nature that would illuminate human intelligence and character, and thereby provide unerring moral guidance. And now nearly three hundred years later, the published ethical guides for the communication profession are still informed by these basic eighteenth-century beliefs, particularly those democratic notions that espouse the dignity

and freedom of the individual and the essential need to safeguard truth. This essay thus focuses chiefly on eighteenth-
century British writers whose search for a high standard shed
some of the brightest light on the meaning of "taste" and
"truth" as these notions affect ethical conduct.

Good taste and truth: the moral/aesthetic imperative

What exactly is taste? Usually we think of taste in regard
to fashion. It is tasteless, for example, in American culture to
wear white sweat socks with a navy blue suit. It is tasteless
to mix plaids and stripes. It is tasteless to wear a red and
purple tie with an orange shirt. Ersatz tudor is tasteless.
Fake Rolexes are tasteless. Madonna is tasteless. Rap is tasteless. In branding something as tasteless, we are saying that
item, person, event, or circumstance offends our aesthetic
sense. Our idea of the beautiful has been violated. The function of taste, then, is to apprehend beauty, to distinguish that
which is beautiful from that which is not. *Good* taste approves
of the shapely, the handsome, the beautiful. *Bad* taste approves of the misshapen, the deformed, the ugly.

But in equating taste with fashion, we have devalued the
power of the term by drastically narrowing its meaning. Such
restricted interpretation has not always been the case. Eighteenth-century notions of taste, for example, were much
broader and thereby richly informative. In *An Enquiry Concerning the Principles of Taste* (1785), Frances Reynolds, sister of famed eighteenth-century British painter Joshua
Reynolds, asserts that fashion and ornamentation occupy the
lowest order of taste. She prefers, in fact, not even to use the
term "taste" to identify this sphere. Instead, because fashion
encourages "the general love of novelty and superfluity" (42),
two corruptors of *true* taste, Reynolds uses the term "Fancy."
A lesser form of imagination because it does not concern itself
with sublime or grand notions, Fancy, in her words, "seems
an undisciplined offspring of Taste" (43). Taste as the arbiter
of acceptable and unacceptable fashion—what for most of us
is the *only* meaning of the term—becomes for Reynolds the
least important meaning, so insignificant that she prefers not
even to designate it an aspect of taste.

In distinguishing taste from fancy as she has, Frances
Reynolds clarifies its least important aspect. The most impor-

tant aspects, she elevates to two greater orders: the divine
and the social. The divine order consists of those objects or
people "which the natural virtuous affections of the soul inspire." These are friendship, filial piety, and the like affections that "unite the moral sentiment to the divine." Our
ethical or moral sentiments and acts are thus infused with
divine sanction in Frances Reynolds' highest order of taste.
The social sphere or second level of taste consists of "order,
beauty, and honour," those "effects of true taste, or moral
virtue" that make relationships among humans both functional
and elegant (42). An honourable person, for example, is a
virtuous person whose behavior is, by definition, *truly* tasteful. The dishonorable person, the liar, the cheat, the scala-
wag, is by definition morally ugly and therefore *tasteless*
(truthless) to persons of virtue.

Reynolds, reflecting the classical humanistic tradition, has
expanded the notion of taste to include morality, thereby mar-
rying the aesthetic sense to the moral sense. These two senses
belong together for a writer like Reynolds and, in fact, cannot
be separated because they work toward the same predetermined
end: perception of the Ideal character. The senses, memory,
imagination, judgment, and reason work in concert to give us
the ultimate vision, the Truth, or (in Platonic terms) the Ideal.
For Frances Reynolds, taste is sometimes seen as the unifying
impulse, involving nothing less than the human soul itself:

> Taste seems to be an inherent impulsive tendency of the soul
> towards true good, given by nature to all alike, and which
> improves in its sentiment as the reasoning faculties improve
> in their knowledge of what *is* true good.

> All the human faculties are, as one may say, constituents of
> the principle or faculty of taste. But its perception seems to
> be shared between the judgement and the imagination: to
> the former seems to belong the truth, or good, of an object of
> taste; to the latter its beauty or grace; and the stamina vi-
> tae, or radical principles of taste, exist, I imagine, in the
> natural affections of the soul. (35)

Truth and goodness are the ultimate targets of the soul.
All human faculties are united toward that goal within the
single faculty of taste. Reynolds here combines truth and
beauty under the auspices of taste by distinguishing their
separate modes of perception. Truth (or good) is derived

through the cold rational faculty of the "judgement." The intellect uses reason or rationality to throw light upon our actions and thereby determine their morality or immorality (36–37). Beauty (or grace), according to Reynolds, is derived through the imagination (as distinct from its lesser form, the fancy). Alexander Gerard in *An Essay on Taste* goes even further, seeing morality itself as simply "taste of a superior order, by which, in characters and conduct, we distinguish between the right and the wrong" (71). For Reynolds and Gerard, taste and morality are thus unified and internalized. In other words, the operating principles of taste are a given; they exist in the soul itself as the aesthetic sense, in a state of what Reynolds calls "the natural affections." Because these principles are essential to the human condition (both the moral and aesthetic senses are "givens" of our being), we cannot satisfactorily explain these principles or understand their operation. For Reynolds, all we need really know is that "taste is intellectual pleasure, an approving sense of truth, of good, and of beauty. The latter seems the visible or ostensible principle of the two former, and is that in which the universal idea of taste is comprised" (37).

Taste and reason

Taste as an approving sense, or natural affection of the soul, may or may not be intellectual, as such. For other eighteenth-century writers aesthetic sensibility (taste) is sometimes seen as reason's adjunct; sometimes seen as passion, separable from reason; sometimes seen as part of an admixture of reason, imagination, and judgment. David Hume notes, for example, in "Of the Standard of Taste" that "reason, if not an essential part of taste, is at least requisite to the operations" of taste (227). Reason is an adjunct to taste simply because creators or artisans must consider the correspondence of the parts to the whole and ensure that the aim of their work is fulfilled.

Contrary to Hume, Alexander Gerard asserts that taste judiciously blends a reasoned judgment and imagination to give us the power to select the good:

> It [taste] consists in certain *excellences* of our original powers of judgment and imagination combined. These may be

> reduced to four: *sensibility, refinement, correctness,* and the *proportion* or *comparative adjustment of its separate principles.* All these must be in some considerable degree *united,* in order to form *true taste.* (98)

True taste for Gerard seems to depend upon correctness and proportion—restraining the imagination, pruning overactive possibilities. In short, true taste settles things in balance. Thus, while judgment and imagination are combined here, Gerard is biased toward judgment; reason seems to prevail.

William Thomson offers one of the clearest expositions of the hierarchal relationship of the taste and the other mental faculties. In his "Discourse on Taste" he notes that the five senses, "as *purveyors,* or collectors of all our stores of knowledge and information" (16), must be seen as the first mental power because they give rise to the *"simple ideas"* (essentially the Lockean view). The second mental power is *memory;* the third, *imagination* or *fancy;* the fourth, "Taste, whose office it is . . . to determine and pronounce upon whatever is *beautiful, elegant, sublime, pleasing,* or the reverse of these"; the fifth, *judgment* (17). Judgment or reason is last, and chief, because it acts as the regulator of taste. But taste is second only to reason in censoring power: taste selects and discards whatever it finds defective in the impressions presented by the imagination. Taste, in fact, for Thomson, is the sixth sense, "which impels us to every action of the body and application of the mind" (67). Thomson has introduced a motivating aspect to taste that for other eighteenth-century writers becomes an important distinction as well, differentiating taste from reason or judgment, and conferring upon it an altogether different kind of power.

Taste and passion

Writing about this same time, John Donaldson in *The Elements of Beauty* examines the relationship of reason to the passions and takes the opposite tack. Contrary to Reynolds' and Gerard's assertion that taste is a combination of judgment and imagination, and closer to Thomson's idea that taste is a separate and very powerful internal sixth sense, Donaldson emphasizes that "Concerning matters of taste, we appeal to the feelings of the heart, rather than to abilities of the head. Taste prevents judgment and is more beholden to sentiment than to experience" (6). For Donaldson, taste is somewhat midless, chiefly a matter of feeling, of emotion. John Gilbert Cooper in his *Letters Concerning Taste* also emphasizes Taste as a feeling. Taste "seizes the Heart with Rapture long before the Senses, and Reason in Conjunction, can *prove* this Beauty by collating the Imitations with their Originals" (7). An affective impulse, taste comes from the heart, not from the head. Frances Reynolds, Donaldson, Thomson, and Cooper seem to echo the *je ne sais quoi* "School of Taste" that conceived "of taste as non-rational" (Bate 44). Taste for them has a very special emotional power.

While reason, the product of intellect operating upon experience, yields truth in the form of propositions, such truth by itself means little to human beings. The motivating impulse to do good, to behave well, to tell the truth, must come from the heart. Put simply, one must *desire* the truth, not simply *know* the truth. For Thomson "the *motive* is ever found in the *Taste,* the *seat* and *mover* of all the passions" (86); in fact, "love and hatred, desire and aversion, etc. have there their rise and energy, and are all excited by the peculiar feelings or sensations of the *internal sense* only" (94). The danger here, of course, is that taste might be corrupted, for it *is* corruptible, Frances Reynolds reminds us (43), and therefore must be very "carefully attended to" (Thomson 87). Recognizing this vulnerability of Taste, Donaldson makes her "the younger sister of Virtue; the offspring of Taste is Pleasure, that of Virtue is Happiness: it is the grace of sentiment" (83). While not identical with Virtue, Taste is closely related to her (younger and therefore possibly more vibrant, more attractive, more vulnerable?). Her progeny is Pleasure, lower on the moral scale than Virtue's Happiness, perhaps, but still essential to make earthly life worthwhile. For Plato, life without reflection, the unexamined life, was not worth living; for Donaldson and other eighteenth-century writers, the unaesthetic life, ignorant "of beauty, or depravity of taste, is defective animation" (84) and thereby not worth living. To have taste, to "feel" beauty, "is to be alive" to truth (85).

Reason and passion in balance

Some eighteenth-century writers recognize that separating reason and passion relative to taste is not always possible. Edmund Burke, for example, appreciates fully the complexity of taste, noting the intermixture of its elements: perception, imagination, reason, emotion, and behavior. Taste, says Burke, "is partly made up of a perception of the primary pleasures of sense, of the secondary pleasures of the imagination, and of the conclusions of the reasoning faculty, concerning the various relations of these, and concerning the human passions, manners, and actions" (23). Unlike Gerard or Thomson, Burke appreciates taste as a faculty combining the others, more or less as a uniting principle that serves to balance the competing interests of the senses, imagination, reason, passions, social conventions, and human acts.

Yet even Thomson, Donaldson, and Cooper, reminiscent of Hume and Burke, conclude that "right reason and true taste" exist in "perfect agreement." As "reciprocal tests of each other's validity," they seem to form a check upon one another, for whenever we encounter pleasing things of good taste, we enquire as to the causes of our pleasure in apprehending them (Donaldson 6). And Thomson notes that "each of the faculties, watching and accompanying the action of its inferior, generally speaking, corrects its errors during its progress" (19). This notion of balance in our faculties reflects the eighteenth-century fondness for the smooth-running, perpetually moving machine, most notable in the clockwork mechanism. Nature, they surmise, is regulated by immutable principles of physics and mechanics, all of which conform to knowable laws. John Gilbert Cooper likewise emphasizes this balance, what he calls a "happy blend," of all the faculties in the person of taste:

> For *Taste* does not *wholly* depend upon the natural Strength and acquired Improvement of the *Intellectual* Powers; nor *wholly* upon a fine Construction of the *Organs* of the Body; nor *wholly* upon the intermediate Powers of the *Imagination;* but upon a Union of them all happily blended, without too great a Prevalency in either. Hence it falls out, that one Man may be a very great Reasoner; another have the finest Genius for Poetry; and a third be blessed with the most delicate Organs of Sense; and yet every one of these be deficient in that *internal* Sensation called *Taste.* (27–28)

Balance ultimately becomes the overriding concern for Cooper and others. Taste functions as a kind of arbiter over the other faculties; without taste, the other faculties can become over-ripe. Too much reason makes one mechanical; too much passion makes one unstable; too much imagination makes one a dreamer. Taste helps to blend all the faculties into a judicious harmony of human power: sensed, remembered, imagined, censored, and reasoned.

Beyond reason and passion—metaphysical aspects of taste and truth

Unlike Hume, Burke, and those who strove chiefly to adduce the operating principles or standards of taste, some eighteenth-century writers, like Frances Reynolds, John Donaldson, and James Usher departed from the more or less empirical/rational approach and struggled to clarify the relationship of the physical (natural) to the metaphysical (ideal) as established through taste. In attempting to fathom the standards of taste, Usher, writing his *Clio: or, a Discourse on Taste* in 1769, is compelled to establish taste as a means to universal beauty: "Good taste is the inward light or intelligence of universal beauty" (36). For Usher, taste comes from within the soul in the form of light. We possess taste by nature and are not necessarily educted to it, though, of course, we can work to improve our knowledge of its standards. Humans with a native sense of good taste are blessed (literally) with something of a given intelligence capable of apprehending or seeing through to "real" or universal beauty. Those possessing *true* taste cannot be duped by the accidental or adjunctive (associative) beauty of mode or fashion because, like Frances Reynolds' beholders of the first sphere, the divine sphere of true taste, they have an unerring or God-like sense of *true* beauty.

For Usher, recalling Rollin, "True taste discovers with delight the image of nature, and pursues it with a faithful passion. The graceful and the becoming are never found separated from nature and propriety" (38). With the so-called true taste, one is able to know truth through the essential aspects of nature. What is natural is true, what is true *is* natural, Taste for Usher is our universal ability to discover *the truth that is nature.* What is full of grace, what is becoming, is also natural and proper. Thus, rules of correct behavior reflect the natural state of gracefulness to which human beings must aspire. Elegance, gracefulness, and propriety are essential natural conditions, not artificial adjuncts or embellishments. The person of taste is able to demonstrate divine truth literally, through the senses.

Truth is the moral high point for Usher because it reflects the ultimate good: "Virtue and truth are inseparable, and take their flight together." In his own flight of fancy, Usher proclaims that "Truth is the genius of taste, and enters into the essence of simple beauty in wit, in writing, and throughout the fine arts" (63). Thus the person of taste is the virtuous one who knows and speaks the truth. The person of taste, in fact, has no choice but to utter truth, for truth (virtue) stands behind taste as a muse or genius. Truth is a creative principle that informs, that inspires beautiful vision through literally entering "into the essence of simple beauty." Taste itself becomes the finite medium (relative and particular) through which the universal truth (absolute and infinite) is manifest. The abstract universal principle of truth/virtue is thus linked through taste with the concrete particulars that our senses apprehend in nature. As Frances Reynolds also notes, the human creator works with that "beauty which is demonstrable truth, and that truth which is demonstrable beauty." The human creator conjoins the intellectual world of idea (the Platonic Ideal) with the world of sense. In demonstrating truth, the human creator is in contact with the divine creator, standing "as it were, between the visible and invisible world; between that of sense and intellect" (10).

Theoretically, all is well and good. The key problem, however, involves the senses and their quality of apprehension. Our perceptions are only as good as our senses, and our senses are extraordinarily fallible. To assert as do Frances Reynolds and Usher that we can attain a vision of perfection through imperfect lenses demands a leap of faith unacceptable to most of us. Our genetic makeup, our mental alertness, our biography, the notions of the times in which we live, as well as a host of sensory variables too numerous to mention, cloud our ability to apprehend the universal with certainty. Our perception selects only what the mind's gatekeepers—its values, beliefs, attitudes, opinions—let through to consciousness. The best we can hope for are partial glimpses of truths that we can cobble together into some kind of generally acceptable truth. For as Hume notes, only "strong sense, united to delicate sentiment, improved by practice, perfected by comparison, and cleared of all prejudice" can result in "the true standard of taste" (228). One simply must *work* at knowing the truth. That struggle to know truth, and the part that a standard of taste plays in handling truth, has never been more clearly explained than in the writings of Joshua Reynolds.

A standard of taste and universal truth in nature

Joshua Reynolds, a major eighteenth-century British artist, became first President of the Royal Academy upon its founding in 1768. His *Discourses on Art,* Robert Lavine notes, are "the first significant attempt in the English language at what may be called a philosophy of art, and no subsequent works of criticism by an Englishman have enjoyed such widespread and sustained respect" (Reynolds v). Walter Jackson Bate goes so far as to say that "Reynolds's *Discourses* comprise perhaps the most representative single embodiment in English of eighteenth-century aesthetic principles" (79). "Discourse Seven, delivered to the Students of the Royal Academy . . . December 10, 1776" (103), in examining "the reality of a standard of Taste" (xiii), presents one of the most immediately accessible humanistic discussions of the subject ever written. His insights are still valuable to us over two hundred years later.

Reynolds begins "Discourse Seven" by framing the definition of taste in moral terms. Taste, he says, "is a power of distinguishing right from wrong . . . applied to works of art" (106). As he proceeds through "Discourse Seven," it becomes clear that by "art" Reynolds means not only those works we commend as "high" art, but anything humanly created, encompassing fashion and the lower forms of craftsmanship. Today, that would include popular music, fiction, movies, advertising, and design. Those works of art that excite "ideas of grandeur" or dignify humanity, however, he holds in highest esteem (116). Over and against art, the humanly created, are the naturally created—those things found in nature, all subject to "natural" law. Itself the result of natural creation, the human mind too must obey the laws of nature. One of the overriding "natural" laws of the human mind is its quest for truth. This quest is the result of a

> natural appetite or taste of the human mind . . . for *Truth;*
> whether that truth results from the real agreement or equal-

ity of original ideas among themselves; from the agreement
of the representation of any object with the thing represented;
or from the correspondence of the several parts of any arrangement with each other. (109)

All these *real* and *fixed* truths (or, if you will, principles and
laws) for which we long are materialized in nature and can be
known through reason and diligent study. Reynolds, in fact,
assumes "that reason is something invariable and fixed in the
nature of things" and "that whatever goes under the name of
taste, which we can fairly bring under the dominion of reason, must be considered as equally exempt from change" (110).
Thus, the principles that guide us, the laws that govern us,
the so-called *real Truths,* are made evident universally
throughout nature and are thereby knowable by way of our
reasoned efforts in the name of taste.

The comforting notion here is that we have two absolutes:
the immutable laws of nature and the unchanging laws of
human reason and taste. For Reynolds *Truth* is not some distant and unattainable Ideal, or bloodless abstraction, or unre-
alizable goal. Quite the opposite. *Real Truths* are the operating
principles of nature; these principles we know from our senses
and understand through our reasoning taste. Many eighteenth-
century writers equate such principles with beauty. Francis
Hutcheson, for example, explains that

> In the search of *Nature* there is the like *Beauty* in the Knowl-
> edge of some great *Principles,* or universal *Forces,* from which
> innumerable Effects do flow. Such is *Gravitation,* in Sir Isaac
> Newton's Scheme; such also is the Knowledge of the Original
> of *Rights, perfect* and *imperfect,* and *external; alienable* and
> *unalienable,* with their manner of *Translations;* from whence
> the greatest Part of moral Dutys may be deduc'd in the vari-
> ous Relations of human Life. (34)

That which conforms to natural law, with either Newtonian
or political ramifications, is knowable and a potential moral
guide. In fact, knowledge of these "great *Principles,* or universal *Forces*" directs our selection or rejection of the good, in *all*
questions of taste, whether moral, political, or artistic.

But not all truths are primary; a vast number are secondary. The secondary truths, what Reynolds terms *apparent* or
variable truths, consist of opinion or prejudice, those things
most obviously fashionable or current. The danger with vari-

able truth is that, because it is subject to the vicissitudes of
time, we can never be certain that such truth is "real." Our
apprehension of such secondary truth may in fact be illusory;
in time we may find these secondary truths to be false. We
must therefore subject these secondary truths to the test of
time and widespread acceptability, for "in proportion as these
prejudices are known to be generally diffused, or long received,
the taste which conforms to them approaches nearer to certainty, and to a sort of resemblance to real science" (110).
Thus, while fashion in one age and country may fall out of
favor in another time and place, certain constants or generalizable aspects prevail as secondary truths. Today, for example,
wide ties may be "in" or "out" of fashion, but the idea itself of
wearing a tie (whether wide or narrow) gains force as *a secondary truth of civilized dress* the more widely it is adopted
by various contries and cultures through time. Color, pattern,
and width are the accidental characteristics subject to whim
or caprice. Because of these vagaries, however, secondary or
variable truths never obtain the force of "real truth" or general principle.

Given these distinctions, what might be the chief operating principle or standard of taste? What is good taste? What
is bad taste?

> The beginning, the middle, and the end of every thing that is
> valuable in taste, is comprised in the knowledge of what is
> truly nature; for whatever notions are not conformable to
> those of nature, or universal opinion, must be considered as
> more or less capricious. (111)

For Reynolds, ever the neo-classical humanist, whatever conforms to natural law, whatever *imitates* nature most generally
or universally conforms to the highest standard of taste: "It
plainly appears, that as a work is conducted under the influence of general ideas, or partial, it is principally to be considered as the effect of a good or a bad taste" (111). The Ideal, the
most widely generalizable or universal aspects of nature, therefore become real to us. We are morally obligated to select that
which conforms most to nature in its broadest outlines and
reject that which conforms least. Nature itself—sensed, objec-
tified, and generalized—becomes the highest standard.

For this natural standard to become accessible to all,
Reynolds must elevate the common to the Ideal. The common

must become Ideal because it pervades nature and humanity most widely. Reason, he writes, is essentially based upon common sense and the common feelings of mankind. For Reynolds, common sense and common feelings are "of equal authority, and equally conclusive" (117). Because most people literally sense and feel in roughly the same way, human beings can apprehend truth through the common assent of "knowing what are the general feelings and passions of mankind" (118). Taste therefore is liable to a "natural standard" because taste is knowledge "derived from the uniformity of sentiments among mankind, from whence proceeds the knowledge of what are the general habits of nature; the result of which is an idea of perfect beauty" (125).

At bottom, then, for Reynolds principles of taste are solidly founded upon the demonstrable truths of general, universalizable nature. To know these principles requires that one diligently study history, philosophy, literature—the arts and sciences, the accumulated knowledge of mankind, as well as keenly and continually observe the workings of nature and the actions of human beings. The highest standard of truth is good taste, nothing less than wisdom itself. The certain knowledge of nature's primary laws or unchangeable real *Truth* becomes the Ideal to be imitated, the model against which we measure and shape human ethical behavior itself.

Summary

Taste is a powerful faculty. As Gerard notes, the person of taste "acquires authority and influence, and forms just decisions; which may be rejected by the caprice of *some,* but are sure to gain *general* acknowledgment" (98). This authority comes to people of taste because they are empowered to choose the right, the proportionate, and the balanced over the wrong, the disproportionate, and the unbalanced. In fact, as Joshua Reynolds asserts, taste and right reason allow for a direct apprehension of the Ideal as manifest in generalizable nature. Put in metaphysical terms so dear to some eighteenth-century writers on the subject, taste affords a glimpse into the mind of God, and of course, in that mind, only virtue could exist. Thus, physical beauty becomes an earthly demonstration, through the senses, of metaphysical truth. The ideal is made real and judged aright through correct and sensitive taste. As Joshua Reynolds notes, taste, aided by reason and study, allows us to understand the immutable laws of nature, which themselves are manifestations of the real truths that serve as ethical guides. Taste is the mode of apprehending the ultimate truths—in Usher's words, those "absolute and eternal perfections" that have been "stamped on our minds" (12). To some writers, most notably Thomson and Donaldson, our desire for such eternal truth is inflamed by the sense of taste, which ignites our passionate commitment actually to seek and do the good. In eighteenth-century parlance, the highest standards of truth and taste guarantee that the rights of individual liberty, passionately pursued, are balanced against the reasoned responsibility to perform our Moral Duty.

Standards of truth and taste applied today

With this eighteenth-century philosophical backdrop, let us now apply these standards of taste and truth to a twentieth-century communication problem. To keep the discussion as simple as possible, "truth" shall be relegated to an easily observable factual proposition (as opposed to one of value or opinion). Thus, the application will be concerned more with *handling* truth than with *ascertaining* it. To test the truth of the statement, then, we will simply compare it to "reality." Does the proposition's meaning square with experience? Would a reasonable person of sound mind and "common" sense upon confronting the facts assent to the proposition? The true proposition in this instance can also be seen as accurate, thus, the "truth and accuracy" statement of the professional codes offers no conceptual difficulty. For example, I see no advertisements in a particular journal in my office. I state, "This journal has no ads." My proposition can be verified by all who hear it through the direct experience of their own vision. I have told the truth if they too see no ads in the journal. (Upon their seeing an ad, I have either lied, uttered mistakenly, or misperceived the situation—three lamentable conditions that affect my credibility.) If my auditors do not have access to the journal, they may trust a third-party verification of the "fact" that no ads exist. Thus, we have all the basic elements necessary for truth-texting by reason (or judgment) and experience: an object perceived through the senses, a factual proposition about that object, a validity test, and recourse to a trusted third-party verification, if desired.

At this essential level of experience, truth-telling and lying are rather simple affairs. Any prohibition against lying can be easily understood. Assume for example, that a manager has stated that she must inform three of her employees that, because of corporate downsizing, their positions must be terminated. The truth-test is concerned with three conditions: the necessity of termination, the number of employees affected by termination, and the cause of termination. If upon examination all three conditions are verified, the manager has uttered truthfully and accurately, thereby fulfilling the codes' injunction. But the question remains: in satisfying the condition of "truth and accuracy," can we ascertain that the manager has adhered to morally tasteful behavior?

No, we cannot, simply because we have no way of testing the *appropriateness* of her actions against a clear standard of taste, as we were able to test the "truth and accuracy" of her utterance against a clear standard of truth. In this matter of taste, we know that any attempt to comply to an invisible standard is futile. But, then again, *why* should the manager even wish to comply? What, after all does "taste" have to do with the unfortunate situation she faces?

I would argue that in this case, and in millions more that we face everyday, standards of good taste, rightly understood—that is, morally understood, as they have been for thousands of years—provide the means for us to decide the ultimate success or failure of the endeavor. In other words, though in *practice* confusing, the linkage of taste with truth is in fact *philosophically* correct. The eighteenth-century writers gave us a great number of glimpses into just how "taste," rightly understood, in truth-telling ultimately affects the tone of human relationships involved. Let me explain.

I have used the phrase "rightly understood" twice in the preceding paragraph to underscore the importance of carefully defining the term "taste." To understand "taste" in the context of our communication codes of ethics, one must follow the lead of those humanists who link the moral with the aesthetic sense. Their concern, remember, goes beyond mode, fashion, and the lower forms of beauty; they see taste related to a larger natural, social, cosmic (metaphysical), or universalized good. A person of taste *cares* about acting correctly because the aesthetic of proper behavior constitutes the concrete demonstration or particular evidence in nature of universal moral law. If, for example, in the process of termination, the manager treats her three employees with dignity by speaking softly rather than bellowing, by talking in measured tones rather than hysterical, by observing all the conventions of politeness, she has deferred to their dignity as human beings. If they comply with like behavior, their relationship has become a kind of artwork of civility (perhaps intuitively), wherein manager and employees collaborate with each other to choreograph a moral and aesthetic dance, acceptable (if not pleasing) to all parties.

The truth all take for granted; at some point all parties *agree* that they are sharing the truth. Thus, in one sense, they are interested less in the substance of the event (for that is a given) than in how they *play out* their assigned parts (for those follow from the given truth). Artifice, style, protocol, manners, propriety, or what I would term *moral choreography*—these dominate the termination event. Some would argue that the parties have wrongly emphasized appearance over substance. I would agree that they *have* emphasized appearance over substance—but not wrongly. Their situation has simply *demanded* that emphasis. Classical humanists, noted for their sensitivity to the moral and aesthetic dimension of manners, understood this better than we do today. Let us look more closely at the manager and her bad news.

The truth is simple: three people must go. In talking with the three, the manager is concerned only with *how* she will tell the truth, not *if* she will tell the truth. Here precisely is where standards of taste come into play, and where the notions of enlightened humanism will help us. Recall, for a moment, Frances Reynolds' three spheres of taste: the fashionable, the social, and the divine. Fashion being irrelevant in this situation, let us focus on the social and divine. The key to "tasteful" behavior in these spheres for Reynolds was behaving honorably; that is, one must not perform any act or utter any word to impugn integrity, honesty, and forthrightness. Reynolds' standards, against which one measures success or failure in attaining tasteful action, are at bottom *affective,* as are Donaldson's, Thomson's, and Cooper's. For all of them, morally tasteful actions are felt; they come from the heart. Reynolds uses the words "friendship" and talks about "filial piety." Donaldson sees the human heart take on a divine aura; in the other person, we "feel" God. Thomson reminds us that taste gives rise to motivating passion. And Cooper regards taste as rapturous. For all four, our responsibility to the other becomes charged (almost sacredly) by means of our sensitivity to human fellow-feeling.

In terminating these three individuals, Reynolds, Thomson, and Donaldson would have us ask: how would we treat our dearest friend? Our loved ones? How we treat them becomes the measure of how we treat these three employees, or how we treat strangers—or enemies. The care and consideration we give these three people, however, may well differ for each because over time our relationship with them has conformed to both our character (values, needs, and behavior) and their character. Reynolds, Thomson, and Donaldson would remind us that a diseased or broken relationship is simply an accumulation over time of morally "tasteless" behaviors and statements. In other words, our "tasteful" behavior in any relationship is predicated upon something greater than the given moment, something larger than any single act performed or statement uttered. Our behavior ultimately is determined by character, biography, relationships, and the events at hand. How do we know any given behavior is tasteful, that is, correct? By *feeling* the correctness. Because the ultimate standard of taste for these writers is *affective,* they would counsel our manager simply to *feel* the rightness of the situation.

When the burden is put on the heart in this way, however, no prescriptive moral code can guide us. Only the character of the manager, her knowledge of, and sensitivity to, the needs of her fellow human beings, and ultimately her wisdom, will result in a "morally tasteful" outcome. Morality at this feeling level *is* an art—precisely why some people are so much better at managing than others. If professional codes demand that we adhere to the highest standards of truth and behave accordingly, they assume that we know exactly what those standards are (which we do not always) and that we are capable of meeting them (which we may not be). Thus, the affective standard is a good moral refuge for some people, but as a standard it leaves many of us still in the dark. Most managers need more explicit guidance. Such guidance we may find not in our hearts but through our senses and in our reason, which, motivated by judiciously tempered passion, impel us to search for universalizable natural law. This "natural" view of truth and moral taste provides a more explicit standard than does the affective view.

In the "natural" view, Joshua Reynolds reminds us, for our manager to give the truth of the bad news tastefully, she must first speak from *common* sense and from *common* feelings. She is responsible to act based upon her own senses, memory, imagination, reason, and feelings, of course, but these must not be whimsical or errant. She must herself become something of an artist, constructing graphic mental sensations and subjecting them to the internal sense, taste, as she prepares to select and reject alternative responses to the moment. The "good" alternatives conform to generalizable natural law; the "bad" alternatives do not. Sometimes called empathy, or empathic fusion, this mental mode is extraordinarily taxing because it makes demands of the *whole* mind.

For example, it would be immoral (morally tasteless) for our manager to be abrupt and curt with an employee whom she has empathically identified as one who thrives upon patient and nurturing responses. Theoretically, the generalizable law would go something like this: *nurturing people usually prefer to receive as well as give nurturing attention.* If our manager can perceive the evidence that indicates employee A to be a nurturing type, and can understand that type from the inside (empathically through memory and imagination), she is able to respond in the relationship imaginatively and instantaneously. Her senses, memory, imagination, and reason help her to select and reject morally tasteless behaviors or statements that violate the conditions of the universalizable law momentarily pertaining in the relationship. What is the chief danger our manager faces in selecting and rejecting her behaviors? Inappropriate or unbalanced response.

Above all, our manager's empathic response, as Thomson, Donaldson, and Cooper remind us, must be balanced. The harmony of the mental abilities, what Cooper called the "happy blend," should produce a balanced and humane response. Behavioral good taste, then, would assure that our manager did not respond too mechanically, too coldly—or too emotionally, too warmly. In other words, the full potential range of responses cannot be predicted or forecast, except in the most general terms, because "tasteful" morality in handling truth is determined by the interplay of the particular humans involved. The manager, for example, may elect to treat person A more warmly than persons B and C, recognizing that A needs such warmth while B and C are made uncomfortable by it. Taste dictates varied responses. Hence, judgment, that censoring faculty, as an element of taste, or closely allied to it, becomes key.

What all this boils down to is that matters of taste, moral and aesthetic, involve almost limitless possibilities that extend over the full range of human perception, intelligence, and feeling. High standards of truth (and taste) must therefore be interpreted according to time, place, and value (both cultural and personal). Even in apparently clearcut matters like this one, where ascertaining truth is simple, *handling* it is extraordinarily complex. Yet we must never quit trying to define the best ways of handling truth. The challenge of our communication codes, as with all professional codes, is in their interpretation. Fortunately, our humanist tradition is rich in possible interpretations of human character and relationships.

There *are* answers to the problems we face in ascertaining the highest standards of truth. They just are not easily gotten. Joshua Reynolds, Hume, Burke, Thomson, Usher, and other humanists remind us, however, that we must have faith in our power to reason and in our ability to fathom the generalizable laws of human nature, for these are the *only* certainties we have. Oh, yes, there is one more: diligent study. No general code of professional conduct can give us all the answers to every situation. Such codes serve only to offer bold outlines of good behavior. Their higher function is, through a necessary uncertainty or tentativeness, to tease us into thought. That thought is disciplined and enriched through studying books, of course, but even more through constantly attending to the actions and reactions of our fellow human beings, for we can never be absolutely certain about them.

As my title reminds us, linking truth and taste can result in the highest of ethical standards. Knowledge of a high ethical standard is absolutely necessary, because the times in which we live are so precarious. But, then, all times are precarious—few ever more so, perhaps, than the eighteenth century. A great number of eighteenth-century thinkers strove mightily to find the solid philosophical bedrock upon which to build effective political and human relationships. They understood that freedom and individual rights, so essential to democracy, depend utterly upon moral behavior. And moral behavior derives from clear insight into the essential principles, Jefferson's self-evident truths. Our recognition that each of us, through reasoned judgment and high moral taste, is personally responsible to discern and adhere to those principles, humanistically links the eighteenth century to our own.

References

Bate, Walter Jackson. *From Classic to Romantic: Premises of Taste in Eighteenth-Century England.* 1945. New York: Harper, 1961.

B/PAA Code of Ethics. Alexandria, VA: Business/Professional Advertising Association (B/PAA).

Burke, Edmund. "On Taste." *Edmund Burke.* Harvard Classics. Edited by Charles W. Eliot, v. 24. New York: Collier, 1910: pp. 11–26.

Code of Professional Standards for the Practice of Public Relations. New York: Public Relations Society of America (PRSA), 1988.

Cooper, John Gilbert. *Letters Concerning Taste, and Essays on Similar and Other Subjects.* 1757. New York: Garland, 1970.

Donaldson, John. *The Elements of Beauty. Also Reflections on the Harmony of Sensibility and Reason.* 1780. New York: Garland, 1970.

Gerard, Alexander. *An Essay on Taste.* 1764. New York: Garland, 1970.

Hume, David. "Of the Standard of Taste." *English Essays from Sir Philip Sidney to Macaulay.* Harvard Classics. Edited by Charles W. Eliot, v. 27. New York: Collier, 1910: 215–234.

Hutcheson, Francis. *An Inquiry into the Original of Our Ideas of Beauty and Virtue.* 1726. New York: Garland, 1971.

IABC Code of Ethics. San Francisco: International Association of Business Communication.

Reynolds, Frances. *An Enquiry Concerning the Principles of Taste and of the Origin of our Ideas of Beauty.* 1785. New York: Garland, 1972.

Reynolds, Sir Joshua. *Discourses on Art.* Robert Lavine, introduction. New York: Collier, 1961.

Thomson, William. *An Enquiry into the Elementary Principles of Beauty, in the Works of Nature and Art. To Which is Prefixed, an Introductory Discourse on Taste.* 1798. New York: Garland, 1972.

Usher, James. *Clio: or, a Discourse on Taste.* 2nd edition. 1769. New York: Garland, 1970.

Willey, Basil. *The Eighteenth Century Background: Studies on the Idea of Nature in the Thought of the Period.* 1940. Boston: Beacon Press, 1961.

Corporate Language and the Law: Avoiding Liability in Corporate Communications

❖

Kristin R. Woolever

Although corporate writers recognize the power of language as a marketing tool, they often fail to realize the legal implications of their words. Liability issues have become a prime concern in four areas where language plays a major part: (1) investment information, (2) goods and services marketing, (3) safety information, and (4) employee handbooks. Understanding the legal problems attendant to these areas will allow corporate writers to better avoid language that risks litigation.

Corporate language implies a contract with the consumer

When writers publish information for the public, their words establish a kind of contract with the audience—a bond of faith based on truth and mutual understanding. Corporate writers especially need to become more aware of this link and realize the multiple possibilities for their words to miscommunicate, thereby breaking faith with the audience. In corporate liability suits involving language, consumers usually claim intentional miscommunication on the company's part, while the company denies any such intent. Somewhere in the transfer of information, the truth has become lost and the courts are left to decide who is to blame for the misunderstanding.

As early as 400 B.C. classical rhetoricians recognized the need for writers and speakers to maintain faith with their audiences, or communication could become a morass of deceit. It's worth noting two short passages, one from Plato and one from Aristotle, that can serve as touchstones for establishing clear lines of communication with an audience. In the *Phaedrus,* Plato explains the steps necessary to create mutual understanding between writer and reader. According to Plato, writers need to do more than a cursory audience analysis; they need to examine the audience's essential character (what Plato calls "the soul") to determine what effect various words will have. He gives a three-step method for thoroughly connecting with the audience:

> [The rhetorician] will first describe the soul with perfect accuracy and make us see whether it is one and all alike, or like the body, of multi-form aspect; for this is what we call explaining its nature. . . . And secondly, he will say what [the soul's] action is and toward what it is directed, or how it is acted upon and by what. . . . Thirdly, he will classify the speeches and the souls and will adapt each to each other, showing the causes of the effects produced and why one kind of soul is necessarily persuaded by certain classes of speeches and another is not. . . . Until [rhetoricians] write and speak by this method we cannot believe that they write by the rules of art.

While Plato focuses on understanding the audience, Aristotle turns his attention to the writers themselves. In this passage from *The Rhetoric,* he discusses how writers—or "speakers" in the classical world—can best win their audience's trust and what causes them occasionally to mislead that audience:

> The speakers themselves are made trustworthy by three things; for there are three things, besides demonstrations, which make us believe. These are intelligence, virtue, and good will. Men are false in their statements, and their counsels, from all or one of the following causes. Either through folly they have not the right opinions; or having right opinions, they say through knavery what they do not think; or they are sensible and honest, but not well-disposed, whence they may happen not to advise the best course, although they may see it.

Central to liability cases are the two issues Plato and Aristotle identify: Is the message designed specifically enough for the intended audience? Does the writer intentionally mislead the audience? These questions are essential to any discussion of corporate language, and the writers' chief concern should be to anticipate them and design prose that does not violate the audience's trust.

Corporate liability is most prevalent in the four areas of communication where these questions play the greatest role: (1) investment information, (2) goods and services marketing, (3) safety information, and (4) employee handbooks. In each of these areas, writers run a great risk of making the "false statements" that Aristotle mentions, thereby precipitating legal action. An investigation into these categories illustrates some of the problems corporate writers face as they try to write for a company and for an audience at the same time— all the while remaining "trustworthy," and "writing by the rules of art."

Investment information

For financial writers the rules are more black and white than they are for writers in other areas. Though writing about the stock market invites trouble, specific rules govern financial communications.

In 1934, Congress passed the Securities Exchange Act which regulates all stock exchange in the country. Especially pertinent to corporate writers in the investment field is Section 10(b), Rule 10b-5 which says "it is unlawful for any person, directly or indirectly, by use of any means or instrumentality of interstate commerce or of the mails, to use *Sales Literature* which is *Materially Misleading* in connection with the offer or sale of securities issued by an investment company." The law defines "sales literature" as any communication used to offer to sell or induce the sale of investment company securities. According to Rule 10b-5, such literature is "materially misleading" if it contains an untrue statement (if it lies) or omits a material fact (if it tells a half-truth). Also included under the rule are stipulations about how writers can legally represent stock performance, benefits from services, quotations of yield, ranking, market indices, and so forth without being "misleading." The guidelines even go so far as to specify type size for footnotes and scale-size for charts.

While this rule guides financial writers, it also ties their hands. In May 1988 the Securities Exchange Commission

(SEC) amended the rule to apply to such things as investment newsletters, pamphlets, and other so-called dealer materials. Traditionally, investment company newsletters have given advice to investors. At Fidelity Investments, for example, the newsletter has always been careful to present information without giving any sales pitches for mutual bond funds. In the past, as long as the writers did not promote Fidelity and as long as they quoted from many sources in addition to Fidelity, the newsletter complied with the law. Now, however, the new SEC guidelines have made it difficult for the newsletter to be fully informative. According to the new standards, financial writers are not permitted to write anything that would alter the way their readers view stock. That means they are not allowed to give performance information on mutual funds, nor can they publish any investigative journalism articles because such pieces would influence the audience. Understandably, the writers argue that the SEC is requiring them to keep information from the public and is compromising the newsletter's function.

While the SEC standards are complicating the lives of financial writers, they are protecting the audience. Because of the law, consumers are shielded from such misleading information as exaggerated earnings predictions, concealed information, and insider trading. For example, GCA Corporation, a semi-conductor manufacturing firm in Massachusetts, announced a short while ago that they were "recession-proof" and then went bankrupt, leaving thousands of stockholders holding worthless paper. In another instance, geologists working for Texas Gulf Sulfur discovered a mineral field and the company withheld the information allowing only those "in the know" to buy stock before the announcement. And at the other extreme, Lotus Development Corporation's delay in announcing that their new version of 1-2-3 would miss its scheduled release date by nearly a year caused a flurry of lawsuits claiming that general stockholders should have been made aware sooner. Plaintiffs suggested that insiders delayed the public announcement until they had already sold their own stock.

As these examples illustrate, careless use of language, intentional misuse of language, and even poor timing of information may result in litigation. To avoid liability, writers in the investment field follow these National Association of Securities Dealers (NASD) guidelines in determining whether a communication is misleading:

GENERAL CONSIDERATIONS. In judging whether a communication, or a particular element of a communication, may be misleading, writers should consider several factors, including, but not limited to:

(a) The overall context in which the statement is made. A statement made in one context may be misleading even though such a statement could be perfectly appropriate in another context. An essential test in this regard is the balance of treatment of risks and potential benefits.

(b) The audience to which the communication is directed. Different levels of explanation or detail may be necessary depending on the audience to which a communication is directed, and the ability of the writer, given the nature of the media used, to restrict the audience appropriately. If the statements made in a communication would be applicable only to a limited audience, or if additional information might be necessary for other audiences, it should be kept in mind that it is not always possible to restrict the readership of a particular communication.

(c) The overall clarity of the communication. A statement or disclosure made in an unclear manner obviously can result in a lack of understanding of the statement, or in a serious misunderstanding. A complex or overly technical explanation may be worse than too little information.

(d) Use of legends and footnotes. Material disclosure relegated to legends or footnotes realistically may not enhance the reader's understanding of the communication.

As these guidelines indicate, financial writers' main concerns parallel the classical rhetoricians' "rules of art": to analyze the audience and then adapt the prose accordingly. When language creates a problem, in almost every instance the difficulty arises because the writer has either failed to realize the prose's effect on the reader or has deliberately concealed some information. Both indicate the writers' disrespect for the audience—the former by failing to "describe the soul with perfect accuracy," and the second by "not advising the best course, although [they] may see it."

Goods and Services Marketing

Sales and marketing writers have a tougher time because there are no clear legal guidelines, though their profession is

a mine field of potential law suits. The main legal issue for
marketing writers is product liability. It's interesting that
once again the writers' primary attention should focus on the
audience rather than the product, even in potential product
liability situations. Under the Uniform Commercial Code
(UCC), companies are held to an "express warranty of description," which means that the description of a product is
an important element in the buyer's decision to buy. If the
marketing language makes false claims or in anyway deceives
the buyer, the company is liable—even if writers have included a disclaimer in the advertising literature. For example,
a company may claim that the exterior housepaint they sell
will last ten years without peeling. In the fine print, they add
the disclaimer that various conditions may affect the paint's
longevity. Nonetheless, because the ad's main thrust is the
promise of long paint life, the buyer can bring suit if the
paint peels sooner than expected. Consequently, marketing
writers—like financial writers—must be aware that their language may be misleading, and the audience has the ultimate
right of interpretation.

The recent cola wars provide a good example of companies
wisely avoiding possible legal action. In widely distributed
commercials, both Diet Coke and Diet Pepsi claimed their
respective sodas beat the other in independent taste tests.
When various consumer affairs groups began investigating
these tests, both companies pulled the ads. Why? According to
a Massachusetts study done at the request of the state consumer affairs secretary Paula Gold, Coke conducted taste tests
in ten cities—all in the eastern half of the country. Pepsi only
questioned people within one hundred miles of four of the
company's processing plants. The study also revealed that the
tests unfairly controlled who was eligible to take part in the
samplings, that the questionnaires were designed to elicit predetermined answers, and that Pepsi used specially manufactured soda for the tests. Both commercials were discontinued
last summer.

In addition to including product marketing, this category
also encompasses the marketing of services, a quagmire of
potential liability. Companies such as engineering firms responsible for writing proposals, reports, and compliance statements are especially vulnerable. Though it's natural for writers
in these situations to put the company's best foot forward and
to concentrate on the company's image, that impulse is at the

root of many potential miscommunications. For instance, the following problem areas may lead to litigation for engineering firms:

> (a) Writers have a tendency to use extreme words as if the communications world were black and white.
>
> (b) Engineering firms have a "can do" attitude; they think they can solve any problem. From a technical standpoint this may be justified, but time and budget constraints may impede their success rate. The key is for writers to recognize the proper occasions for cautious expressions.
>
> (c) This general tendency to want to please sometimes leads writers to make promises when there's no need to do so or when it's impossible to fulfill the commitment made. In these instances, the verb "to be" (is, are, will, shall) must be qualified.
>
> (d) In some circumstances, the "good guy" syndrome may lead writers to admit blame to be a good sport. The general rule, of course, is to delay admissions of blame pending a thorough investigation. It is almost impossible to retract an "it is my fault" statement.

A further concern for writers in these situations is that words they do use in an attempt to be cautious may lead to miscommunication because of their multiple meanings. Some of the words so prone to misunderstanding, particularly in engineering reports, are as follows:

> "Inspection" has a broader meaning than just "looking," and means to examine carefully or critically, investigate and test officially, especially a critical investigation or scrutiny. *State es rel. State Farm Mutual Auto Ins. Co. v. Rickhoff,* Mo. App. 509 S.W. 2d 485, 487. Preferable words are "review," "study," "tour the facility."
>
> "Determine" means to come to a decision, to decide, to resolve. *Norwood Hospital v. Howton,* 26SO 2d 427, 432, 32 Al. App. 37. Preferable words are "evaluate," "assess," "analyze."
>
> "Assure" has several meanings. It is a synonym for the word "promise." *Van Hook v. Southern California Waiters Alliance, Local 17,* 323 P.2d 212, 220, 158. Ca. 2d 556. In business documents, generally, it means a pledge or security. *Utilities Engineering Institute v. Kafad,* 58 N.Y.S. 2d 743, 745, 185 MISC. 1035. It also means to render safe, to make secure, and to give confidence to, to put a person beyond doubt, to

> cause to feel certain, give confidence to and convince. *Colonial Trust Co. v. Elmer C. Breuer, Inc.* 69 A.2d 126, 128, 363 Pa. 101. Preferable words are "to facilitate," "to provide further confidence," "to enhance the reliability of."

Though this is a partial list, even these few examples show the care engineering writers need to take in choosing specific words to avoid miscommunication. Here is one more example illustrating how a writer can revise a complete statement to avoid potential liability:

> **Original:** "The engineer will thoroughly inspect the premises and certify that the construction has been completed in complete conformity with the contract documents, or that no hazardous wastes or hazardous waste residues exist at the facility."

> **Revision:** "Upon completion of services, the engineer will prepare a report for the owner. The report will include an opinion regarding the conformance of the completed work to the plans and technical specifications the engineer prepared. The engineer will also prepare a statement of opinion regarding the presence of hazardous wastes or hazardous waste residues at the portions of the facility the owner identifies."

In marketing goods and services, then, writers need to focus more attention on the buyer than on the seller. Because liability claims generally come from the consumer, writers must take extra precautions to understand what motivates their audience and what language will persuade them without creating false signals.

Safety Information

As in the previous two categories, writers concerned with safety information must analyze the audience carefully to make sure that the language used will successfully communicate. But in this category, writers are not only dealing with potential liability, they are also protecting people from physical harm. It's essential that their prose both communicates that danger exists and compels people to take the necessary safety precautions. The governing rule for writers in this area is from torts law:

In order to prevent the product from being unreasonably dangerous, the seller may be required to give directions or warnings, on the container, as to its use. Where warning is given, the seller may reasonably assume that it will be read and heeded; and a product bearing such a warning, which is safe for use if it is followed, is not in defective condition, nor is it unreasonably dangerous. (Restatement of Law Second, Torts 2d, American Law Institute, 1965, Section 402A.)

For a warning to be effective, it must do more than communicate danger; it must also tell people how to operate the product safely. From the writer's perspective, that means the language must do more than convey a passive message; it must also induce action. Because the language used in warnings must perform a dual function, Plato's advice that the writer should determine "what [the audience's] action is and toward what it is directed, or how it is acted upon and by what" applies here more than to the other categories.

Understanding how words act upon the audience, then, is an important part of knowing how the language can ultimately move the consumer to act rather than just read. If the warning or caution does no more than indicate a danger, it fails in half of its purpose; similarly, if the warning is present but not prominently displayed, it also fails to achieve its goal and the company could be liable for any injuries that may result.

This category has received a great deal of attention lately in the technical communications field. Current research on speech/act theory and semiotics is enabling writers to better understand how language functions as both communication and motivation. Because this topic has been covered extensively elsewhere, only a short checklist is necessary here. Following are the principal factors writers need to consider when designing effective warnings and safety instructions:

Writers of effective warnings must:

- Comply with the legal basis of the duty to warn, including consideration of the nature of the product, its use, the experience of the user, the frequency and seriousness of the potential injuries, who should be warned, the obviousness of the danger, the foreseeability of misuse, and the feasibility of warning.
- Consider the existence and compliance with appropriate standards.

- Consider the urgency, specificity, and clarity of wording.
- consider the appropriate location and durability of the warning.
- Consider the likelihood that the information will reach the ultimate user.

Employee Handbooks

The final category where language may invite liability includes material published for employees. In wrongful termination cases, plaintiffs may look to employee handbooks or other employee information to corroborate their claims. If, for example, the company handbook contains a statement such as "At XYZ Company, we encourage hard work and team spirit by rewarding everyone who does a good job," they have made it extremely difficult to discharge any employee. Because the courts look to the context of the language to interpret its meaning, any employee may successfully argue that he or she did a good job and the result was not the reward promised. The claim that the company has broken faith with the employee may be valid. To avoid such misunderstanding, the company should carefully examine the implied contracts contained in their handbooks. Is the language in these in-house documents trustworthy, or is it marketing hype?

Aristotle's definition of trustworthy applies here. According to Aristotle, writers are "false in their statements" for three reasons: through folly they don't hold the right opinions, through "knavery" they say what they do not think, or through poor choice they do not give the best advice. Certainly the first statement has no bearing here; we can assume that the writers are not stupid enough to hold the wrong opinions. If we also assume that the writers are not intentionally lying, then that leaves the third reason as the only possibility: the writers have made a poor choice. In so doing, they have chosen language that may create a false impression for the employees, though the intent was to project a pleasant corporate image.

For example, consider this statement from a New York publishing company's handbook:

> Reimbursement of employees' out-of-pocket expenses shall be limited to those that are authorized and reasonable.

'Reasonable' means making the expenditures as though the funds were personal and to duplicate the standard of housing and meals on a basis comparable to that maintained at home. It does not mean luxurious accommodations.

There are two problems with this directive. First, it definitely favors those employees who maintain a higher standard of living at home. Second, an employee can spend the company's money with abandon and argue that s/he would do the same thing for a special evening at home. In this statement, the corporate image of generosity conflicts with the reality of fiscal responsibility, producing ambiguous language that is not legally enforceable.

Writers responsible for these handbooks should be aware of how the audience may misinterpret their words or even look for loopholes. Employees read the information in the most beneficial way possible and trust that the implied promises are valid. Therefore, while the writers' impulse is usually to present the company in the best light and to make statements that will encourage employee loyalty, they must edit the copy for such potentially dangerous language. Instead of using marketing terminology in handbooks and other internal documents, writers should realize that they do not have to "sell" the company to the employees. Office politics and employee relations have no place in official documents that serve as a sort of expressed contract and may be invoked in unexpected and unpleasant ways.

Language liability is a matter of interpretation

Corporate language and the law is not a black and white issue. Writers cannot depend on a series of checklists to determine if their words meet the legal standards necessary to avoid liability. Instead, almost all litigation involving language is a matter of interpreting what was said, what was meant, and what was understood. Given the ambiguity of these situations, writers must sit down with their project teams before they write and grapple with the timeless questions of classical rhetoric: what is the nature of the audience, what is the nature of the message to be conveyed, and, to use Plato's words, how can they "adapt each to each other?" In the end, corporations bear the legal burden of proof that their prose is trustworthy. Such ultimate responsibility requires responsible prose in the first place.

References

Aristotle. *The Rhetoric*. Translated by Richard Clavehouse Jebb. Cambridge: Cambridge University Press, 1909.

E. C. Jordan Company, Consulting Engineers. "Clear Communication." Pamphlet 8.87.81. Portland, ME.

Moll, Richard. *Product Safety and Liability Prevention: The Role of Warnings and Instructions Conference Bulletin*. February 1989.

National Association of Securities Dealers (NASD). "Guidelines Regarding Communications with the Public about Investment Companies and Variable Contracts." Washington: February 1982.

Plato. *Phaedrus*. Translated by H. N. Fowler. Cambridge, MA: The Loeb Classical Library, Harvard University Press.

NIMBY: Defining and Dealing with the Not-In-My-Backyard Syndrome

❖

Nancy Blethen

> Today, any institution that wishes to expand, change or con-
> struct just about anything—a highway, housing development,
> water tower or manufacturing facility—will encounter the
> NIMBY, or Not-In-My-Backyard, syndrome. The people who
> comprise NIMBY groups are our neighbors, friends, and fami-
> lies; perhaps even you may have joined a NIMBY effort at
> one time or another. Because the people who form NIMBY
> groups are motivated by a genuine concern for their neigh-
> borhoods, they must be considered seriously when planning
> and implementing any communications effort.

During the past fifteen years, my firm has been called
upon to address the concerns of NIMBY groups that have
formed to oppose our clients' projects. As a result, we have
learned what it takes to develop a successful community-
acceptance program.

Coleman & Pellet Inc. is a public relations firm based in
Union, N.J., counseling corporations, trade associations, utilities and government agencies. In addition to the aforemen-
tioned community acceptance campaigns, we plan and
implement crisis management, public policy and corporate
identity programs for companies in the pharmaceutical, insurance, automotive, chemical, utility, and waste management
industries. Among our major clients are the New Jersey Health
Products Council, the New Jersey Insurance News Service,
Merck & Co., Inc., Hoffmann-La Roche, Inc., Elizabethtown
Water Company, and BMW of North America.

NIMBYism today

To understand the person who joins a NIMBY group, it is important to first look back at the trend-setting events of the past few decades. The women's movement, the civil rights protests, the Vietnam War and Watergate demonstrated to people that changes can begin at the grass-roots level. Although no single event of the past twenty years is responsible for NIMBYism, their cumulative impact taught people that authority figures and institutions could be challenged successfully.

During the 1980s, NIMBYism took on a new focus—primarily due to the public's growing fear of chemical pollution and the cancer it might cause. And now that lawmakers are enacting legislation like SARA Title III, which establishes planning and reporting requirements in connection with the use and release of hazardous substances, NIMBYism will be strengthened and become more legitimate.

More than ever before, people are concerned about what risk an existing manufacturing facility or new construction project will have on their lives, children, water, air, soil and even the value of their homes and property. Although most people will agree that new facilities, such as resource recovery plants, are needed and that the function they perform is essential to modern life, very few people are eager to have one of these plants located in their neighborhoods, despite the inclusion of environmental and health safeguards.

In some cases, this concern is justified, but for the most part, NIMBY groups are simply reflecting a genuine mistrust of business and government and a fear of change. Usually, this mistrust causes everyone involved to lose. Society loses a needed product or service. Developers lose a profitable business opportunity. Local government loses ratables, which could be used toward community programs. And the residents lose job opportunities and tax benefits.

Frequently, public relations professionals were brought in to conduct community relations or risk communication programs only after the public was very angry and project developers were very frustrated.

That situation used to be the case more often than not. But during the 1980s, largely because of community relations failures, companies have become more conscious of the concerns and needs of the people residing in host communities.

Armed with this new knowledge, companies are communicating earlier and more often with their important publics.

Risk Communication

The first important factor to understand when communicating with the public—whether the project in question has a real risk element or not—is that you are dealing with emotions, which are genuine regardless of the merits of the project. And unless you recognize this and empathize with community members, you will not gain their trust.

I have come to realize that to build trust you have to be a *person* before you can be a *spokesperson.* We have learned that statistics do not reduce public fear and skepticism—shared concern and understanding do. Only when you establish a personal relationship with the people in a neighborhood can you begin to reverse any misconceptions that may have developed.

The beginning of communication is when community members and project developers look at each other face-to-face and say, "I know where you are coming from." When that openness occurs, a project that deserves to be accepted by a community usually moves forward.

From our experience I have learned that there is an emotional process to gaining acceptance. The analogy that best describes this process is that it is a lot like the steps experienced by a person grieving the loss of a loved one.

- First—denial. "This can't be happening to me. Maybe it will go away."
- Next—anger. "Why is this risk being inflicted on me? Why did they propose the project in my community?"
- Then—bargaining. "How can we deal with it?" Once people become resigned to the situation, they begin to accept the project and think about how to deal with it through a more rational approach: "If I must have this in my community, what's in it for me?"
- Sometimes—depression. That emotion is often felt when people realize what was given up. "Did I do enough? Will people understand?"
- And finally—acceptance. Just as a grieving person comes to terms with the inevitable and realizes that

death is a part of life, so too do communities come to accept new facilities as a part of progress.

It is the job of the public relations counselor to help people work through these stages. By learning and addressing community concerns, listening to suggestions and involving the public in the development of the project, opposition to a project can be minimized. Sometimes, opponents even become supporters.

Coleman & Pellet has been involved in several controversial projects where facilities were finally sited. In Union County, for example, we coordinated the campaign to site a resource recovery facility that resulted in one of the few such referendum victories in the nation. We did that in 1985 when the city of Rahway voted to become host to Union County's resource recovery facility. And in Middlesex County we organized a broad-based coalition of media, business and environmental groups to support the county when it announced its decision to site a landfill and resource recovery facility. The coalition served as a counterpoint to NIMBY groups formed to oppose the sitings.

Because we have been able to develop strategies that result in successful community acceptance programs, Coleman & Pellet has been retained to promote a major energy project right here in Morris County. It is a project I would like to use as a case study.

A case study: The Mt. Hope Waterpower Project

In May 1988, Halecrest Company—a development company located in Edison, N.J.—selected Coleman & Pellet as its public relations counsel to plan and implement a comprehensive community, media and government relations program to build support for the Mt. Hope Waterpower Project in Rockaway Township, N.J. This pumped-storage hydroelectric facility will have a capacity of 2,000 megawatts of much-needed power for peak-demand periods.

At the time we were retained, some officials had already announced their opposition to the project. Through comments made at the first public hearing, we also learned that most residents wanted more information before forming an opinion.

The objectives of the program we recommended are:

- To familiarize residents and policy-makers with the need for additional peaking power for New Jersey and the region;
- To present pumped-storage waterpower as an economically and environmentally sound, clean, safe and reliable solution to the problem of assuring peak-load capacity;
- To address public concerns regarding increased traffic generated by the project, environmental considerations, construction noise, dam safety, plant size and location, and property values, among others;
- To create strategies that will bring the Mt. Hope Waterpower Project to fruition through the issuance of a Federal Energy Regulatory Commission (FERC) license and other necessary permits.

The information program that Coleman & Pellet has developed for the Mt. Hope Waterpower Project uses a variety of communication tools to convey client messages to their key publics.

- A slide presentation dealing with all phases of the Mt. Hope Waterpower Project is the centerpiece of the community relations program. Currently, the slide show is being presented to local civic, religious, and political groups by company officials.
- A leaflet that highlighted how the project will benefit Rockaway Township was mailed to approximately five thousand area residences in March 1989. A larger brochure about the project also will be produced, and quarterly newsletters addressing controversial issues are planned. These publications will also be mailed to area residents.
- A half-hour cable TV program was written and produced by Coleman & Pellet and aired as part of a four-part series. The series was coordinated by a local civic organization and cable television channel with eighty-four thousand potential viewers. Included in the cable program is an excellent example of the people-to-people communication we like to use when possible. We were

able to obtain on-camera testimonials from residents of Blairstown, N.J., who live near the Yards Creek pumped-storage waterpower project. This facility, which is very similar to the one proposed for Mt. Hope, has been operating for some twenty-five years.

- One of the most successful methods of informing the public about a proposal or complex technical project is through the creation of a Citizens Advisory Council (CAC). We plan to organize a CAC, composed of representatives of local organizations as well as neighbors of the project, who will meet regularly with representatives of the Mt. Hope Project. The CAC gives residents a forum to discuss concerns and make recommendations that would make the project more acceptable.
- Coleman & Pellet also has developed and is implementing an aggressive media relations program, which is an essential ingredient of any site-acceptance assignment. The program will include regular briefing sessions with reporters and editors, and the issuance of press kits and periodic releases. To guarantee that the company's message will be carried accurately and with proper focus and emphasis, newspaper advertisements addressing key aspects of the project will be prepared as well.
- In addition, the information program will include a series of tours of the Mt. Hope project site and the Yards Creek pumped-storage facility for government officials, media representatives, and interested citizens.
- Furthermore, Coleman & Pellet has recommended that Halecrest engage in a series of meetings with the government agencies involved with the project and with interested federal and state elected and appointed officials. We also are seeking the support of business, environmental, and civic organizations.

The fact that the state recently convened a Governor's conference on energy has provided our program with a sense of urgency. The Board of Public Utilities predicts that New Jersey will need ten thousand megawatts of additional electricity by the year 2010—the Mt. Hope Waterpower Project can provide two thousand megawatts of this essential power.

Summary

Although the jury is still out on the Mt. Hope Waterpower Project, we believe we have learned how to communicate effectively with residents of communities where controversial projects have been proposed. What it takes is a lot of patience, genuine concern, a bit of luck, and a great deal of hard work.

Further Reading

Anderson, Jerry W. Jr. *Corporate Social Responsibility.* Westport, CT: Quorum Books, 1989.

Brody, E. W. *The Business of Public Relations.* Westport, CT: Praeger Publishers, 1987.

The Foundation Directory. New York, NY: The Foundation Center. Annual.

Kruckeberg, Dean, and Kenneth Starck. *Public Relations and Community: A Reconstructed Theory.* Westport, CT: Praeger Publishers, 1988.

Lowengard, Mary. "Community Relations—New Approaches to Building Consensus," *Public Relations Journal* (October 1989): 24–30.

Mack, Charles S. *Lobbying and Government Relations: A Guide for Executives.* Westport, CT: Quorum Books, 1989.

Research Centers

Center for the Advancement of Applied Ethics, Carnegie Mellon University.

The Foundation Center, New York, NY and branch offices in major cities across the United States.

4

Corporate Identity

❖

Michael B. Goodman

Overview

Images of American business and business leaders are not hard to find in our literature and entertainment media. For example, if you go to the classics of American literature, Twain's *A Connecticut Yankee in King Arthur's Court* (1889) is a damnation of business technology and industrialism over the human spirit. Melville's Captain Ahab in *Moby Dick* (1851) is often seen as the megalomaniacal leader of the "American" ship of state. Whole industries were fair game in books like Upton Sinclair's *The Jungle* (1906), an expose of Chicago meatpacking written in the period when journalists were called Muckrakers, the turn of the century investigative reporters.

Award winning plays such as Miller's *Death of a Salesman* (1949) and Mamet's *Glengarry Glen Ross* (1981) paint a bleak and predatory image of entrepreneurship and American business. And movies and TV create the image of the unethical or often diabolical corporation and equally villainous corporate leader. Here is a short list of image making entertainment: Gordon Gekko in *Wall Street* (1987), Henry Potter in *It's A Wonderful Life* (1946), *The Man in the Gray Flannel Suit* (1956), the executives in *The China Syndrome* (1979).

The villains in recent sci-fi are corporations, the mining company with its operations on Mars in *Outland* (1981), and the space salvage company in *Alien* (1979), and the company that enforces law with *Robocop* (1987). *Network* (1976), *9 to 5* (1980), and *Working Girl* (1989) all use corporations or executives as villains.

Local and network news focus on financial and business misdeeds, small and monumental. Almost every station has a consumer advocate who gets to the bottom of scams, frauds, and cheats.

In a simpler time the Western was a staple for books, movies, and TV. The good guys wore white hats and the bad guys wore black. Whether or not you feel that corporations are rightly or wrongly portrayed in literature and the media, it remains a state of the contemporary environment, a sort of popular culture reality, that in telling a story of fiction, the villain in a business suit has come to be plausible.

How does any corporation fight such negative images of business in general? One place to begin would be to build an image more compatible with the community's sense of a good neighbor and corporate citizen. Companies that enjoy a positive image in the minds of the public and their own employees are generally good companies. The identity and the image cannot be too far apart from one another.

A positive corporate identity and image can be created and perpetuated through coherent and thoughtful programs directed internally and to the public at large.

Corporate identity is a combination of more than the sum of these parts: mission statements and corporate philosophies; logos, letterhead, and annual reports; advertising; internal perception programs; external communication and public perception of company image. People learn to recognize a company by everything it does, from the products and services it sells, to its buildings and employees.

The mergers and acquisitions of the 1980s and the downsizing and restructuring that followed have treated corporate reputation and image rather roughly. From GM to IBM the face of business has changed dramatically. The need to build corporate identity has never been more important to a company's survival.

Mission statements and corporate philosophies

The corporation's mission statement is the first formal act of the creation of an organization's identity. The written mission statement defines the corporation, its goals and operating principles, and its values and beliefs. The first of the three parts is relatively straightforward and brief. Here's an example from Schering Research, a part of the Schering-Plough Corporation:

> Schering Research is engaged in the discovery and development of unique pharmaceuticals that save, enhance, and prolong life. To achieve that mission, the scientists of Schering research are extending the limits of medical knowledge in their search for pharmaceuticals that provide significant therapeutic advantages for a wide range of diseases. (*Schering Research,* Kenilworth, New Jersey, 1986, Inside Front Cover).

The presentation of goals and operating principles calls for more detail and of course each company or organization's discussion will vary according to the products and services it creates and the communities and customers it serves. Here is an example from CBI—the Confederation of British Industry:

> Most industrialised *(sic)* countries have a national spokesman for their business communities—Britain's is the Confederation of British Industry, the CBI. Founded in 1965, the CBI is an independent, non-party political organisation *(sic)* funded entirely by its members in industry and commerce.
>
> It exists primarily to voice the views of its members to ensure that governments of whatever political complexion—and society as a whole—understand both the needs of British business and the contribution it makes to the well-being of the nation.
>
> The CBI is acknowledged to be Britain's business voice and, as such, is widely consulted by government, the civil service and the media. But it is not solely concerned with major national issues—an important part of its task is to represent business interests at local levels, too. It is also directly involved in providing essential information and research services for its members. (CBI Brochure, 1991).

The expression of a company's values and beliefs, which is also covered in a larger context in the chapter on Corporate Culture below, is the most difficult of all since it is an effort to express the corporate philosophy. It is difficult because we generally associate values and beliefs with philosophical or religious activities, not commercial ones. The clash between the world of commerce and the world of philosophy requires clear and articulate expression to maintain believability in the skeptical environment we described at the beginning of this chapter.

Johnson & Johnson's "Credo" provides an excellent model:

> We believe our first responsibility is to the doctors, nurses and patients, to mothers and all others who use our products and services. In meeting their needs everything we do must be of high quality. We must constantly strive to reduce our costs in order to maintain reasonable prices. Customers' orders must be serviced promptly and accurately. Our suppliers and distributors must have an opportunity to make a fair profit.
>
> We are responsible to our employees, the men and women who work with us throughout the world. Everyone must be considered as an individual. We must respect their dignity and recognize their merit. They must have a sense of security in their jobs. Compensation must be fair and adequate, and working conditions clean, orderly, and safe. Employees must feel free to make suggestions and complaints. There must be equal opportunity for employment, development, and advancement for those qualified. We must provide competent management, and their actions must be just and ethical.
>
> We are responsible to the communities in which we live and work and to the world community as well. We must be good citizens—support good works and charities and bear our fair share of taxes. We must encourage civic improvements and better health and education. We must maintain in good order the property we are privileged to use, protecting the environment and natural resources.
>
> Our final responsibility is to our stockholders. Business must make a sound profit. We must experiment with new ideas. Research must be carried on, innovative programs developed, and mistakes paid for. New equipment must be purchased, new facilities provided, and new products launched. Reserves must be created to provide for adverse times. When we operate according to these principles, the stockholders should realize a fair return. ("Our Credo," Johnson & Johnson).

Johnson & Johnson's expression provides a benchmark for others to follow since it includes everything experts agree should make up a clear statement of corporate philosophy.

The expression of a corporation's philosophy is often aligned with the mission statement and in practice it is difficult to draw a clear line marking the end of a mission statement and the beginning of a corporate philosophy. Generally, however, such statements cover a company's commitment to:

quality and excellence;
customer satisfaction;
stockholder return on investment;
profits and growth;
employee relations;
competition and competitiveness;
relations with vendors;
ethical behavior;
community relations and corporate citizenship;

and recently:

diversity in the workplace;
preservation of the environment and resources.

Often a complex corporate code of conduct, ethics policy guidelines, or handbook of business practice follows the company statement of philosophy. The written code acts as an implementation guide. Such codes, guidelines, or policies often include a section on:

- applicability and purpose;
- policy regarding general business conduct; disclosure, compliance and disciplinary action;
- workings of the corporate business ethics committee;
- compliance with laws:
    securities—inside information; financial inquiries
    disclosure of company information
    political contributions
    relations with government officials, domestic
    relations with government officials, foreign
    commercial bribery—kickbacks, gifts, etc.
    recordkeeping
    anti-trust—Sherman Antitrust Act, Clayton Act
    mergers and acquisitions
    international operations
- bidding, negotiation, and performance of government contracts
- conflict of interest
- equal opportunity
- working conditions
- the environment

Logos, letterhead, and annual reports

The logos of companies such as AT&T, Coke, and IBM are familiar to you by design. If you do not recognize the company name instantly, the logo has done a poor job of graphic communication. Even if the logo is a graphic design of the letters of the company name, it is the artwork that you recognize time and time again to reinforce your reaction to the visual stimulus. The logo and the company colors build corporate image by giving a non-verbal message that reinforces the company image in the mind of the viewer.

Shape, use, color, and placement are all tightly and centrally controlled to build and maintain a corporate identity. Even in an age of decentralized management practice, the central control of the corporate graphic images is an essential strategy in successfully building and keeping a corporate image.

The annual report, aside from its primary function as the marketing tool to persuade investors that the company is a sound place to put capital, promotes corporate image and identity. It is the one publication that is given freely to introduce the company to the outside world.

It is also the publication, the corporate report card, that provides information on the company's progress and accomplishments for the investment community, stockholders, employees, and the general public. An indirect but essential goal of the annual report, and one other way to justify its expensive production, is its role in the perpetuation of the image and identity of the organization. Copies of the report not only go to all registered stockholders, but also to Wall Street analysts, the business press, students, libraries, vendors, trade associations and professional groups. The report is often a requirement in new business proposals to clients and the government, and frequently used for employee recruiting.

Given all these uses, every element of the annual report, including: the artful covers, the letter from the CEO, the list of officers, the excellent photography and artwork, the summary of the year's accomplishments, the discussion of plans for the coming year, the operation statement, the balance sheet, the ten-year comparison of financial highlights, the statement from the auditors, even the footnotes to satisfy all Securities Exchange Commission (SEC) regulations and guidelines, is designed to contribute to the positive image of the company.

Advertising and company perception

Corporate advertising, different from product advertising, is designed to create a positive image of the corporation in the mind of a particular group, from investors to the general public. Corporate advertising presents a general image of the company or presents an issue with which the company wants to be associated.

Corporate advertising can feature issue advocacy as well as the presentation of views on social issues such as the environment, recycling, conservation, acid rain, and world hunger. It could be found in special sections of the Sunday newspaper magazine, market-prep or issue ads on the Sunday morning news analysis shows, on the Corporation for Public Broadcasting documentaries, sponsorships of special art and museum exhibitions, or sporting events and concerts.

Some examples include print and television commercials from: AT&T, IBM, Mobil Oil, Boeing, and General Electric. According to the Association of National Advertisers annual survey *Corporate Advertising Practices 1992* (17), the intended audiences for corporate advertising continue to be customers first. Then the trade, employees, Wall Street, and Washington are all very close together, but over thirty percent behind customers. This is a significant change since 1990 when the gap was less than twenty percent.

Internal perception programs

Programs such as Total Quality Management are used to create a feeling of comradery, or even family among the company employees and managers. Internal communication programs are often motivational and developmental. One spinoff of these programs is the creation and definition of the company values and beliefs for the employees. The next chapter goes into more detail on corporate culture.

These internal programs generally begin with an orientation to the company itself, its history, policies and procedures, mission, and philosophies. In this direct manner the members of the company understand clearly what it means to be a member of that organization.

External communication and perception of company image

Programs for the community create a perception of the organization in the minds of the people who are customers, but also neighbors. Macy's throws a traditional parade on Thanksgiving Day as a way to entertain the community, but also to emphasize its commitment to everyone in the family.

Many corporations sponsor literacy and reading programs to demonstrate their commitment to the society around them. In fact, many of the corporate citizenship efforts noted in chapter 3 are efforts to project the company image as a good citizen and neighbor.

These external programs had been the public relations efforts for an organization. The stories generated by the media have been regarded as more valuable than advertising since such discussion of the company as news draws the reader into an objective view of the company. Most people approach advertising with at least some degree of skepticism.

Selected essays and comment

The essays and case studies selected for this chapter are from the presentations at the annual Conference on Corporate Communication at Fairleigh Dickinson University. Each of the authors focuses on a part of communications theory and practice in some aspect of creating, developing, or perpetuating corporate identity.

Professor Richard Doetkott explores the use of the CEO in corporate video. He explains the pitfalls and benefits of using corporate officers over actors in video because of the problems that amateurs bring to the effort. He then discusses some principles and techniques for using corporate amateurs in video effectively.

Dr. Donald Cushman surveys the revolutions in organizations that call for new organizational communication processes. He presents the theory of high-speed management as a response to global changes in business. He explores the transformation that has taken place in small group communications within corporations engaged in continuous improvement programs. The four communication processes he presents are: 1) a linking and negotiation process; 2) a New England town meeting process; 3) a cross-functional teamwork process; and 4) case studies in world class benchmarking processes.

Mr. Jay Morris examines the employee-owned company Weirton Steel Corporation. The paper discusses the communications plan to persuade the employee-owners to invest money in the plant for tomorrow, instead of putting it in their pockets today.

Using CEOs and Other Amateurs in Corporate Videos

❖

Richard Doetkott

It is generally agreed that one of the most effective means of persuasion in media is to use "real" people in real situations. If you are trying to convince the stockholders that the company is solvent, for example, you put the CEO on your video to say so. That being said, it also must be said that producers of corporate video have been reluctant to use corporate officers over actors because of the problems that amateurs bring to the party. This does not have to be the case, and this paper discusses a few of the principles and techniques in using CEOs and other amateurs in corporate videos effectively.

Why bother?

Aristotle observed that of the modes of persuasion furnished by the spoken word there were three kinds. The first depended on the personal character of the speaker; the second on putting the audience into a certain frame of mind; the third on the proof provided by the words of the speech itself (*Rhetoric*. I. 2. 1356).

Aristotle further allowed that of the three, the character of the speaker was the most effective means of persuasion. Or to put it the Madison Avenue way, "People like to buy from somebody they like" (Doner 50).

According to this view, the person or persons shown in a corporate video would be more effective if the audience could identify them as being of "good" character, that is, worthy of being believed. It follows that actors playing roles are at an obvious disadvantage, unless they are as famous as, say, Jimmy Stewart, whose screen image is that of a "good" man. But even an actor of the stature of Stewart is not as effective in the Aristotelian sense as a "real" CEO such as Lee Iacocca of Chrysler Motors. Iacocca was used as the official media spokesman during the most critical period in the history of that company. This turned out to be a brilliant decision, but one that would not have surprised the lecturer from the Lyceum a bit.

Honesty in corporate media is catching on. Many corporations are using a true documentary approach. Burlington Northern made the rather courageous move of sending documentary film maker David Ellis to record the carnage at a recent company train derailment for a video magazine they produce for their employees (Rodkin 23). According to *Advertising Age,* CEOs are even going so far as to talk about their own heart attacks in order to sell TV dinners ("Con Agra Tries Health Claims" 4).

If the power of using CEOs and other amateurs is clear, the methods of so doing are not. Rather than deal with the problems, media professionals at all levels tend to avoid the issue. And yet most of the problems encountered can be solved with common sense. The purpose of this paper is to draw upon a few of the techniques used successfully by the author.

First, we must understand that the amateur we are contemplating using is an amateur in the use of the media, not an amateur in life. In fact, it is a truism that the CEO or other corporate officer is skilled in oral communication and has achieved his or her success at least partly for that reason. These skills vary as to degree and type, but they are always present and usually honed to a fine degree. One CEO will be most effective entertaining a visitor with a tour of the facilities. Another will be extremely effective in a casual situation, such as a company picnic. Yet another does formal speechmaking particularly well. Still another does best "one on one."

The basic premise

The basic premise in using amateurs is to utilize their native communication skills without destroying these positive attributes through the mechanical demands of the media being used, in this case, video. This means that it is not wise to take amateurs and attempt to make them media actors in one glorious swoop. In fact, "acting" should never enter into the equation. Think of the video production as a documentary, where people are observed, not as a theatrical film, where actors perform. This must be communicated strongly to the amateur, who will, if not prevented, invariably approach the production as he or she would a school play.

The first order of business is for the director/producer to carefully observe the CEO or other amateur in question as he or she carries out oral communications to groups in the real world. The strengths must be noted—these will form the matrix for the job to be done in the media. For example, most educated and successful people are rather surprisingly poor at reading from the printed page. If your CEO is typical, it is suicide to have him or her attempt to learn to use a teleprompter. The stilted delivery that results will undercut any note of confidence the CEO might convey to the audience and you will wish that an actor had been employed.

It may be that memorization of lines will be equally unsatisfactory. This all hinges on whether the CEO or other amateur normally is comfortable, as well as effective, using this mode of transmission. If this is not the case, do not use a memorized word for word script. Some executives are comfortable with a memorized outline; others may prefer the use of a "key word" list. Whatever the amateur is used to is the best bet for the production in question.

What else is left? Conversation. Conversation one on one, which virtually every CEO and other corporate officer must have as a communication skill, is no different when it is "one on camera." The advantage of being able to cut and edit in media can contribute greatly to the success of such a conversation with the viewer, since it can be edited to fit a time frame and to make a point quickly.

The amateur can be presented as conversing with some other person on camera, or to the camera itself. If the latter, it is helpful to present the camera not as a substitution for a person, but as an extension of the real person behind it, who should be introduced to the CEO as the other side of the conversation. Another way this can be done is for the director to have the amateur speak directly to the director through the camera and on to the monitor which the director watches during the takes. This should take place within the view of the CEO, but not in such a way as the CEO can see his or her own image, which can lead to all sorts of bizarre behavior.

It is a good idea not to have the amateur view his or herself on tape for the same reason. If this cannot be avoided, take several takes, and when an appropriate rest period is indicated, then all should sit down and watch the takes together as an audience. The audience will tend to mitigate the anguish the amateur will feel of "not being good enough." Of course, the director must be honest, but always positive. It is a great help if the director carefully points out exactly what he or she is looking for in the scene before any viewing is done by anyone but the director. Playback for the director should be done with earphones, since the sound of one's voice to an amateur is extremely traumatic.

The importance of the script

The script plays an important part in using amateurs, even if it is not providing all of the words that will be eventually used in the video. The script should demonstrate the skills of the amateur, as ascertained by the producer before any writing commences. This is extremely important, since the effectiveness of the corporate officer will be compromised if the script calls for him or her to perform as someone other than who or what he or she is. If the officer is terrible at formal speech situations, then bend over backwards to avoid any tendency to put him or her in that environment or use that style of delivery.

However, many producers have a very limited view of what the CEO or other corporate officer can do. If the amateur has a hobby such as skydiving, running, raising flowers, or sailing—use it! Not only will it catch the attention of the audience, but it will improve confidence and delivery. If the CEO normally does not talk to the firm's employees from behind a desk, then why force him or her to do so in a video? If the CEO likes to relate to an audience on the shop floor, or at a staff picnic, or in the hall—then write a scene that takes place there. Find out where he or she likes to be in the company workplace and place your locations to take advantage of it.

Technical considerations

Of course there are always technical details to be taken care of in order to get good images. But here again common sense should prevail. Use a "stand in" and never have the CEO wait for lighting to be set up or changed. If this is unavoidable, the director must take the amateur aside to discuss the script or perform other useful duties while the changes are being made on the set. And only one director, please! Be sure to have an assistant take care of all of the other details and problems, hopefully without interrupting the director and the amateur in their conversations.

Keep lighting levels low to have a cooler set. Keep the size of the crew to a minimum. Use fill light that is greatly diffused in order to avoid glare. Have the slate done unobtrusively, or better, use another method of marking scenes and takes that does not tend to "throw" the amateur performer. Consider rehearsals without the crew present in order to build the confidence of the performer that he or she can do the job. Use the technique of allowing the camera to just run without stopping between takes as you work with the amateur to try to achieve the performance you want.

The common attempt to "project" the voice is the greatest killer of naturalness in amateurs. It helps to explain that the mike is very sensitive and will pick up a whisper. A useful technique is to stand very close to the performer and have him or her run through the performance, talking only to you, not the camera. Then step out of the picture and have the amateur attempt to duplicate the level, as well as the style of delivery just practiced.

Other considerations

Of course, one of the most important aspects of using CEOs and other amateurs in corporate videos is that they learn the real truth about media production. Indeed, one of the side benefits of using corporate officers is that they will gain a real appreciation for what media professionals do and the hard work necessary to obtain any kind of effective results. So never give the impression that any production will just take a minute or two of their time or that they can just dash it off. Naturally this must be balanced with the constant encouragement that they can do the job; indeed, that they can do it better than anyone else. Many CEOs respond well to a written list from the director as to what he or she is looking for. In summary, be firm and consistent in your demands and accentuate the positive always.

Mention should probably be made here of the difficulty some media producers and managers have in approaching their CEOs and other high corporate officers. Because of the typical rigidity of corporate structures in the business world, you may feel that it would be presumptuous for you to insist on any aspect of the production with the CEO. However, you must insist on that which you know is important. You are the expert. You must take charge. Leadership will be responded to by any corporate officers, because they both understand and respect it.

It is helpful to observe the use of CEOs and others in television advertising. Note that where the company or product must have absolute creditability, a corporate officer is invariably used as was the case with Chrysler Corporation. You may find that with repetitions, the amateur becomes very professional in his or her efficiency with the medium. Ronald DeLuca, president of the Bozell advertising agency which carries the Chrysler account, was quoted in *Advertising Age* (79) to the effect that Lee Iacocca had become so good in Chrysler commercials that it would be hard to find a pro who could do it better!

Observing television commercials will also give you plenty of ideas about production techniques designed to maximize the strengths of the corporate officer without creating a situation where the weaknesses are exposed. Write down the ideas you think are effective, particularly those that create an interest in the CEO being something other than a person behind the desk in an office on the top floor.

You may find, with enough work and practice that you, as well as the Chrysler Corporation, can make a media star of a corporate officer. Not only will this enhance your own position, but it will make your corporate videos much more effective.

Aristotle would be proud.

References

"Con Agra Tries Health Claims." *Advertising Age* 2 October 1989: 4.

Doner, W. B. *Likable Advertising.* Internally published book. Quoted in "Likable Advertising Sells." *Advertising Age* 12 June 1989: 50.

"How Bozell Helped Save Chrysler—Agency's Bet on Chrysler Paid Off." *Advertising Age* 27 February 1989: 3.

Rodkin, Dennis. "In Corporate Video, What's Up? Docs." *Advertising Age* 3 July 1989: 23.

High-speed Management: A Revolution in Organizational Communication in the 1990s

❖

Donald P. Cushman
Sarah Sanderson King

A series of revolutions have taken place within the global economy which has transformed the theoretic basis for organizational coalignment and thus all information and communication processes. This essay tracks the principled basis for that transformation. It then explicates a new theory of organizational communication—high-speed management. High-speed management has as its goal the achievement and maintenance of sustainable competitive advantage by the innovative, flexible, efficient and rapid response to environmental change. This essay then details the transformation high-speed management has made in small group communication processes by exploring organizational continuous improvement programs. Continuous improvement programs aim at establishing and maintaining a sustainable competitive advantage through four communication processes: (1) a linking and negotiation process, (2) a New England town meeting process, (3) a cross-functional teamwork process, and (4) case studies in world class benchmarking processes.

Regardless of which corporations or nations emerge as leaders in the high-technology race, the world high-technology market has given rise to a new system of management which is revolutionizing the way work gets done. This new high-speed management system is a set of principles, strategies, and tools for coming up with a steady flow of new products, making sure they are what the customer wants, designing and manufacturing them with speed and precision, getting them to the market quickly, and servicing them easily in order to make large profits and satisfy consumer needs (Pepper, 1989). High-speed management which began in the high technology sector is now diffusing to all public, private, and nonprofit sectors of the world economy with promising results (Stalk, 1988). High-speed management systems have at their core a new conceptualization of the role information and communication must play in organizational functioning, a role which generates an unique form of sustainable competitive advantage and is grounded in a new set of principles, strategies and techniques of organizational communication (Cushman and King, 1992).

It will be the purpose of this essay to provide a broad outline of the theory of high-speed management and of the principles, strategies, and techniques which undergrid its effectiveness. In so doing we will (1) briefly explore the convergence of four trends which has led to the emergence of high-speed management, (2) outline the general theory of high-speed management, and (3) explore some of the transformations high-speed management has brought about in the traditional conceptualizations of organizational communication processes.

Four trends that have led to the emergence of high-speed management

Prior to entering into the main body of our analysis, we shall explore four trends whose convergence has led to the restructuring of the global economic environment, placing new demands on corporate management and giving rise to high-speed management systems.

First, a series of breakthroughs has taken place in information and communication technologies which have dramatically changed how organizational manufacturing, marketing, and management work.

Second, this information and communication revolution has helped facilitate a dramatic increase in world trade, the emergence of a global economy, and the development of three large core markets.

Third, these technological breakthroughs and increases in world trade have created a volatile business climate characterized by rapidly changing technology, quick market saturation, and unexpected competition, making succeeding in business difficult.

Fourth, to compete successfully in such an environment requires that executives employ management theories and practices which emphasize innovation, adaptation, flexibility, efficiency, and rapid response.

Let us explore each of these trends briefly and in turn.

Breakthroughs in information and communication technologies

A series of technological breakthroughs has taken place which make possible the generation, processing, and instant delivery of information and communication throughout the world, creating a revolution in organizational manufacturing, marketing, and management. At the center of this revolution is a constellation of new management tools based on computers and telecommunications and classified as new (a) manufacturing, (b) marketing, and (c) management technologies. Taken collectively, these tools provide a new way of thinking and acting in regard to all the problems which confront management in dealing with a rapidly changing economic environment.

New manufacturing technologies employ computer-aided and telecommunication-linked engineering, manufacturing, and resource planning processes to allow for the rapid development, production, sales, and service of customized new products at low cost, high quality, and easy service throughout the world (Young 1990). Allen Bradley, a Milwaukee manufacturer of industrial controls, possesses one of the world's most modern computer-aided and telecommunication-linked engineering, manufacturing, and resource planning facilities. This facility can produce one of a product or 100,000 of the same product at the same per unit cost. This plant can receive the specifications for an order one day and deliver the product at its destination the next, cutting the average turnaround time on orders from four weeks to two days. Under such a system, engineering and manufacturing costs decreased 40 percent while profits increased by 32 percent and product quality increased by 200 percent (Port, *Business Week,* June 16, 1986: 100–108).

New marketing information technologies employ computer-aided and telecommunication-linked environmental scanning, electronic test marketing, and real-time merchandising for speed in providing customers with world class products when and where they want them in order to increase market shares (Young 1990). Campbell Soup Company, for example, can scan the environment to determine customer desire for a new soup; then computer model its contents; simulate its production; calibrate its cost, price, profit, and sales potential; develop an artificial intelligence system to control its rate and quality of production; pretest its name, taste, shelf placement, the type and content of its advertising; and run its test markets—reducing a management decision process which used to take years to a matter of two or three days. These new marketing technologies cut the cost of this process by 30 percent while increasing product success rates by 80 percent (Russell, Adams, Boundy, 1986).

New management information technologies employ computer-aided and telecommunication-linked decision support, operational research, artificial intelligence, and group technology systems to integrate, coordinate, and control management processes in order to create competitive advantage. American Express recently implemented an artificial intelligence system which provides decision support for managers making authorization decisions on individual purchases from 400,000 shops and restaurants throughout the world. This expert system reduced by 20 percent the turnaround time per transaction, reduced by 50 percent the number of authorizations in trouble ninety days after approval, while providing annual savings of $27 million (Feigenbaum, McCorduck and Nii, 1988). New manufacturing, marketing, and management information technologies, when appropriately employed, allow for more effective integration, coordination, and control of all organizational processes creating the potential for competitive advantage (Young, 1990).

These then are some of the new information and communication tools which when taken collectively are creating a new way of thinking and acting in regard to all management problems. They have in common the technology that allows organizations to track and respond in real-time to the interests of managers, stockholders, workers, customers, and competitors throughout major portions of the globe. Similarly, such a world class information and communication capability allows organizations to track and respond in real-time to international changes in the cost of capital, labor, raw materials, consumer taste, and competitor response.

Breakthroughs in information and communication technologies are increasing world trade

The ability of corporations to track in real-time the needs of customers and changes in the cost of capital, labor, and raw materials throughout the world has led to (a) a rapid increase in world trade, (b) the emergence of a global economy, with (c) strong regional markets. Driven by information and communication technologies and the comparative advantage they create, world trade over the past four decades has grown much faster than the world's gross national product. International exports and imports were about one-fifth the world GNP in 1962, one-fourth in 1972, one-third in 1982, and are projected to approach one-half in the world GNP by 1992 (The Global Giants, September 21, 1990).

Over the past decade a single model of economic development has emerged that is influencing economic policies throughout the nations involved in the emerging global economy.

The generalization of such a model does not imply all governments nor all economies are alike; it merely suggests broad central tendencies in the economic policies of most nations as they begin to participate in the global economy. This model includes seven general features: (1) control of inflation through fiscal austerity and monetary restrictions; (2) reduction of labor costs as a percentage of product cost; (3) increased productivity and profitability through the effective use of information and communication technology; (4) restructuring of industrial and service sectors by disinvesting from low profit areas and investing in high growth, high profit areas; (5) privatization and deregulation of some aspects of the economy by withdrawing from state ownership and control in favor of open market forces; (6) relative control over the pricing of raw materials and energy, assuring the stability of pricing systems and exchange flows; and (7) opening up gradually to world markets and increased internationalization of economies. As Castells (1986:300) argues:

Such a model is not necessarily linked to a particular political party or administration, or even to a country, even though the Reagan or Thatcher governments seem to be the closest examples of the fulfillment of these policies. But very similar policies have developed in most West European countries, in those governed by Socialists, and even in Communist-led regions (Italy) or Communist-participating governments (France, for a certain period). At the same time, in most Third World countries, austerity policies, inspired or dictated by the International Monetary Fund and world financial institutions, have also developed along the same lines, establishing not without contradictions and conflicts (Walton, 1985) a new economic logic that is not only capitalistic but a very specific kind of capitalism.

With the emerging global economy, comparative advantage is shifting towards those regions of the world with (1) a large core market, (2) a strong scientific and technological workforce, and (3) a private and public economic sector which can attract the capital necessary to provide the infrastructure needed for increased growth and technological changes. The U.S./Canadian core market, the EEC core market, and the Japanese area of influence in Asia appear to meet these criteria (Baig, 1989).

The information and communication revolution and the rise in world trade has created a volatile business climate

"Rapidly changing technology, quick market saturation, unexpected global competition—these all make succeeding in business, particularly a high technology business, harder than ever today" (Fraker, 1984). The volatile business climate engendered by the information technology and communication revolution and the globalization of economic forces has led to a significant realignment of individual corporate resources. In order to understand this corporate realignment we will (a) explore the unique problem this realignment creates for individual corporations, and (b) outline the new corporate perspective for responding to this problem.

The Unique Problem of the Shrinking Product Life Cycle

Most of the environmental forces precipitating the need for rapid change in corporate operations arise from a single problem; namely, the fact that firms are confronted by shrinking product life cycles. The product life cycle is the period of time available from the inception of an idea for a product until the market for that product is saturated or disappears due to new product development. A product life cycle normally involves several stages—product conceptualization, design, testing, refinement, mass production, marketing, shipping, selling, and servicing.

Dominique Hanssens, a professor in UCLA's Graduate School of Management, has studied the product life cycle in electrical appliances for years. He reports (Fraker, 1984) that years ago the product life cycle for refrigerators took over thirty years to mature, providing considerable time for each phase of the product life cycle to develop. However, all of this has changed. The market for microwave ovens has taken ten years to mature; CB radios, four years; computer games, three years; etc. Perhaps the most dramatic example of shrinking product life cycles as a result of rapidly changing technology, quick market saturation, and unexpected competition, can be found in the computer industry (Berlant, Browning and Foster, 1990).

The first commercially successful computer, containing an 8-bit memory chip came to market in 1977; four years later in 1981 the 16-bit memory chip appeared; two years later in 1983 came the 32-bit memory chip; and one year later in 1984 came the 64-bit memory chip. By 1987 we witnessed the appearance of the one megabyte memory chip, by 1989 the four megabyte memory chip, and by 1990 the development of a sixteen megabyte memory chip was well underway. The industrial shakedown from such rapid changes has taken its toll. Large U.S. companies, once dominant in their respective markets such as Hewlett Packard, MacIntosh, and DEC, who were unable to respond effectively to the end of one product life cycle and the beginning of a new one, lost their market position, with still other firms going out of the computer business.

How can a company manage to avoid these unpleasantries and prosper? What new techniques and skills must managers master to respond to this challenge? Only recently have executives who have responded successfully to this challenge begun to report a consistent pattern of attack that shows promise of providing a foundation for a new corporate perspective on how to respond to rapid environmental change.

A New Corporate Perspective on Rapid Change

Fraker (1984) argues that a rapidly changing technology, quick market saturation, and unexpected competition have led to the emergence of a new corporate perspective for coping with a volatile business climate.

- First, companies must stay close to both their customers and their competitors. Successful companies always know what the customer needs and attempt to provide it. When products and manufacturing processes change rapidly, it is crucial to keep up with the investment strategies and product costs of rival companies. In order to accomplish this, companies must develop and maintain a rapid and accurate intelligence system capable of preventing surprises.
- Second, companies must think constantly about new products and then back that thinking with investment, fast. A good new product strategy requires a large, active, and focused research and development team with ready access to and prudent use of large amounts of capital.
- Third, rapid and effective delivery requires close coordination between design, manufacturing, testing, marketing, delivery, and servicing systems. The interdependence of these systems combined with the short lead time in product delivery makes certain that any error within or between systems will delay product delivery endangering market penetration. Close cooperation between these systems requires strong, quick, and responsive integration, coordination, and control systems.
- Fourth, product quality, user friendliness, ease of service, and competitive pricing are essential for market penetration. In an environment where consumer and investor representatives compare, rate, and effectively communicate product differences, market penetration depends on quality, utility, and readily serviceable products. This in turn requires the active monitoring, testing, and checking the servicing of one's own and one's competitive products.
- Fifth, companies that introduce new products must consider the processes and costs required to cannibalize their own products and to retrench the workers involved. Companies faced with rapidly changing technology, quick market saturation, and unexpected competition must be prepared to change or withdraw their own products rather than let their reputation and

market shares be eroded by a competitor. Corporate planning for new products must include contingencies for shifting, retraining, or retrenching large product sectors rapidly.

- Sixth, a corporate vision must be developed which emphasizes change, allows for the assimilation of new units with alternative values, and encourages members to learn from mistakes without reprisal. Corporate cultures that cannot change rapidly will impede market adaptation. Corporations faced with stiff competition will often acquire other corporations with alternative values that will have to be integrated without delay into their corporate culture. Finally, a certain number of new initiatives are doomed to failure for all the reasons previously cited. Talented members of an organization must learn quickly from their failures and press on to new projects.
- Seventh, a corporate strategy must be developed which scans the globe for potential acquisitions, joint ventures, coalitions, value added partnerships, and tailored trade agreements which can give a corporation a technological edge, market access, market control, and/ or rapid response capabilities. Such a pooling of corporate resources is necessary for survival in a rapidly changing, highly competitive, international economic environment.

Each of these seven issues form the basis for a new set of corporate assumptions and practices.

Successful organizations are employing new management assumptions

Rapid environmental change creates organizational problems, but it can also create organizational opportunities. An organization's management system, with its integration, coordination, and control processes must have certain specifiable characteristics in order to respond to the opportunities created by successive, rapid, environmental change. A management system which capitalizes on environmental change must be (a) innovative, (b) adaptive, (c) flexible, (d) efficient, and (e) rapid in response . . . a high-speed management system.

Innovative management refers not only to product development, but innovation in corporate structure, manpower utilization, outsourcing, inventory control, manufacturing, marketing, servicing, and competitive positioning.

Adaptive management refers to an organization's appropriate adjustment to change in employee values, customer tastes, investor interests, government regulations, the availability of global economic resources, and the strategic positioning of competitors.

Flexible management refers to the capacity of an organization to expand, contract, shift direction on products and competitive strategy, and to assimilate acquisitions, joint ventures, coalitions, and to excise unproductive or underproductive units.

Efficient management refers to maintaining the industry lead in world class products, productivity, investors' equity, return on investment, employee satisfaction, customer support, product quality, and serviceability.

Rapid response management refers to setting and maintaining the industry standard in speed of response to environmental change.

The organizational benefits that flow from a high-speed management system can be breathtaking.

First, order of magnitude changes occur in response time. General Electric reduced from three weeks to three days the amount of time required to deliver a custom-made circuit breaker. Motorola used to turn out electronic pagers three weeks after the factory order arrived; now the process takes two hours (Ruffin 1990).

Second, order of magnitude changes occur in productivity, product quality, and market shares. A recent survey of 50 major U.S. corporations by Kaiser and Associates, a large consulting firm, found that all listed time-based management strategies at the top of their priority list (Dumaine, 1989:54). Why? Because speed of response tends to provide order of magnitude improvements in productivity, profits, product quality, and market shares.

Third, order of magnitude changes occur in profits. McKinsey & Company management consulting group demonstrates that high-tech products that come to market six months late earn 33 percent less profit over five years than coming out with a product on time, while 50 percent over budget increase in product development cuts profits only 4 percent when the product is on time (Vesey, 1991:25).

The focus of this new corporate perspective and thus the goal of high-speed management is the use of the new information technologies and human communication process to rapidly develop, test, and produce a steady flow of low cost, high quality, easily serviced, high value products which meet the customers' needs and of quickly getting these products to market before one's competition in an effort to achieve market penetration and large profits.

An outline of the theory of high-speed management

Competitive advantage in a rapidly changing economic environment will depend upon a corporation's capacity to monitor changes accurately in external economic forces and then to rapidly reorder a firm's internal resources to respond effectively to these external economic forces. In order to monitor changes accurately in external economic forces, an organization must have a world class information and communication capability. A world class information and communication capability must allow an organization to track and respond in real-time to international changes in the cost of capital, labor, and raw materials as well as changes in consumer taste and competitor response.

Similarly, sustainable competitive advantage in the 1990s will depend upon a corporation's capacity to rapidly orient and reorient a firm's product development, purchasing, manufacturing, distribution, sales, and service systems in response to volatile environmental change. To understand and systematically employ a high-speed management system, we are in need of a theoretic framework to guide the development and maintenance of such a world class information and communication capability. It is the purpose of this portion of our essay to explicate such a general theoretic framework. Our explication of this framework will proceed in two stages.

First, we shall explore a theory of environmental scanning as an information and communication framework for monitoring and evaluating rapid changes in an organization's external economic forces.

Second, we shall explore value chain theory as an information and communication framework for rapidly orienting and reorienting an organization's internal resources in response to changing external environmental forces.

A theory of environmental scanning

Environments create both problems and opportunities for organizations. Organizations must cope with changes in the cost of capital, labor, raw materials, shifts in consumer taste, governmental regulations, political stability, and unexpected competition. Similarly organizations depend upon the environment for scarce and valued resources, for developing strategic alliances such as coalitions, licensing, acquisitions, joint ventures, consortiums, value added partnerships, and tailored trade agreements aimed at improving a firm's R&D, manufacturing, distribution and service, and sales capabilities. An organization's environment, perhaps more than any other factor, affects organizational strategy, structure, and performance. However, whether changes in organizational strategy, structure, and performance lead to positive or negative consequences rests almost entirely upon the speed, accuracy, and interpretation of the information and communication regarding various environmental changes and the rapid reorientation of an organization's strategy, structure, and resources in order to take advantage of such changes. Our analysis of environmental scanning will be explored in two stages: (1) an explication of an environmental scanning framework and (b) an example of environmental scanning by a high-performance firm.

An Explication of a Theory of Environmental Scanning. If environmental scanning is an essential information and communication process for reorienting organizational strategy, structure, and resources, then how is this monitoring to be achieved?

Each industry and market in which a firm operates will contain its own unique underlying dynamic based upon what one's competitors are doing to influence sales and the influences to which one's customers are responding in buying products. Thus environmental scanning of industry and market forces must track the organizational strategies, structures, and resources employed by one's competitors and the tasks, inclinations, products, and potential products which one's customers will want or demand.

Once the competitive dynamics of an industry and market are understood, then top management normally scans the economic, technical, political, and social forces at work in the global economy which might be employed by one's competitors and/or self to influence these competitive dynamic. For example, capital can frequently be borrowed from Japanese banks at 3 to 5 percent less than other sources; skilled labor can be obtained in Singapore, Taiwan, and Korea at 30 to 60 percent less than in the U.S.-Canadian and European economic community core market; parts and manufacturing processes can frequently be subcontracted from other firms less expensively than provided in house. These global forces can significantly influence the competitive dynamics of an industry and market and are central to reorienting one's own firm to achieve a competitive advantage.

Environmental Scanning in a High Performance Organization. Environmental scanning is at once a simple and complex process. It is simple in that the critical information required to analyze the underlying dynamics of an industry and market are frequently readily available by all the competitors. It is complex in that the number of areas monitored to effect this dynamic may be large. Let us explore the elements in this process in a concrete example. Jack Welsh, CEO of General Electric, a very successful global competitor, describes the two levels of environmental scanning and their effect on corporate alignment in his firm. Once a year at the annual meeting of GE's top 100 executives, each of the firm's fourteen business leaders is required to present an environmental scanning analysis of his or her respective businesses. Each business leader is asked to present one-page answers to five questions:

1. What are your businesses' global market dynamics today and where are they going over the next several years?
2. What actions have your competitors taken in the last three years to upset those global dynamics?
3. What have you done in the last three years to effect those dynamics?
4. What are the most dangerous things your competitors could do in the next three years to upset those dynamics?
5. What are the most effective things you could do to bring about your desired impact on those dynamics?

Welsh concludes:

Five simple charts. After those initial reviews, which we update regularly, we could assume that everyone at the top knew the plays and had the same playbook. It doesn't take a genius. So when Larry Bossidy is with a potential partner in Europe, or I'm with a company in the Far East, we're always there with a competitive understanding based on our playbooks. We know exactly what makes sense; we don't need a big staff to do endless analysis. That means we should be able to act with speed.

Probably the most important thing we promise our business leaders is fast action. Their job is to create and grow new global businesses. Our job in the executive office is to facilitate, to go out and negotiate a deal, to make the acquisition, or get our businesses the partners they need. When our business leaders call, they don't expect studies, they expect answers.

Take the deal with Thomson, where we swapped our consumer electronics business for their medical equipment business. We were presented with an opportunity, a great solution to a serious strategic problem and we were able to act quickly. We didn't need to go back to headquarters for a strategic analysis and a bunch of reports. Conceptually, it took us about 30 minutes to decide that the deal made sense and then maybe two hours with the Thomson people to work out the basic terms. (Tichy and Charzon 1989:115)

Environmental scanning allows us to focus on the forces external to an organization that significantly influence its internal relationships. Value chain theory allows us the opportunity to reorient an organization's internal relationships in an effort to influence an organization's response to external forces.

An explication of value chain theory

We are in need of a theoretic framework for analyzing the kinds of international markets, the types of competitive advantage, and the issues involved in configuring and linking a firm's activities relative to one's competitors so as to obtain a sustainable competitive advantage. Particularly useful in this regard is value chain theory. We shall therefore: (a) explicate value chain theory, (b) apply value chain theory to analyze competitive advantage in the international auto industry, and (c) draw out the implications of this analysis for high-speed management.

The basic unit of analysis in understanding international competition is the industry, because it is in the industry that market shares are won or lost. In order to analyze how international competition functions, we must explore various market strategies, types of competitive advantage, and how value chain theory can serve as a theoretic approach for developing the sources of competitive advantage within an organization's functioning.

The forms of international competition within an industry range from multidomestic to global. A multidomestic approach to markets treats each country or core market as a unique arena and adjusts a firm's strategy for obtaining a competitive advantage to the specific issue in that market. When a firm takes this market-by-market approach, its international strategy is multidomestic. A multidomestic firm views its industry as a collection of individual markets. In such instance, a firm normally operates relatively autonomous subsidiaries in each market.

A global approach to markets is one in which a firm's competitive position in one country or core market is significantly affected by the firm's competitive position in other countries or core markets. International competition in a global industry is more than a collection of independent subsidiaries located in individual markets with unique strategies for obtaining competitive advantage in each market. A global approach rests on a series of interdependent activities which are integrated, coordinated, and controlled so that competitive advantage in one part of the world can be leveraged to obtain competitive advantage throughout the linkage system.

Competitive advantage can be viewed conceptually as emanating from four sources:

First, a product or service which provides customers with comparable value at lower cost than one's competitors creating low cost competitive advantage. Japanese automakers have consistently produced cars at $750–$950 per unit lower cost than comparable American manufacturers leading to low cost competitive advantage (Treece & Howr, August 14, 1989:75).

Second, a product or service that is comparable in cost but which contains some unique quality, styling, service, or functional features relative to one's competitors creating differentiation competitive advantage. Toyota and Honda automobiles require less repairs, are easier to service, and have more standard features included in the product price, such as air conditioning, power brakes and steering, and AM-FM raidos, and thus create higher customer satisfaction than similar U.S. and European cars and a product differentiation competitive advantage.

Third, a firm may provide a broader range of products or services than one's competitors thus creating scope competitive advantage. The Ford Motors Corporation provides its customers with small, medium, large, luxury, sport, and station wagon cars to select from as well as a broad range of trucks and mini-vans creating competitive advantage relative to the Chrysler Corporation based on product scope.

Fourth, due to the high demand for certain products or services, the first producer into the market with a quality product can dominate the market, and obtain high-end pricing and maximized profits based on speed of response creating a time competitive advantage. The Chrysler Corporation's development, production, and marketing of mini-vans beat its competitors to market by one year, allowing Chrysler to capture all of the market for mini-vans for one year and get high-end pricing for maximum profits, and to hold a majority of the market (51 percent) for the next two years due to its time competitive advantage.

Most top international firms seek to exploit competitive advantage from all four sources. To diagnose where the sources of a firm's competitive advantage are and how each organization's functional units and business processes add value or fails to add value to products, we are in need of a theoretic framework for disaggregating a firm's discrete activities and evaluating their value added contribution to an organization's products. Particularly useful in this regard is value chain theory. Managers term the discrete activities involved in producing a product or service the value chain and arrange them into functional unit activities and business processes (see Figure 4.1).

In examining an organization's functional unit level of the value chain, notice that the two circles which denote suppliers and customers are normally found outside the organizational structure while the square boxes denote functional activities performed within an organization's structure. In examining an organization's business process level, note how each process includes some activities unique to each business process and some activities which overlap with other business processes.

Functional units and business processes may be located anywhere on the globe where they can gain competitive advantage from their location. Product development processes are normally located in regions where firms have access to a steady supply of state-of-the-art engineers such as the U.S., Japan, and Germany where competitive advantage can be obtained from product differentiation. Product delivery processes are normally located near sources of inexpensive and skilled labor and automated production facilities such as Korea, Singapore, and Taiwan, where competitive advantage can be obtained from low cost production. Customer service and management teams are normally located in the core market's firm services in order to obtain competitive advantage from rapid response time. A firm may obtain competitive advantage and/or value added contributions from one or more of these sources. However, competitive advantage and value added activities gained in one functional unit or business process can be added to or cancelled out by an organization's performance in other functional units or business processes. This is what is meant by value added or value diminishing chains of activities. If a functional unit or business activity fails to provide a source of competitive advantage or add value to an organization's products, then it needs to be improved or replaced. A primary function of management is to employ information and communication to monitor, evaluate, and improve the value chain in order to gain competitive advantage. This is essentially a communication process. Section three of this essay will explore the information and communication component of this process in detail.

Functional Business Unit Level

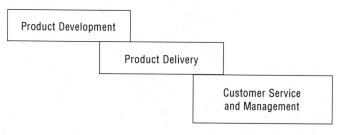

Business Process Level

(Revised from Rockart & Schort, 1989:12)

Figure 4.1 An Organization's Value Chain

An Application of Value Chain Theory to the Global Auto Industry. The international auto market is a multi-billion dollar industry. Ten firms account for approximately 78 percent of world sales. Table 4.1 provides a profile of their September 1988 to September 1989 global performance.

Table 4.1
World Auto Market, September 1988–September 1989

				World Wide Productions		
Trucks	World % of Market Shares	Auto Revenues U.S. $ Billions	Net Earnings U.S. $ Thousands	Vehicles Thousands	Autos %	%
1. GM	17.7	99.7	$3,831	7,946	74	26
2. Ford	14.6	76.8	4,259	6,336	70	30
3. Toyota	9.4	53.8	2,836	4,115	76	24
4. Volkswagon	6.6	34.4	921	2,948	93	7
5. Nissan	6.4	36.4	945	2,930	77	23
6. Chrysler	5.4	30.8	629	2,382	48	52
7. FIAT	5.4	26.4	2,453	2,436	90	10
8. Peugeot	4.6	22.8	1,518	2,216	88	12
9. Renault	4.2	26.4	1,451	2,053	80	20
10. Honda	4.0	25.2	945	1,960	86	14

(Borrus, 1990)

The top three firms—General Motors, Ford, and Toyota—account for over 40 percent of the world auto market. We shall, for reasons of space, limit our analysis to the international competition between the top three firms in the U.S. core market. The central competitive dynamics operating in the global automobile industry, according to Harold Poling, CEO of Ford Motor Corporation, are "vehicle attributes, customer satisfaction and value for money" (Poling, 1989). Vehicle attributes refers to styling, power train performance, and road handling. Customer satisfaction refers to vehicle comfort, safety, quality, ease of maintenance. Value for money refers to cost, standard features, gas mileage, insurance costs.

Table 4.2. provides the relevant high-speed management data upon which our analysis for the U.S. Market is based.

The General Motors Corporation is the world's largest producer of automobiles. Its U.S. market shares have fallen from 45 percent in 1980 to 35 percent in 1989. A one percentage

Table 4.2
High-Speed Management Data
(for U.S. Market)

	GM	Ford	Toyota
% Market Shares 1980	45	20	6
% Market Shares 1989	35	22	7
% Market Shares 1990	35	21	9
Productivity 1990 (Worker Hours Per Car)	20	17	12
AV Replacement Time 1990 (Years Per Model)	5	5	2
Factory Utilization (% 1990 Capacity)	70	78	110
Productivity Increase 1990 (%)	4.8	6.2	10.2

(Compiled from *Automotive News* 1989–1990)

point drop amounts to 114,526 cars. GM's market shares at
the lower end auto price range have been eroded by Ford
Escort and Toyota Tercel; at the middle price range by Ford,
Taurus, and Tempo and the Toyota Corolla; and at the upper
price range by Ford Lincoln and Toyota Camry. GM has invested $46 billion in plant modernization (a sum equal to the
amount needed to purchase Toyota Motors in 1990) and is
still the high-cost producer. GM in the past three years cut
$15 billion from its operating budget, closed several plants,
laid off workers, but still ran its remaining plant at 70 percent compared to 78 and 110 percent for Ford and Toyota. As
you can see from the high-speed management data, GM requires more worker hours per car, more model replacement
time, and has a lower productivity increase than its two competitors. In addition GM's Cadillac, Oldsmobile, and Buick
cars ranked 7, 8, 9 in quality ratings, while Toyota's Corolla
and Camry ranked 2 and 3, with no Ford cars appearing in
the top ten (Taylor, February 26, 1990).

The Ford Motor Corporation is one of America's most successful global competitors in the 1980s. Ford's market shares
increased from 20 percent in 1980 to 22 percent by 1989. Ford
produces vehicles at $200 less per unit than GM but trails
Toyota by $650 per unit in cost. Over the past five years Ford
has invested $21 billion in plant modernization and has sig-
nificantly improved its production capabilities. It is evident
from our high-speed management data that Ford outperforms
GM in productivity, replacement time, factory utilization, and
productivity increases in 1989. However, Ford still trails
Toyota in all categories (Taylor, November 19, 1990).

Toyota Motors has established itself as the low-cost, high-quality, and best-value automobile producer among the top three. Toyota's cars cost $675 to $950 less to produce than Ford and GM (Treece and Howr, 1989). In addition Toyota leads Ford and GM in all high-speed management measures. It costs less, takes less worker hours per car, less time to replace a car, and on average, Toyota workers are more productive than Ford and GM. That may be why Toyota has gone from 6 percent of the U.S. market in 1980 to 9 percent in 1990. In 1989, Toyota's market shares increased 3 percent in the United States, 3 percent in the European Economic Community, and 4 percent in Japan yielding a 10 percent increase worldwide, an increase in sales of over one million cars. A one percentage point gain amounts to 114,526 cars. While Ford and GM have lost market shares in the last ten years, Toyota has gained. Toyota's innovative, adaptive, efficient and rapid response systems according to Taylor, November 19, 1990) accounted for the firms competitive advantage in product cost, differentiation, scope and timing.

Implications For High-Speed Management. While environmental scanning and value chain theory appear to be useful as analytic tools for exploring the types and sources of competitive advantage employed in the auto industry, two questions arise regarding the framework's generalizability.

First, can the appropriate use of environmental scanning and value chain theory to analyze change in the environment and quickly adjust an organizations value chain to meet these changes separate successful from unsuccessful international competitors based on configuration and linking processes irrespective of industry?

Second, can environmental scanning and value chain theory demonstrate that firms which have a competitive advantage based on time also have improved performance ratings on all forms of competitive advantage?

Marquise Cvar (1984) attempted to answer the first questions when he undertook a study at twelve international corporations in 1984. For his research, Cvar selected eight successful and four unsuccessful firms for study. Four of the successful firms were American, while one each was Swiss, British, Italian, and French. Three of the four unsuccessful firms were American and one was Swiss. These twelve firms each competed in separate industries. Successful firms were distinguished from unsuccessful firms by their high investment in information and communication technology and by the effective use of information and communication to analyze and evaluate quickly changes in the external organizational environment and then to reorient rapidly its internal resource in responding to those changes.

Smith, Grimm, Chen and Gannon (1989) attempted to answer our second question in their study of 22 top-level managers from high-technology electronics firms. They explained major portions of the variance in organizational performance or increases in profits and sales from decreases in response time to environmental change. They found that an external orientation by a firm, a rapid response to competitor threat, and the radicalness of the change initiated in the organization were all positively related to increased profits, sales, and the general performance of an organization. Decreases in response time to external change were highly correlated with communication systems improvements in an organization's R & D, manufacturing, and marketing.

Value chain theory does appear to be capable of (1) separating successful from unsuccessful international firms, and (2) revealing how competitive advantage based on integration, coordination, and control improves overall organizational performance. We are now in a position to explore the transformations the general theory of high-speed management has brought about in the traditional conceptualization of organizational communication processes.

High-speed management transformations of traditional organizational communication processes

Within every organization there are tacit assumptions about how individuals and groups must share information and interact through communication in order to perform organizational tasks. These tacit assumptions create an organization's mind set and define how members of that organization perceive and interact with an organization's stakeholders. These tacit assumptions that govern and guide perception and interaction create an organization's information and communication climate. What has our analysis thus far taught us about the broad outline of such a set of necessary assumptions in successful high-speed management organizations?

The first section of this essay argued that a series of breakthroughs have taken place in information and communication technology that have dramatically altered how organizations do work. This information and communication revolution in organizational processes has led to a dramatic increase in world trade, the emergence of a global economy, and the development of three large core markets anchored by the U.S., Germany, and Japan. This dramatic increase in world trade has created a volatile business climate characterized by rapidly changing technology, quick market saturation, and unexpected competition making succeeding in business very difficult. To compete successfully in such an environment requires that organizations employ management assumptions which emphasize innovative, adaptive, flexible, efficient, and rapid response to change—high-speed management assumptions.

The second section of this essay argued that obtaining competitive advantage in a volatile business environment will depend upon an organization's capacity to rapidly and accurately monitor changes in an organization's external environment and then to quickly reorient an organization's internal and external resources in order to effectively respond to that change. Rapidly and accurately monitoring an organization's external environment requires the real-time tracking of changes in consumer taste, competitor strategies, global economic forces, and core market demand. Quickly reorienting an organization's external and internal resources requires scanning the globe for acquisitions, joint ventures, strategic alliances, and exploiting the value added potential of one's own organizational activities. Finally, a world class information and communication capability or high-speed management system is required in order to successfully employ such an environmental scanning and value chain alignment capability.

It is the purpose of this final section of our essay to explore the (1) philosophical rational, (2) theoretic principles, and (3) practical basis for such a world class information and communication capability and to indicate how high-speed management has transformed the traditional conceptualizations of organizational communication.

Philosophical rationale for the transformation of organizational communication processes

While it is clear from our previous analysis that a successful global competitor carefully monitors changes in global economic forces and then quickly reorients an organization's value chain to meet those changes in ways which create value added activities and thus competitive advantage, it is far from clear what the philosophical rationale is for guiding the communication activities involved in these organizational adaptation processes. Fortunately, several well-developed studies have explored this problem in detail with convergent results (Rockert and Schort, 1989; Venkatraman and Prescott, 1990; Cvar, 1986; Smith, et al., 1989).

The Center for Information Systems Research at the MIT Sloan School of Management in 1989 summarized these convergent studies when it stated that an organization's ability to continuously improve its effectiveness in managing organizational interdependencies was the critical element in successfully responding to the competitive forces of the 1990s (Rockert and Schort, 1989). Effectiveness in managing organizational interdependencies refers to an organization's ability to achieve coalignment among its internal and external resources in a manner which is equal to or greater than existing world class benchmarks for responding to environmental change.

Coalignment is a unique form of organizational interdependence in which each of a firm's subunits clearly articulates its needs, concerns, and potential contributions to the organization's functioning in such a manner that management can forge an appropriate value added configuration and linkage between units. An appropriate value added configuration and linkage between units is one which integrates, coordinates, and controls each unit's needs, concerns, and contributions so that the outcome is mutually satisfying to the units involved and optimizing in value added activities to the organizational functioning as a whole.

World class benchmarking refers to the standards one holds in setting goals for improvement. These benchmarks or goals to be met in improving an organization's innovation, adaptation, flexibility, efficiency, and rapid response to environmental change must be set at world class levels. They must reflect the highest standards of the best companies in the world. Only then will improvement in an organization's coalignment process provide for the value added gains necessary for sustainable competitive advantage.

Our analysis of the philosophical rationale for the primary function of communication within its organizational context suggests that communication serves to continuously improve organizational effectiveness in managing a firm's coalignments between its internal and external resources benchmarked against world class standards in responding to environmental change. Coalignment is a unique communication relationship in which each of a firm's stakeholders clearly articulates its needs, concerns, and contributions in such a manner that management can forge an appropriate value added configuration and linkage between stakeholders which is mutually satisfying and optimizing to the value added activities of the organization when benchmarked against world class standards, thus creating a sustainable competitive advantage.

While such a philosophical rationale seems clear and responsive to a volatile economic environment, what theoretic principles are available to guide this continuously improving communication process of organizational coalignment and world class benchmarking?

The theoretic bases for the transformation of organizational communication processes

Four dynamic communication processes, each with its own theoretic rationale, currently form the basis for such a continuous improvement of organizational coalignment processes based on world class benchmarking. These are: (1) negotiation linking, (2) a New England town meeting, (3) a cross-functional teamwork, and (3) a best practices case study program.

(1) A Negotiated Linking Program

A unit or function is created within an organization whose purpose is to continuously scan the globe in order to locate resources in the form of customers, partners, technologies and/or consultants which are capable of enhancing an organizations competitiveness. Such resources may include land, labor, capital, market entry, distribution channels, technology, training, etc. This unit then

- interacts with the unit holding the potential resource in order to locate its interests, concerns, and contributions to coalignment.

- develops the form of coalignment preferred by both units, such as acquisition, joint venture, alliance, partnership coalition, collaboration, licensing technology leasing, transfer, and/or training.
- determines the world class benchmarking targets in market shares, productivity, quality, flexibility, and/or rapid response time to be met before coalignment can take place.

The organizational negotiated-linking program then formulates the negotiated coalignment agreement aimed at mobilizing external resources for organizational usage.

(2) A New England Town Meeting

A unit or function is created within the organization to implement a worker continuous improvement program within a New England town meeting format. Its goal is to improve an organization's productivity, quality, flexibility, adaptability, and/or response time. It is an attempt to eliminate nonessential, non-productive, or "bad work" and replace it with "good work." These New England style town meetings last from one to three days. They begin with the division head calling together 20–100 workers, suppliers, and/or customers.

The meeting then proceeds in the following manner:

- the division head opens the meeting with a presentation of key market issues, the organization's vision in responding to these issues, how the organization and its competitors are responding to this vision, and specific organizational needs for increased productivity, quality, flexibility, adaptability, and rapid response time. The division head leaves at this point in the meeting.
- teamwork facilitators take over and generate a list of bad work to be eliminated and good work to be undertaken in responding to the various areas of concern.
- the group is then divided into teams of 5 to 10 members to analyze, discuss, and debate potential areas for improvement.
- each team then provides a cost/benefit analysis and action plan for the solutions recommended.
- the division head then returns and listens to a cost/ benefit analysis and action plan from each group.

The division head acts on all high yield ideas by selecting a team champion, training the team champion in project management, empowering a team to implement the change, setting performance targets, measurement criteria, time frame, and feedback procedures. The worker improvement team then implements the action plan.

(3) A Cross-Functional Teamwork Program

A unit or function is created to set up cross-functional teams whose goals are to map and then improve cross-functional organizational processes. Many of the most significant improvements in organizational performance have come from mapping important cross-functional organizational processes and then asking those involved in the process to simplify and/or improve the functioning of that process. This approach has been very profitable for organizations since many of these processes have developed and expanded overtime without anyone examining the entire process and exploring its improvement.

Here cross-functional teams are set up and assigned the task of mapping the decision, implementation, and review levels of important organizational processes. The cross-functional team is then asked to evaluate and make improvements in the process mappings. This is accomplished in four steps:

- developing a clear understanding of the process goal
- identifying the necessary and sufficient critical success factors for achieving that goal
- mapping and improving the essential sub-processes to meet these critical success factors
- rank ordering each sub-process and evaluating its productivity, quality, flexibility, adaptability, and how to make improvements.

The unit and/or function then implements the change process and fine tunes its sub-processes.

(4) A Best Practice Case Study Program

A unit or function is created to scan the globe for world class competitors and to study how various parts of these organizations succeeded in setting world class benchmarking standards in regard to productivity, quality, flexibility, adaptability, and response time. This unit usually

- locates such organizations and makes a site visit
- develops a case study of the processes involved
- trains personnel at its own organization in ways to adapt these innovations to its organization

This unit then sets up monitoring and feedback procedures for and implements the change.

These then are our four dynamic communication processes, each with its own theoretic rationale for developing an organizational continuous improvement program employing environmental scanning and value chain theory aimed at achieving coalignment between an organization's external and internal resources.

The practical bases for such a world class information and communication capability

Continuous improvement programs aimed at improving organizational coalignment through negotiated linking, cross-functional teamwork. New England town meetings, and case studies in world class benchmarking are necessary elements in establishing a world class organizational information and communication capability. Continuous improvement programs are essential information and communication processes in high-speed management which have rapidly defused to small and large organizations in the private and public sectors of the world economy. Let us therefore examine the practical bases of continuous improvement programs by exploring the four dynamic communication processes functioning first in a small local organization, the Danville, Illinois Bumper Works, and second in a large multinational organization such as the General Electric Corporation.

The Danville, Illinois Bumper Works.

In 1978 Mr. Shahid Khan, a naturalized U.S. citizen from Pakistan, borrowed $50,000 from the Small Business Loan Corporation and took $16,000 of his own savings to establish the 100 person Bumper Works in Danville, Illinois. This company designed and manufactured truck bumpers. Between 1980 and 1985, Mr. Khan approached the Toyota Motors Corporation on several occasions attempting to become a supplier of bumpers for their trucks but without much luck.

In 1987, the Toyota Motors Company called together a group of 100 potential suppliers and released their design, quality, quantity, and price range specifications for the product. The officials at Toyota Motors also indicated that they expected increased quality and a reduction in price each year from the supplier. By late 1988, only Mr. Khan's Bumper Works company could produce a product which met Toyota Motors exacting requirements. In 1989, Toyota Motors sent a manufacturing team to Danville, Illinois to negotiate the contract and coalignment agreement between the two firms. The negotiations failed because the Bumper Works could not produce 20 different sized bumpers and ship them in a single day. If they could not do this, it would slow down the production of all Toyota trucks, increasing their price dramatically (White, 1991:A7).

Mr. Khan called a New England town meeting of workers from his own and Toyota Motors Japanese factories to explore how this problem might be solved within Toyota's design, quality, quantity, and price requirements. It was decided that the Bumper Works would have to switch the factory from a mass production to a batch production line and that a massive stamping machine which took 90 minutes to change each cutting die would have to be modified so as to make such changes in 20 minutes (White, 1991:A7).

Next, the workers at both the Bumper Works and Toyota Motors set up cross-functional teams to make a process map of current production procedures. They studied, simplified, and restructured the process so as to allow for batch production. The large stamping machine was studied for modifications that would speed up die changes. All this was done with considerable help from Toyota Motors who had solved these same problems, but in a different way, back in Japan (White, 1991:A7).

Then, the Bumper Works' remodeled assembly line was ready to begin production. For six months employees with stop watches and cost sheets observed the restructured process and benchmarked its operations against the world class standards of the Toyota Plant in Japan—but still could not meet Toyota's quality, quantity, and speed of delivery specifications. They videotaped the process, studied it, modified it, and sent it to Japan for review. In July 1990 Toyota Motors sent a team over to help retrain the workers. They returned again in December of 1990 to fine tune the process, meeting Toyota Motors contract requirements.

The new production line increased productivity 60 percent over the previous year, decreased defects 80 percent, cut delivery time by 850 percent, and cut waste materials cost by 50 percent. A manual and videotape of the manufacturing process were prepared for training, the first of their kind at Bumper Works, and continuous improvement teams were formed in order to meet contract requirements for Toyota Motors of increased quality and decreased costs for each subsequent year.

Now that representatives of each unit involved in the value chain linking the Bumper Works and Toyota Motors had communicated their interests, concerns, and contributions to the coalignment process, each firm's management was able to forge a linking process that was satisfactory to the units involved and optimizing to the value added activities of each organization in order to create a sustainable competitive advantage. Mr. Khan, the owner of Bumper Works, has profited from this experience and is building a new plant which will employ 200 workers in Indiana and will supply truck bumpers for a new Isuzu Motors plant located there (White, 1991:A7).

The General Electric Corporation

In 1990, General Electric had $58.4 billion in sales, $4.3 billion in profits and had 298,000 employees worldwide. As Stewart (1991:41) indicates:

Few corporations are bigger; none more complex. GE makes 65 cent lightbulbs, 400,000 pound locomotives, and billion dollar power plants. It manages more credit cards than American Express and owns more commercial aircraft than American Airlines. Of the seven billion pounds of hamburger Americans tote home each year, 36 percent keep fresh in GE refrigerators, and after dinner, one out of every five couch potatoes tunes in GE's network, NBC.

This is the organization which CEO Jack Welch, Jr. wants to be lean, agile, and aggressive to run like a small business. His corporate goal is to make GE the most competitive corporation in the world by having each of its 13 businesses ranked number 1 or 2 in world market shares, while increasing sales 15 percent, profits 10 percent, productivity 5 percent per year, and decreasing costs by 5 percent per year. It goes without saying that Jack Welch Jr. is a strong advocate of continuous improvement programs. Let us explore GE's continuous improvement program.

Since 1981 GE has divested itself of $5.9 billion in low growth businesses and acquired $11.1 billion in high growth businesses in order to maintain its number 1 or 2 world market shares in each of 13 businesses. It is a difficult task for an environmental scanning unit to locate such a large number of potential acquisitions capable of performing at the level required by GE and then to negotiate the linking agreement so that the acquisition is quickly brought up to speed. For example, Philips Corporation of Holland purchased Westinghouse's lighting business; Electrolux of Sweden purchased White consolidated major appliance division; and Brown and Bovevi of Switzerland and ASEA of Sweden merged their power systems divisions. Each of these acquisitions and mergers threatened GE's number 1 or 2 market shares ranking in the lighting, major appliances, and power systems industries. In each case GE scanned the globe for potential linking arrangements which could restore their market dominance and which could meet their world class growth, productivity, product quality, and rapid response targets. Acquisitions were located, linking arrangements negotiated, and coalignment processes put in place so that market shares and performance targets could be met. Over ten years, such acquisitions amounted to 11.1 billion dollars.

In order to become the most competitive corporation in the world, Jack Welch realized that his business leaders had to find a better fit between their organization's needs and their employee's capabilities. To reorient this fit, GE in 1987 established a New England town meeting program called "Workout." The purpose of workout town meetings according to Welch were:

> To see a team work together to face its problems and candidly discuss issues which negatively affect their work by giving each employee the power to define and shape his job, to give it meaning so he can feel responsible for it, get value from it, and have it be an enriching experience instead of a draining, numbing nuisance. In the end, each employee will have worked to create more customers, more job security, and more job satisfaction. That's our ultimate goal for the 1990s at GE (Workout, Dec. 1989:1).

By the end of 1991 over 50,000 GE employees will have participated in three day workout town meetings with remarkable results. In GE's plastic division alone, over thirty workout teams have been empowered to make changes. One team saved GE plastics $2 million by modifying one production process, another enhanced productivity fourfold, while a third reduced product delivery time 400 percent (Workout, Sept. 1991:1 & 2). Another business, NBC, used workout to halt the use of report forms that totaled more than two million pieces of paper a year (Stewart, 1991:44). GE Credit Services used workout to tie its cash registers directly to the mainframe, cutting the time for opening a new account from 30 minutes to 90 seconds. Similar results have been reported from workout projects in GE's other business demonstrating a remarkable company-wide reorientation of coalignment processes between worker capabilities and organizational needs.

While this internal transformation of GE's value chain was taking place, Jack Welch also realized that some other global organizations were achieving greater productivity, quality control, flexibility, adaptability, and rapid response time than GE, even with the workout program in place. In the summer of 1988, GE began its "Best Practices Program" aimed at locating those organizations which had outperformed GE in a given area, developing a case study of how they did it, and then employing these case studies as world class benchmarks for improving GE's performance.

GE scanned the globe and located twenty-four corporations that had in some areas outperformed GE. They then screened out direct competitors, and companies that would not be credible to GE employees. Welch then invited each corporation to come to GE to learn about its best practices and in return allow GE people to come to their companies and study their best practices. About one-half of the companies agreed. They included AMP, Chapparral Steel, Ford, Hewlett Packard, Xerox, and three Japanese companies. GE sent out observers to develop case studies and ask questions. These best practices case studies have been turned into a course at Crotonville, GE's leadership training center, and is offered to a new class of managers from each of GE's 13 businesses each month (Stewart, 1991:44–45).

Finally, as GE's top management team reviewed the projects which had been successful from both their workout and best practices program, they noticed a difference in the types of projects which saved up to a million dollars and those which saved 100 million. The latter always involved changes in organizational processes that spanned the entire value chain. They cut across departments and involved linking with suppliers and customers. All emphasized managing processes, not functions. This led GE to establish its cross-functional teamwork program aimed at mapping and then improving key organizational processes. Such process maps frequently allowed employees for the first time to see and understand organizational processes from beginning to end. They also demonstrated the need for a new type of manager, a process manager who could coalign an organization's total assets. It allowed employees to spot bottlenecks, time binds and inventory shortages, and overflows.

Since implementing such a cross-functional teamwork program, GE appliances has cut its 16 week manufacturing cycle in half, while increasing product availability 6 percent and decreasing inventory costs 20 percent. The program has cost less than $3 million to implement and has already returned profits 100 times that (Stewart, 1991:48). Product-mapping programs have also provided an empirical basis for changing how GE measures its management and workers' performance. GE now employs world class cross-functional process benchmarking standards to evaluate its various business performances and to award its bonuses and merit awards for process improvements.

Continuous improvement programs like those we explored at Bumper Works and General Electric are using negotiated linking, New England town meetings, cross-functional teamwork, and case studies of world class benchmarking to revolutionize how the practical basis for communication effects the coalignment of organizational processes in order to obtain a sustainable competitive advantage.

Summary

Our rather long journey into the theory of high-speed management is over. In summary we began this essay by noting how the convergence of four trends has created a volatile business environment. Next we explored how the general theory of high-speed management attempts to give managers some control over rapid change through the use of environmental scanning theory and value chain theory. Finally we explored how organizational coalignment was effected by four theoretic and practical communication processes: (1) negotiated linking, (2) New England town meetings, (3) cross-functional teamwork, and (4) case studies of world class benchmarking.

Our goal throughout this essay has been to explicate a *macro* theory of organizational communication processes (environmental scanning and value chain theory) and demonstrate how that macro theory can guide the development of *micro* theories and research on continuous improvement programs and their communication processes. This macro theory can be employed to reorient micro organizational communication theories of leadership, corporate climate teamwork, etc. (Cushman and King, 1992). High-speed management thus shows promise of providing a new approach to all organizational communication issues, strategies, and techniques, through an information and communication approach to organizational processes.

References

Automotive News (1989–1990), all issues.

Baig, E. (July 13, 1989). Where Global Growth is Going, *Fortune*, 120:71–88.

Berlant, D., Browning, R., and Foster, G. (January–February 1990). How Hewlett-Packard Gets Numbers It Can Trust, *Harvard Business Review*, 68:178–182.

Borrus, A. (May 7, 1990). Japanese Streak Ahead in Asia, *Business Week*, 31:54–55.

Castells, M. (1986). High-Technology, World Development and the Structured Transformation: The Trends and Debate, *Alternatives*, 11:297–342.

Cushman, D. P., and King, S. S. (1989). The role of communication in high technology organizations: The emergence of high-speed management. In S. S. King (ed.) *Human Communication as a Field of Study*, chapter 12. Albany, New York: SUNY Press.

Cushman, D., and King. S. (1992). *High-Speed Management: Organizational Communication in the 1990s*, in process.

Cvar, M. (1986), *Case Studies in Global Competition Patterns of Success and Failure*. In M. Porter (ed.) *Competition in Global Industry*, Boston, MA: Harvard Business School Press, pp. 483–517.

Dumaine, B. (February 13, 1989). How Managers Can Succeed Through Speed, *Fortune*, 119:54–59.

Feigenbaum, E., McCorduck, P. and Nii, P. (1988). *The Rise of the Expert Company,* New York: Times Books.

Fraker, S. (February 13, 1984). High-Speed Management For The High Tech Age, *Fortune,* 119:34–60.

The Global Giants, *Wall Street Journal* (September 21, 1990), R27.

Pepper, C. B. (February 1989). Fast Forward, *Business Month,* pp. 25–30.

Poling, H. (November 7, 1989). An Interview with the CEO Designate of Ford Motors Company, *Automotive News,* E8.

Port, O. (June 16, 1986). High tech to the rescue. *Business Week,* pp. 100–108.

Rockart, J., and Schort, J. (Winter 1989). IT in the 1990s: Managing Organizational Interdependencies, *Sloan Management Review,* 30:7–17.

Ruffin, W. (January 1990). Wired For Speed, *Business Month,* pp. 56–58.

Russell, E., Adams, A., and Boundy, B. (Winter 1986). High-Technology Test Marketing Campbell Soup Company, *The Journal of Consumer Marketing,* 3:1:71–80.

Smith, K. G., Grimm, C. M., Chen, M. J. and Gannon, M. J. (1989). Predictors of Response Time to Competitive Strategic Action: Preliminary Theory and Evidence, *Journal of Business Research,* 19:245–258.

Stalk, Jr., G. (July–August, 1988). Time—The Next Source of Competitive Advantage, *Harvard Business Review,* 66:41–51.

Stewart, T. (August 12, 1991). GE Keeps Those Ideas Coming, *Fortune,* pp. 41–49.

Taylor, A. (February 26, 1990). Can American Cars Come Back? *Fortune,* 121:62–65.

Taylor, III, A. (November 19, 1990). Why Toyota Keeps Getting Better, *Fortune,* 122:66–79.

Tichy, N., and Charzon, R. (1989). Speed, Simplicity, Self-Confidence: An Interview with Jack Welch, *Harvard Business Review,* 67:112–120.

Treece, J., and Howr, J. (August 14, 1989). Shaking Up, *Business Week,* 24–80.

Venkatraman, N., and Prescott, J. (1990), Environment-Strategy Coalignment: An Empirical Test of Its Performance Implications, *Strategic Management Journal,* 11:1–23.

Vescy, J. (1991). The New Competitors: They Think in Terms of Speed-to-Market, *Academy of Management Executive,* 5:22–33.

Walton, J. (1985). The IMF Riot, Paper delivered at the I.S.A. Conference on the Urban Impact of the New International Division of Labor, Hong Kong.

White, J. (September 9, 1991). Japanese Auto Makers Help U.S. Suppliers Become More Efficient, *Wall Street Journal,* pp. A1 and A7.

Workout (December 1989 and September 1991). Special Edition of *GE Silicones News.*

Young, J. (Spring 1990). An American Giant Rethinks Globalization, *Information Strategy,* pp. 5–10.

Perspectives on Communicating Corporate Culture to Employee-Owners— A Case Study: Weirton Steel Corporation

❖

Jay Morris

The Reagan years will be remembered for big business mergers and an increasing number of giant multinational conglomerates, but a smaller, yet growing trend, also developed—employee-owned companies or ESOPs (Employee Stock Ownership Plans). ESOPs demanded that we re-think the ways and methods in which we communicate to our new employee-owners. This paper focuses on the largest fully employee-owned company, Weirton Steel Corporation (WV) and the implementation of a unique communications plan. In a time of record-setting profits and production for the company, the employee-owners were asked to give concessions in order to fund a $650 million capital investment plan. The communications team's obstacle in developing a successful communications plan was unenviable—convince prosperous and productive employee-owners to put money into the plant for tomorrow instead of in their own pockets today.

Why Weirton Steel became an employee-owned company

During World War II, Weirton Steel made steel bomb casings as their contribution to the war effort, but no amount of familiarization with explosives could have prepared their employees for the "bombshell" news that their parent company delivered in Spring 1982. National Steel Corporation announced that the steel-making division in Weirton would be downsized to a finishing mill. Employment at the Weirton plant would drop from 10,000 to 1,000.

Options were few. It soon became apparent that no buyers would step forward during a period of depressed steel prices. The only alternative left to the employees was untested and risky—an employee buyout of the plant from National Steel under an Employee Stock Ownership Plan (ESOP). An ESOP of this size had never been attempted; Weirton would also be the first ESOP venture for a steel plant.

In order to get the Weirton ESOP off the ground and make it attractive to its customers, an ESOP study advised that each new employee-owner take a 32 percent wage and benefits cut. In return, the employee-owners would receive a 35 percent profit sharing provision and stock in the new company.

In January 1984, "We Can Do It!" became the rallying cry for the ESOP vote that passed by an overwhelming margin, and Weirton Steel became the nation's largest fully employee-owned company.

Weirton Steel's first five years as an ESOP

Despite the dour predictions of most steel industry analysts, Weirton Steel's ESOP showed a profit each quarter from its inception. The profits peaked in 1988 when Weirton Steel set its own profit and shipping records. However, the unforeseen profitability caused a dilemma for the future of the plant. Under the original ESOP agreement of 1984, a trigger mechanism was put in place once the company reached $250 million in equity. The company unexpectedly reached that figure after only four years triggering 1) an increase in profit sharing from 35 percent to 50 percent; 2) a stock repurchase obligation allowing employee-owners to cash in their shares of the company (estimated stock liability—$37 million).

On the surface it would appear that Weirton Steel was now a prosperous company, and the 8500 employee-owners would now have a chance to regain the concessions of four years ago. However, Weirton Steel was an aging company (one of the biggest factors of National Steel's pullout dealt with its unwillingness to pump revenues into modernization of Weirton's steel-making facilities). CEO Herbert Elish and his management team developed a $650 million capital program that would include renovation of the hot mill and construction of a continuous caster. Continuous casting allows for better quality, more speed, and flexibility in meeting specifications of customers in comparison to old methods of pouring molten steel into molds. Upon completion of the renovations, Weirton Steel would be positioned as a state of the art steelmaker, and long term profitability and job security would be the likely end result.

The scenario of increased profit-sharing and stock repurchase obligation would cause long term problems for Weirton Steel by negating the $650 million capital investment plan because all cash reserves of the company would be needed to cover the stock repurchase obligation. The 50 percent profit-sharing provision further cut into the pool of revenue that the company could re-invest into the plant. With the company's cash reserves used up, and a profit-sharing payout of 50 percent, Weirton Steel was not in an attractive position in order to borrow $650 million from bankers and investors.

In order to fund the capital re-investment plan, Elish and investment bankers developed a three-pronged plan:

1. a public offering of common stock allowing employee-owner shares to be sold on the open market thus eliminating stock repurchase obligation by the company itself.
2. modify current ESOP charter ensuring employee-owner control.
3. modify profit-sharing from 50 percent back to the previous level of 35 percent.

All proposals, no matter how practical or beneficial to the good of the company, had to be approved by vote of the employee-owners. As you can now see, a new dilemma faced the company: Would employee-owners, who already had given a company 32 percent of their salary and benefits during the bad times just four years ago, now make concessions again during times of record profits?

The task of educating and informing the employee-owners about the new plan was monumental, and the internal communications and public relations departments were asked to complete their task in just six weeks from implementation to vote.

The communications plan

A massive "selling" job was necessary, and even though upper level union representation was firmly behind the plan, a multifaceted communications approach still needed to be developed and implemented throughout the plant. Initial opinions from the employee-owners seemed overwhelmingly negative toward the plan. Typical responses to the plan resulted in comments like, "We've already given up all that we're going to give up. We want what was promised us. We kept our end of the deal." Other employee-owners expressed skepticism that a company that just completed a record-setting year could be in long term financial trouble. The rumor mill began to grind out tall tales, which snowballed into even taller tales. The communications process had already begun informally throughout the plant, and much misinformation and half-truths ensued. Now, the company had to react and react quickly.

The development of the Financial Plan Communication Campaign was a joint effort among management, union officials, internal communications, and public relations departments. The plan centered around electronic, print and face-to-face communications, but "education" became the key word to the plan. Elish and Independent Steelworkers Union president Virgil Thompson both believed that if the employee-owners fully understood the complex issues involved, they would support the capital investment plan and vote for the changes that would allow it to be implemented.

Internal communications: face-to-face and one-on-one

The first line of communications was developed around face-to-face and one-on-one communications. Select spokesmen from both union and management were chosen and trained to explain the financial issues of the new plan. Each spokesman needed to be well-versed on the issues, but it was also essential that they could then communicate that information properly. The investment bankers and members of the board of directors helped keep the spokesmen informed and up-to-date, while teaching them how to break down complex issues into layman's terms.

A structure was already in place that allowed the CEO and upper level management and union representatives to tour the plant to gain firsthand knowledge about employee-owners' concerns. The meetings are called in-plants, and they were developed during the education process of the initial ESOP in 1982. In the six weeks of the Financial Plan Communication Campaign, 42 in-plant meetings were conducted. All areas of the mill and offices were given an opportunity to discuss the plan firsthand at these in-plant meetings. The in-plant meetings were structured with an opening presentation and explanation about the capital investment plan and concluded with a question and answer session. Most questions were answered by the representatives present at the in-plant, but any question that could not be answered during the meeting itself were usually answered over the telephone and in most cases, within 24 hours. Approximately 3000 of the 8500 employee-owners attended the in-plant meetings.

Of course, all employee-owners' concerns could not be answered during in-plant meetings, so an additional one-on-one communications tool was initiated—a 24-hour telephone bank. The phone bank was manned live during a four-hour period Monday through Friday by a group of representatives from management and union. During the remaining hours, all calls were recorded, and responses were given to employee-owners usually during the next business day. The phone bank's function was to serve as a 24-hour feedback tool for employee-owners about the financial plan. The phone bank received in excess of 2,200 calls pertaining to 160 different concerns.

Communications "S.W.A.T." teams supplemented the efforts of the in-plant meetings and the 24-hour phone bank. The "S.W.A.T." teams were designed to visit plant and office areas where misinformation, misunderstandings and rumors were especially prevalent.

Internal communications: print communications

The *Independent Weirton* is a 12 to 16 page informational newspaper that was also developed initially to educate employee-owners about essential stories dealing with the ESOP. Under the Financial Plan Communication Campaign, the *Independent Weirton* was utilized almost exclusively to deliver general announcement information; thoughts of employee-owners, customers, and government officials; and comments from Elish, Thompson, and the investment bankers pertaining to the financial plan.

"Straightforward" is a new publication that was designed to communicate additional, more in-depth and timely information specifically relating to the financial plan. "Straightforward" is printed weekly and is typeset entirely in-house on the internal communications new Macintosh desktop publishing system. Specific segments dealt with question and answer columns, event information, and updates on the mechanics of the voting process. Each issue was mailed to the homes of all employee-owners. Ten issues of "Straightforward" were published relating to the financial plan.

Other print materials developed for the Financial Plan Communication Campaign:

1. Bulletin board releases were distributed when immediate dissemination of information was needed. Bulletin board coordinators were already in place, so in most cases, information could reach bulletin boards plant-wide within 24 hours.
2. Posters were developed promoting the phone bank, event schedules, voting information and instructions, and general information about the financial plan. Posters were also distributed via bulletin boards.
3. Special billboards were designed and posted on the five local billboards that the company uses on a regular basis. The billboard's message—"We Can Do It Better!"—played upon the theme of "We Can Do It!" from the initial ESOP push in 1982.
4. A cash flow primer was developed to define and explain complicated terms relating to cash flow and economics. The primer was distributed to employee-owners in department meetings.

Internal communications: video communications

When many companies began cutting back on expensive communications items such as videotape equipment and accessories during the 1980s, Weirton Steel expanded their videotape communications capabilities. Weirton Steel's video distribution system includes 140 television monitors and videocassette recorders throughout the plant. A newscast entitled "News and Views" relating to the company and the steel industry is distributed weekly. Specific segments included during the campaign were an entire newscast devoted to an Elish and Thompson discussion; an investment banker interview; a phone bank demonstration; press conference highlights; and "Understanding Wall Street" segments.

External communications: retirees, spouses, and business and communities informational meetings

Special informational sessions were designed to outline the financial plan and answer the questions of the retirees, the employee-owners' spouses, and business and community groups. Much like the in-plant meetings in format, representatives from management and union tailored each presentation to the specific group's needs.

Of the company's 1000 retirees, 600 attended the three informational sessions for retirees.

External communications: media and advertising

In order to reach the employee-owners and the area communities in large numbers, several call-in talk shows with Elish and Thompson were scheduled on local television and radio stations. A 30-minute round table discussion that also included representatives from Weirton Steel's legal department and from banking specialists and stock analysts was broadcast on the NBC affiliate in Steubenville, Ohio.

The public relations department also invited local radio, television, and newspaper media to a press conference to highlight the upcoming financial plan and company-wide vote. National media features about the financial plan appeared in *The Wall Street Journal, Business Week, Forbes,* and *USA Today.*

Information statement

Prior to mailing out the ballots, an information statement was released to all employee-owners and retirees of Weirton Steel. The 21-page booklet was prepared with assistance from Weirton Steel's financial advisors. It explains in detail the financial proposal and the voting procedure. Also included in the statement is a summary of proposed amendments, an explanation of the proposed public stock offering, the charter and by-law amendments, ESOP amendments and profit sharing adjustments.

Due to the complex nature of the economic terminology involved with the financial plan, additional explanations were spelled out about dividends, future stock issuances, elections to the company's board of directors, and income tax consequences. Finally, the information statement deals with the effects that non-approval of the financial plan would have upon the future of Weirton Steel.

The overall objective of the information statement was to tie together all information and explanation material that employee-owners would need in their decision-making process. Special emphasis was paid to areas that were discovered to need additional clarification from questions asked during the previous in-plants and informational sessions.

The outcome of the vote

Most communications plans are devised and implemented, but their outcomes are difficult to evaluate and analyze. When the culmination of a communications plan is a company-wide vote, the end results are easier to judge. In the case study of Weirton Steel, the final vote proved that the Financial Plan Communications Campaign was a success. The decision to allow a public stock offering and to modify the ESOP was approved by an 85–15 percent count, and the reduction of the profit sharing was approved by a 79–21 percent count.

Herb Elish expressed his confidence in the future of the company to the employee-owners during Weirton Steel's Shareholders Meeting, "This is a major achievement in Weirton's remarkable history. We will now have the financial structure to support our commitment to technical excellence. The opportunity for long term success is ours, and we intend to make the most of it."

Finally, union employee Jim Andreozzi has the last word for skeptical critics who doubt the long-term viability of ESOPs, "The critics all said the telling point would be whether we put our money to work or put our money in our pockets. Our employees made the right choice, to put the money back in the plant. We've got to spend money to make money. This ought to put the critics to bed."

Spoken like a well-informed businessman.

Epilogue

Weirton Steel has posted profits every quarter from the inception of the company becoming an ESOP in 1984 until the last quarter of 1990; but like thousands of other American businesses, the 1990s have not been kind to Weirton Steel. Strapped with soft prices for steel, a recessionary business climate for its customers, and massive outlays of capital into modernization programs, Weirton Steel has posted losses totalling $119 million since the last quarter of 1990.

The company's financial report shows hope for the rest of the decade. Losses for 1991 totalled $74.7 million, while losses dropped significantly each quarter in 1992 for a total loss of $31.8 million for the year.

Losses of $31 million for the year hardly is a harbinger of prosperity, but CEO Herbert Elish is optimistic because the modernization plan's programs are now almost complete and most of the kinks have been worked out making Weirton Steel a high-quality, low-cost producer. The order book is full for 1993 and if the economy recovers, Weirton Steel is ready to face the future. "We want to assure Weirton Steel's future, not just for the next few years, but well into the twenty-first century, and we believe that Weirton Steel is taking the steps necessary to make a bright future possible," said Elish.

References

Azzarello, Sue. "Weirton Steel Officials Emphasize Importance of Ratifying Agreement," *Weirton Daily Times,* Jan 26, 1989, pg. 1.

Carbasho, Tracy. "Weirton Steel's '92 Losses Cut," *Wheeling Intelligencer,* Jan. 29, 1993.

Chu, Patrick. "Employee-Owned Weirton Steel May Go Public," *USA Today,* Mar. 9, 1989, pg. B-2.

DiCesare, Anthony. "Weirton Steel Agreement Explained," *Weirton Daily Times,* Jan. 26, 1989, pg. 1.

DiCesare, Anthony. "Weirton Steel Corp. Employees Vote Yest," *Weirton Daily Times,* Mar. 7, 1989, pg. 1.

DiCesare, Anthony. "Vote Shows That Democracy Works," *Weirton Daily Times,* Mar. 8, 1989, pg. 1.

Harris, Linda. "Weirton Steel Shareholders Meeting—Celebration of People," *Wheeling Intelligencer,* Mar. 8, 1989, pg. 1.

Hicks, Jonathan. "Weirton Steel Sets Plan to Sell Stock," *New York Times,* Jan. 26, 1989, pg. 14.

Lafferty, Charles. *Financial Plan Communication Campaign,* Weirton Steel Corporation, Jan. 1989.

Schroeder, Michael. "Has Weirton's ESOP Worked Too Well?" *Business Week,* Jan. 23, 1989, pg. 66.

Wartzman, Rick. "Weirton Steel Plans to Offer Public a Minority Stake," *The Wall Street Journal,* Jan. 26, 1989, pg. 5.

Further Reading

Falsey, Thomas A. *Corporate Philosophies and Mission Statements: A Survey and Guide for Corporate Communicators and Management.* Westport, CT: Quorum Books, 1989.

Garbett, Thomas. *How to Build a Corporation's Identity and Project Its Image.* Lexington, MA: Lexington Books, 1988.

Gray, James G. *Managing the Corporate Image: The Key to Public Trust.* Westport, CT: Quorum Books, 1986.

Roalman, Arthur R. *Investor Relations Handbook.* NY: American Management Association, 1974.

Winter, Elmer L. *A Complete Guide to Preparing a Corporate Annual Report.* NY: Van Nostrand Reinhold, 1985.

5

Corporate Communication and Corporate Culture

❖

Michael B. Goodman

Overview

Often in your business career you have been at a conference or trade show or business meeting involving numerous companies and you noticed a person in the crowd or at a coffee break. Without speaking to that person or reading the name tag, you knew the company that person represented.

That's corporate culture.

Corporate culture has become a concept that, used appropriately, offers the intellectual tools for insightful analysis into an organization's beliefs and behavior. Used improperly, it devolves into jargon and faddism.

In an anthropologist's terms, all human groups by their nature have a culture—the system of values and beliefs shaped by the experiences of life, historical tradition, social or class position, political events, ethnicity, and religious forces. In this context, a corporation's culture can be described, understood, nurtured, and coaxed in new directions; but rarely created, planned, or managed in the same way a company creates a product or service. Nevertheless, an organization's culture plays a powerful role in its success and in its failure. For this reason, the discussion of a corporation's culture offers a foundation for the understanding of the group's behavior, and suggests ways to either perpetuate or change the cultures.

Defining a Corporation's Culture

Terrence Deal and Allen Kennedy popularized the term corporate culture in 1982 with the publication of their book *Corporate Cultures: The Rites and Rituals of Corporate Life.* In the book, however, they only approach a definition of this concept with: "Values are the bedrock of any corporate culture." Equally circuitous is J. Steven Ott's definition of organizational culture as " . . . the culture that exists in an organization." However, Ott redeems himself with this additional explanation: " . . . and consists of such things as shared values, beliefs, assumptions, perceptions, norms, artifacts, and patterns of behavior."

In analyzing a corporation's culture, we can divide Ott's list into three levels: 1) artifacts and patterns of behavior that can be observed, but whose meaning is not readily apparent; 2) values and beliefs that require an even greater level of awareness; 3) basic assumptions about human activity, human nature and human relationships, as well as assumptions about time, space, and reality. The last group is often intuitive, invisible, or just below the level of awareness.

Examples of the first group abound: corporate logos, the company headquarters, annual reports, company awards dinners, the annual golf outing, the business attire at the home office. The artifacts and behavior can be observed. Often these are outward manifestations of what the corporation believes and values, no matter what it says its values and beliefs are.

Examples of the next group, the values and beliefs, may be articulated in a slogan or an ad campaign, such as Ford's decades old "Quality is Job 1," or GE's "We bring good things to life." These are simple yet effective ways to put into words what may often be very complex and difficult to articulate simply. Both examples present a sort of complex pledge from the company to its customers to create products that improve their lives. Companies that actually write a values statement find the task difficult because the written presentation to often sounds like the values statement of almost any company. Cliches and platitudes can make the most honest presentation seem hollow.

Basic assumptions, the third group, is even more difficult to articulate because it requires the analysis of both what the company says and an observation of what it does, then a synthesis to determine conflicting ideas. One example of a fatal conflict between the projected basic assumption and what lay beneath the surface was the demise of investment houses E. F. Hutton and Drexel Burnham. Both companies quickly lost clients' trust when scandals surfaced that undermined the integrity a client is supposed to feel toward the central character trait of their investment bank.

Other aspects of corporate culture fall into the first category, but are often illustrations of company values and basic assumptions. Company heroes, stories, legends, and myths reinforce the corporate culture in the same way that religious stories present patterns of behavior and beliefs and values to members of the congregation. For instance, a high-technology organization that submits complex proposals to the U.S. government often presents a story to its proposal teams about a hapless fellow from a competing company who delivered a proposal a half hour late, thinking the submittal was due at the close of business, 3:00 p.m. His dawdling cost the company a shot at the contract, and him his job. The lesson of the story for the corporate audience is crystal clear: the proposal effort is very serious business to our personal and corporate survival.

Quality Programs and Corporate Culture Changes

TQM, or Total Quality Management, and other change programs have become a major preoccupation with the business community in the U.S., particularly those involved with technical goods or services. In present practice in the U.S. and throughout the world, the quality process derives from W. Edwards Deming whose theories of statistical quality control took root in post-World War II Japan, not in his native America. U.S. corporations embraced the quality process as the tool to use to combat the Japanese challenge for world industrial supremacy.

In 1987 the Malcolm Baldridge National Quality Improvement Act made the trend official. The Act also established the Malcolm Baldridge Quality Award, similar to the Deming Award for quality given in Japan since the early 1950s. The European Community is now at work on similar quality initiatives called ISO 9000. To underscore the power of such programs in the United States, such giants as Xerox, IBM, and Cadillac have pursued and won the Baldridge Award.

In American corporations, quality programs have an impact on the corporate culture and the relationships among all members of the corporation. The process emphasizes a change in management practices from hierarchical, authoritarian relations between managers and employees, to a consensus approach to management which is focused on quality action teams empowered to identify and solve problems.

Communications and a new customer-orientation are the cornerstones of the culture change in both company attitudes and practices. These new attitudes and practices required corporations to make massive changes in the way people in the corporation communicated with one another and with those outside the company.

Diversity and Workforce 2000

The workforce in America is becoming more diverse in ethnicity, race, gender, and age. Numerous government publications such as *Workforce 2000* underscore the fundamental changes in the make-up of Americans at work.

The need for individuals to work in groups or teams at work has increased as a result of greater technological complexity in the nature of work itself. Even before the building of the Pyramids of Egypt or the building of Roman roads, large projects demanded group efforts. Technological effort in the 1990s and into the next century implies that individuals from a wide variety of backgrounds work together in groups. The quality process itself depends on groups of professionals and technicians at all levels working together to achieve the common goals of the group.

Interpersonal communication skill, which begins with understanding and respect for each of the people in the group, is the key to successful group performance. In a corporate culture of decision-making by consensus, the efficient and effective interaction of members of a group is essential for communication.

Prejudice and bigotry have no place in corporate America.

Training (Human Resource Development) and Perpetuating Corporate Culture

If corporate culture can be understood through analysis and observation, and if it can be modified through change programs, then corporate training can be used to nurture and perpetuate a culture that is desirable.

Several methods on how a culture tends to perpetuate itself, afford an opportunity for training:

- preselection and hiring of new employees
- socialization of members
- removal of members who do not fit in
- presentation of behavior appropriate to the culture
- justification of behavior that is beyond the norm
- communication of cultural values and beliefs

Many corporations have a clear idea of the kind of people they wish to hire and that profile provides them a guide for recruiting. The analogy is a sports team that drafts players with certain talents and skills, but also with the ability to fit in with the other players. A corporation does the same thing.

Once a person is recruited and hired, the corporation requires the socialization of its new member through a formal orientation program, followed by less formal socialization in the first few weeks and months on the job. Some organizations go further by instituting a mentoring program to reinforce the corporate culture.

Sometimes the match does not work out, so the member who does not fit must be removed. For new employees, this is usually done within some initial probationary period. For employees and managers this can be done with careful record keeping and a pattern of performance that demonstrates the employee. The performance appraisal has come to be the instrument for perpetuating the corporate culture.

The behavior appropriate to the corporate culture is generally written down in a formal employee handbook, a guide to ethical behavior, and a company code of conduct. These documents generally function as the formal presentation of the company culture. The informal code is in day to day activity, tradition, and company custom.

When a member of the company breaks the customs, the corporation must justify this apparent deviation from acceptable behavior. If the top salesperson looks a bit unkempt, collar unbuttoned and tie loosened, or wears a sweater instead of a suit to the office, the company must justify the violation by clearly saying that the sales force must often dress to fit the client, rather than to fit in with the corporate culture.

Communicating the culture happens everyday in small and large ways. Giving awards at the annual recognition ceremony, publishing news of employees who have had personal accomplishments, posting signs in corridors and lobbies, inviting discussion at meetings, and a hundred more actions communicate what is of value to the company, and what is not.

Perpetuating the culture is also vital to the survival of the corporation, if the culture is compatible with the business and economic environment. Of the hundreds of automobile makers in America just seventy years ago, only three major ones remain. Since chance and luck can happen to anyone, the survivors must have developed a culture that evolved with the changes in the market and technology. For any corporation to survive, its culture must continue to evolve to meet the rapid changes in the global marketplace.

Selected Essays and Comment

The essays and case studies selected for this chapter are from the presentations at the annual Conference on Corporate Communication at Fairleigh Dickinson University. Each of the authors focuses on a part of corporate communications theory and practice that is related to corporate culture.

Dr. Margaret Whitney suggests the use of ethnographic analysis—observation, interviewing, and collecting situational data—to unlock the meaning of an organization's culture. Her essay explores how the understanding of the culture of an organization can promote beneficial change.

Dr. Ann Bohara and Mr. Patrick McLaurin present research findings related to communication in a diverse workforce. They examine how communication styles and the perceptions of those styles help people to assess how competently women and ethnic minorities communicate in organizations.

Dr. Loretta Harper and Dr. Lawrence Rifkind examine the impact of the increased interest in sexual harassment issues had on fostering a productive work environment. Their essay emphasizes the paradox created by immediacy, which establishes interpersonal warmth and closeness, and sexual harassment policies which are designed to reduce employer liability.

Ms. Jeanne Steele examines ways employees express resistance through commonplace corporate activities as the annual picnic, talent shows or Follies, underground newsletters, and anonymous dirty jokes in suggestion boxes. She suggests that managers can use their interpretations to help identify productive actions to break down barriers among members of the corporation.

Analyzing Corporate Communications Policy Using Ethnographic Methods

❖

Margaret A. Whitney

Those interested in creating or refining corporate communication policies should consider ethnographic analysis—observation, interviewing, and collecting situational data—to understand the complex web of meanings that make up organizational culture. Such an analysis can provide diagnoses of organizational policies and procedures as well as a deeper understanding of communication behavior in organizations. As such, ethnographic analysis can promote beneficial change in policy issues.

Introduction

Communication is more than an important organizational function. It reflects corporate values, maintains them, and even creates them. Communication can build or shake morale. While some see it as only one part of the organizational structure, others understand communications as the network by which the organization is held together. Organizational life is constituted by means of communication. If we view the interactions of individuals within an organization as crucial, then we can see that communication policy issues as a guiding force in the company as a whole.

Scholars have realized the importance of communications policies within organizations. Since information is a crucial commodity in a company, the way in which it is conveyed can either help or hinder company goals. Much of the time, there is too little ordered information, resulting in multiple, contra-dictory, and vague communication practices and procedures (Wildavsky, 1983). Such information uncertainty has led to calls for improvement. Sigband (1969) suggests that corporate communications policies reflect the philosophy of the organi-zation as a whole. Koten (1984) notes that "excellent" compa-nies have communications policies that are the concern of top executives as well as other employees within the corporation. Studies also suggest that experienced employees as well as newcomers use communication policies as guides and models in their written communications in order to fit their messages with the "ethos" of the company (Duffy, et al., 1987; Bandes, 1986). "Good writing" corresponded to company guidelines, pro-cedures, and policies.

Despite the fact that communication policies have proved useful and important, they are not universally found nor uni-versally valued in corporations (Gilsdorf, 1987). If, however, a company wishes to improve existing policies or create new ones, how does it go about doing so? How do we create and maintain communication policies that reflect good practices within the corporation? This paper suggests that a method for determining beneficial policies and eliminating detrimental ones is ethnography, a technique usually reserved for anthro-pological research, but recently employed in the study of cor-porate culture.

Organizations as Communications Networks

Before we consider the ethnographic method of organiza-tional analysis, we must redefine our conception of the orga-nization itself. In addition, we must consider the position of corporate communication policies within the organization. Too often in the past the task of creating and maintaining com-munication policies has fallen to middle management. Accord-ing to Bloom (1983), they have problems formulating policy because of the following factors:

1. Thoughtless and mechanistic restatements of previous policies and procedures.
2. Lack of coordination and cross references with other corporate, divisional, functional, departmental policy and procedure statements and manuals.

3. Poor criteria for the selection of policy or procedure from existing corporate documents.
4. Lack of formal control over the issuance of policy and procedure statement and updates.
5. Little or no feedback about the weaknesses or ambiguities from informal policy and procedures.

Solutions to such difficult issues may be found. First, however, we must redefine and reconceptualize the way in which we view organizations. Typically, attempts to understand organizational functioning have been viewed in terms of productivity or efficiency. This focus was managerial and tended to assume that streamlined policy could produce a more efficient company.

Another approach, however, rests on the premise that "communication creates and constitutes the taken-for-granted reality of the world" (Pakanowsky and O'Donnell-Trujillo, 1982). In such a view, the concept of organization is severed from its managerial moorings and considered more abstractly. Organizations are interlocked actions of a group. Social activity, human interaction, and communication cannot be separated. Humans not only create an organizational reality by means of coordinated actions, they also communicate by means of symbols, the most important of which is language. As a result, the study of communication in organizations involves more than a mere segment of the company; it is the company itself.

Organizations as Cultures

In considering organizations as communications cultures, we have both enlarged and complicated the study of the organization. We have agreed that the study of organizational culture is a legitimate domain of inquiry for those interested in communications. We have agreed that organizational cultures may be "contexts" to be interpreted. Researchers and those interested in corporate communications can therefore interpret culture by considering, as Geertz (1973) indicates, the "web of meanings" in which humans are suspended. "Thick description" and close analysis will reveal the nuances of sense-making in the culture. Those developing corporate guidelines can take this perspective if they wish to provide policies and procedures that are in keeping with the ethos of the organization: communication policies provide one way in which corporations incorporate, maintain, and reify the culture of the organization.

The fact that textual material such as policy, procedures and manuals form an important means by which the culture is made public has been recently noted. Freed and Broadhead (1987) suggest that internal company documents codify institutional norms, rules, and regulations. Written policies and procedures promote four important cultural functions: standardization, autonomy, historicity, and vitality. First, texts, handbooks, policy manuals and statements are means by which an organization establishes and defines itself. Secondly, such standardization encourages, fosters, and promotes autonomy. Cultures need to be seen as unique and different from others. Thirdly, both standardization and autonomy further an interest in the history and traditions of the culture, a desire to understand the reasons for its present shape and practices. Finally, all of these encourage vitality. Texts, manuals, and written communication policy statements become part of networks using language to perform the culture's vital functions. Policies can provide the norms to which communicators adhere in order to be considered competent within the culture.

Developing Communications Policies

Because organization culture is complex, and written material can be considered codifiers of the culture, developing policies that reflect the corporate culture demand different methods of investigation, data gathering, and analysis. Producing corporate communications policies illustrating an understanding of organizational culture requires more than "top-down" analysis, decrees by management, and obedience by the workforce. We must consider different ways in which to produce meaningful and accurate policy, mirroring the practices of a highly-educated and well-trained workforce.

An assumption, however, is that adoption of the corporate culture perspective will prompt us to ask certain types of questions, examine certain indicators of organizational life, and conduct investigations or research that will access the web of meanings in an organization.

The first step in such a developmental process is to ask basic questions:

1. What are the key communication activities?
2. How have people made sense of these?

Examination of certain cultural indicators will help answer such questions. This will more reliably inform our development of policies. Pakanowsky and O'Donnell-Trujillo (1982) state that there are seven indicators of the way in which individuals within organizations make sense of their surroundings. These should be considered in investigations of communications and corporate culture:

Relevant Constructs

Examine the general aspects of organizational understandings. These may be objects, individuals, or processes such as "The Monday morning budget meeting," or "The Report Editing session."

Facts

Examine the system of facts that explain how and why an organization communicates the way it does. This "social knowledge" comprises relationships among people, problems, and actions. These social facts make the relevant constructs concrete and recognizable to participants.

Practices

Look for practices for getting the job done. Tasks may be formally assigned by supervisors but often are made particular and personal by individual members as they complete them. Though there may be formal policies regulating practices, the way in which these tasks are accomplished may be totally different. Important practices may not be expressed formally but may be practiced informally.

Vocabulary

Examine the vocabulary used by members. It can provide clues to the relevant constructs, facts, and practices of organizational life.

Metaphors

Look at metaphors used by members. These provide an understanding of the ways individuals within the organization structure their experience communicatively.

Stories

Ask about stories. These are other ways in which members structure the experience of the culture, and these may function as future scenarios or as bits of "folklore."

Rites and Rituals

Examine rites and rituals that orient members and serve as sense-making opportunities. Participation in such rites and rituals provides access to a shared sense of organizational reality.

As participants reveal cultural indicators, they are also uncovering parts of their organizational culture. These can become part of the analysis and help to explain how such culture is communicated to members. Individuals examining organizational culture in order to explicate and formulate communication policies more clearly and accurately must move back and forth between the part and the whole. They must understand that each part only achieves meaning in relation to the entire network of meanings. In this way they will be able to establish patterns that give meaning to organizational life.

Ethnography and Organizational Culture

So far we have seen that in order to develop corporate communication policies that model and reflect the ethos of the organization itself, we must consider the organization a culture. We must also examine specific components in order to understand culture more completely. Since we have the theoretical background and the units of analysis for such an examination, we should now turn to method.

Traditionally, ethnographic methods have been used in cultural analysis (Geertz, 1973). Recently, they have also been used in organizational analysis (Smircich, 1983a) and in communication research (Doheny-Farina & Odell, 1984; Pakanowsky

& O'Donnell-Trujillo, 1982). Those interested in improving corporate communications policies can use such techniques as participant observation, interviewing, and collecting organizational documents to piece together the multifaceted meaning systems in organizational contexts.

While ethnographers have been accused of lack of rigor in their studies, recent scholarship has shown that structured techniques of ethnographic analysis can be both intuitive and produce valid research results. One reason for this is the use of "triangulation," which, according to Goetz and LeCompte (1984), allows the investigator to check the reliability of his or her data:

> Just as a surveyor locates points on a map by triangulating on several sights, so an ethnographer pinpoints the accuracy of conclusions drawn by triangulating with several sources of data. Triangulation prevents the investigator from accepting too readily the validity of initial impressions; it enhances the scope, density, and clarity of constructs developed during the course of the investigation. It also helps in correcting biases that occur when the ethnographer is the only observer of the phenomenon under investigation.

An Overview of Ethnographic Methods

OBSERVING

The most common method of collecting ethnographic data is participant observation. The key to successful observation is freeing oneself as much as possible from the filter of one's own cultural experience. For those investigating communication policies within their own organizations, the observational task may be made more difficult, but it is not impossible. Attempts at being an objective observer, in describing but not evaluating communication behavior, and in not drawing hasty conclusions are essential. In later analysis, conclusions may be based on observations, but the most important part of the observational techniques is objectivity.

GETTING KEY INFORMANTS

In order to get pertinent and reliable information from participants, those investigating corporate communications policies will have to rely on key informants. Spradley (1979) indicates that these individuals should possess several characteristics in order to increase their reliability:

1. Key informants should be thoroughly acculturated. Good informants know the culture well and no longer have to think about performing routine tasks. They do things automatically from years of practice.
2. Key informants should be currently involved in the cultural scene. In this way, they can use their expert knowledge to guide their actions.
3. Key informants can provide you with an adequate amount of time to answer questions.
4. Key informants should be nonanalytical. They should be able to describe and explain procedures and practices without analyzing them in psychological, sociological, or organizational ways. They can "speak the language" of the culture and communicate that language to the investigator.

INTERVIEWING

As Spradley indicates, ethnographic interviews are carefully structured and organized. While they can be friendly and casual, their purpose is to ascertain the knowledge systems of participants of the culture. As such, they involve expert purpose and direction. Two types of interviewing techniques may be used: the ethnographic explanation and the ethnographic question.

First, during the ethnographic interview, the questioner is certain to make the purpose of the meeting clear and direct the conversation so that it will reveal the cultural knowledge of participants. The interviewer also offers various explanations to the informant as the interview progresses. The goal is to make the informant the "teacher," imparting knowledge to the investigator. Five types of explanations can be used:

1. Project Explanations: These include explanations of the entire project. Statements like "I am interested in the types of communication that take place in this organization," or "I'd like to know what types of communication you take part in every day" might elicit knowledge of the culture of communication in the organization.

2. "Recording" Explanations: These include comments about the necessity of note taking while interviewing or the necessity of recording interviews: "I'm going to write this down," or "Would you mind if I taped this interview?"

3. Native Language Explanations: These encompass explanations of the ways in which the informants interact with others in their own cultural context. Questions like: "If you were going to speak to a customer, what would you say?" "How would you sign that type of letter?" "What would you call this type of phone call?" can give the investigator ideas of ways in which communication is accomplished on a day to day basis. Informants are encouraged not to translate such answers but simply describe what happens.

4. Interview Explanations: These provide information by having informants draw maps or sort information on cards. Schall (1983), for example, derived information about power influences within organizations and synthesized these on cards for informants for verification. Such techniques could also be applied to corporate communication policy.

The main tool of the ethnographic interview, however, and the primary one with which the investigator discovers the cultural knowledge of participants, is the ethnographic question. Spradley lists thirty types, but places them in the following three categories:

1. Descriptive Questions: These are the easiest to ask and imply: "Tell me as much as you can in great detail." Samples of descriptive questions: "Could you describe a typical working day in this organization?" "Could you describe the typical communications you make daily, weekly, monthly?" "Could you draw a map which would explain to me the path of this particular communication?"

2. Structural Questions: This type of question allows the investigator to find out how participants have organized their knowledge. "What are the different types of communication used in this organization?" "What are the stages in the preparation of this report?" "What types of communication activities would you do as a

manager, writer, administrator, secretary, etc.?" In this
way, the individual interested in formulating corporate communication policy based upon the real practices of the organization might discover basic units or
categories of the participants' knowledge within the
organization.

4. Contrast Questions: These types of questions enable
   the investigator to discover how participants distinguish between one contextual construct or item and
   another. They allow you to find out what a participant
   "means" by using one term or another. Questions like
   "What's the difference between a sales meeting and a
   document review meeting?" might give ideas about the
   nature of differing communications and help distinguish between various symbols in their world.

Both explanations and questions provide logical, reasoned,
and methodologically rigorous ways in which to investigate
communications within an organization. Investigators should
keep careful records of interviews and observations in field
work journals and attempt to get a verbatim record of what
people say and do.

COLLECTING DOCUMENTS

Collecting printed material on communication practices
and values is also an important ethnographic technique in an
analysis of corporate communications policies. Much necessary background material may be found in written sources,
and, as mentioned earlier, written documents may function as
"sacred texts," guides for individuals as they navigate the cultural waters. Furthermore, as investigators compare the way
documents are actually used by participants, they will be able
to understand how participants in the culture transcend,
modify, or ignore texts, documents, written rules, and procedures within the context of the situation.

Analysis of all these techniques can lead to an appraisal
of the meanings individuals have constructed within organizations. Because communication activities are at the heart
of organizational culture, using them as the basis of analysis provide valid data with which to develop new policies,
alter counterproductive ones, or keep those that are useful
and efficient.

Consequences of an Ethnographic Analysis of Communication Policies

According to Smircich (1983b), the consequences of an interpretive theory of organizations and the use of ethnographic analysis in the examination of organizational communication are twofold:

First, since the type of knowledge ethnographic analysis provides is focused on intersubjective meanings, this technique is concerned with "relationships within their specific contexts." It is also particularistic and specific. As such, ethnographic approach of corporate communication policies can be diagnostic. It asks how the organization works and what it means to be organized and consequently provides the means of answering such questions. It can point, therefore, to aspects of communication that are beneficial and suggest changes for those that are detrimental. We may subsequently pattern policy after good practices, remediate dysfunctional practices, and keep those practices that work for the individuals involved.

Secondly, ethnographic analysis of communication within organizations attempts to do what few research agendas do—uncover the structures of meaning in the setting, synthesize a picture of the group's reality, and make it available for consideration. Perceptions of participants become the basis for analysis; these are interpreted by researchers and investigators and in turn are reflected back to the group. The goal of ethnographic research is, after all, to see the world as the organizational members see it, to learn the meanings of actions and behaviors within the culture, and portray them accurately.

Because of this interpretive and intuitive agenda, Smircich maintains that "within a particular setting, the analysis of the organization as culture may serve the same purpose as that served by therapy for an individual." Because the researcher illustrates and reflects the culture to those involved, a deeper understanding of human behavior can be gained. Increased insight may lead to beneficial change within the organization. Communication policies that truly reflect organizational practices can be seen. Ethnographic analysis highlights their functionality (or lack of it) within the communication networks. The methodology provides a more humanistic rationale for the study of organizations and suggests practical and reasonable reasons for change, taking into account the web of meanings that make up corporate culture. For these reasons, ethnographic analysis can be a viable analytic tool in the development and revision of corporate communication policies.

Works Cited

Bandes, H. 1986. Defining and controlling documentation quality: Part I. *Technical communication,* 33, 6–9.

Bloom, S. 1983. Policy and procedure statements that communicate. *Personnel journal,* 62, 711–718.

Doheny-Farina, S., and L. Odell. 1984. Ethnographic research on writing: Assumptions and methodology. In L. Odell and D. Goswami, eds., *Writing in nonacademic settings* (pp. 503–530). New York: Guilford.

Duffy, T., T. Post, and G. Smith. 1987. An analysis of the process of developing military technical manuals. *Technical communication,* 34, 70–78.

Freed, R., and G. Broadhead. 1987. Discourse communities, sacred texts and institutional norms. *College composition and communication,* 38, 154–165.

Geertz, C. 1973. *The interpretation of cultures.* NY: Basic Books.

Gilsdorf, J. 1987. Written corporate communication policy: Extent, coverage, costs, benefits. *The journal of business communication,* 24, 35–52.

Goetz, J., and M. LeCompte. 1984. *Ethnography and qualitative design in educational research.* NY: Academic Press.

Koten, J. 1984. Corporate communications: All together now. *Business horizons,* Jan./Feb., 18–20.

Pakanowsky, M., and N. O'Donnell-Trujillo. 1982. Communication and organizational culture. *The western journal of speech communication,* 46, 115–130.

Schall, M. 1983. A communication-rules approach to organizational culture. *Administrative science quarterly,* 28, 557–581.

Sigband, N. 1969. Needed: corporate policies on communications. *S.A.M. Advanced management journal,* 34, 61–67.

Smircich, L. 1983a. Concepts of culture and organizational analysis. *Administrative science quarterly,* 28, 339–358.

Smircich, L. 1983b. Studying organizations as cultures. In G. Morgan, ed., *Beyond method* (pp. 173–187). Beverly Hills, CA: Sage.

Spradley, J. 1979. *The ethnographic interview.* NY: Holt, Rinehart & Winston.

Wildavsky, A. 1983. Information as an organizational problem. *Journal of management studies,* 20, 29–40.

ESSAY

Perceptions of Communicative Competence in Organizational Settings: The Influence of Styles and Stereotypes

❖

Ann M. Bohara
and
Patrick McLaurin

This essay examines how communcation styles and perceptions of those styles help shape assessments of communicative competence for women and ethnic minorities in
organizational contexts. We present a model which posits
several types of communication styles—from technical to
relational (task-oriented to other-oriented)—and correlates
these styles with contextual factors—loci of power, hierarchical relationships, role and task expectations. More interestingly, the model posits listener response to the adoption
of particular styles and predicts evaluations of competence-
based on the expectations or stereotypes at play in a given
interaction. Finally, the model offers some insights on how
antagonisms can escalate when co-workers interpret style
and context differently.

Over the past twenty years, American corporations have
increasingly found it necessary to open their doors to employees who represent cultural or racial minorities: women, African Americans, Hispanic Americans, Asian Americans.
Currently, non-traditional workers, women and minorities,
form the fastest growing segment of the labor pool. The Bureau of Labor Statistics predicts that in the twenty-first century, white males will form a minority of the U.S. workforce.
The inclusion of large numbers of women and minorities in

199

the workforce raises issues of assimilating these diverse groups into the culture of the workplace. For both organizations and individual employees, the process of acculturation poses problems.

For organizations the challenge of "managing diversity" has become the focus of much corporate training. This focus reflects not simply a benign, "human relations" stance but the corporate recognition that the challenges posed by a diverse workforce strike at the heart of organizational intent—to coordinate individual activity into productive, collective behavior. To accomplish this goal, organizations attempt to render more predictable the behaviors of their employees; communication that works can help reduce uncertainty and enhance predictability. But diversity means less predictability. Employees with divergent backgrounds, from different speech communities, bring to the workplace different expectations about communication, interpreting the messages they receive through their own frames of reference. Communication—up, down, sideways—becomes more difficult and distorted. The potential for miscommunication exists not only on the shop floor or assembly line, where English may be spoken as a second language, but also in the offices of middle managers and in the executive suite, where apparently small or subtle differences in communication styles can be both confusing and divisive.

In this environment, many women and minority men and women at managerial levels are finding the process of assimilating to organizational cultures bewildering and sometimes hostile. As R. Roosevelt Thomas, Jr., Director of the Diversity Institute in Atlanta, describes (1990):

> Once again blacks, Hispanics, women and immigrants are dropped into a previously homogeneous, all-white, all-Anglo, all-male, all native-born environment, and the burden of cultural change is placed on the newcomers (p. 29).

Diversity initiatives and training programs, while communicating professed corporate attitudes toward difference, are failing to address the problems of acculturation—assimilation, accommodation, and identification—as experienced by both majority and minority employees.

A crucial but often ignored aspect of cultural change for newcomers is the ability to interact with peers and superiors. While the corporate response has called attention to the need for communicative competence of newcomers, much of this effort has focused on job related or formal communication contexts. For the most part, women and minorities have been on their own—with varying degrees of success—in attempting to assimilate the communicative styles associated with the informal ranges of interaction within mainstream culture.

The purpose of this essay is to examine how communication styles and perceptions of those styles help shape assessments of communicative competence for women and ethnic minorities in organizational contexts. Specifically, we have observed female and minority managers during the early phases of their careers struggling as they seek to develop a communication competence—both for formal and informal contexts—which will be effective in their organizations.

Based on these observations and interviews, we present a model which posits several types of communication styles—from technical to relational (task-oriented to other-oriented)—and correlates these styles with contextual factors—loci of power, hierarchical relationships, role and task expectations. More interestingly, the model posits listener response to the adoption of particular styles and predicts evaluations of competence based on the expectations or stereotypes at play in a given interaction. Finally, the model offers some insights on how antagonisms can escalate when co-workers interpret style and context differently.

The Problem: Relational versus Technical Competence

In our interviews, female and minority students in one of the country's top MBA programs report experiences of professional frustration; these individuals have often returned to school in the hopes of obtaining the credential that will enable them to break through the "glass ceiling." Whether the degree will help them do this is uncertain; preliminary interviews with recent female and black alumni indicate that the invisible barriers may still be in place for them. It is important to emphasize these "top" women and minorities are individuals whose training and education ought to make their histories models of successful assimilation.

The problem, then, does not seem to be related to training, education, or technical competence. Rather, our interviews point to issues in the nature and quality of upline and

peer relationships. The relationship between career advancement and the ability to manage superiors is relevant to all
professionals regardless of race and gender. This wisdom is
clearly stated by George Berkley (1985):

> Although some authorities still like to cling to the cliche
> that good performance speaks for itself, nearly all those who
> have worked in or studied organizations of any kind believe
> differently. While competency in discharging one's duties is
> usually necessary for working one's way upward, it is rarely
> the sole ingredient or even the most important one in deter-
> mining organizational success (8).

This sentiment is supported by the results of a longitudinal
study which found "successful" managers, those who had been
promoted quickly, and "effective" managers, those who have
satisfied and committed subordinates, had little in common
(Luthans, 1988). The study measured success by dividing a
manager's level in the organization by length of service. Effectiveness was measured on two criteria: getting the job done
with high standards and having committed subordinates. For
successful managers, only networking had a statistically significant relationship with their achievement.

Establishing an organizational career that is both effective and successful is a challenge for any manager, but research indicates that minorities and women on managerial
paths in historically white male organizations encounter special difficulties (Jones, 1986). These obstacles arise both from
the traditional ways that power is generated and dispersed in
organizations and from differences in behaviors and expectations of majority and minority managers. One such obstacle is
Jones' (1986) notion of "Colorism" "an attitude, a predisposi-
tion to act in a certain manner because of a person's skin
color. This means that people tend to act favorably toward
those with skin color like theirs and unfavorably toward those
with different skin color." In Jones' analysis, colorism may
influence decisions about promotion, assignments, rewards—
all subjective decisions, especially at the middle- and upper-
management levels:

> Those who seek to step into upper management are playing
> a new and more complicated game. The stakes are higher
> and the rules are often less well defined, if they exist at all.

So it is here in the middle management passage where the issue of prejudice is most accute (89).

As Jones rightly notes, advancement in organizations depends on the individual's ability to develop and exploit, "informal networks of cooperative relationships." Perhaps the most important informal relationship a young manager can establish is that with a corporate mentor. Jones asserts that many black managers remain outsiders because few are able to "win bosses or mentors." A more recent study by Thomas and Alderfer (1987) supports this conclusion; the study cites the difficulties that racial and gender differences pose to the growth of mentoring relationships and reports that cross-race, cross-gender relationships face the greatest obstacles. Thomas and Alderfer also discuss the societal basis of these obstacles:

> The taboos of race and sex are deeply embedded in feelings and practice, and people consciously hoping to treat one another fairly may nonetheless enact the system of suspicion, mistrust, and devaluation that shapes the basic relationship between the races in the United States (107).

Jones, Thomas, and Alderfer underscore the significance of gender and race to interpersonal and mentor relationships in organizations. We would suggest that many critical problems inherent in cross-race and gender organizational relationships derive from the communication processes at work in these interactions. Specifically, we argue that women and minorities often fail to build productive peer and up-line relationships because of substantive differences with white males in the use and interpretation of communication styles. One crucial difference centers on methods of balancing both the task and relational dimensions of communication, especially in interpersonal contexts and informal ranges.

Communicating Task and Relational Dimensions

Organizational Demands

The ability to manage both task and relational dimensions of communication is a necessary skill for all speakers;

that effectiveness requires attention to multiple goals is one
of the commonplaces in theoretical discussions of communicative competence. One way of conceptualizing these goals is
the need for both the clear communication of information
(the task function of communication) and the concern for
maintenance of the relationship. The notion of task and relational dimensions has been instrumental in the work of
numerous theorists (Clark & Delia, 1979; Hart & Burke, 1972;
Kipnis & Schmidt, 1980; 1983; Wiemann, 1977).

A second way of looking at multiple goals is the management of "face" demands within interactions. Face as described
by Goffman (1955), is "the positive social value a person effectively claims for himself by the line others assume he has
taken during a particular contact" (213). Building on these
ideas, Brown and Levinson (1978) developed their "politeness theory" which accounts for how people support (or
threaten) the positive and negative face of each other. Positive face is the degree to which a person wishes to be seen
with approval in terms of attributes relevant to self-identity, while negative face is the degree to which an individual
wishes to feel free to define a course of action unimpeded by
others also in terms relevant to self-identity.

Within organizational contexts, the attempt to influence
superiors requires the effective balance of task and relational
dimensions. Upward influence attempts require special consideration be paid to the face of both the influencer and the
target individual. Studies indicate that subordinates employ
a variety of styles when making upward influence attempts.
Kipnis and Schmidt (1983) suggest four styles: "shotgun"
managers used a wide variety of tactics, "tactician" managers emphasized reason, "ingratiator" managers relied most
on friendliness, and "bystanders" used the fewest tactics when
attempting to influence their superiors.

The evaluation of competence in managing these mul-
tiple-goals of interaction is highly culture-specific. Even the
most proficient language users may overlook the subtle nuances that balance the need to convey the functional aspect
of the message with the relational demands of the interaction. For those from different cultures or with different signalling cues of involvement, the chance for giving offense is
great.

Communicating Task and Relational Dimensions

Cultural Differences

Many observers have focused on the relationships between cultural variables and communication behaviors. For instance, Hall (1976) claims that all cultures can be placed on a scale of low-context to high-context with communication styles varying accordingly:

> High-context cultures make greater distinctions between insiders and outsiders than low-context cultures do. People raised in high-context systems expect more of others than do the participants in low-context systems. When talking about something that they have on their minds, a high-context individual will expect his [or her] interlocutor to know what's bothering him [or her], so that he [or she] doesn't have to be specific. The result is that he [or she] will talk around and around the point, in effect putting all the pieces in place except the crucial one. Placing it properly-the keystone-is the role of his [or her] interlocutor (98).

D. Levine (1985) argues that Hall's low-context, high-context dimension is equivalent to Hofstede's (1980) categorization of cultures as individualistic, at one end of the range, to collectivist on the other: low-context cultures are individualistic, high-context are collectivist.

About communication, Levine asserts that cultures in each of these categories demonstrate a consistent preference for either directness or indirectness, for certainty or ambiguity, in communication. For example, Levine suggests that in the U.S., an individualistic, low-context culture communication seeks directness:

> The [North] American way of life, by contrast, affords little room for the cultivation of ambiguity. The dominant [North] American temper calls for clear and direct communication. It expresses itself in such common injunctions as "Say what you mean," "Don't beat around the bush," and "Get to the point." (28).

In describing actual behavior, Levine observes the following features of direct (univocal) versus indirect (ambiguous) communication styles:

Univocal verbal communication is designed to be affectively neutral. It aims for the precise representation of fact, technique, or expectation. Univocality works to strip language of its expressive overtones and suggestive allusions. Ambiguous communication, in contrast, can provide a superb means of conveying affect. By alluding to shared experiences and sentiments, verbal associations can express and evoke a wealth of affective responses. The exploitation of ambiguity through wit and jokes can convey a wide array of feelings. The clandestine ambiguities of ironic messages have the capacity to transmit sentiments of enormous power (32).

Hall, Hofstede, and Levine all are examining conversational style and cultures within the broad perspective of comparisons between nationalities (or, at times, civilizations: Western, Eastern, African); but some of their insights are equally helpful when analyzing differences within cultures. Certainly within a culture as diverse as that of the U.S., groups will have differing expectations about the propriety or effect in a given situation of a direct versus indirect style. For instance, urban U.S. African American culture has been characterized by its use of indirection as a stylistic feature of discourse (Abrahams, 1976; Kochman, 1986; Labov, 1976; Mitchell-Kiernan, 1969).

Complementing these studies based on broad comparisons of culture and expectations are inquiries that focus on specific differences in communication features and cues. For example, Gumperz (1982) demonstrates that speakers signal what activity they are engaging in, i.e., the metacommunicative frame they are operating within, by use of paralinguistic and prosodic features of speech such as intonation, pitch, amplitude, rhythm, and so on. Gumperz calls these features, when they are used to signal interpretive frames, "contextualization cues."

Given the variety of cues Gumperz lists and how deeply embedded in social process is the acquisition of these cues, we must expect that cross-cultural communication will be difficult; individuals coming together, each with a different frame of reference or, perhaps more important, different styles or ways of signalling that frame, must meet difficulty in seeking to negotiate a new, mutual perspective. It is, of course, much easier for individuals of similar history to communicate; as Tannen (1984) points out:

The fact that people understand each other's ways of signalling meaning is in itself proof of shared background and context. The implication is not that speakers necessarily or consciously attempt to invoke solidarity when they speak, although that may be the case, more or less consciously, when a recognizably in-group style or code is used. Rather habitual forms of talking make use of verbal devices that honor rapport and considerateness in conventionalized ways. Because of the paradoxical nature of closeness (and consequently of communication), speakers must constantly observe both the need for involvement and the need not to impose, or expressed positively, for considerateness (27).

The problem for speakers from high-context speech communities is often in developing competence in the signalling cues associated with the low context culture of mainstream North American communication: specifically, in the management of the perceived need to be "direct" while still maintaining the "appropriate" relational tone of closeness and consideration. Communicators who reduce the relational emphasis are often seen as having a cold and distant communicative style.

Lakoff (1975) uses the categories of "involvement" versus "considerateness" as opposing ends on a continuum of interpersonal preferences: a style demonstrating "involvement" emphasizes camaraderie or relatedness and is appropriately chosen in "situations in which the emotional involvement between speakers and between them and their subject matter is maximal." A style of "considerateness" emphasizes distance or a preference not to impose on the listener; at its extreme, "only the content of the message is important; speakers evidence no involvement with each other or the subject matter."

Many speakers, making the transition from high to low context speech communities, initially identify the need for directness to be primary in interactions. These speakers find that utilizing a "univocal" style—or Lakoff's considerateness style—is the most effective way of communicating with their mainstream interlocutors. Another appeal of this style is that, to some extent, it is also the "safest" in that relational signalling is reduced. For many minorities and women entering hostile work environments, relational issues are often mine fields they prefer not to enter. What such a strategy does, however, is sacrifice signals of rapport, solidarity, and considerateness.

A Synthetic Perspective

To bring together these disparate scholarly insights in a form more readily accessible, we offer a figural interpretation or model: in line with standard discussions of interpersonal communication, we propose that each communication event or interaction has both task and relational dimensions. Asking the cafeteria attendant for "coffee, please" reflects both these goals. Moreover, we would argue that the speaker's decision to say "please," as opposed to "May I have coffee, please?" or even to reverse the phrase, "Please, coffee" indicates a choice concerning the extent of solidarity or of deference, positive or negative face, appropriate to assume in this everyday interaction. Most job-related interactions are, of course, longer and more complicated; and the less concrete the task at hand, the more evaluative or managerial, the more difficult to dissect. But we would begin our analysis along a task versus relationship matrix (see figure 5.1). Onto this matrix, we would map three of the categories derived by Kipnis & Schmidt in their study of upward influence in organizations. And we would add a category, "technician" representing a fifth communication style/preference.

"Bystanders" (LR/LT) and "Ingratiators" (HR/LT) in Kipnis and Schmidt terminology both assume communication styles that de-emphasize task or function—or the speaker's organizational role—but the Bystander also makes no claims on relationship while the ingratiator seeks to accomplish task goals by highlighting relational connections. We put Kipnis and Schmidt's Tactician in the upper right quadrant (HT/HR). This group represents an organization's most successful influencers. We would assert that these people are successful because they know not only what to say (task) but how best to say it (relation) balancing the mixture of solidarity and deference, closeness and distance, imposition and respect. Our fourth quadrant (HT/LR), we term "technician," reflecting a communication style in which the message is paramount and relational issues seemingly neglected.

By mapping onto this grid some of the dimensions proposed in sociolinguistic literature, we can begin to categorize specific differences in conversational or interpersonal styles (see figure 5.2). To make this matrix more concrete, we can describe each style and its relationship to the dimensions of conversational analysis (see Appendix A).

This matrix can be helpful in explaining how individuals shape and respond to the dynamics of power and influence within organizations. Furthermore, we believe that individuals are constrained by their histories—race, gender, culture— to occupy certain quadrants of the matrix; they find themselves within organizations effectively limited to certain roles and their attendant communication styles. Violating these constraints can have serious consequences, particularly for assessments of overall competence.

For example, Kipnis and Schmidt (1983) report that "upward-influence style plays a role in the performance evaluations and salary achieved at work. How large a role is unknown." They found that males using a "tactician" style (of influence) were evaluated most highly but that women using this style did not receive the most favorable performance evaluations; rather, the "ingratiator" style was favored by superiors. Kipnis and Schmidt postulate that socialization of gender roles causes men to expect women to be passive or ingratiating, and not to use logic as a persuasive appeal. Kipnis and Schmidt also hypothesize that female subordinates who emphasize reason and logic may be perceived as acting inappropriately and thus evaluated less competently than Ingratiators.

As with the cross-racial pairs interviewed in Thomas and Clayton's mentor study, it would seem that feelings associated with sexual identity—beliefs concerning the appropriate rules of behavior for women and men—are also deeply embedded. Violating these expectations by stepping out of role is apt to cause discomfort for one or both parties in an interaction, and in the corporate setting, is also likely to result in either official or unofficial sanctions.

An Illustration

This matrix can be helpful in explaining the kinds of communication problems encountered between co-workers of different races and genders. To illustrate its application, we offer the following excerpt from a role-playing dialogue taped in an MBA class on conflict resolution.

Two first-year MBA students, a black woman (playing "Alisha") and a white man (playing "Jim"), conducted the dialogue. The role-playing situation gave them a brief history of working together as internal auditors for a large company; both are at the same job level in the company, but he (Jim) has four years of experience and she (Alisha) has only one. Under a new department-wide system, their immediate boss has assigned them to conduct client audits together in an informal trainer-trainee relationship. On their first trip together. Alisha found Jim unjustifiably authoritarian and patronizing (even criticizing her in front of the clients); Jim found Alisha's work careless and her attitude uncooperative. Each student receives a role-play that describes his or her character's perceptions and feelings; they are instructed to choose strategies that will help the pair negotiate a mutually acceptable resolution.

(Alisha joins Jim in his office)

Jim: Alisha, good morning. You look great.

Alisha: Thanks, I was hoping we could discuss how things went . . .

Jim: Yeah, I suppose we do need to get some things ironed out.

Alisha: . . . in Kansas City.

Jim: You know, I think that trip was rough on both of us, although they [the clients] seemed happy . . .

Alisha: Specifically, I'd like to get some clarity on our reporting relationships. I realize you are my trainer, but I was hoping we could lay some clearer ground rules for operating on the road.

Jim: I don't know what you mean, reporting relationships; I was assigned your trainer because our boss thought I could teach you something.

Alisha: Yes, I realize you have more experience, and I have some things to learn, but I was hoping we could work out some better procedures for communicating.

Jim: What did you have in mind?

Alisha: Well, first, I think we ought to debrief after the meeting . . .

Jim: I thought we did.

Alisha: . . . and I think you should save any criticism or correction of my presentation until after.

Jim: Fine, but if a mistake is made in something I think is important to the client, my obligation is to bring it up right there . . .

The role play proceeded and, as this excerpt suggests, both players became entrenched in their viewpoints. The student playing "Jim" became increasingly adamant about his obligations to his clients and to his trainee; the student playing "Alisha" became more definite about the need for rules and procedures to govern their work together. Ultimately, "Jim" assumed an authoritarian stance, insisting on his rights as the senior trainer to conduct their audits as he saw fit, compromising only so far as to promise not to "reprimand" Alisha publicly.

The non-verbal and paralanguage messages accompanying this dialogue were revealing. From the start, "Alisha" seemed to control her voice and posture firmly: she sat straight-backed, used few gestures, and spoke in a voice of great clarity but little modulation. These characteristics intensified as the dialogue proceeded. "Jim," on the other hand, began the interaction while leaning back in his chair; his greeting to "Alisha" was accompanied by a smile and some warmth in his tone. Midway through the excerpt, however, he assumed a straight-backed position and suppressed, by and large, the initial animation in his voice. In fact, nonverbally, "Jim" began to reflect "Alisha."

After viewing the videotape, the two participants and their classmates discussed their perceptions of the interaction. Ironically, both "Alisha" and "Jim" described identical goals for what each had hoped to achieve through the meeting: to reestablish a mutually beneficial working relationship and to avoid recourse to the boss, a move which would make both "look bad." The class attributed the pair's failure to arrive at a collaborative, mutually satisfactory solution to several factors: "Jim's" sexist greeting and his inability to listen sensitively to "Alisha's" concerns; "Alisha's" perceived "coolness" and her inability to unbend and consider "Jim's" viewpoint. Overall, the class found fault with their mutual boss who had created the ambiguous structure of their reporting relationship. Make the rules clear, clarify who works for whom, who has final authority, these MBA students argued, and "Jim" and "Alisha" would know where they stood and be able to adjust their behavior accordingly.

Both participants had envisioned a meeting that would resolve the current issues and establish groundwork for collaboration; but because each chose divergent strategies to reach that goal, their mistrust and dislike deepened. While the immediate problem was patched up—neither wanted the boss's involvement—the student playing "Jim" admitted to being angry with "Alisha's" 'attitude,' while the student playing "Alisha" claimed that the interaction would prompt her to start sending out resumes. We would suggest that beyond the sources of conflict built into the roleplay's script, these two demonstrated the increased potential for misunderstanding between work pairs of mixed gender and race. Their conflict escalates because of differing expectations about interpersonal communication.

Applying the Matrix

The literature review would suggest that the interaction between "Jim" and "Alisha" described in our illustration is typical of most cross-race and cross-gender interactions, and the communication obstacles both encounter are predictable. As we have said, most novices or junior members of any profession, white, black, male, or female, will initiate communication in the "Technician" quadrant. Here, they do not risk presuming too greatly on short-lived relationships with listeners, especially senior members; they thus show appropriate deference. This style also allows novices to demonstrate content mastery and technical competence, while displaying their understanding of the formal rules which govern discourse in this quadrant. Our "Alisha," the junior member in the roleplay, locates herself in this quadrant. Some junior or new members of an organization may, however, assume an "Ingratiator" style. As Kipnis and Schmidt suggest, this style apparently works effectively for white women as a vehicle of upward influence, and less well for white men, given, they hypothesize, the white, mainstream expectations of how men and women should communicate.

While advancing through an "Ingratiator" style may be problematic for many white professional women, we suggest that for minority managers, this style is seldom an option. For these professionals, the "Ingratiator" quadrant is "off-limits." For men and women of color, assuming the "Ingratiator" style is dangerous: they risk assuming a solidarity with the listener ("you and I are more alike than different") that the listener may reject; they may misread or misapply the informal signals which control this communication quadrant; finally, they risk being perceived as all "fluff" with no chance to display "professional" demeanor or technical competence. White women, while enjoying more effectiveness in the "Ingratiator" quadrant, may encounter similar dangers as they attempt to move into the "Tactician" quadrant and adopt its style of communication.

Thus, many white women find themselves constrained in organizational interactions to either the "technician" or "Ingratiator" styles; many men and women of color are typically forced to adopt the "technician" style. We might argue that the ability to shift, as need be, among the four styles presented, to move freely between quadrants, is the mark of the competent corporate communicator, and the move into the "Tactician" quadrant reflects the progress of a successful career. But opportunity for this kind of movement is not equal, given differing cultural expectations about appropriate communication: white men and women share the same understanding about conversational styles—that men and women appropriately communicate wants and exert influence differently; men and women of color may find it hard to perceive or exploit nuances of relationship in what appears to be the "univocal" majority style. All members of the organization thus enter into work relationships constrained by their expectations of appropriate style.

"Alisha," reading the context of her interaction with "Jim," begins in quadrant I: she is a technician, all-business, focusing on the task at hand, getting the "procedures" clear, allowing no relationship concerns into the picture. "Jim," in contrast, starts out in quadrant III, the "Ingratiator." "Alisha" chooses her style because she is concerned about maintaining her power in the relationship—power she perceives as less than "Jim's"—and saving her (negative) face. Her experience suggests that with this style she will be, at least, safe, at most, able to secure a formal division of authority. "Jim" is concerned about smoothing the relationship and helping both Alisha and himself save (positive) face. He has fewer fears about his source of power or authority; moreover, the "Ingratiator" style is the behavior he would expect from a white woman in "Alisha's" position. "Jim's" strategy is to assume a solidarity with his partner; but when "Alisha" fails to respond in kind, "Jim" quickly moves into a "technician" style of his own, again saving (negative) face. Although both are now communicating in the same style, they fail to reach mutual understanding; their issues are both task- and relationship-centered, a High-Task, Low-Relationship style limits them to a short term solution.

Individual and Organizational Outcomes

The long-term implications for individuals and their organizations are critical. "Jim" may, over time, slip into Quadrant II, the Bystander mode, in his relationships with black women within his workgroup, and attribute his noninvolvement to their "negative attitudes" despite his attempts at inclusion. "Alisha" might also become a "Bystander"—or leave the organization altogether. R. R. Thomas, Jr., describes the outcome of a "real-life" cross-gender, cross-race work relationship:

> In one case, an ambitious young black woman was assigned to a white male manager, at his request, on the basis of her excellent company record. They looked forward to working together, and for the first three months, everything went well. But then their relationship began to deteriorate, and the harder they worked at patching it up, the worse it got. Both of them, along with their superiors, were surprised by the conflict and seemed puzzled as to its causes. Eventually, the black woman requested and obtained reassignment. But even though they escaped each other, both suffered a sense of failure severe enough to threaten their careers.

Thomas does not address the "causes" of this failure; our diagnosis is one of divergent communication styles and expectations, a divergence that, unexamined by the participants, can only result in escalating confusion, conflict, and, ultimately, disappointment on both sides. This divergence, we believe, can go far to explain why, for instance, "Alisha" and "Jim," despite shared intentions to collaborate, fail to construct a mutual solution to their shared problem.

Thomas suggests that employees trying to negotiate these new and challenging relationships are "pioneers" who need support as they work "at the cutting edge of race and gender relations." Organizations ought to look carefully at the nature of this support, however. Training programs or intervention strategies aimed at raising awareness and changing racist or sexist attitudes are not sufficient to address conflicts arising from divergent interpersonal communication behaviors. Even for those sincere in their efforts to confront racism and sexism, communication styles and perceptions of those styles constrain the growth of interpersonal relationships necessary for career development and organizational success. We believe that the combination of insights represented in the research reviewed here can serve as due warning of the pitfalls of seeking to manage diversity without attending to the complex communication dynamics such diversity entails.

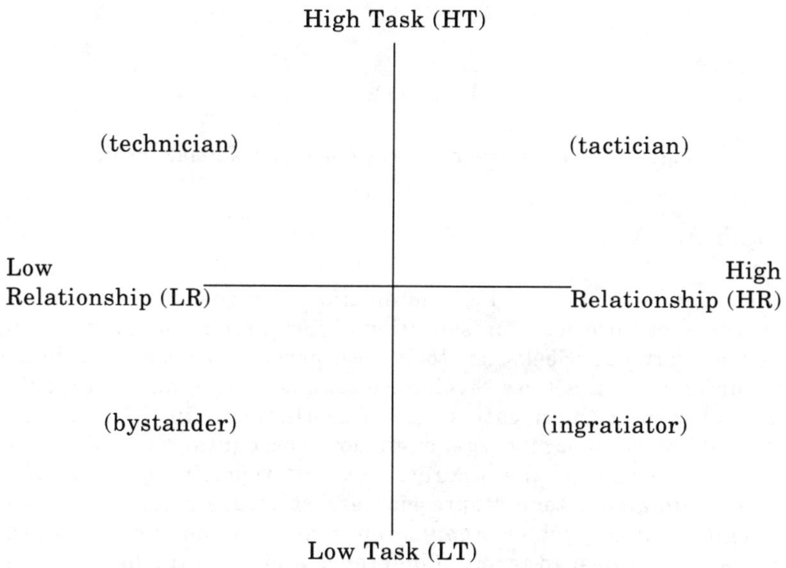

High Task (HT)

(technician)   (tactician)

Low   High
Relationship (LR)   Relationship (HR)

(bystander)   (ingratiator)

Low Task (LT)

Figure 5.1. Task vs. Relationship Matrix

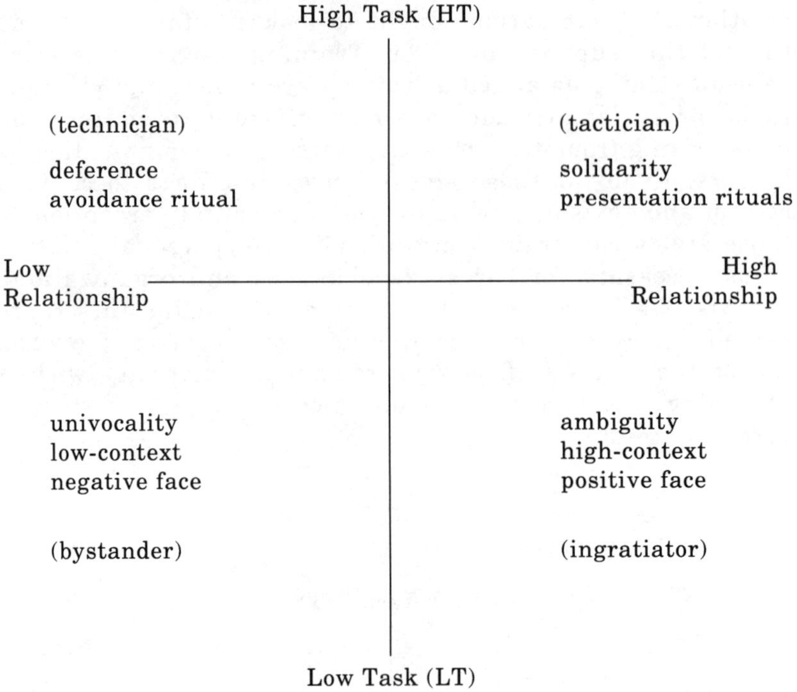

High Task (HT)

(technician)

deference
avoidance ritual

(tactician)

solidarity
presentation rituals

Low
Relationship

High
Relationship

univocality
low-context
negative face

ambiguity
high-context
positive face

(bystander)

(ingratiator)

Low Task (LT)

Figure 5.2. Interpersonal Style and Task vs. Relationship

Appendix A

Technician: Uses univocal communication, designed to be affectively neutral; seeks precise representation of facts; strips language of suggestive overtones. Seeks not to impose personal concerns on listeners (deference): practices "avoidance rituals," using formality, rules, titles to respect the negative face of the listener. In this quadrant, we would place the archetypal engineer or accountant, one who seeks his or her impact by the accurate, "expert" reporting of data—often conveyed in a monotone, 'expressionless' style. Here, also, the novice or beginner in any job or organization may be found, since this technical style is safest in terms of deference and since the formal 'rules' of any group are those easiest to identify and copy.

Bystander: Like the technician, tends to use a univocal. formal style in professional contexts, less, however, out of deference to his or her listener's negative face than to protect his or her own and ensure autonomy. In this quadrant, we would place, like Kipnis and Schmidt, those managers who appear to have withdrawn from seeking to influence organizational decisions.

Ingratiator: Uses "ambiguous communication"; alludes to shared experiences and sentiments, uses verbal associations to express and evoke affective responses. Exploits ambiguity through wit and jokes; affirms solidarity and seeks to affect the positive face of listeners. Performs "presentational rituals" salutations, invitations, compliments and minor services. Speaks in a varied, emphatic tone, much animation and gestures. Here we would place the archetypal marketing or sales executive or trainee.

Tactician: In many ways, the hardest category to define, but here we would place executives or managers who appear to be CEO material, combining the image of being highly task (or bottom-line) oriented with the ability to evoke relational histories and bonds. These are the people with "strategic vision": "strategic" reflecting their task competence or technical expertise; "vision" reflecting their skill at involving listeners in their perspective.

References

Abrahams, R. D. 1976. *Talking Black*. Rowley, Mass.: Newberry House.

Berkley, G. 1985. *How to manage your boss*. Englewood Cliffs, N.J.: Prentice Hall.

Brown, B. R. 1977. Face saving and Face restoration in negotiations. In D. Druckman, ed., *Negotiation: Social psychological perspectives* (pp. 275–300). Beverly Hills: Sage.

Clark, R. A., and J. G. Delia. 1979. Topoi of rhetorical competence. *Quarterly Journal of Speech, 65*, 187–206.

Gumperz, J. J. 1982. *Discourse Strategies*. Cambridge: Cambridge University Press.

Hall, E. 1976. *Beyond Culture*. Garden City, N.Y.: Anchor Press.

Hart, R. P., and D. B. Burke. 1972. Rhetorical sensitivity and social interaction. *Quarterly Journal of Speech, 39*, 75–91.

Hofstede, G. H. 1980. *Culture's consequences: International differences in work related values*. Beverly Hills: Sage.

Jones, E. W. 1986. Black Managers: the dream deferred. *Harvard Business Review*, April-May, 84–93.

Kipnis, D., S. Schmidt, and I. Wilkinson. 1980. Intraorganizational Influence Tactics: Explorations in Getting One's Way. *Journal of Applied Psychology, 65*, 440–452.

Kipnis, D., and S. Schmidt. 1983. An Influence Perspective on Bargaining Within Organizations. In M. Bazerman and R. Lewicki, eds. *Negotiating in Organizations*, 303–319. Beverly Hills: Sage.

Kochman, T. 1986. Strategic Ambiguity in Black Speech Games: Cross-Cultural Interference. *Text, 6,* 153–170.

Labov, W. 1976. Rules for Ritual Insults. In T. Kochman, ed. *Rappin & Stylin out: Communication in Urban Black America.* Chicago: University of Illinois Press.

Lakoff, R. 1975. *Language and Woman's Place.* New York: Harper & Row.

Levine, D. 1985. *The Flight from Ambiguity.* Chicago: University of Chicago Press.

Luthans, F. 1988. Successful vs. Effective real managers. *Academy of Management Executive, 2,* 127–132.

Mitchell-Kiernan, C. 1969. Language Behavior in Black Urban Community. *Monograph 2, Language Behavior Research Laboratory,* Berkeley: Univ. of California Press.

Tannen, D. 1984. *Conversational style: Analyzing talk among friends.* Norwood, N.J.: Ablex Corp.

Thomas, R. R. 1990. From Affirmative Action to Affirming Diversity. *Harvard Business Review,* March-April, 107–117.

Thomas, D., and C. Alderfer. 1987. *The Influence of Race on Career Dynamics: Theory and Research on Minority Career Experiences.* Working Paper #712; The Wharton School, University of Pennsylvania, PA.

Wiemann, J. M. 1977. Explication and test of a model of communicative competence. *Human Communication Research, 3,* 195–213.

Sexual Harassment and Immediacy Behaviors in the Multicultural Workplace: A Communication Paradox

❖

Loretta F. Harper
and Lawrence J. Rifkind

Increased interest in sexual harassment issues has drawn attention to the multicultural nature of the workforce in the United States. Corporations must comply with federal guidelines on sexual harassment while fostering a productive work environment in the multicultural workplace. Immediacy communicates approachability and availability. Interpersonal relationships are crucial to job effectiveness and satisfaction. Increased concern about sexual harassment in the workplace creates a paradox which indicates that while immediacy behaviors can establish a positive workplace environment, sexual harassment policies can serve to inhibit such behaviors. As a result, there are implications for corporate decision makers in the arenas of training policies and procedures. This essay addresses immediacy behaviors that are appropriate within the context of sexual harassment policies in the interculturally diverse workplace. Emphasis is placed upon the paradox created by immediacy, which establishes interpersonal warmth and closeness, and sexual harassment policies which are designed to reduce employer liability.

Introduction

The U.S. Bureau of Labor Statistics' forecast for the American workforce between 1986 and 2000, projects some rather startling changes in the American workplace. For instance, they indicate that only 32% of the workers entering the labor force will be white non-Hispanic males, while 51% of the workers entering the workforce will be females. Furthermore, females will constitute 47% of the total workforce. As a consequence, these individuals will be entering a more multiculturally diverse work environment. Thus, according to Schmidt (1991), we are becoming more of a "salad bowl" than a "melting pot."

Sex-role stereotypes have been firmly held by most cultures for centuries. According to Borden (1991), "sex" is biological with two categories: female and male. "Gender" is psychological, with three categories: masculine, feminine, and androgynous. The close association between gender and sex-based characteristics is reinforced by all of society. Men are hypothesized to perceive themselves as possessing the masculine characteristics. They are aggressive, forceful, strong, rational, self-confident, competitive, and independent. Women are hypothesized to perceive that they possess feminine characteristics. They are warm, kind, emotional, gentle, understanding, aware of others' feelings and helpful to others (Fagenson, 1990).

There are three variables in the equation for sex-role differentiation: biological characteristics, psychological characteristics, and cultural characteristics; or sex, gender, and tradition. When we consider that sex, gender, and culture all have a part in shaping the role that each sex will be pulled toward, we must be aware that all roles in the United States appear to be moving in the direction of more objectivity/less subjectivity, more production oriented/less relation oriented, and more monetary success oriented/less caring oriented (Borden, 1991).

It would appear that the interpersonal relationships that are established in the workplace are crucial to job effectiveness and satisfaction. Two variables that appear to be closely linked to this concept are sexual harassment and immediacy. The process by which sexual harassment came to be recognized and defined as a form of sex discrimination began in movement politics and was developed through interest group politics in the executive and judicial branches of government (Fowlkes, 1987).

Sexual harassment

In the final stages of the Civil Rights Act of 1964, "sex" was added to Title VII, which addressed discrimination in employment. However, almost immediately after the Civil Rights Act was passed, the "sex" provision was dropped. The Equal Employment Opportunity Commission (EEOC) was established to implement and oversee the act's provisions. According to Jo Freeman (1975, 54):

> The first executive director of the (EEOC), Herman Edelsberg, publicly stated that the provision was a 'fluke' that was 'conceived out of wedlock.' He felt 'men were entitled to female secretaries.'

During the late 1960s, the alliance of liberal politics and tolerant sexual attitudes began to weaken. Major writers of the women's movement began to argue that sex, which the sexual revolution had presented as an activity to be enjoyed by men and women alike, was more often an arena in which dramas of oppression against women—from harassment to spouse abuse—were played out (Garnett, 1991). Feminists developed the label "sexual harassment" to describe certain behaviors of men toward women and the consequences of that behavior. The consequences are that women both as individuals and as groups are humiliated by being treated as objects often, not always, as sexual objects, but always as objects for the use of men. Furthermore, stereotypical expectations that women are passive and unable to defend themselves may lead some men to think that they, as Georgie Porgie in the nursery rhyme, can sexually harass women as long as there are no other men around to stop them (Wise and Stanley, 1987).

In 1966, women within the newly formed EEOC and women meeting at an annual conference of state commissions on the status of women attempted to get "sex discrimination" recognized by the EEOC, but to no avail. The National Organization for Women was founded at this conference. Eventually, these individuals prevailed in their efforts with the EEOC. It was not until 1976 in the case of Williams v. Saxbe that the federal courts declared sexual harassment illegal sex discrimination under Title VII of the Civil Rights Act of 1964. EEOC guidelines were issued in 1980.

According to EEOC guidelines, unwelcome sexual advances, requests for sexual favors, and other verbal or physical conduct of a sexual nature constitute sexual harassment when:

- Submission to such conduct is made either explicitly or implicitly as a condition of an individual's employment;
- Submission to or rejection of such conduct by an individual is used as the basis for employment decisions affecting that person;
- Such conduct has the purpose or effect of unreasonably interfering with an individual's work performance, or creating an intimidating, hostile, or offensive working environment.

Although this definition is gender neutral, the victim of sexual harassment is far more likely to be female than male. For example, a survey of charges filed with the Illinois EEOC found that ninety-four percent of those filing sexual harassment charges were women (Terpstra, 1989).

Claims of sexual harassment can be expensive to organizations. For example, in October 1988, five women who were sexually harassed by the same supervisor were awarded $3.85 million (Frierson, 1989). Since the courts and EEOC have found that sexual harassment exists even if physical contact is not present, defining sexual harassment becomes more difficult. Needless to say, sexual harassment is a complex problem with psychological, interpersonal and socio-cultural causes and consequences (Thomann, 1989).

The Civil Rights Act of 1991 made sexual harassment a matter of federal law. The legislation provided additional remedies for intentional discrimination and unlawful harassment in the workplace by permitting the complaining party to recover both compensatory and punitive damages (in addition to any relief permitted by the Civil Rights Act of 1964) from a respondent who has engaged in unlawful intentional discrimination. Compensatory damages range from $50,000 to $300,000 per complaining party, depending upon the number of employees in the organization. The law does not provide limits on punitive damages.

Needless to say, sexual harassment is not always easy to define, much less to combat. Some progress has been made in developing a system to define and address the problem. EEOC has interpreted the formal definition to include sexual joking, certain compliments of a very personal nature, and gratuitous touching. However, the definition continues to be somewhat vague and abstract. As a consequence, it is often subject to individual perception and interpretation.

Immediacy

Mehrabian (1969) defines immediacy as that communication which enhances closeness to another. Andersen (1985) states that immediacy behaviors indicate approachability, signal availability for communication, increase sensory stimulation, and communicate interpersonal warmth and closeness. In his development of the immediacy construct, Mehrabian demonstrates that the major communicative function of immediacy behaviors is that they reflect a more positive attitude of the sender toward the receiver. He points out that immediacy and liking are two sides of the same coin. That is, liking encourages greater immediacy and immediacy produces increased levels of liking.

Mehrabian uses an approach metaphor to describe the immediacy construct. He points out that people have a tendency to move toward that which they like and away from that which they dislike. Therefore, approach indicates preference and positive evaluation, while avoidance indicates dislike. Burgoon et al. (1984) found that high eye contact, close proximity, forward body lean, and smiling convey greater intimacy, attraction, and trust. Conversely, low eye contact, backward body lean, and the absence of smiling and touch communicate greater detachment. Thus, if immediacy behaviors indicate approach, openness to communication, and warmth, it seems logical that such communication would enhance interpersonal relationships in the workplace.

Immediacy occurs both verbally and nonverbally. A person's choice of words can indicate approachability to communication, as well as avoidance. The use of first person plural pronouns, such as "we" and "us," as well as the use of humor, self-disclosure, initiating conversations with others, providing praise for work performed, and asking questions that solicit viewpoints or opinions are examples of verbal immediacy cues. Nonverbal immediacy cues include eye contact, relaxed body position, gestures, smiling, vocal expressiveness, and physical proximity (Andersen, 1979).

Multicultural dimensions of immediacy

According to Andersen's (1985) arousal-valence theory, culture does have a definite impact upon immediacy. This theory posits that for immediacy to have effects, it must be perceived by a receiver. Once perceived, immediacy generates an arousal change in the receiver. Extremely high levels of arousal result in aversion, while extremely low levels of arousal result in no behavioral change. However, moderate levels of arousal are valenced either positively or negatively, resulting in behavioral responses. Andersen indicates that culture is a primary influence on valence. In other words, if the arousal change is a result of culturally inappropriate behavior for the receiver, negative valence will occur.

Communication patterns tend to differ across cultures. Hecht and Ribeau (1984) found that Black, Hispanic, and White respondents differed significantly in the type of communication that they found satisfying. Hispanics found communication to be a bonded relationship with internal rewards, whereas Whites viewed communication as more self-oriented with external rewards. Satisfying communication for Hispanics seems to revolve around nonverbal communication and acceptance of self.

Whites and Blacks tend to stress the future of the relationship and confirmation that the message and possible relationship are accepted. Black respondents required deeper, more intimate topical involvement than White subjects. Satisfaction for Blacks revolved around having their own goals fulfilled through the actions of others. Conversely, Whites placed more emphasis on emotional aspects and tended to be more future oriented.

For Hispanics, immediacy seems to signal relational confirmation and warmth. This group tends to prefer informality and relational bonding in advisement contexts. Perhaps immediacy plays an important role in the affilial orientation of Hispanics. For Whites, these findings indicate that expressiveness, as transmitted by immediacy, has a particularly positive effect. These results suggest that expressiveness influences the perception of clarity and affect toward others for Whites. This finding seems to support Kelley and Gorham's (1985) position that immediacy relates to positive arousal, especially for Whites.

There would appear to be communication differences across gender in the area of immediacy behaviors. The empirical research concerning sex differences in kinesic nonverbal behaviors seems to provide support for the possibility that there is a "male style" and a "female style" of interaction (Arliss, 1991). Stereotypically masculine bodily actions tend to communicate dominance and power, while stereotypically feminine bodily actions tend to communicate affiliation and warmth. These findings seem to suggest that all individuals who behave according to sex-appropriate prescriptions are substantially limited to the extent that men are less capable of communicating warmth and women are less capable of communicating power.

Haas and Sherman (1982) suggest that men report a higher frequency of talk about money, news, spectator sports, and participation in sports. This further indicates that nearly every study of conversation topics conducted in the last six decades conclude that most clearcut is the sex difference in talk about sports. Other common male topics surround public as opposed to personal business. Men report talking about news and money, presumably topics that can be discussed on a less personal basis than more popular female topics. Women seem to demonstrate their interest and expertise in private matters such as people, relationships, and clothing; they do not report talking often about sports, news, or money. Moreover, men are following tradition by discussing less personal matters; specifically, talking less about their relationships with others.

Discussion

Paradoxically, the increased concern about sexual harassment in the workplace seems to indicate that immediacy behaviors can contribute to an environment in which sexual harassment is likely to occur or to be alleged. Men and women are taught from infancy to use language differently, thus creating mistrust and misunderstandings between the genders (Emerson, 1991). The cultural difference in the use of language as well as the other differences between genders seem to lead to increased difficulties in coping with issues and definitions of sexual harassment.

Lakoff (1973) reports distinct female linguistic patterns. Generally, women seem to employ an extended vocabulary in referencing color, in expressing their emotions verbally, and in evaluating the world. She suggests that women seem to be unwilling to use grammatical constructions, or the way speakers put words together, expressing certainty, while men are typically more straightforward. Perhaps the strongest evidence of this distinction lies in the documented female tendency to use polite forms. Her research indicates that female speech is, by prescription, more polite than male speech, with politeness involving an absence of strong statements. Thus, a female, even in a position of superiority, would be likely to use polite speech to achieve the same end as her less polite male counterpart.

Subsequent research has endorsed the assertion that women are more likely than men to phrase imperatives as questions. McMillan et al. (1977) found that females used this type of construction three times as often as males in peer group interaction. In addition, women have been observed to add obligatory polite forms, such as "please" and "thank you." Crosby and Nyquist (1977) examined communication behavior across status relationships and concluded that both gender and status proved are useful in predicting the use of polite speech. As might be expected, being female and being subordinate are conditions that statistically increased the likelihood of being polite.

Sexual harassment is generally characterized as an abuse of either role power or sexual power. Stringer et al. (1990) have identified types of power from sociological models and how these types of power lead to a better understanding of sexual harassment. The first and most obvious source of power as it relates to sexual harassment is that of formal role power based on the person's rank or position within the organization. This type of power is achieved power.

Women have less formal and informal power in organizations than men, confront more obstacles on their path to developing organizational power, and have fewer opportunities to acquire organizational power (Kanter, 1977). Wood and Conrad (1983, 308) indicated that even when women hold positions of formal power, men interpret women's behavior "as congruent with powerless roles," and define women in terms of traditional stereotypes.

The second type of power is ascribed power resulting from an attributed characteristic over which a person has no control. Two sources of ascribed power relative to the workplace

are gender and ethnicity. Stringer et al. (1990, 45) have described gender power as follows:

> ... is fundamental to sexual harassment. Virtually all re-
> search indicates that this culture attributes more power to
> men simply because of their gender. In work settings, men
> are viewed as more competent, responsible, committed and
> valuable than women. Even when a woman has role, infor-
> mation or money power in an organization, she does not have
> access to the societal value placed on the male gender.

They further state that although societal values have begun to change, employers must understand that differential
values placed on men and women by most Americans continue
to impact the workplace. As concerns ethnic power, they state:

> Because whites are more powerful and valued in this culture
> than people of color, complaints or concerns of ethnic minor-
> ity victims are often not taken as seriously, investigated as
> appropriately, or reprimanded as strongly as those complaints
> of white victims. Ethnic minority harassers of white women,
> on the other hand, are often disciplined more severely.

Indeed, ascribed and achieved powers can be combined
through the sources of power of sexuality and physical size
and strength. One's sex is biologically determined, but one's
perception of sexuality and sexual practices is learned through
one's culture. Stringer indicates that men and women act differently toward sex and power in the workplace. Men tend to
occupy positions of power, thus making it easier for them to
demand sex from a less powerful person, usually a woman.

Furthermore, because men are generally larger and stronger than women, they may use their size to consciously or
unconsciously intimidate or control women whom they are harassing. Numbers and territoriality are sources of situational
power in the workplace. In attempting to maintain the homogeneity of the workforce, the only woman, the only homosexual,
or the only ethnic minority become targets of harassment.

Women and men are not as separated by size as the myth
would have us believe. The range of heights and weights for
American women and men tends to overlap considerably and
the averages continue to grow closer (Henley, 1986). Therefore, it seems unlikely that we unconsciously award less space
to women because of their diminutive size. Rubin (1970) posits

that women tend to hold their bodies in such a way that they take up less space. Men assume sitting and standing positions consistent with the contention that they command a larger portion of the surrounding space than their female counterparts who sit and stand in more restricted positions.

The concept of crowding can also be applied to the violation of one's invisible personal space—the distance others are expected to keep. The violation of proxemic expectations results in consistently disruptive effects on the communication between two or more people (Argyle and Williams, 1969). Those individuals who place a high value on distance and are most accustomed to separation find spatial invasions most upsetting. Therefore, it should come as no surprise that men have consistently been viewed as responding more negatively to invasions of their personal space than women (Ellyson et al., 1981).

Davis and Weitz (1981) provide empirical verification for the contention that people usually perceive male kinesic behavior as indicative of dominance and female kinesic behavior as indicative of submissiveness. Females are also rated as warmer and more partner-oriented. This study demonstrates that kinesic behaviors, such as facial expressions, eye contact, gestures, posture, and movement, are seen as support for the prevailing mythology about masculinity and femininity in our culture.

This research confirms that individual behaviors tend to correspond with cultural standards of masculine and feminine display. Males sit with widened postures, show a greater range of movement, and use more gestures than females. Females use more head movements, however, along with greater amounts of gaze and smiling.

Nieva and Gutek (1981) identify four general models for women's work situation: the individual deficit model, the structural institutional model, the sex role model, and the intergroup model. Tangri, Burt, and Johnson (1982) identify three models or explanations for sexuality at work: the natural-biological model, the organizational model, and the sociocultural model. Gutek (1985) concludes that none of these models can offer an adequate explanation of sexual harassment and that they are unlikely to be able to explain the concept of sexuality. Therefore, Gutek and Morasch (1982) propose the sex role spillover model to emphasize the effects of sex role expectations in an organizational context.

Sex role spillover is a term used by Nieva and Gutek (1981) to denote the carryover of gender based roles into the workplace. Gutek (1985, p. 16) explains this effect for men and women as follows:

> Sex role spillover occurs, for example, when women are expected to be more nurturant or loyal than men in the same position. Sex role spillover also occurs when women are expected to serve as helpers (as in laboratory helper),... without ever advancing to head of the laboratory, manager of the office, or principal member of the research staff.
>
> When men are expected to behave in a stereotypical manner—to automatically assume the leader's role in a mixed-sex group, pay for a business lunch with a female colleague, or confront a poorly performing colleague—sex role spillover also occurs.

In terms of sexual harassment, the sex object aspect of gender roles is the most relevant. Being a sex object is central to the female sex role, but it is not clear whether there is a comparably strong aspect to the male sex role unless it is sexual aggressiveness or assertiveness (Gutek, 1985). Katz and Kahn (1978) define a work role as a set of expectations associated with tasks to be accomplished at work. Sex role is a set of expectations of the behaviors of men and women.

Birdwhistell (1970) is credited with recognizing that many movements function as "gender displays." According to this analysis, all animals need to identify potential mates. However, humans are relatively unimorphic, so it may be difficult to be sure who's who based solely on visual information. For example, because humans are "civilized" creatures, the situation is confounded by the custom of concealing with clothing the biological information that distinguishes people as male or female. We cannot rely on olfactory information like dogs, for instance, so each society seems to have developed "patterned social-behavior" gender displays (Zimmerman and West, 1975).

In our culture, women tend to be more facilly expressive than men. Ekman and Friesen (1975) explain that the female stereotype allows for a wider range of emotional expressions, including positive expressions such as giggling and negative expressions such as crying. The tendency for women to be more facially expressive both supports and perpetuates the stereotypes that females are emotional and men are rational. As a result, Buck et al. (1974) conclude that women appear to be more outward in their emotive displays, or externalizers, and men are more inward in their emotive displays, or internalizers of emotion.

Sex differences in eye contact can be summarized rather simply: women look in the direction of their conversational partners more than men and, logically, participate in more mutual gaze during interaction. Mehrabian (1971) argues that women are more interested than men in establishing positive interaction; thus, they tend to be more affiliative. Availability for mutual gaze is but one of several affiliate behaviors. Women score higher than men on self-report tests intended to measure the affiliative tendency and also demonstrate this effect in their nonverbal communication.

Additional research seems to lend support to the affiliative explanation. Females who score high on affiliative tendency display more eye contact that females who score low on the same measure (Rubin, 1970). There is reason to believe that pairs who believe they share a positive relationship will display more eye contact, particularly when discussing a positive topic (Exline and Winters, 1965) and pairs who believe they are engaged in negative interaction will display less eye contact (Exline, Gray, and Schuette, 1965). Competition between partners, which counters the affiliative tendency, has been suggested as a cause of the reduction in the amount of eye contact in female-to-female interaction.

Tannen (1991) suggests that a "cultural divide" separates men and women in our society. She posits that relation-centered females can get short shrift in the office that is dominated by confrontational and competitive males. The intergender confusion that follows can indeed spill over into the workplace. Men and women are working in new relationships for which a set of rules has not been developed (Stringer et al., 1990).

Hacker (1981) explains that self-disclosure must be understood as involving two dimensions: intimacy and power. Status does affect the sharing of information such that self-disclosure is likely to be somewhat unidirectional in nonpeer relationships, with the subordinate revealing more personal information than the superior. Presumably, keeping personal information secret helps to distance a superior. On the other hand, a subordinate has more to lose by disclosing too much information to someone with the power to damage or improve their position.

Generally, the literature reports that women disclose more than men and they receive more disclosure from others (Cozby, 1973). Of course, other studies report no apparent differences across genders in self-disclosure (Hacker, 1981). It may be most telling that no study has reported that males disclose more than females (Arliss, 1991). Overall, the research can be summarized as substantiating the myth that females participate in self-disclosure and males may or may not participate as frequently or as openly in self-disclosure, depending on the conclusions of the particular study.

A more interesting contradiction has emerged regarding the same-sex effect on self-disclosure. Research hypothesizes that people tend to disclose more freely to others they perceive as similar to themselves. This seems logical since we can assume that someone who shares our experiences probably understands our perspective best. For instance, a disgruntled employee would be more likely to seek out a disgruntled peer to whom they might disclose attitudes about work. The same reasoning indicates the likelihood that a woman would disclose to another woman and a man would disclose to another man (Nierenberg and Calero, 1973).

Some studies suggest that while females disclose most often and more openly to other females, males disclose more often and more fully to females as well. Specifically, in terms of the depth and breadth of information shared, female-female relationships have been ranked first in most studies, followed by male-female relationships, with male-male relationships rated the lowest on degree of intimacy (Spiegel and Machotka, 1974). Thus, it would appear that both men and women prefer to self-disclose to women, which is consistent with the findings that women are more other-centered in their communication. It may be that women are perceived as more supportive and understanding, and therefore, as better recipients of self-disclosure.

Conclusion

Ours is a culture that is preoccupied with dividing the human race into males and females, regardless of age and status. The lack of such information can result in intense anxiety, particularly in a work environment. Perhaps this need to know another person's sex is predicated on the conditioning that we receive that causes people to understand and evaluate behavior as sex appropriate. Once we classify another individual as male or female, we begin to draw inferences about certain emotional and psychological attributes.

According to Arliss (1991), the process by which we learn and teach sex-appropriate behavior is assumed to be part of the larger communication process by which we come to understand our world and the extent to which we fit within it. Therefore, communication is thought to be the process by which we learn to be male or female and the product of our attempts to behave sex appropriate. Until we become aware of the standards by which we differentiate appropriate male from appropriate female behavior, it seems unlikely that we will become fully aware of the boundaries of sexual harassment and the subsequent paradox that exists between such behaviors and immediacy within the context of the workplace. Ironically, few of those standards exist in a permanent form. Rather, many of our judgments about sex-appropriate behaviors are based on implicit standards. We learn and teach these standards, often times on an unintentional level, through communication.

The paradox created by concern over sexual harassment and immediacy behaviors has implications for corporate decision makers in the arenas of training policies and procedures. It is recommended that training programs go beyond merely informing supervisors and workers about the definitions of sexual harassment and explanations of policies by also addressing the multicultural nature of the workforce. Training programs must include information about immediacy behaviors and their meaning relative to gender and ethnic background.

Specifically, training programs should be segmented into two sections. The first section should include, but not be limited to, discussions of definitions of sexual harassment, descriptions of specific behaviors that may be perceived as harassing, and discussions of the cultural differences between men and women and how they use language (both verbal and nonverbal) accordingly. Topics in the program should also focus on the appropriate ethnic behaviors depending upon the ethnic composition of the workforce.

The second section of the training must concentrate on disseminating the organization's policies and procedures relative to sexual harassment. Copies of policies and procedures must be distributed along with detailed instructions of how to comply with them. However, before they can become part of training, great care should be exercised to ensure that the corporation's policies and procedures are clear and in compliance with EEOC guidelines.

There should be provision for a grievance procedure that can be utilized by victims of perceived harassment without fear of reprisal. Specifically, policies should include the following: (a) definitions of sexual harassment; (b) statement that sexual harassment is prohibited by the corporation; and (c) disciplinary actions that will be taken against offenders.

In addition, procedures must clearly outline the following:

(a) process by which a victim can file a claim of sexual harassment,
(b) the steps to be followed in investigating the claim,
(c) the steps to be followed in resolving the matter,
(d) sanctions against the offender if warranted, and
(e) the steps to be followed by the victim to appeal the results of the investigation.

Provisions must be made in the written policies and procedures to ensure that confidentiality is maintained throughout the claims of sexual harassment.

The corporation must be clear in its statement that sexual harassment is prohibited in the workplace. Attention must also be given to the development of training programs that will provide better understanding of not only the sexual harassment policies and procedures but also the cultural differences between genders. Implementation of these recommendations will lessen the potential for legal liability and costly settlements particularly in the multicultural workplace.

As our society becomes increasingly multiculturally diverse and the composition of the workplace changes accordingly, the need for members of the workforce to understand the varying ways in which immediacy behaviors can function differently for people of diverse cultural backgrounds, including males and females, becomes increasingly critical. Greater attention needs to be given to ways in which worker ethnicity influences both the patterns and expectations for communication behavior in an environment affected by sexual harassment policies. Thus, workers will be better able to adapt their communication behaviors to these major cultural shifts.

References

Andersen, J. F. 1979. Teacher immediacy as a predictor of teaching effectiveness. In D. Nimmo, ed., *Communication Yearbook 3* (543–559). New Brunswick, NJ: Transaction Books.

Andersen, P. A. 1985. Nonverbal immediacy in interpersonal communication. In A. W. Siegman and S. Feldstein, eds., *Multichannel Integrations of Nonverbal Behavior*. Hillsdale, NJ: Lawrence Erlbaum.

Argyle, M., and M. C. Williams. 1969. Observer or observed? A reversible perspective in person perception. *Sociometry*, 32, 396–412.

Arliss, L. P. 1991. *Gender Communication*. Englewood, NJ: Prentice Hall.

Birdwhistell, R. L. 1970. *Kinesics and Context*. Philadelphia: University of Pennsylvania Press.

Borden, G. A. 1991. *Cultural Orientation: An Approach to Understanding Intercultural Communication*. Englewood, NJ: Prentice Hall.

Buck, R., R. E. Miller, and W. F. Caul. 1974. Sex differences in parental directives to young children. *Sex Roles*, 8, 1123–1139.

Burgoon, J. K., D. B. Buller, J. L. Hale, and M. A. DeTurch. 1984. Relational messages associated with nonverbal behaviors. *Human Communication Research*, 10, 351–378.

Cozby, P. 1973. Self-disclosure: A literature review. *Psychological Bulletin*, 79, 73–91.

Crosby, F., and L. Nyquist. 1977. The female rejecter: An empirical test of Lakoff's hypothesis. *Language and Society*, 6, 313–322.

Davis, M., and S. Weitz. 1981. Sex differences in body movements and positions. In Clara Mayo and Nancy M. Henley, eds., *Gender and Nonverbal Behavior*. NY: Springer-Verlag.

Ekman, P., and W. V. Friesen. 1975. *Unmasking the Face*. Englewood Cliffs, NJ: Prentice Hall.

Ellyson, S. L., J. F. Dovidio, and B. J. Fehr. 1981. Visual behavior and dominance in women and men. In Clara Mayo and Nancy M. Henley, eds., *Gender and Nonverbal Behavior*. NY: Springer-Verlag.

Emerson, B. 1991. He said, She said, *The Atlanta Constitution*. D1.

Exline, R. V., D. Gray, and D. Schuette. 1965. Visual behavior in a dyad as affected by interview content and sex of respondent. *Journal of Personality and Social Psychology*, 1, 201–209.

Exline, R. V. and L. C. Winters. 1965. Affective relations and mutual glances in dyads. In Silva S. Tomkins and Carroll Izard, eds., *Affect, Cognition, and Personality*. NY: Springer.

Fagenson, E. A. 1990. Perceived masculine and feminine attributes examined as a function of individuals' sex and level in the organizational power hierarchy: A test of four theoretical perspectives. *Journal of Applied Psychology*, 75(2), 204–211.

Fowlkes, D. 1987. Notes on sexual harassment, unpublished paper.

Freeman, J. 1975. *The Politics of Women's Liberation: A Case Study of an Emerging Social Movement and its Relation to the Policy Process*. NY: David McKay.

Frierson, J. G. 1989. Reduce the costs of sexual harassment, *Personnel Journal*, 79–85.

Garnett, S. 1991. Thomas fiasco sullies the image of government, *The Atlanta Journal-Constitution*, G1.

Gutek, B. A. 1985. *Sex and the Workplace*. San Francisco: Josey-Bass Publishers.

Gutek, B. A., and B. Morasch. 1982. Sex ratios, sex role spillover, and sexual harassment of women at work. *Journal of Social Issues*, 38(4), 55–74.

Haas, A., and M. A. Sherman. 1982. Reported topics of conversation among same-sex adults. *Communication Quarterly*, 30, 341.

Hacker, H. M. 1981. Blabbermouths and claims: Sex differences in self-disclosure in same-sex and cross-sex friendship dyads. *Psychology of Women Quarterly*, 5, 385–401.

Hecht, M. L., and S. Ribeau. 1984. Ethnic communication: A comparative analysis of satisfying communication. *International Journal of Intercultural Relations*, 8, 135–151.

Henley, N. 1986. *Body Politics: Power, Sex and Nonverbal Communication*. NY: Touchstone Press.

Hofstede, G. 1984. *Culture's Consequences: International Differences in Work-Related Values.* Beverly Hills, CA: Sage Publications.

Kanter, R. M. 1977. *Men and Women of the Corporation.* NY: Basic Books.

Katz, D., and R. L. Kahn. 1978. *The Social Psychology of Organizations,* 2nd edition. NY: Wiley.

Kelley, D., and J. Gorham. 1985. Effects of immediacy on recall of information. *Communication Education,* 37, 198–207.

Lakoff, R. 1973. Language and woman's place. *Language in Society,* 2, 45–80.

McMillan, J. R., A. K. Clifton, D. McGrath, and W. S. Gale. 1977. Women's language: Uncertainty or interpersonal sensitivity and emotionality? *Sex Roles,* 3, 545–559.

Mehrabian, A. 1969. Some referants and measures of nonverbal behavior. *Behavior Research Methods and Instruments,* 1, 213–217.

Mehrabian, A. 1971. *Silent Messages.* Belmont, CA: Wadsworth.

Nierenberg, G. I., and H. H. Calero. 1973. *How to Read a Person Like a Book.* NY: Pocket Books.

Nieva, V. F., and B. A. Gutek. 1981. *Women and Work: A Psychological Perspective.* NY: Praeger.

Rubin, Z. 1970. Measurement of romantic love. *Journal of Personality and Social Psychology,* 16, 265–273.

Rubin, Z. 1970. Measurement of romantic love. *Journal of Personality and Social Psychology,* 16, 265–273.

Schmidt, W. V. 1991. Diversity, intercultural communication, and the global advantage. Paper presented at the Florida Communication Association Convention, Vero Beach, FL.

Spiegel, J., and P. Machotka. 1974. *Messages of the Body.* NY: Free Press.

Stringer, D. M., M. Remick, J. Salisbury, and A. B. Ginorio. 1990. The power and reasons behind sexual harassment. An employer's guide to solutions. *Public Personnel Management,* 19(1), 43–52.

Tangri, S. S., M. R. Burt, and L. B. Johnson. 1982. Sexual harassment at work: Three explanatory models. *Journal of Social Issues,* 38(4), 33–54.

Tannen, D. 1986. *That's Not What I Meant! How Conversation Style Makes or Breaks Your Relations with Others.* NY: Ballantine Press.

Tannen, D. 1991. *You Just Don't Understand: Women and Men in Conversation.* NY: Ballantine Books.

Terpstra, D. E. 1989. Who gets sexually harassed? Knowing how to educate and control your work environment. *Personnel Administrator,* 84–88.

Thomann, D. A., D. E. Strickland, and J. L. Gibbons. 1989. An organizational development approach to preventing sexual harassment: Developing shared commitment through awareness training. *CUPA Journal,* 34–43.

Wise, S., and L. Stanley. 1987. *Georgie Porgie Sexual Harassment in Everyday Life.* NY: Pandora Press.

Wood, J. T., and C. Conrad. 1983. Paradox in the experiences of professional women. *Western Journal of Speech Communication,* 47, 305–322.

Zimmerman, D. H., and C. West. 1975. Sex roles, interruptions and silences in conversations. In Barrie Thorn and Nancy Henley, eds., *Differences and Dominance.* Rowley, MA: Newbury House.

CASE STUDY

Carnival, Resistance, and Transgression in the Workplace

❖

Jeanne Rogge Steele

This case study applies the concepts of carnival, resistance, and transgression to such commonplace corporate activities as the annual employee picnic or field day, homegrown talent shows and Follies, underground newsletters, and the anonymous epithets and dirty jokes that inevitably turn up in employee suggestion boxes. The author shows the reader where to look for friction points between management and employees, suggests new ways of interpreting resistant practices, and identifies how corporate management can use this new way of seeing for good or ill.

Historical, theoretical, and political definitions of carnival, resistance, and transgression are summarized, then adapted for application to the corporate world. The author suggests that management can use employee resistance and transgression as a lens to help identify counterproductive management actions and policies and to break down barriers between people separated by their real, or perceived "high/low" positions on the corporate ladder.

"The limitations of any field of study are most strikingly revealed in its shared definitions of what counts as relevant."

——James C. Scott

It's an election year and corporate America is engaged in a no-holds-barred search for ways to reignite the economy

239

and inspire American workers. That's a project far too grand for me.

I do, however, have an idea that may help to avoid problems and move organizations toward the ideal of purposive, productive partnership between management and employees. It centers around a new approach to seeing, hearing, and interpreting the actions of subordinates—particularly the little things that make managers, from the top on down, feel threatened.

The people in charge and we corporate communicators who advise them could learn a great deal, I believe, by paying attention to the role of the "carnivalesque," "resistance" and "transgression" in the workplace. Learning to recognize and interpret these characteristic reactions to dominance will give management a tool that can be used in positive ways.

Definition by example

If you are at all like me, you associate "carnival" with the circus or state fair; "resistance" with revolution; and "transgression" with sexual behavior that deviates from accepted norms. Such terms can be usefully applied in other contexts as well. Here are a couple of examples to illustrate what I mean.

I am writing this piece in first person. It's a form of resistance—my way of questioning, resisting, or contravening, on a very small scale, the accepted academic practice of writing scholarly articles in the third person, thereby distancing the author from assertions made. One can certainly contest whether what I have to say qualifies as scholarly. But that's not the point. The question is one of agency and responsibility, not scholarship. The views expressed are mine, and I take full responsibility for them; hence, I use the first person.

As a second example, let me breach corporate and academic decorum by making a personal statement about who I am. I'm the bird in figure 1, the buzzard with the flower on her head. "I'm 51 percent sweetheart and 49 percent bitch. So don't push it."

It is a proclamation I would have loved to make on numerous occasions, but I've never dared. Only friends have been privy to this transgressive assertion, a fact that contradicts the self-description. Nevertheless, the cartoon captures a very

Figure 5.1. I'm 51 percent sweetheart and 49 percent bitch. Don't push it.

real aspect of who I am. That's why I tacked it, in my pre-academic, corporate life, to the back of my office door—as a silent rejoinder to the powers-that-be.

I got the bird from a woman who was Vice President for Medical Affairs at a mid-sized medical center in New England—an upper-management position held by very few women in 1989. We met in the winter when I was doing a market research project for her hospital's parent corporation, and the only place to hang a coat was on the hook on the back of her door. I spotted the cartoon, taped right below the hook, when I hung up my coat. I asked her for a photocopy when I left.

It wasn't until I started writing this article that I sought to understand what was so appealing about the cartoon. Once I started thinking about it, I discovered a few things. My behavior—posting the cartoon in an unobtrusive spot and sharing it only with friends—tipped me off to the resistance at work. In private, I had a desire to be tough, to let those above me on the corporate totem pole—men mostly—know that I didn't take kindly to their exercise of executive privilege, or the unspoken demand to pay it lip service. Publicly, however, I kept my rebellious side quiet. I made sure that my "public" persona fit the presumably gender-free corporate image of how a communications professional should behave. Now I realize that the cartoon was my silent "critique of power," a form of both transgression—upper level managers don't say "bitch" in public, particularly when they're women—and resistance, i.e., "oh, yes, we do."

And what about carnival? Does it exist in the workplace? I argue, yes, that ritualized sales meetings, annual employee picnics, retirement roasts and similar corporate events fit the category of carnival. In addition, aspects of the "carnivalesque" are characteristic of the anonymous epithets and spiteful remarks that turn up in employee suggestion boxes. And the uneasy laughter triggered by ethnic- or gender-specific jokes is also carnivalesque. "Blonde" jokes, I would wager, were as popular in the men's room as they were in the high school cafeteria, and it didn't take but a minute for 'Busheru' jokes to hit the streets of Tokyo following the President's untimely "upchuck" at a state dinner.

What these mindless, little three-liners have in common is their focus on the hidden codes that separate "proper" from "improper," "smart" from "dumb," and "classy" from "trashy." Calling attention to such dichotomies and taking pleasure in the levelling of the "high" to the plane of the "low" is an integral part of carnival. In other words, we take satisfaction in knowing that not even the president of the United States is immune from throwing up when he has the flu.

From whence the hypothesis comes

This line of reasoning was sparked by political, literary, feminist and, increasingly, communications theories of carnival, resistance, and transgression. Of the three, "resistance" appears most frequently in the literature—no doubt because resistant behavior is so much a part of the daily give-and-take between dominant and subordinate groups. In *Weapons of the Weak* (1985), James C. Scott uses the term to describe the way peasants or the poor typically respond to those who hold power over them. The material measure of that power—whether it's based on ownership of one more cow, or an entire colonial regiment—matters little. Its effects are felt simply by virtue of the hierarchical arrangement that results in a dichotomy between "haves" and "have-nots." Scott characterizes resistance as an everyday tactic, a natural and often strategic reaction to being the underdog (Scott, 1990, xii).

Resistance is usually not blatant. In fact, it is frequently silent and can be easily mistaken for something other than what it is—a reaction against the indignity of being subordinate. That reaction may take the form of repressed anger, the kind of "slow burn" most of us are familiar with. Or, it may take the form of self-defense, a silent distancing mechanism that protects the psyche from the humiliation of being less than equal (Scott, 1990, 137).

Rarely is resistance overt. Peasants, for example, in the face of oppression rely on "the ordinary weapons of relatively powerless groups: foot dragging, dissimulation, desertion, false compliance, pilfering, feigned ignorance" (Scott, 1985, xvi). Such forms of resistance work well, he argues, because "they require little or no coordination or planning; they make use of implicit understandings and informal networks; they often represent a form of individual self-help; they typically avoid any direct, symbolic confrontation with authority" (xvi).

Picking up on the same theme but in a different context, radical feminist Sarah Lucia Hoagland (1988) takes issue with history's depiction of black slaves as "lazy, docile, and clumsy" because they "frequently broke tools." A rational woman under slavery, Hoagland asserts, makes no effort to safeguard tools because she "comprehends that her situation is less than human, that she functions as an extension of the will of the master" (Hoagland, 1988, 42). Breaking a tool was a subversive activity, according to Hoagland, akin to sabotage undertaken "to differentiate herself from the will of the master."

In many African countries, resistance to state-imposed tariffs and export crop quotas has resulted in a "second" or "off-the-books" economy (Newbury & Schoepf, 1989, 100), where peasant farmers, many of them women, grow only enough food to feed their families, barter with one another for necessities, or cross borders and trade at markets in neighboring countries in order to circumvent exploitation. When the Central African Republic tried to force peasant farmers to grow cotton, and when Idi Amin's government forced growers to deliver coffee against their will, the peasants responded with silent forms of resistance. "The coffee may be neglected; perhaps the seeds will fail to sprout. The coffee somehow is not properly dried" (Barker, 1989, 169).

There are good reasons for sidestepping the system rather than confronting it head on. As Scott points out, "most subordinate classes throughout most of history have rarely been afforded the luxury of open, organized, political activity. Or, better stated, such activity was dangerous, if not suicidal" (Scott, 1985, xv). Nevertheless, resistance can turn violent as it did early this century in British Kumaun, a colonial territory bordering Tibet and Nepal. For decades, the hill people of this area had lived simple, law abiding lives. But when the state, under the aegis of forest management, began to curtail their customary rights of access and use of the forest for grazing and gathering firewood, everyday tactics were transformed into more militant forms of resistance. A strike against forced labor was followed by an organized campaign of deliberate burning that claimed hundreds of square miles of tropical forest. Although no one could prove it, British officials believed at least two-thirds of the fires were intentionally set (Guha, 1989).

Even when not violent, organized campaigns can force the hand of those in power. In the 1970s leaders of Senegal's Muslim brotherhoods urged their kinsmen to grow food for their families first and to pay their debts to state peanut cooperatives second. This "peanut revolt" moved the government to raise producer prices and do away with the unpopular practice of paying for peanuts with chits rather than cash (Barker, 165).

I cite these examples, which are far removed from the carpeted, white-walled offices so many of us occupy, in the belief that familiar patterns are sometimes easier to recognize if seen from a distance. Scott reminds us that problems associated with power relations belong to us all. In *Domination and the Arts of Resistance* (1990), he focuses on the most blatant conditions of powerlessness and dependency in order to illuminate divergences between what he calls the public and hidden transcripts. He builds his case from studies of slavery, serfdom, and caste subordination, arguing that structurally similar forms of domination will elicit comparable reactions and patterns of resistance. "In the interest of delineating some broad patterns," he chooses to deliberately overlook the "great particularity of each and every form of subordination" (xi) and to focus instead on ways "we might more successfully read, interpret, and understand the often fugitive political conduct of subordinate groups" (xii). The catalyst pushing Scott was an awareness that he, too, acted differently when someone had power over him. He found that frequently he had to choke back responses in the name of prudence. But on those "rare occasions" when his anger or indignation got the best of him, he "experienced a sense of elation despite the danger of retaliation. Only then did I fully appreciate why I might not be able to take the public conduct of those over whom I had power at face value" (x).

Building on the foregoing studies, examples and insights, I offer the following working definitions as a guide for applying the concepts of carnival, resistance and transgression to the workplace.

Carnival: Traditional corporate events or occasions that are defined as out of the ordinary, where the usual, hierarchical constraints of the workplace are suspended. Similarly, any behavior, language or expression that breaches what is commonly held to be acceptable, workplace decorum can be considered "carnivalesque."

Resistance: Actions or expressions, verbal or nonverbal, that give voice to the stifled anger and sense of "lowness" that result from the employer-employee, high-low, management-staff dichotomies that *de facto* characterize the corporate workplace. Resistance is a "striking back," an oft-times symbolic gesture of indignation over exploitation, inequity, or loss of autonomy.

Transgression: Actions, postures or expressions that push to the limit or actually cross over the unwritten boundaries of socially (and hence corporately) acceptable behavior and good taste.

Sites of resistance

Scott's experience of the release that comes from striking back, even if that resistance is silent, led him to formulate the concept of "public" and "hidden transcripts." The public transcript represents conduct and discourse played out in public. He uses the term as a "shorthand way of describing the open interaction between subordinates and those who dominate" (Scott, 1990, 2). There is no reason to hide the public transcript since these expressions reinforce accepted, hegemonic social norms. From the time we were children, we have been taught how to behave in various situations. Both dominant and subordinate players know the rules—both explicit and implicit—for navigating power relationships. Play according to those rules constitutes the public transcript.

The hidden transcript, in constrast, is much more difficult to get at. It is the veiled response or reaction of people in subordinate positions to "more or less compelled performances" (Scott, 1990, 108). This hidden transcript is like a shadow or flicker; it fades in and out of view. When we see it, we get a glimpse of a concrete, oppositional reality that is at odds with the social conventions mandated by the dominant power structure. But because the hidden transcript is deliberately masked, it is possible to discount our momentary discomfiture at realizing the world may not be the way we want it to be. In its simplest form, the hidden transcript is the muted complaint, the forced smile, the cartoon on the back of the door. As often as not this "work of negation" (Scott, 1990, xi) is expressed openly, but in disguised or anonymous form. Examples are the raised eyebrow, the exchange of glances, or the sentence left hanging when a "higher-up" unexpectedly appears in the doorway of the employee lounge.

Sometimes, the hidden transcript takes on a multiplicity of meanings and is all the more threatening as a result. A good example is the anonymous April Fools' Day newsletter that surfaced in the doctor's lounge at a hospital where I used to work. In no time at all, copies of the newsletter, which parodied the 'official' house organ, turned up in employee lounges and on administrators' desks. Just as quickly, all copies disappeared—snatched up by physicians, nurses, technicians and administrators alike. Viewed by top management as subversive and mean-spirited, the newsletter was filled with operating room humor and jabs at the president. Reportedly, it was cleverly done—so clinically witty, in fact, that the hospital president and his top advisors were convinced it was the creation of a small group of doctors whom they had previously pegged as troublemakers. Rather than laugh at the parody and heed the discontent that inspired it, management immediately sought to "contain" the presumed potential for damage to its image by destroying all newsletters that they managed to get their hands on. So successful was the containment effort that copies of the underground newsletter were literally impossible to find later the same week.

Scott suggests that we can judge the fragility of ideological hegemony by how hard dominant groups work to wipe out the hidden transcript and the autonomous social sites that make its production possible. Building on that insight, I argue that we can identify corporate trouble spots by paying attention to efforts to minimize, erase, or counter communications that challenge management's image of itself. In the case of the newsletter, the hospital administration went to great lengths to determine its creators—even resorting to a crude deconstruction of grammar and syntax in an effort to identify the culprits. It is hard to say what would have befallen the perpetrators had they been positively identified, but my hunch is that management would have kept silent—using the information to feed the paranoia that too frequently invades the subconscious of people at the top.

I relate all of this in order to make several points. For one, Scott notes that the "elaboration of hidden transcripts depends . . . on the active human agents who create and disseminate them. The carriers are likely to be as socially marginal as the places they gather" (Scott, 1990, 123). The first part of that statement is relatively obvious. *People* resist, not words or images. But the second assertion carries an inherent irony. The hospital-wide consensus was that the newsletter was written by one or more doctors. Categorizing the authors and the doctor's lounge as "socially marginal" puts an enlightening twist on the incident. Historically, community hospitals were owned by doctors. They were established by physicians so that they could care for their patients more efficiently. Today, however, in the technocratic world of heavily regulated healthcare, many doctors feel powerless in institutions that could not survive without them. In essence, the newsletter was a sure sign that in that hospital, at that time, the hospital administration was the dominant elite and the physicians were striking back.

Transgressive behavior

Interestingly, physicians from this same hospital come to mind when I turn to the topic of transgression. Seven or so doctors, ranging in age from barely thirty to near-retirement, were performing a burlesque-type spoof in modified drag (somewhat transgressive in itself) for the hospital's semi-annual Follies, an amateur-talent fundraiser traditionally choreographed by a professional brought in from New York. The entire show was a far cry from 42nd St., but the doctors brought down the house when, at the end of their act, they turned around and one by one bared their buns to the audience. They didn't actually drop their drawers, but a few of them were wearing jockey shorts that were the briefest of brief. Like burlesque star Lydia Thompson and her troupe of "British Blondes," who took the New York stage by storm in 1868, the doctors appropriated "the existing tradition of burlesque—parodic, inversive send-ups of works of high culture—and rechanneled it" through the spectacle of the Follies (Allen, 1991, 45). Only in the doctors' case, the inversion parodied the chorus line, now a socially-accepted form of family entertainment. The transgression occurred when they "mooned" their audience—pushing to the limit the unwritten boundaries of acceptable behavior and good taste. Those boundaries are particularly rigid for members of the medical profession, to some extent because of their own efforts to remain aloof, not only from their patients but also from non-physician colleagues and acquaintances. Like most stereotypes, the foregoing observation deserves an in-depth examination to see if it holds some measure of truth, but that is a task for someone else.

Carnival connections

For now, the vision of the doctors' backsides provides a fitting transition to carnival: that fun-filled, colorful moment of "never-never time-space" which history professor Samuel Kinser (1990) describes as a "way of dreaming with others, publicly and responsively. Its qualities of inversion, of ambivalence, of conspicuous consumption and excess have to do with removal and escape from social calculations" (xvi) . . .

All but the most unfortunate among us have experienced carnival somewhere, sometime. Some have savored its southern flavors and undulating rhythms in New Orleans, Mobile, or Rio. Others have braved the frigid winds of the North to imbibe the irresistible high spirits of Winter Carnival in Quebec or St. Paul, MN. From the bingo tent at the small-town church dinner to the teeming Midway at a midwestern state fair, carnival is both an event and an ambiance, a place where day-to-day frustrations are banished in the pure exuberance of it all.

In *Carnival, American Style,* Kinser picks up on themes trumpeted by Mikhail Bakhtin, Victor Turner and, more recently, Peter Stallybrass and Allon White. In addition to qualities of inversion, ambivalence, and excess, carnival's themes typically include a fascination with the body, particularly its little-glorified or "lower strata" parts, and dichotomies between "high" or "low."

If anyone deserves credit for the academic community's current fascination with carnival, it is Bakhtin, a Russian theoretician who wrote *Rabelais and His World* during the late thirties. The book was submitted as a thesis to the Gorky Institute of World Literature in 1940 but was not published until after the Second World War. The English translation appeared in 1968, the same year as Chicago's bloody Democratic National Convention and France's equally tumultuous *evenements du mai* (Turkle, 1968). It may have been the shock of the 1960s uprisings, of familiar worlds turned upside down and inside-out, that caused both American and European intellectuals to pay close attention to Bakhtin. He himself voiced this caution: "No dogma, no authoritarianism, no narrow-minded seriousness can coexist with Rabelaisian images; these images are opposed to all that is finished and polished, to all pomposity, to every ready-made solution in the sphere of thought and world outlook" (Bakhtin, 1968, 3).

Carnival calls attention to "barriers omnipresent in daily life" (Kinser, 1990, xvii) . . . It deals in a range of "thou shalt not's" and calls attention to our less-than-admirable propensity for establishing our places in the world by repudiating the "low" (Stallybrass and White, 1986). Too often, it seems, we build our identities, our self-images on being "better" than someone else. It is this aspect of carnival—this high/low opposition—that holds particular fascination for Stallybrass and White. In *The Politics and Poetics of Transgression,* they urge the academic community to pay attention to the *binary extremism* (26) that affects our society, a binary extremism defined by the 'high' and the 'low.' These "underlying structural features of carnival," they argue, "operate far beyond the strict confines of popular festivity and are intrinsic to the dialectics of social classification as such" (26).

And I, in turn, suggest that it is these very structural features that spark acts of resistance and transgression in the workplace. Until recently, most of us have had neither words nor theories to explain the hidden transcript, the carnivalesque laugh, or the political humor of a buzzard on the back of a door. We probably haven't looked for them; instead we have lashed out or sought to quash "signs" that we don't understand. Hence, when the doctors voiced resistance by publishing an underground newsletter, management did its very best to snatch up every copy. Clamping down rather than asking "what's amiss?" has been the typical response.

It is not that the themes of these political scientists, literary theorists, or cultural critics have been absent from the corporate culture literature. We just haven't "seen" them for what they are. Armed with this new vocabulary, however, we can be on the lookout for evidence of the carnivalesque, resistance, and transgression in our organizations. The following bracketed guide to Townsend's (1970) *Up the Organization* demonstrates how it can be done.

In his opening salvo, Townsend invites readers to dip into *Up the* [billingsgate: Bakhtin's term for "curses, oaths, slang, humour, popular tricks and jokes, scatalogical forms, in fact all the 'low' and 'dirty' sorts of folk humour" (Stallybrass and White, 1986, 8)] *Organization* wherever the spirit moves them. "If you don't get at least a hollow laugh [carnivalesque] *and* a sharpened need to kick that 200-foot sponge you work for [resistance and transgression], then throw the book away . . . There are already too many organizational orthodoxies [high/low] imposed [by the dominant] on people, and I don't want to help the walking dead [grotesque body] institute another one" (Townsend, 1970, 9).

Bakhtin was fascinated with the grotesque. He was struck, Stallybrass and White observe, by the "compelling difference between the human body as represented in popular festivity and the body as represented in classical statuary in the Renaissance. He noticed how the two forms of iconography 'embodied' utterly contrary registers of being" (Stallybrass and White, 1986, 21). Picture, for example, the silky lines and exalted physique of Michelangelo's David. Compare that image with the grotesque, teeming, dirty bodies that crowd the sixteenth century canvases of Hieronymus Bosch or Bruegel (Stallybrass and White, 21). The contrast is a vivid reminder of how we put certain members of our corporate structures up on pedestals and at the same time constantly remind their subordinates of their "puniness" (Bazin, 1959) by continuing to use such organizational anachronisms as uniforms, time clocks and mandated lunch times.

Townsend's solution for a corporate America that has become "a nation of office boys," is nonviolent guerrilla warfare. "Start dismantling our organizations where we're serving them," he advises, "leaving only the parts where they're serving us. It will take millions of such subversives to make much difference" (Townsend, 1970, 11). Updated in 1984, *Further Up the Organization* is as insightful and fun to read today as its forerunner of twenty years ago. Its very durability underscores the utility of viewing the corporate world through the lenses of carnival, resistance, and transgression.

"Fun" and "utility" are key words, here. They should drive all that we do. I'll bet Townsend thoroughly enjoyed writing *Up the Organization.* I love his fantasy about the "vice-president in charge of anti-bureaucratization," a transgressive position if ever there was one. Functionally positioned under the heading "INSTITUTION, ON NOT BECOMING AN," this V.P. must have, "a loud voice, no fear, and a passionate hatred for institutions and their practices . . . it's his job to wander around the company looking for new forms, new staff departments, and new reports. Whenever he finds one that smells like institutionalization, he screams 'Horseshit!' at the top of his lungs. And keeps shouting until the new whatever-it-is is killed" (Townsend, 1970, 106).

Looking for signs

Identifying the seams between management prerogative—the 'high'—and employee responsibility or contribution—the 'low'—can be as enlivening as it is serious. But in order to 'see' those seams, we need to know what we are looking for and where to look. Enter *semiotics:* the study of signs. As Arthur A. Berger (1984) says, "We are all semioticians, even if we don't recognize it or understand the technicalities of the subject" (Berger, 1984, x). In *Signs in Contemporary Culture.* Berger, a professor of broadcast communication arts at San Francisco State University, points out that we "all know about status symbols; we all talk about 'images'; and we all read articles in newspapers and magazines about 'body language' and 'dressing for power' " (x).

Going a step further, I suggest that if effective communications requires a thorough understanding of the intended audience, then those in charge of communicating had best pay attention to the 'signs' and 'practices' of that audience—particularly the signs and practices tucked away in hidden transcripts.

Acting on what is seen

This case study has focused on the internal audience, the individuals who people our organizations—each characterized by a unique culture (Jermier, Slocum, Fry & Gaines, 1991). We can learn a great deal about out organizations and how they are perceived up and down the corporate ladder by paying attention to the acts of resistance, carnival, and transgression that imbue the corporate workplace. "Just as an involuntary twitch of the eyelid can be interpreted as a wink by those aware of a code in which doing so counts as a conspiratorial signal, an official culture may be viewed by those aware of deeper meanings entailed as a planned deception" (Geertz, 1973, as cited in Jermier, Slocum, Fry & Gaines, 170).

Scott (1990) calls such deception "artful disguise." I see it as an everyday part of corporate life, present in the cartoons taped to a secretary's "out basket" and in the jibes and jabs of a retirement roast. The challenge is to recognize in such expressive gestures the "points of antagonism, overlap and intersection between the high and the low, the classical and its 'Other'" (Stallybrass and White, 1986, 25). Finding previously unseen "transcripts" should remind us of the fragility of our "precarious and conditional" chains of command (Storey, 1983, 189, as cited in Golding, 1991, 569). Taking a closer look at the friction points between high and low can be illuminating, as illustrated by one last deconstruction of a typical corporate event. Let's turn to the annual employee picnic, a ritualized and sometimes carnivalesque performance engaged in by many of the corporations I've known. Its manifest purposes are several:

- to say thank you to employees and their families for all the time, effort, and loyalty they've invested in the corporation;
- to make visible management's avowed commitment to the egalitarian ideal of full employee participation in the mission of the organization;

- to celebrate a year of hard work with food, drink, and merrymaking.

All well and good, but even better if the organizers 'tune-in' to the themes of carnival, resistance, and transgression. When they do, they will see the ambivalence some employees feel when availing themselves of the opportunity to pummel the supervisor perched atop the 'dunk tank.' Pick up on the 'transgressive remarks' made just within earshot of your CEO, as he flips hamburgers in his just-for-the-occasion bermuda shorts. In theory, a healthy 'levelling' of high and low status occurs when the boss puts on his barbecue hat and apron. In fact, however, the not-for-the-boss's-ears remarks suggest that some employees see the symbolic gesture as a calculated effort to reinforce management's 'high' standing. Management, in turn, would do well to examine its motives for hosting such events.

But rather than spoil all the fun, as Kinser fears he will do by applying historical, cultural, and sociological analysis to Mardi Gras (xi), let me conclude with an observation made by Victor Turner, in his foreword to *Symbol and Politics in Communal Ideology* (1975). He wrote: "The most harmonious-seeming ideologies, cosmologies, ritual systems, legal codes, and political constitutions have the chaos dragon in their hidden hearts" (in Moore and Myerhoff, 1975, 7). When management catches a glimpse of the dragon's fire and feels its hot breath, it can either attack or back-off and consider what's feeding the flames. In the case of the physicians' underground newsletter, hospital management chose the former action and sought to stomp out the problem by eliminating its expression. Had they instead looked for the cause of physician resistance, they might have avoided a subsequent, and far more public expression of discontent by making a genuine effort to work more cooperatively with physicians.

Looking for and seeking to understand the 'chaos dragon' will make us more sensitive communicators and effective advisers. If management can use employee (or subordinate) resistance and transgression as opportunities for identifying counterproductive management actions and policies, and resolving problems, then it will have found a valuable tool. And we corporate communicators will have an easier job and a lot more fun, even if it's tinged with the ambivalence of Bakhtin's carnivalesque laughter.

References

Allen, R. C. 1991. The leg business: transgression and containment in american burlesque. *camera obscura,* 23, 43–71.

Bakhtin, M. M. 1968. *Rabelais and his world.* Trans. by Helene Iswolsky. 1984. Bloomington: Indiana University.

Barker, J. 1989. Peasant farmers as citizens. Ch. 8. In Barker. *Rural Communities Under Stress: Peasant Farmers and the State in Africa,* 162–194. Cambridge: Cambridge University.

Bazin, G. 1959. *A history of art: from prehistoric times to the present.* New York: Bonanza.

Berger, A. A. 1984. *Signs in contemporary culture: an introduction to semiotics.* New York: Longman.

Fiol, C. M. 1991. Seeing the empty spaces: towards a more complex understanding of the meaning of power in organizations. *Organization Studies,* 12, 547–566.

Golding, D. 1991. Some everyday rituals in management control. *Journal of Management Studies,* 28, 569–583.

Guha, R. 1989. Saboteurs in the forest: colonialism and peasant resistance in the indian himalaya. In Forrest Colburn, ed., *Everyday Forms of Peasant Resistance,* 64–92. Armonk, N.Y.: M. E. Sharpe.

Hoagland, S. L. 1988. *Lesbian ethics: toward new values.* Palo Alto: Institute of Lesbian Ethics.

Jermier, J. M., J. W. Slocum, Jr., L. W. Fry, and J. Gaines. 1991. Organizational subcultures in a soft bureaucracy: Resistance behind the myth and facade of an official culture. *Organization Science,* 2, 170–194.

Kinser, S. 1990. *Carnival, american style.* Chicago: University of Chicago.

Moore, S. F., and B. G. Myerhoff, eds. 1975. *Symbol and politics in communal ideology.* Foreword and epilogue. Ithaca: Cornell University.

Newbury, C., and B. G. Schoepf. 1989. State, peasantry, and agrarian crisis in Zaire: does gender make a difference? In Parpart, J. L. and Staudt, K. A., eds., *Women and the State in Africa,* 91–110. Boulder: Lynne Rienner.

Scott, J. C. 1985. *Weapons of the weak.* New Haven: Yale University.

Scott, J. C. 1990. *Domination and the arts of resistance.* New Haven: Yale University.

Stallybrass, P., and A. White. 1986. *The politics and poetics of trans-gression*. Ithaca: Cornell University.

Townsend, R. 1970. *Up the organization*. New York: Alfred A. Knopf.

Townsend, R. 1984. *Further up the organization*. New York: Knopf.

Turkle, S. R. 1968. Symbol and festival in the french student upris-ing (May-June 1968). 1975. In Moore and Myerhoff, eds. *Symbol and politics in communcal ideology* 68–100. Ithaca: Cornell University.

Further Reading

Berne, Eric. *Games People Play*. NY: Grove Press, 1964.

Deal, Terrence E., and Allan A. Kennedy. *Corporate Cultures: The Rites and Rituals of Corporate Life*. Reading, MA: Addison-Wesley Publishers, 1982.

"Does the Baldrige Award Really Work?" *Harvard Business Review* (January-February 1992): 126–147.

Fayol, Henri. *General and Industrial Management* (trans.). London: Pitman, 1916, 1949.

Kanter, Rosabeth. *Men and Women of the Corporation*. NY: Basic Books, 1977.

Katzenstein, Gary. *Funny Business: An Outsider's Year in Japan*. Englewood Cliffs, NJ: Prentice-Hall, 1990.

Kidder, Tracy. *The Soul of a New Machine*. NY: Avon Books, 1981.

Mamet, David. *Glengarry Glen Ross*. NY: Grove Weidenfeld, 1984. (Pulitzer Prize winning play in 1981; movie version, 1992).

Malcolm Baldridge National Quality Award, National Institute of Standards and Technology, U.S. Department of Commerce.

"Organizational Culture: Techniques Companies Use to Perpetuate or Change Beliefs and Values," United States General Accounting Office Report GAO/NSIAD–92–105. Washington, D.C.: GAO, February 1992.

Ott, J. Steven. *The Organizational Culture Perspective*. Pacific Grove, CA: Brooks/Cole Publishing, 1989.

Ouchi, William. *Theory Z: How American Business Can Meet the Japanese Challenge*. Reading, MA: Addison-Wesley, 1981.

Peters, Tom, and Robert Waterman. *In Search of Excellence*. NY: Harper and Row, 1982.

Sathe, Vijay. *Culture and Related Corporate Realities: Texts, Cases, and Readings on Organizational Entry, Establishment, and Change*. Homewood, IL: Irwin, 1985.

Stewart, James B. *Den of Thieves*. NY: Simon & Schuster, 1991.

Symbols and Artifacts: Views of the Corporate Landscape. Pasquale Gagliardi, ed. Belgirate, Italy: ISTUD-Instituto Studi Direzionali, 1990.

Taylor, Frederick. *The Principles of Scientific Management*. NY: Norton, 1911.

Thomas, R. Roosevelt. *Beyond Race and Gender: Unleashing the Power of Your Total Workforce by Managing Diversity.* NY: AMACOM, 1991.

"Woman at Work," *Management Review* (March 1992): Issue devoted to women's issues in changing corporate cultures.

Corporate Culture in the Movies and On TV

"L.A. Law," NBC.

"Murphy Brown," CBS.

"Network," MGM, 1976.

"Roger and Me," Warner Brothers, 1989.

"Tucker," LucasFilm, 1988.

"Wall Street," 20th Century Fox, 1987.

6

Corporate Communication and Meeting the Press

❖

Michael B. Goodman

Overview

You've had a very productive day at your office in the corporation's headquarters of an internationally known maker of low-fat additives for the prepared food industry, and you are leaving for the day. As you unlock your car you are approached in a non-threatening way by an individual who says she represents the local newspaper. She has some concerns about the report she received over the wire service and which she heard repeated that afternoon on CNN that a research laboratory in Sweden has found links between no-fat sweeteners and heart disease in its latest experiments on rats.

What do you do?

Your response in such a hypothetical situation has a lot to do with corporate identity and corporate culture, the issues covered in previous chapters. These two forces will guide you to the action you take no matter what the experts say is the best way to handle relations with the press.

If your corporate culture says your day ends when you leave your desk, you might shrug and say you are going home for the day, offering to see the reporter about it tomorrow. The reporter of course has a deadline and knows that tomorrow will be too late. The other paper in town will have had the story and some comment from the company by then. You meant not to be a block, but the reporter sees you as one. Frustrated, she is determined to find out what you are hiding.

On the other hand if your company has made a point of creating a professional and productive relationship with the press, you might look up a bit puzzled, say you have been buried all day in an annual financial report, but asked the reporter to follow you back to your office where you place a few calls to the R&D department and the public affairs officer and see if the reporter can come to the lab and ask a few questions related to the news wire report and the CNN broadcast.

If the latter is the case, your organization is seen by the press as a source of information and expertise on the topic. Your company becomes a part of the solution, not the problem.

Creating good relations with the media requires constant effort and attention.

Wall Street: The financial press

What is the relationship of corporate communications and the company's bottom line? Most experts and practitioners have come to agree that good corporate communications can improve the company's financial position, keep managers out of trouble with the Securities Exchange Commission, and help protect against unfriendly takeover attempts. Companies must communicate clearly their financial expectations and long term outlook. Investors and investment analysts are interested in just such information in making a decision about investment for themselves and their clients. Annual reports, 10-K and 10-Q reports, and quarterly reports are among the documents required by law for the SEC, the stock exchanges, and stock holders. These fundamental documents can be used to communicate the corporation's vision for the future while providing the detailed financial analysis needed by stockholders, regulators, and the financial press.

The legal policy of "materiality" has evolved through regulatory changes and decisions. It requires a publicly held company to disclose all information that can have an impact on the profit or financial position of the organization. Such disclosures are done through information wire services—Dow Jones and Reuters.

Communication with individual investors and with institutional investors such as pension plans and annuities is also done on a daily and periodic basis through the business and financial press. Relations with the financial press usually means *The Wall Street Journal, Business Week, The Financial Times, Barrons, Forbes,* and other periodicals devoted to general business news. Firms invest a great deal of effort to develop positive relations with these media so reporters and editors come to them for information about the company or the industry. Also corporations place ads in these periodicals for a variety of goals, from greeting a new corporate officer, to setting the record straight for investors on issues and rumors about the company.

Placing articles explaining a corporation's position on a merger, acquisition, restructuring, or downsizing can have a positive impact on the image the company creates in the minds of the investor community. These management decisions reflect how well the organization manages changes and the stress that accompanies it. A solid relationship with the press can benefit the organization through an objective report in the press.

Main Street: The hometown media

The newspapers and local radio and TV stations will cover your company from the local angle. If your organization has a substantial presence in the community, any slight change in the size of your national workforce or global strategy will make the front page on Main Street, U.S.A. With this in mind, make sure the corporation's representatives in the community and the ones at the home office have had substantial contact with one another before the information is reported. Such conversation ensures consistency in the information given to the reporters. The implication is for careful planning. Good relations with the press are nurtured.

A local media strategy is just as important as a global one. A process approach can be applied locally as well as globally. The process follows a problem-solving model and is simple to remember.

First, define the problems or issues. Write the problem down as a statement, and analyze the situation it is in. The analysis requires research—the gathering, processing, and interpretation of information. The most fundamental research method is listening and observing. Many Total Quality programs are based on the dictum, "listen to your customer," and your customer may be a fellow employee as well. Everyone you contact should be considered your customer. Other forms of research include: Delphi groups (experts in the field), surveys, interviews, focus groups, advisory committees and boards, media content analysis, analysis of incoming mail, government or commercial poll results. Your interpretation of the information you gather helps you to confirm the problem statement, or to restate it in light of your interpretations. The results of your analysis should lead to planning the next step in the problem-solving model.

Second, planning demands articulating goals and objectives and developing a program of actions and activities to achieve the goals. It also consists of identifying the audiences or "publics," the goals for each, the message and media strategies determined to meet the goals, and the budget schedule and other resources that must be committed to the program. Planning also involves planning for the evaluation of the performance of the program.

Third, implement the plans and communicate the messages. Here the fundamentals of the communication process offer the key to successful implementation of the plans. Understanding the corporate goals and objectives, fitting them to the audience needs and expectations, and being mindful of the context in which the communication occurs applies here and in all communication efforts. The goal is to change the thinking and behavior of the audience. To meet that goal the audience 1) becomes aware of the idea or message, 2) becomes interested and seeks more information, 3) evaluates the pros and cons of the idea and decides to try it, 4) applies the idea on a trial basis, and 5) if the idea is acceptable, it is adopted into normal behavior or practice.

Fourth, evaluation of the process. The evaluation of the effectiveness of the program can vary from the number of column inches or the number of minutes on the air the effort generated; to the increased awareness of the issues measured in the target audience; to changes in attitudes, opinions, or behaviors; to evidence of economic, social or political change. The criteria and evaluation methods must be determined as the program is planned and as it evolves.

Park Avenue: National newspapers

We have only a handful of national newspapers that claim as their mission the daily reporting of news of the U.S. and the world. *The New York Times* and *The Washington Post,* and to a lesser degree *The Los Angeles Times* [*The Wall Street Journal* is included in the financial press, but you could easily include it in the general news category since business is involved in everything], consider themselves newspapers of record. They report any event of importance for the country and the world and generally make their reports available to the world through their wire services.

Corporations of any size scan these newspapers every morning for stories and information. They create a company briefing book of the clips and circulate it among their officers, alerting them of any news related to the corporation, its products, the industries it is a part of, or stories related to its core business strategy.

These few national newspapers have enormous impact on public opinion and on general attitudes. The stories they run tend to set the agenda for other media, particularly television news programs and cable network programming. Even though broadcast media cover late breaking stories very well, they are weak in the coverage of business, economic, and financial news. How often do you see on TV news of trade negotiations such as the GATT (General Agreement on Tariffs and Trade) or the International Monetary Fund (IMF) discussions of loans to Russia? Even scandals such as insider trading, BCCI, and the S&L failures are often reduced to pictures of the defendants coming or going to a courtroom or hearing. It is the print media that still covers business in depth, with the exception of cable news programs devoted to business issues. Even *USA Today,* as a national newspaper, is more like a series of sound bytes or headlines that you might see on CNN Headline News.

Industrial Boulevard: The trade publications

Trade and industry specific newspapers and periodicals offer businesses a medium specific to their business. These publications are mainly closed circulation periodicals; that is, the people who receive the publication are involved in the industry in some way. Further, the publications have either paid or free subscriptions. The free subscription periodicals are generally regarded as promotional vehicles for the industry or trade, giving advertisers a controlled audience. The paid publications generally work with a clear journalistic separation between the editorial content of the reporting and the advertising department. Such publications are seen as more objective and thus containing more reliable information. Examples include *Aviation Week and Space Technology* for the aerospace industry and *Publishers Weekly* for the book and magazine industry.

Research Plaza: Professional journals

Professional journals have long been the main vehicle for communication of research findings in every field. Their very existence and value depend on objective editorial policies. Most do not accept advertising because of hint of bias. Some however, accept ads from professional organizations and groups for conferences, books and other publications. We might put *Harvard Business Review* in this group for general management theory even though it runs ads for upscale automobiles and liquor.

The best way to develop relations with such publications is through support in a general way of professional societies and organizations which in turn support the publications.

Broadway: Entertainment media

Social events related to charity functions are often the only time a corporation appears in the entertainment media, unless of course the corporation is part of the entertainment industry.

Corporations are often included in the entertainment media if they become sponsors of media happenings such as the opera, philharmonic, or Shakespeare Company; or the Super Bowl, The Olympics, or other sporting events.

Selected Essays and Comment

The essay and case study selected for this chapter are from the presentations at the annual Conference on Corporate Communication at Fairleigh Dickinson University. Each of the authors focuses on a part of corporate communications theory and practice that is associated with meeting the press.

Dr. Dulcie Straughan examines the actions by the Food and Drug Administration (FDA) in regulating the public relations actions by pharmaceutical companies in promoting prescription drugs. Her article explores the impact of considering such activity commercial speech or fully protected speech under the First Amendment. Ruling on commercial speech has involved advertising, not public relations.

Dr. Nancy VanArsdale looks into the editorial policy decision of *Time* magazine to take a stand on the environment in 1988, but also to offer solutions to the problem. The magazine also sponsored a public relations program, "The Environmental Challenge," to create awareness on the environmental crisis facing planet earth. The case study examines the public relations program in relation to two trends, advocacy journalism and environmental business communications programs.

Public Relations and Commercial Speech at the Crossroads: Implications for the Pharmaceutical Industry and for the Profession

❖

Dulcie Murdock Straughan

In recent years the Food and Drug Administration has begun to regulate closely public relations activities by pharmaceutical companies on behalf of their prescription drug products. This paper examines FDA actions over the past eight years to determine whether the agency is acting within its regulatory bounds or whether it is encroaching on pharmaceutical companies' First Amendment rights to free speech. The paper will address whether public relations activity by pharmaceutical companies would be considered commercial speech by the courts, or whether it would be afforded full First Amendment protection, thereby limiting the FDA's power to regulate it. Commercial speech case law will be reviewed to provide some context for answering this question. Because no commercial speech case to date has involved public relations activity per se, but rather advertising, this paper will discuss how the courts might apply decisions from key U.S. Supreme Court commercial speech cases to a public relations case.

Growth of public relations activities by pharmaceutical companies

Content analysis studies of U.S. newspapers over the years have shown an increased amount of space devoted to health-related news. One such study by a public relations agency found that as much as one-quarter of newspapers' newsholes were devoted to health stories (Dilenschneider, 1983: 10). Health-related stories that have received extensive newspaper coverage in the past few years cover a wide variety of topics, from the discovery, spread and treatment of AIDS to the development of a successful hair-growing drug to treat balding men, to studies of drugs designed to treat various types of cancers.

National news magazines also have increased health coverage. An example is the cover story of the March 16, 1990, issue of *Newsweek,* which extols the development of a new "breakthrough drug" for depression (1990: 38).

More frequent media coverage of health-related news is due in part to an increased interest in such news on the part of the public. The *Physician's Desk Reference,* which provides detailed information on prescription drugs and was once available only to physicians and pharmacists, is now one of the largest selling books in the country (Rheinstein, 1982: 332).

Increased monitoring of FDA activities by special interest groups concerned with issues of drug safety and efficacy also created more media interest in covering prescription drug development and approval.

Additionally, the past thirty years have been a time of significant drug developments, such as AZT (the AIDS drug), drugs to treat various cancers and psychotropic drugs for the treatment of mental illnesses.

Finally, there has been an increased push by consumers to get more information from their physicians about new drug therapies and from the pharmaceutical companies that develop and market prescription products.

What has this meant to pharmaceutical companies? Where they used to concentrate their efforts on informing their traditional publics—physicians, pharmacists and other health care professionals—about their prescription drug products, and to rely on reports of prescription drug developments in medical journals or on their pharmaceutical sales representatives to persuade physicians to prescribe their products, they now spend more time and money informing the consumer directly (Pines, 1989).

Together, U.S. pharmaceutical companies spend approximately $150 million a year on public relations activities (Hyman, 1990: 22).

It is precisely these activities that the FDA has begun to regulate. In every instance of FDA action against a pharmaceutical company for what it has considered to be violations, the company in question complied with the agency's orders. But company officials have questioned whether the FDA has the authority to regulate their public relations activities.

Authority of FDA

The FDA is the federal regulatory agency charged with reviewing and approving for marketing prescription and over-the-counter drugs. And, since 1962 when the Food, Drug and Cosmetic Act was amended, it was given authority to review advertising for prescription drugs to make certain it was not false and misleading (21 CFR 312).

Public relations activities are not mentioned in that Act, so when the FDA first began to regulate public relations efforts by pharmaceutical companies, it did so by existing regulations from the advertising and labeling sections of the act. Section 201(m) of the Act defines labeling as, "All labels and other written, printed, or graphic matter (1) upon any article or any of its containers or wrappers, or (2) accompanying such article." (21 CFR 312) Section 502(n) cites specific requirements for prescription drug advertising.

The FDA has the authority to declare a drug misbranded, which means that the agency can actually seize the drug product and prevent it from being sold. Section 502(a) of the Code states that a drug "shall be deemed to be misbranded if its labeling is false and/or misleading in any particular."

Before a drug receives approval for marketing from the FDA, the pharmaceutical company and the agency agree on wording for the information that appears on the product label and on the package insert. Typically, information about how the drug should be used, who should take it, and potential adverse effects is included. These statements are also used by pharmaceutical sales representatives and for advertising copy in medical journals (Salitsky, 1984).

Much of the public relations activities occur at the time of a new drug's approval for marketing by the FDA. More recently, public relations activities may occur while drug studies in humans are being conducted. Preliminary results of drug testing in humans may be reported in medical and scientific journals, or may even receive wider coverage in the lay press, as has been the case in recent years with a number of important drugs, such as AZT.

Is public relations activity labeling?

The FDA's claim that public relations activities are labeling and subject to content regulation dates from 1982 when FDA official Kenneth Feather said in a speech to the Pharmaceutical Manufacturers' Association that the FDA began to treat press releases and press kits as labeling when pharmaceutical companies started to release information about new drugs to the public that it considered inappropriate (1982). In recent months, said Feather, a number of press releases issued by companies about new drugs contained false and misleading information, said Feather. And, while the FDA did not want to regulate all press kits and require pre-clearance of public relations materials, "we want it known that the FDA feels these press releases are labeling. . . . " (1982).

Feather made clear that the FDA considered press releases to be commercial speech, noting that, "They (the Supreme Court) have firmly established that commercial free speech can be regulated to make sure it is truthful and not misleading" (1982).

Since 1982, the FDA has taken action against pharmaceutical companies' public relations activities in more than 20 instances. Actions have included official citations and corrective orders to three drug companies for false and misleading press kits; issuance of a warning letter to a company that had sponsored a series of medical seminars, which the agency said violated rules concerning exchange of information regarding investigational drugs; and issuance of a warning letter to a company that paid for a press conference called by one of the drug's researchers to announce preliminary results of an ongoing drug study.

In each instance, the pharmaceutical company in question has complied with FDA demands for corrective action. But many companies questioned FDA authority to regulate public relations activities.

The first significant instance of FDA regulatory action over a pharmaceutical company's public relations activities occurred in 1982, when the FDA ordered Eli Lilly to issue a press release correcting an earlier one it had sent out about its newly approved arthritis drug.

A short time after the drug was approved for marketing by the FDA, the agency received reports of a number of deaths of people who had been taking the prescription drug. The FDA was concerned that the people who died had not been good candidates for taking the drug, but had received the drug because they put pressure on their physicians after hearing positive reports about it in the media.

In a regulatory letter to the pharmaceutical company, the FDA said that it was evident from media coverage that the company had communicated false and misleading information to the public through its press kit materials, which it said constituted misbranding of the drug. The FDA ordered Lilly to issue a corrective press release to all media outlets that had received the first press kit materials. More than 6,000 were distributed (Halperin, 1982).

In reply to the FDA order, Lilly's legal counsel stated that it was the company's opinion that the FDA had incorrectly applied labeling regulations to press kit materials, therefore making it inappropriate for the FDA to regulate that material. Counsel cited a passage from a 1978 FDA draft of working guidelines on company press releases for new drugs, which reads: "Press releases which mention prescription drugs by brand or generic name will not be regulated as promotional communications (e.g., advertisement or promotional labeling) unless the pharmaceutical supplier (or persons acting on their behalf) makes or offers payment for the insertion into any media, in which case it will be regulated as some form of advertising (advertisement of promotional labeling). Also regarded as advertising will be press releases that fail to label investigational uses and unapproved claims as such or which is not representative of what is known or should reasonably be known to the sponsor about the product discussed" (Holt, 1982).

Lilly's counsel acknowledged that media reports may have exaggerated the effectiveness of the drug. But, he stated, " ... media reports which may be oversimplified or erroneous are, to some extent, unavoidable whenever reporters write for laymen about complex scientific and medical matters. The only sure way of preventing this situation would be to ban the issuance of such information to the media, a course of action

that would obviously be foreclosed by the First Amendment"
(Holt, 1982). Lilly's counsel added that Lilly did not pay the
media to use the press kit materials they were sent.

Before this case was resolved, Lilly pulled the drug off
the market and the FDA rescinded its order for corrective
action (*Time,* 1982: 83).

In 1987, the FDA seemed to expand its definition of what
it considered to be labeling when it questioned ICN Pharmaceuticals about its relationship to *Pediatric Virology,* a medical journal that had published an article about Virazole, an
ICA drug that had been approved by the FDA in 1986. Although the drug was being tested for use in treating a variety
of conditions, the FDA's approval had limited its use to treatment of respiratory viral infections in infants. The journal
article discussed unapproved uses of the drug.

In its warning letter to the company about the journal
article, the FDA stated that it considered the medical publication to be labeling under the FDC Act because, "... your
firm provides sole sponsorship of the publication and the fact
that editorial independence is suspect because of the close
relationship of the publication's two editors to your firm." Both
editors were researchers for ICN, said the FDA (Rheinstein,
1986).

ICN complied with FDA's requests. It continued to support the publication financially, but stated it would not have
any other involvement with the publication, including submission of articles to the journal by ICN employees. In its
response to the agency ICN noted that, "ICN does provide
financial support for the publication, but does not exercise
any voice in its editorial policy or in the selection of articles
for inclusion. ... Moreover, we believe ICN has the right to
provide financial support to publications to ensure that physicians in this specialty area have access to information on
current developments" (Staffa, 1987).

More recently, the FDA has turned attention to pharmaceutical company sponsorship of scientific seminars and sponsorship of press conferences by researchers who wish to release
information about drugs under study. Its concern is with pre-
approval promotion of a drug.

The FDC Act gives the FDA authority over pre-approval
promotion. A pharmaceutical company may not disseminate
promotional material stating that a drug under investigation
is safe or useful. However, the Act states that "this regulation

is not intended to restrict the full exchange of scientific information concerning the drug, including dissemination of scientific findings in scientific or lay communications media . . . " (Subchapter D, Part 312.7, FDC Act). This exception raises questions about where promotion ends and scientific exchange begins.

The FDA took issue with a press conference held by a University of Michigan researcher to announce his findings of a study of Retin-A, a cream approved by the FDA for treatment of acne, but found to have beneficial effects on aging skin. Dr. John Voorhees' study examined use of the drug for repairing sun-damaged skin, an unapproved use of the drug. Ortho Pharmaceutical Corporation, makers of the drug, paid for the press conference.

The press conference was held the day after the *Journal of the American Medical Association* published an article on Dr. Voorhees' study of Retin-A.

The FDA objected to the press conference, stating that the researcher issued positive information about the results of one study for an unapproved use of the drug (Feather, 1988). In a regulatory letter to Ortho's legal counsel, the FDA stated, "Your firm, as the sponsor of Retin-A, is fully aware that it is illegal to promote a marketed drug for unapproved indications. While we understand that Dr. Voorhees was at liberty to hold a press conference and/or provide press materials on his own, your firm had the option of refusing to sponsor this activity." (Feather, 1988).

As a result of the FDA action, the company's affiliate, Johnson & Johnson, issued a release stating that it "wanted to put into perspective the widespread media interest in the past few days in a prescription skin cream that appears capable of improving the condition of skin aged by the sun" (1988). The release went on to say that the study was one of several clinical trials of the drug and its effects on aging skin.

These examples of FDA actions show that the agency has become more aggressive in seeking to control public relations activities by pharmaceutical companies. Is a court case imminent as pharmaceutical companies begin to question whether the FDA is overstepping its regulatory bounds?

If a case were to be heard, a court would have to consider whether public relations activities such as those mentioned are commercial speech or speech deserving of full protection under the First Amendment.

The FDA has stated quite clearly that it considers public relations activities to be commercial speech and, as such, subject to FDA regulation. That position was underscored by Kenneth Feather in a November 1988 speech. "Our position is that most company-sponsored public relations activities dealing with their product(s) can be considered to be promotional activities (i.e., commercial speech) which are subject to our regulation." He added, "We are considering cases on which to begin to take regulatory action based on that position."

Public relations: is it commercial speech?

Key commercial speech cases decided by the U.S. Supreme Court show how this area of the law has evolved and may indicate how the Court might look at public relations cases.

Commercial speech case law began in 1942, when the U.S. Supreme Court upheld a New York statute that prohibited the distribution of any "handbill, circular . . . or any other advertising matter whatsoever in or upon any street" *(Valentine v. Christensen).* In a similar case heard in 1951, the Court upheld the conviction of an individual who had violated an ordinance that prohibited door-to-door solicitation of magazine subscriptions *(Breard v. Alexandria).* The Supreme Court took the position that commercial expression is not entitled to First Amendment protection.

But in 1975 the Court modified its stance and began to offer limited protection for commercial speech.

In *Bigelow v. Virginia,* the Supreme Court said that advertising was entitled to First Amendment protection. The "relationship of speech to the marketplace of products or services does not make it valueless in the marketplace of ideas" (1975).

The Court reversed the conviction of the editor of a student newspaper at the University of Virginia for violating a state statute prohibiting the circulation of a publication that encouraged or promoted abortion. The newspaper had run an advertisement by a New York abortion referral service (1975).

The U.S. Supreme Court sought to define further commercial speech in a decision a year later. In *Virginia State Board of Pharmacy v. Virginia Citizens Consumer Council,* the Court nullified a state statute that forbade pharmacists from advertising prescription drug prices, noting that information such as this had value to the consumer (1976). In striking down the statute, the Court said that commercial speech, or "speech that proposes a commercial transaction," was deserving of some protection. However, commercial speech that is false or misleading may be regulated by the state (1976: 1830).

That consumers have a right to receive certain kinds of information like that classified as commercial speech was the emphasis in a number of cases involving advertisement of professional services.

In a 5-4 decision, the Court decided in *Bates v. State of Arizona* that "advertising by attorneys may not be subject to blanket suppression" (1977: 350). This decision effectively struck down the longstanding tradition of no advertising by attorneys, but did not really help to clarify just what constitutes commercial speech.

That same year the Court found in *Ohralik v. Ohio State Bar Association* that a lawyer's in-person solicitation of a client constituted commercial speech and therefore had "a limited measure of protection commensurate with its subordinate position in the scale of First Amendment values" (1977:456).

In a key case in 1980, the Supreme Court further clarified the distinction between commercial and fully protected speech and also laid out a four-step procedure on which courts could analyze commercial speech cases.

In *Central Hudson Gas & Electric Corporation v. Public Service Commission,* the Court held that a state regulation that banned utilities from advertising to promote electricity use violated that utility's First Amendment rights (1980:565). In attempting to delineate the differences between commercial and free speech, the Court described commercial speech as "speech related solely to the economic interests of both the speaker and the speaker's audience" (p. 561). The Court noted that, "Commercial expression not only serves the economic interest of the speaker, but also assists consumers and furthers the societal interest in the fullest possible dissemination of information" (p. 561).

In deciding commercial speech cases, the Court said, a court must examine four areas: First, to receive (limited) protection under the First Amendment, commercial speech must concern lawful activity and must not be misleading. If the court finds this to be the case, then it must determine whether the asserted government interest (in regulating the speech in question) is substantial. Then, the court must determine whether the regulation (that affected the speech) directly advances the government interest asserted, and finally; whether the regulation is more extensive that necessary to serve that interest (p. 566).

The Supreme Court acknowledged in a 1983 decision that determining whether certain speech is commercial or fully protected is not always easy. In *Bolger et al. v. Youngs Drug Products Corp.,* the Court said that advertising that links a product to important public issues or topics currently under discussion does not necessarily give it full protection under the First Amendment as noncommercial speech would have (p. 68).

The case involved a federal statute that prohibited the mailing of unsolicited ads for contraceptives. The Youngs Co., manufacturers of Trojan condoms, mailed informational pamphlets and advertisements to members of the public; the materials discussed the dangers of sexually transmitted diseases and the importance of using condoms to help reduce the spread of disease. In making its determination that the speech in question was commercial speech, the Court examined each of the pieces mailed. Most of the material included in the mailing fit the "core notion of commercial speech 'speech which does no more than propose a commercial transaction,'" said the court (p. 64).

But the pamphlets could not be so easily categorized, it added. "The mere fact that these pamphlets are conceded to be advertisements does not compel the conclusion that they are commercial speech" (p. 66). Neither does the fact that reference was made to a specific product or the fact that Youngs clearly is economically motivated. But, said the court, the combination of these factors provides strong support for their being labeled commercial speech, regardless of their discussion of sexually transmitted diseases (p. 66).

In its most recent decision involving commercial speech, the Supreme Court in *Board of Trustees of State University of New York v. Fox* (1989) seemed to narrow its definition of what constitutes commercial speech. The case involved a written policy of the University that prohibited private commercial enterprises from operating in university facilities. A Tupperware party held in a student's dorm room was stopped by the campus police. The salesperson was arrested and charged with trespass, soliciting without a permit and loitering (p. 3028).

The Court struck down the university policy. In its discussion, the Court stated that commercial speech is that "which proposes specific commercial transactions, which is the test for identifying commercial speech" (1989:3031).

In its decision, the Court excluded "paid speech providing job counseling, tutoring, legal advice and medical consultation," from the commercial speech category (p. 3029).

Clearly, the Court is not yet satisfied with its own definition of what constitutes commercial speech. What does this mean for pharmaceutical companies and their public relations activities?

Implications for public relations activities

While there are no definitive guidelines that distinguish clearly between commercial and traditional free speech, an examination of the key cases provides broad characteristics of commercial speech. In the major decisions, the content of speech defined as commercial involves a message that promotes a demand for a product or service. It also typically refers to a specific product or service and may discuss its attributes, such as price and quality. In *Bolger* (463 U.S. 60, 1983) the Court said that information about the health effects associated with a product may classify it as commercial. Finally, commercial speech is paid for by an individual or an organization.

While press kits about new products are distributed by organizations to help provide information to the media and the public, their purpose also is to promote a demand for a product. Such was the case in the Eli Lilly/Oraflex example mentioned earlier, and indeed, became the major focus of the controversy. As a *Time* magazine article noted in a story about the FDA action against Lilly, "Lilly had taken the bold course of promoting its product directly to the consumer, and the misleading claim was trumpeted in newspapers and on television" (*Time*, Sept 27, 1982: 83).

The story said that the widespread media coverage, based on press kit materials that implied the drug could retard the course of arthritis, caused a huge demand for the drug.

But there are significant differences between the Lilly case and commercial speech cases to this point: The media were not paid to use the material Lilly sent them; and the media could modify Lilly's message. Unlike advertising copy, which is controlled by the source, press release materials may be used in their entirety, edited, or simply thrown away.

These differences could have an impact on how the courts view such speech by pharmaceutical companies.

The courts have stated that all corporate speech is not commercial speech (*First National Bank of Boston v. Bellotti,* 1978). As Pratt notes, the courts have given limited First Amendment protection to corporate speech when it involves political discussions (1990: 212).

Also, in two U.S. Supreme Court cases and in a lower court decision, the definition of what constitutes commercial speech has been narrowed. These cases also dealt with activity more like public relations than advertising.

In *Pacific Gas and Electric Co. v. Public Utilities Commission of California,* the U.S. Supreme Court said that the public utility did not have to run an article in its monthly newsletter that stated the views on nuclear power of an opposing organization. The Court found the newsletter deserving of full protection under the First Amendment. Because the newsletter, which is distributed with its monthly bills, contains energy saving tips, recipes and stories, it "extends well beyond speech that proposes a business transaction and includes the kind of discussion of 'matters of public concern' that the First Amendment both fully protects and implicitly encourages" (p. 908).

A U.S. Court of Appeals found that *Ad World,* a community "shopper" distributed door-to-door could not be classified as commercial speech (*Ad World v. Doylestown,* 1982). The Court noted in its decision that "The Supreme Court has confined the category of commercial speech to cases involving purely commercial advertising" (p. 1136).

The U.S. Supreme Court's most recent commercial speech decision, *Board of Trustees of the State University of New York v. Fox,* also narrowed the commercial speech category. The Court found in that case that paid speech providing job counseling, tutoring, legal advice and medical consultation was excluded from the commercial speech category (1989: 3028).

How would these decisions have affected FDA regulatory activity over pharmaceutical companies like ICN, cited by the FDA for its financial sponsorship and close editorial ties to the medical journal, *Pediatric Virology?* It is possible the Court might have determined that the material contained in the journal was deserving of full protection under the First Amendment, given its reasoning in *Pacific Gas* or in *Ad World*.

What about a pharmaceutical company's sponsorship of a press conference where a researcher announces the results of a drug study? Counsel for the company could point to the Supreme Court's most recent decision in *SUNY v. Fox* and argue that speech by a researcher who presents study results at a press conference arranged for and paid by a pharmaceutical company would fall into a similar category.

But a strong argument for finding public relations activity by pharmaceutical companies to be commercial speech and therefore deserving of less protection under the First Amendment, is that of public safety.

A case involving the Federal Trade Commission and its regulation over nonprescription drug advertising provides evidence as to how the courts might rule in a case involving public relations promotional activity by a pharmaceutical company. In *Sterling Drug Co. v. FTC* (1985), the Supreme Court upheld an FTC order that barred unsubstantiated advertisements of superiority claims for certain nonprescription drugs. The Court said, "When drug advertising is at issue, the potential health hazards may well justify a more sweeping order than would be proper were the Commission dealing with a less consequential area." While this involved advertising, pure and simple, it is clear that the Court has concerns about prescription drug information.

Clearly the FDA has a stake in trying to ensure that the public is safe from harmful drugs. There is a danger that an unwary public may be exposed to misleading messages about a drug that could result in its inappropriate use. As one trade magazine article notes, "There is one qualitative distinction: unlike with advertising, the consumer is at a distinct disadvantage when evaluating the credibility of media that directly result from public relations efforts. If people are unaware of the real source of a message (i.e., the drug company or public relations firm), they may be more accepting of the message and perceive it as unbiased, compared to advertising channels, where the source of the message is understood" (*Perspectives*, March-April 1985: 8).

Judging by statements made by FDA official Feather last year, the FDA considers the question of payment a key factor in determining whether public relations activities by pharmaceutical companies would be classified as commercial speech. In a speech made to the Pharmaceutical Manufacturers' Association in March 1989, Feather said, "The space for a newspaper article may not be paid for, but the press materials and press conference lying behind the article from which the reporter got his/her information, are certainly paid for by the sponsor."

If at some future date the courts determine that public relations activities by pharmaceutical companies do constitute commercial speech, and thus may be regulated by the FDA, then other problems arise. The most troublesome one, for the federal agency and for pharmaceutical companies alike, will likely be the need for a formal review process for promotional materials.

Although FDA officials stated categorically in the early 1980s that they did not wish to get involved in pre-clearance of press kits, in recent years the FDA routinely asked to review companies' public relations materials announcing FDA approval of new drugs before they are released to the media. Although the FDA has no authority to do so under the Code, companies have been complying with the agency's request.

If press kit materials were considered to be speech deserving full protection under the First Amendment, such a review process would be considered prior restraint and therefore not allowed. But as the U.S. Supreme Court noted in *Central Hudson,* "we have observed that commercial speech is such a sturdy brand of expression that traditional prior restraint doctrine may not apply to it" (1980: 571).

However, if a review process were instituted, then it would have to contain safeguards for the pharmaceutical companies to assure that materials would be reviewed in a timely manner, as the court directed in *Freedman v. Md.* (1965). Publicly held companies also must follow SEC regulations on timely release of information.

Implementing such a system may prove difficult for the FDA, whose staff is already overworked and where the drug review process alone may take more than two years. And the more practical matter of providing the media with timely information may be more difficult, given the potential delays in FDA review of materials.

Also, the FDA needs to clarify its position on the difference between promotion and exchange of scientific information. Today, where there is strong media and public interest in health-related stories, and where leading medical journals issue press releases to the lay press about medical studies reported in their publications, therefore creating interest and demand for more information, pharmaceutical companies may be forced into playing a similar game. But the rules of the game need to be clearer.

Pharmaceutical companies and public relations practitioners must share the responsibility for adhering to the highest ethical standards in providing accurate information to the mass media about new drug therapies. There is no question that there have been abuses by public relations agencies and their clients in the past. If a pharmaceutical company uses a public relations agency to develop press materials, its own public relations and legal staff must review those materials carefully before they are distributed to the media.

One thing is certain: The FDA has stepped up its surveillance of public relations activity and moved to a position where, as one FDA staff member in the Division of Drug Advertising and Labeling said, " . . . to the fullest extent possible we believe that 'false and misleading' and 'fair balance' standards should be extended to press statements as well as advertising." With this attitude, it seems only a matter of time before a test case comes before the courts.

References

Ad World v. Doylestown, U.S. Ct. of Appeals, Third Circuit, 1982 627 F. 2d 1136 (3rd Cir.) cert denied, 456 US 975 (1982).

Bates v. State Bar of Arizona, 433 U.S. 350 (1977).

Bigelow v. Virginia, 421 U.S. 809 (1975).

Board of Trustees of the State University of New York v. Fox, 109 S. Ct. 3028 (1989).

Bolger v. Youngs Drug Products Corp., 463, U.S. 60 (1983).

Breard v. Alexandria, 341 U.S. 622 (1951).

Central Hudson Gas & Electric Co. v. Public Service Commission, 447 U.S. 557 (1980).

Consolidated Edison Co. v. Public Service Commission, 447 U.S. 530 (1980).

Dilenschneider, Robert L. "Pre-approval promotions and guidelines," *Medical Marketing and Media,* Vol. 18, No. 6, 10–14 (June 1983).

F.D.C. Reports, Aug. 9, 1982, p. 5.

Federal Food, Drug and Cosmetic Act, 21 CFR 202.1 (1) (2), 201(m), 501(a).

Feather, Kenneth R. In speech to Pharmaceutical Manufacturers' Association, Washington, D.C., March 14, 1989.

————. In speech to New York State Bar Association, N.Y., N.Y., Jan. 19, 1989.

————. In speech at Pharmaceutical Marketing Symposium, Washington, D.C., Nov. 10, 1988.

————. In speech to Pharmaceutical Manufacturers' Association, Washington, D.C., Sept. 15, 1982.

————. Acting Director, Div. of Drug Advertising and Labeling, Office of Drug Standards, FDA, in letter to Russell Hume, Executive director, regulatory affairs, Ortho Pharmaceutical Corporation, March 10, 1988.

Freedman v. Md., 380 U.S. 51 (1965).

Friedman v. Rogers, 440 U.S., 1 (1979).

Halperin, Jerome A., in FDA regulatory letter to Richard Wood, chairman of board and president, Eli Lilly and co., July 27, 1982.

Holt, John, legal counsel for Eli Lilly, in letter to Arthur Yellin, FDA, Aug. 25, 1982.

Hyman, Don. "Pharmaceuticals: Balancing the demands of diverse publics." *PR Journal,* Oct. 1990, 22–25.

Molotsky, Irvin. "F.D.A. tells company to revise drug description." *N.Y. Times,* April 13, 1986, p. 14Y.

Morris, Louis A. Div. of Drug Advertising and Labeling, FDA, in speech to Pharmaceutical Manufacturers' Association, Washington, D.C., June 1989.

Newsweek. "The power of Prozac," March 26, 1990. 38–41.

Ohralik v. Ohio State Bar Association, 98 S. Ct. 436 U.S. 447 (1977).

Pacific Gas and Electric Co. v. Public Utilities Commission of California, 106 S. Ct. 903 (1980).

Pines, Wayne. "Overview of current industry communication activities," from *Proceedings of the workshop of Innovations in pharmaceutical promotion: marketing public relations and advertising.* Sponsored by the Food and Drug Law Institute, Oct. 4, 1989.

Pratt, Catherine A. "First amendment protection for public relations expression: The applicability and limitations of the commercial and corporate speech models." *Public Relations Research Annual.* Vol. 2, 1990, 205–217.

Rheinstein, Peter H. "A head start, a broader audience, and an emphasis on difference: the new frontiers of prescription drug promotion." *Food, Drug and Cosmetic Law Journal* 37 at 332 (1982).

———. Director, Office of Drug Standards, Center for Drugs and Biologics, in regulatory letter to Milan Panic, Chairman of Board, ICN Pharmaceuticals, Inc., March 24, 1986.

Salitsky, Ann, member, legal counsel, Burroughs Wellcome Co. Personal interview. Dec. 8, 1984.

Staffa, Jeffrey A. Vice President, regulatory affairs, Viratek, Inc., in letter to Kenneth R. Feather, Dir. of Drug Advertising and Labeling, Office of Drug Standards, FDA, July 30, 1987.

Sterling Drug Co. v. FTC, 741 F.2d 1146 (9th Cir. 1984), cert denied, 470 U.S. 1084 (1985).

Time, "Excess marks the spot," Sept. 27, 1982, 83.

Virginia State Board of Pharmacy v. Virginia Citizens Consumer Council, 425 U.S. 748 (1976).

Washington Drug Letter, Vol. 14, No. 48, Nov. 29, 1982.

Case Study of a Public Affairs Program: *Time* Magazine's "Environmental Challenge"

❖

Nancy VanArsdale

In 1988 *Time* modified its year-end tradition; instead of selecting an individual, the editors named "The Planet of the
Year." Their choice was linked to a new commitment to more
provocative journalism in an increasingly competitive era of
news source proliferation. In that article and others that
followed, *Time* not only probed environmental problems, but
also tendered solutions. Media experts elsewhere pointed to
the approach as an example of the emerging trend in advocacy journalism and questioned the ethics involved. *Time* editors responded that such positions should be scrutinized, but
one topic clearly could be advocated without question: the
preservation of planet earth. Subsequently, the publisher announced the magazine's sponsorship of a public relations program, "The Environmental Challenge," that would further
heighten awareness of the crisis. This paper will examine
the components of that public affairs program in relation to
two trends, advocacy journalism and environmental business
communications programs.

Green marketing, green journalism

On January 29, 1991, *Advertising Age* published its first
special issue devoted entirely to coverage of "The Green Marketing Revolution." The contents of the issue contained reports on such marketing giants as Procter & Gamble, Mobil
Corporation, and McDonald's Corporation. But in addition to

reporting on advertising and marketing news, the trade magazine transcended the bounds of its traditional forum, print, to hold a "Green Marketing Summit," a conference for marketing executives on environmentally-linked business efforts. Moreover, for the first time, the trade publication produced the whole issue on recycled, coated paper stock. The environmental initiatives already undertaken by the business community were at the center of the publication's interest, but not its only interest. In effect, *Advertising Age* used the conference as an educational meeting to encourage and stimulate increased activism in environmentalism among marketers and advertisers. Indeed, the publication had used the occasion as an opportunity to explore recycling options within its own offices. The editorial contents, the public relations efforts and the magazine's internal business policies were all linked by a common objective: the advocacy of the environment.

Advertising Age, however, was not the first publication with an editorial mission clearly distinct from environmentalism to commit its journalistic, public relations and internal communications forces to the preservation of the planet. In fact, during the two years preceding the special issue, *Advertising Age* had reported on the multifaceted efforts of another magazine to heighten awareness of the environmental crisis. That major magazine was *Time.*

The most widely-read, general-interest news magazine in America, *Time*'s advocacy of endangered earth began with the modification of its own year-end tradition, the naming of the "Man of the Year." In 1988, instead of selecting an individual, the editors named "The Planet of the Year" and featured on the cover the controversial artist Christo's rendition of the environmental crisis, a desk globe wrapped in polyethylene and rope.

Journalism intended to generate publicity

"The Man of the Year" tradition needs to be analyzed as one of the media world's own significant publicity inventions. *Time* founded the tradition at the end of 1927 as a way of generating interest during a typically slow news week, that which falls between the Christmas and New Year holidays. On that occasion, the editors, perhaps still embarrassed by their oversight of not placing Charles Lindbergh on the cover just after his trans-Atlantic solo flight months earlier, declared the American hero to be "Man of the Year." The hastiness of the editorial decision to name the first "Man of the Year" is best revealed not by the cover image of Lindbergh, but by the accompanying article inside. Containing virtually no news about the then current status of Lindbergh, the article amounted to less than a complete magazine page.

Regardless, the tradition caught on and *Time* editors, who today deliberate their selection for weeks and even months in advance, are evidently still keenly aware of the publicity-value of the issue. Controversy magnifies publicity. Therefore throughout the history of their selections, the editors have frequently chosen surprising figures as the most influential newsmakers of their times. The magazine does not view selection necessarily as an honor, but as a consequence of generating headlines throughout the past year. So in addition to leaders generally respected by the magazine's readership, e.g., Winston Churchill, Franklin D. Roosevelt, John F. Kennedy, the selections have also included leaders with notorious reputations such as Adolf Hitler, Joseph Stalin and the Ayatollah Khomeini. Other choices have included groups of people; the objective in such instances has often been to reflect social change. "Women of the Year," a cover in effect devoted to the women's movement, was such a selection.

The tradition was also altered in 1983 with the naming of the computer as the "Machine of the Year," a choice intended to focus on the impact of the personal computer in institutions and the home. Even the two most recent selections, in 1989 and 1990, featured quirky mutations of the lable. Mikhail Gorbachev was declared "Man of the *Decade,*" as opposed to the *year* at the end of the eighties, a distinction many readers evidently believed should have been belonged to Ronald Reagan. The most recent selection featured George Bush as "Men [sic] of the Year," a designation intended to represent his "two-faced" decision-making style.

The naming of "The Planet of the Year" therefore needs to be viewed within the dual disciplines of journalism and publicity. Publisher Robert L. Miller introduced the issue with a statement of justification in his column to the magazine's audience: "This week's unorthodox choice of Endangered Earth as Planet of the Year, in lieu of the usual Man or Woman of the Year, had its origins in the scorching summer of 1988, when environmental disasters—droughts, floods, forest fires, polluted beaches—dominated the news" (3). But this same column also made quite clear the issue's intentions to advocate solutions to the environmental crisis. The top editor presented his vision in a direct quotation within the text: "The new journalistic challenge,' says managing editor Henry Muller, 'was to help find solutions, and that by definition meant international solutions'" (3). Environmental solutions were thus first discussed, contemplated and proposed at an environmental conference hosted by *Time* prior to the special issue's publication date, a conference attended by "26 journalists and 33 experts" (3), the latter group composed of "scientists, administrators and political leaders from five continents" (3). The names and titles of the guest participants were published in this introductory column; conference attenders included E. O. Wilson, a Harvard professor of science; Fyodor Morgun, the chairman of a Soviet committee on environmental protection; Albert Gore, Jr., the now vice president; and Sir Crispin Tickell, the British representative to the United Nations.

The subsequent 35-page report examined the environmental crisis from an international perspective and focused on four specific problem areas: biodiversity, global warming, waste and overpopulation. In addition to an in-depth article on each problem area, the magazine also presented "solution boxes" with the headings "What Nations Should Do." Each "solution box" contained four or five steps which *Time* suggested should be implemented by every nation around the world. For example, the first suggestion in the "solution box" of the overpopulation report read: "1. Make birth-control information and devices available to every man and woman" (25). Even the more general overviews of the lengthy article contained proposals for action. In the two-page section entitled "Hands Across the Sea," for instance, a "solution box" recommended that the Nobel Prize organization establish a new award category for environmental activism (29).

Like other international news and media organizations, *Time* measured public response to its unusual issue in two principal ways: coverage of the announcement by other news vehicles (network and cable television, newspapers, other magazines and trade journals) and public response to the issue. In fact, the magazine's initial announcement of the "Planet of the Year" selection was officially made, not in the magazine itself, but on a television documentary produced by *Time* and aired across the nation. According to a sales brochure distributed to the advertising community, the "Planet of the Year" selection generated more reactions from readers than any prior "Man of the Year" issue. Moreover, throughout 1989, there were five times the number of letters and calls concerning the magazine's environmental coverage compared to the previous year's tally (Brochure, 1989). By all measures, the selection of Endangered Earth as a substitute for a Man of the Year had been a success.

Indeed, *Time*'s issue dated December 18, 1989, almost a year after the publication of the feature story, included an eight-page "Endangered Earth Update." Again, the magazine had convened a conference to probe what progress, if any, had been made. The magazine introduced the second feature article with a statement reflecting its own active involvement in the process:

> As a follow-up to our Jan. 2, 1989, Planet of the Year issue, *Time* invited 14 environment experts and policymakers to Alexandria, Va., for a one-day conference. Its aim was two-fold: to take stock of the environmental progress that had been made around the world during the year, and to develop an agenda for the future. This special report sums up our conclusions—and some proposals for action (60).

The pattern of advocating solutions was thus re-established. For example, one statement in a box headlined "What Can Be Done" recommended: "Promote 'resource accounting,' so that economic yardsticks include the costs of pollution and the depletion of resources" (62).

A year after *Time* had published the second major environmental article and two years after the "Planet of the Year" issue, the *Columbia Journalism Review* (Nov./Dec. 1990) featured its own story on "The Greening of the Media." Written by Holly Stocking and Jennifer Pease Leonard, the article recognized *Time*'s role in instituting a transition to increased coverage of environmental issues throughout the media. The authors found a shared commitment by large and small media organizations. They observed,

> In the last two to three years, in particular, beats have been expanded in major media. *The New York Times,* for example, has added a second full-time reporter to cover environmental issues. . . . All of the networks have beefed up their coverage, and NBC has designated a coordinating producer for environmental coverage" (37–38).

The research focused on activity outside of New York reflected a similar pattern: "The media have been greening in
small markets as well. In one recent survey, nearly 70 percent of the editors of newspapers with circulations under
50,000 said that, over the past two years, they had increased
environmental coverage" (38).

Maximizing the environmental initiative with public relations

In the last page of the *Time* "Endangered Earth Update,"
writer Jeanne McDowell looked four months ahead to Earth
Day 1990, set to occur on April 22. McDowell recognized the
strategic operations for the international event as they were
being coordinated under the direction of Dennis Hayes, a San
Francisco lawyer who was chairing the 115-member American
board of directors and who had helped organize the first Earth
Day in 1970 when he was enrolled at Harvard's law school.
Although McDowell's article clearly reported on the planning
process from a journalistic stance, her text ultimately promoted the objectives:

> One of the main goals of Earth Day 1990 is to help broaden
> the environmental movement far beyond its upper-class, bird
> watcher base. . . . The challenge of the next decade will be to
> channel that concern into strong and sustained action to save
> endangered earth (71).

During this period of time, members of the sales, marketing and promotion staff at *Time* had begun to meet to discuss
ways the public relations arm of the magazine could associate
the publication more directly with Earth Day events. Because
a mass market publication generates revenues from two main
sources, paid advertising and paid subscriptions, the internal
group was considering options which would help publicize the
magazine's environmental initiative to its two main constituencies: advertisers and readers, as well as to the public at
large. The group considered ways of getting the magazine directly involved in Earth Day events, but ultimately decided to
explore other routes. The reasons were twofold. First, *Time*
wanted to continue to be unique in its environmental activism; since so many other companies were planning to partici-

pate in Earth Day, the notion of proprietorship was missing. Second, the editors would cover Earth Day as a news event whether or not the public relations department was involved. Was there not a way to develop a separate public affairs event that itself was newsworthy? This group of corporate communicators proposed that *Time*'s public relations initiative could be announced around the events of Earth Day, but should in fact be a distinct program, linked more directly to the magazine's own ability to communicate to the public on a regular basis through its own pages.

Thus, the idea of the campaign was conceived and named "The Environmental Challenge." The campaign would consist of two fundamental components, each directed to a separate constituency. The first component was a competition to be held among American advertising agencies; each agency was given the opportunity to create an advertisement on behalf of "Client Earth" which would then be judged by a panel of creative leaders. The ten winning advertisements would appear in space donated by *Time*. Although the specific environmental message of each advertisement was left to the discretion of the creators, each winning advertisement was required to ask concerned readers to donate money to an "Environmental Challenge Scholarship Fund." The second component of the program therefore focused on the outreach to the magazine's general audience through fundraising in the pages of the magazine itself—though in this case, the pages would represent public service advertising, not journalistic reports.

Component 1: targeting the advertising community

Just before Earth Day, *Time* invited approximately two hundred creative directors from leading advertising agencies to attend a special luncheon program in its New York-based headquarters. During the previous summer of 1989, the magazine's parent company, Time Incorporated, had merged with the parent company of Warner Studios and Columbia Records to become Time-Warner Inc., the largest communications and entertainment company based primarily in the United States. The invitation from *Time* reflected the impact of the merger; the publisher of the magazine and the chief executive of the new entity were both listed as hosts of the event. In addition, the invitation listed the names of two

special guests associated with the music and movie industries, Paul Simon and Dustin Hoffman. The corporate facility
was filled to capacity; press personnel covering the event were
numerous; a television crew from *Entertainment Tonight* filmed
segments of the event to air on that evening's broadcast.

Although the major proportion of the program was devoted to the stars who talked about their personal commitment to environmental activism, the publisher of *Time*
announced the "Environmental Challenge" program. Each executive received a kit which contained rules and an entry
form for the advertising competition, reprints of the "Planet
of the Year" and "Endangered Earth Update" articles and a
post card requesting their intent to participate.

During the subsequent weeks, thousands of the kits were
mailed to large and small advertising agencies across the
nation and a hot line number was established at the company to answer questions about the competition. Although
thousands of kits were mailed, each agency or branch office
was instructed that it could officially enter only one submission to the competition by the August 1 deadline. Consequently, several major agencies staged competitions within
their own offices to determine which advertising concept from
among their creative teams would be entered into the competition. In the meantime, *Time* had made arrangements with
an independent professional advertising organization called
The One Club to serve as an independent judging panel for
the competition.

The history of promotional programs at the magazine
reveals that the "Environmental Challenge" program was not
the first advertising competition sponsored by *Time* on behalf of a cause. During the refurbishing of the Statue of
Liberty, for instance, the magazine had organized a similar
competition to raise funds for the restoration. That earlier
competition (as well as two others in the seventies) had
proven to *Time* management that advertising agencies wel-
comed the opportunity to create truly powerful, provocative
print advertising messages for worthy non-profit causes, *not*
just to sell a client's goods. Moreover, the range of previous
submissions from large and small agencies across the country had reinforced the notion that agencies on and off Madison Avenue should compete. Thus in establishing the rules
of the competition for the "Environmental Challenge," *Time*

had decided to encourage a range of regional agencies to enter by guaranteeing that winners would reflect the geographic diversity of the publication's own advertiser and subscriber base.

By the August deadline, more than 325 advertising agencies had officially entered the competition. The independent judges evaluated the entries and selected the ten winners. By mid-September, another invitation was in the mail to all agencies that had entered. *Time,* now in collaboration with the Advertising Club of New York—the largest professional organization of advertising executives in the metropolitan area—planned to host an industry luncheon program at the famed Plaza Hotel in order to announce the winners. Set for October 10, the program took place in the hotel's Grand Ballroom, a facility which could serve six hundred attenders. Attendance was near maximum levels.

Prior to the event, *Time* had notified the ten winning agencies. Interviews with the creative teams, typically a single copywriter and an art director, were conducted and recorded in person or over the telephone. *Time* thus prepared both an audio-visual presentation and an accompanying print brochure to showcase the winning advertisements and to provide insights into the creative strategies used to produce them. Table 6.1 lists the winning agencies.

Table 6.1
Winning Advertising Agencies
(or Branch Offices) by Cities
The Environmental Challenge Competition

City	Agency
Annapolis	Crosby Communications
Boston	Della Femina, McNamee WCRS, Inc.
Detroit	J. Walter Thompson
Houston	Taylor Brown Smith & Perrault Inc.
Los Angeles	HDM
New York	Altschiller Reitzfeld Davis/Tracy-Locke
	BBDO
	Lord Einstein O'Neill & Partners
San Francisco	Mandelbaum Mooney Ashley
Wichita	Sullivan Higdon & Sink

The luncheon program was featured as a news story in such notable trade publications as *Advertising Age* and *Adweek*. The winning agencies were not only announced in *Time* itself, but in other national news vehicles including *USA Today*.

The initial announcement of the competition and final announcement of the winners had given the magazine two ideal opportunities to address the advertising community. Moreover, two themes were embedded within the communications. First, the advertiser-relations effort had touted the magazine's commitment, as a journalistic entity and as a corporate citizen, to the ecological movement. Second, it had emphasized that the power of print advertising was still an effective way to move people to action, a message related to its routine business efforts.

Component 2: targeting the general public

The ten winning advertisements were striking; they best speak for themselves. Three of them directly addressed the individual in terms of the first steps he or she could take to help the earth. In effect, these three advertisements were the equivalents of the "solution boxes" which had run within the *Time* articles. For instance, one advertisement featured an illustration of eighty glasses of water and the headline: "If you had to drink all the water wasted every time you brushed your teeth, you'd never get out of the bathroom." The body copy simply advised the reader to turn the water off next time, "unless of course, you're very thirsty."

Seven of the other advertisements attempted to arouse the sensations of fear or embarrassment, sometimes via humor, other times via panic. One advertisement showed the eight other planets in the solar system; its headline stated: "If the earth isn't worth saving, consider the alternatives." A second advertisement featured an image of the Statue of Liberty buried in a pile of trash. Its headline sought to arouse a national sense of guilt: "Throughout history, many great civilizations have been buried. None, however, by their own garbage." A third advertisement displayed a photograph of an Egyptian pyramid, provoking American guilt for cultural contributions of fast food and long-lasting trash. In this case, the headline read: "Your cheeseburger box will be around even longer." (Note: a few weeks after *Time* revealed the "Environmental Challenge" winners within the magazine, McDonald's announced its plan to phase out the use of non-recyclable packaging.)

Each advertisement shared the same call-to-action tagline asking the reader to contribute to the Environmental Challenge Fund. At the time this article was written, *Time* had not yet officially released information about the amount of funds raised for the scholarship fund or about the colleges or institutions which would oversee the scholarships. But a spokesman inside the company indicated that "thousands" of dollars had already been raised, that the advertisements were still running when space was available in the magazine, and that public response to the program had been quite positive. Moreover, the executive indicated that one of the most generous contributions made to date had actually been donated by one of the advertising agencies which had entered, but not won, the advertising competition held during the summer.

As a public relations campaign targeting advertisers and readers, the "Environmental Challenge" was already deemed a successful campaign.

Riding the green wave, internally and externally

The special issue on green marketing published by *Advertising Age* (January 1991) included a survey of the one hundred leading national advertisers focused on their internal and external environmental initiatives. Out of one hundred corporations, only eight chose not to respond to the survey.

The synopsis on Time-Warner Inc. reflected a diversified commitment to environmental activism throughout the corporation's divisions in Hollywood and New York, but did *not* mention the "Planet of the Year" issue which, in fact, had represented the first major instance of advocacy. Instead, the *Advertising Age* report mentioned a Time-Warner television special broadcast just prior to Earth Day and internal efforts to promote recycling and to research "the feasibility of Time Inc. magazines eventually being published on recycled paper" (43). At present, the company's magazines are not printed on recycled stock; nor can they be recycled by most communities because of the color-processing chemicals and glossy paper stock used. Nevertheless, the public affairs program, "The Environmental Challenge" was mentioned and commended:

"Flagship *Time* challenged ad agencies to create compelling print ads to raise public awareness of the environmental crisis" (43). A public relations program conceived about a year earlier and fully implemented just two and a half months before the publication of *Advertising Age*'s special issue had evolved to represent a major symbol of corporate concern for the environmental crisis.

References

"Endangered Earth Update." *Time* 18 Dec. 1989: 60–71.

The Environmental Challenge: Competition Guidelines (corporate brochure). New York: The Time Inc. Magazine Co., 1990.

The Environmental Challenge: A Portfolio of Advertising in Support of Endangered Earth (corporate brochure). New York: The Time Inc. Magazine Co., 1990.

If You Care about our Future on Endangered Earth (corporate brochure). New York: The Time Inc. Magazine Co., 1989.

"Planet of the Year." *Time* 2 Jan. 1989; reprint of feature article available from the company.

"Special Issue: The Green Marketing Revolution." *Advertising Age* 29 Jan. 1991.

Stocking, Holly, and Jennifer Pease Leonard. "The Greening of the Press." *Columbia Journalism Review* Nov./Dec. 1990: 37–44.

Further Reading

Corrado, Frank M. *Media for Managers*. Englewood Cliffs, NJ: Prentice-Hall, 1984.

Evans, Fred J. *Managing the Media: Proactive Strategies for Better Business-Press Relations*. New York: Quorum Books, 1987.

Herman, Edward S. *Beyond Hypocrisy: Decoding the News in an Age of Propaganda, Including the Doublespeak Dictionary*. Boston: South End Press, 1992.

Lesley's Handbook of Public Relations and Communications, 4th Edition. Philip Lesley, ed. Chicago: Probus, 1991.

McKibben, Bill. *The Age of Missing Information*. New York: Random House, 1992.

Moore, David W. *The Super Pollsters: How They Measure and Manipulate Public Opinion in America*. New York: Four Walls Eight Windows, 1992.

Parenti, Michael. *Make-Believe Media: The Politics of Entertainment*. New York: St. Martin's Press, 1992.

Parry, Robert. *Fooling America: How Washington Insiders Twist the Truth and Manufacture the Conventional Wisdom*. New York: William Morrow, 1992.

Postman, Neil, and Steve Powers. *How to Watch TV News*. New York: Penguin, 1992.

Ridgway, Judith. *Successful Media Relations: A Practitioner's Guide*. New York: Ashgate Publishing, 1984.

7

Corporate Communications and Media

❖

Michael B. Goodman

Overview

The previous three chapters on corporate identity, corporate culture, and meeting the press cover different ways corporations communicate their messages to audiences with diverse needs. The use of media is an effective, cost-efficient way of sending messages in a consistent and timely manner. In this chapter *media* refers to the tools and methods used to send messages within the organization, as well as to communicate with outside audiences.

Corporations have seized the opportunity to influence audiences internally and externally with media, ever since Marshall McLuhan opened the eyes of the world to its power. The power of public opinion became part of the strategy of large businesses with the rise of corporations during the twentieth century. Newspapers and magazines were the only mass media.

Forward thinking organizations developed strong relationships with the media, partly in response to the negative attitude toward business that followed the so-called muckrakers such as Upton Sinclair and Ida Tarbell. These journalists were reacting to a public need for information about large organizations that almost exclusively at the turn of the century held firm to the notion that what they did was not the concern of the general public.

The obvious lack of what we now know as corporate citizenship created an adversarial relationship between business and the media that continues to exist today—though now the relationship between business and the press is somewhat more symbiotic than in the past. The media depends on business for information related to the company, so an atmosphere of mutual benefit has emerged.

Broadcast media—radio and television—and telephone and computer networks have changed the relationship once more. This section examines the ways in which corporations use media to communicate internally and with external audiences.

Broadcast news networks

Gone is the era in which the three national networks dominated the television screens of America. Major markets have a dozen or more stations, and when you count cable the number goes well above fifty.

Nevertheless, the national network news still plays a major role in bringing the business news to most people. Creating good relations with the national networks and their local affiliates is fundamental to an effective corporate communication strategy. Providing timely information to the news media is also part of that strategy since the reporter has to meet a deadline. If your organization returns a call late in the day or early the next morning, the reporter is likely to say something like, "XYZ Corporation did not return our telephone call." Such a phrase while true, appears to the viewing public as if your corporation had something to hide and was dodging the reporter's questions, when the truth may have been just the opposite. You may have been checking your facts.

Reporters work under pressure of the deadline and an effective relationship with them considers their deadlines in all conversations. This is particularly true when we consider that the content of business reporting on nightly news often is related to some sort of crisis or emergency. (Chapter 8 is totally devoted to crisis and emergency communication so this section will concentrate on other aspects of business communication.)

Generally corporate use of the national networks is related to the building of corporate identity and corporate image, an area covered in chapter 4. This is not to imply that television does not play an important role in major organizations. Many companies use television on a daily basis for meetings, informational sessions, training, and annual meetings. Though they use closed or business networks, the production of an interview with the vice president for marketing on what new products will be offered in the next year requires the same techniques as putting Larry King on the air.

Corporate television must have the same look and feel of broadcast television because the audience is video literate and sophisticated and expects high production quality in the programs it sees. The audience needs drive the level of quality for corporate programs to be very high.

Public broadcasting and corporate sponsorship

In recent years public television in the U.S. has become a bit more more commercial, allowing some short ads from the corporate sponsors to appear before and after a show. Corporate support of programming on public television has long been considered part of corporate philanthropy or corporate citizenship. As such, corporate communications participates in public television as another effort at building corporate identity and image.

Corporate sponsorship extends also to sporting and cultural events like broadcasts of the local or regional symphony or performances of a visiting ballet or foreign circus. Sports sponsorship has long been a method to create awareness of the company and its products and services. A tennis match, automobile race, football game, basketball tournament—all attract a corporate presence.

Sponsorship requires a high degree of coordination between advertising and public relations. More and more, these functions which have traditionally been separated are now combined. Putting advertising and public relations together helps build corporate identity and image, as well as building awareness of the corporation. The goal of such integration is to have the company speak with one voice, tone, and look to customers and employees. Often the company advertising theme drives all its communication themes.

Public television in the U.S. follows the European model for placing ads on the air. However, Europe is a few years behind the U.S. in the spread of cable networks and programming. The trend is now toward more advertisements even on the BBC as the air medium becomes more competitive.

As the European Community removes barriers to programming, the changes offer an opportunity to reach almost everyone in Western Europe. The implication of broadcast efforts in the European Community are discussed further in the essays in chapter 9.

Radio

Radio in the age of television has become an "outlaw" medium. It is very personal and focused on niche markets. Certain products and services can be discussed and advertised on the radio with relative ease. For instance, condom manufacturers advertise during dating hours such as Friday and Saturday nights on rock stations for an audience predominantly sixteen to twenty-four years old.

Radio stations appeal to smaller and smaller audiences with ever increasing diversity. Advertising and sponsorship of shows is a bargain compared to television network rates. A corporation may routinely sponsor a radio broadcast of a sports or cultural event, such as the long running Texaco opera series.

Radio is also used to inform employees of events at a local factory or corporate headquarters, in the case of natural disasters and plant closings. Radio talk shows are a sort of grass-roots therapy session for the community.

Cable network

Like radio, cable television has so many stations, in some areas over seventy, that its audiences are smaller and more diverse. Advertising for local businesses makes economic sense in these markets. Cable stations focus on types of information—sports, weather, financial reports, world affairs, political events in congress, court trials, and call-in talk shows.

Cable also covers business news and events more closely than the national broadcast networks because it follows the all-news format of the radio and can devote some time to business issues. Also, business related programs make up much more of the programming on these stations.

The infomercial, or long-form commercial, has become a very popular device on cable network stations. The company buys an entire half hour or hour and sells a product, but presents it as if it were a talk show or game show. Diet programs, investment schemes, automobile polish products, kitchen counter top gadgets are some of the staples of this form. However, Ross Perot's use of the long-form format during the 1992 presidential election suggests that the form may begin to have an impact on mainstream products and audiences.

The infomercial allows more details and discussion. The appeal of the Perot presentations is that people reacted to the presentation of detail as a way to cut through the clutter of the 15 second ads on network television. It also suggests that the appeal of the ads is to an audience that receives most of its information through the broadcast media, not newspapers, books, or periodicals.

Video and satellite news releases

Traditional communication with newspapers called for the circulation of a written press release usually sent by mail or FAX. If the information was considered very important or particularly newsworthy, the company would hold a press conference.

Now many organizations use video and satellite technology to provide information about the company and its products and services to local news stations, the national networks, and cable companies. In effect, the corporation prepares a video news story that the outlet can run in its entirety or can use clips in developing its own story.

The practice has benefits for both the company and the news organization. It allows the company to provide detailed information in a visual format that it can monitor and control. It offers the news program a feature without the production costs involved in sending a crew out to the company site. Often the company can provide much more dramatic footage than the station has available or could prepare on a daily deadline schedule or budget; for instance, pictures of aircraft in flight, automobiles or other vehicles undergoing testing, or computer simulations of planned buildings within the community.

Corporations also use video internally to provide information to staff and employees. Companies such as IBM have a television network that broadcasts company news daily to major sites around the world. The messages are communicated in a timely and consistent manner to all employees. Often the television monitors are located in high traffic areas, by elevators or near the entrance to the company cafeteria. The screen may have a scrolling message in words, similar to the use of video in hotel lobbies. In addition to this video bulletin board, the monitor may offer short pieces of information from company officers, plant employees, community leaders.

The use of corporate video also involves the orientation and training of employees. We mentioned this in our discussion of the ways to perpetuate corporate identity.

Corporate video can also be used to provide important information to the community. For example, local utilities such as telephone, gas, and electric companies routinely develop information on safety and on how to cope with a natural disaster such as a flood or winter storm. Often they work together with a non-profit organization to produce an informational video for the community.

Corporate video is also used to present product information to potential customers and current owners. Many organizations provide a "set-up" video for the new buyer of a complex or technical product, along with the traditional instruction booklet. Many companies use video to present financial information in what has been called a video annual report. In both cases the use of video meets the needs of an American population that has grown up on television and receives most of its information from the video screen, whether broadcast, tapes played on a VCR, or computer information.

Interactive video has proven useful in providing information to knowledge workers. It works like a computer program and allows the user to select information from a menu by using a light pen, mouse, or the keypad. Such systems are in use in hospitals, factories, hotels, and offices. The combination of computers and video has opened the corporation to new media technologies such as voice-mail, E-mail or electronic mail, and Local Area Networks or LANs.

Voice Mail, E-Mail, and LAN

The 1980s brought a quiet media revolution to the office in the form of personal computers. Now powerful machines and programs made it possible for one or two people to do the work of several. Spreadsheets and wordprocessing and desktop publishing are among the most common computer applications. Larger corporations are now using the computer network as a major communication channel.

Voice mail allows computers to answer telephones and store messages, and users can call in for messages from anywhere in the world and at anytime. The service unknown only a few years ago has become commonplace in business.

E-mail, or electronic mail, is the linking of computers to send messages from one computer to another. The systems have global reach through various networks such as Internet and Compuserv. The advantage of these electronic communication channels is savings of time and distribution costs. You can send a message to a general bulletin board which anyone on the system can have access to, or to a designated distribution list, or to one person on the network. E-mail allows you to send messages tagged for urgency, or to ask for a verification of the message being received and read. In this manner, E-mail has replaced, in many organizations, the use of and the need for informational memos. Using E-mail to replace paper memos and physical distribution of those documents has substantially accelerated the communication of information within organization which use them.

Local Area Networks (LANs) function similarly to E-mail, but they are several computers in a particular location linked to form a computer network that allows the users to share the use of data and programs. LANs have the outward appearance of a centralized computer mainframe set up, but the system functions more like a bundle of cells. The LAN is also a system that is secure because it is not connected to outside users.

Selected Essays and Comment

The essays and case study selected for this chapter are from the presentations at the annual Conference on Corporate Communication at Fairleigh Dickinson University. Each of the authors focuses on a part of corporate communications theory and practice that is associated with using various types of media in a corporate environment.

Ms. Julie Longo explains the use of video to communicate the technology of a company to its customers and its employees. She explores the process and methods of using video in presenting technological information in a corporate environment.

Drs. Ronnie Bankston and Laura Terlip discuss the use of new video technologies as a means of communicating with various external audiences. They explore a case example in the use of cable television and the interactive video technology—the Government Information Channel in Iowa City, Iowa. They evaluate the potential value of the system in relation to the local government's external and internal communication efforts.

Using Corporate Video to Communicate Advanced Technology

❖

Julie A. Longo

Corporate video is a powerful, concise way to communicate the technology of a company if some basics rules are followed. The communicator has to understand the corporate culture of the company; the corporate culture of the customer interested in the technology; and the audience, which may or may not be the same as the customer. The video must have solid technical content, both in the script and the visuals in order to gain credibility with the usually technically literate audience and also must include good camera work, well-designed graphics, and sophisticated use of editing and audio to best represent the company's image. This paper discusses how a video can be successfully used in communicating technology in the corporate environment.

The growing success of corporate video

Prior to the 1980s, the use of video was beginning to be recognized by corporations as an important medium for communicating information. Today, corporate video is entering an era of dynamic, exciting growth. Corporations increasingly are using video programs as a powerful means to improve sales, enhance marketing efforts, support public relations, and motivate employees by means of training tapes and video newsletters. Based on the success of video presentations in corporations, many corporate video departments are being allocated capital to buy state-of-the-art equipment, are allowed greater budgets in producing programs, and are increasing their staffs (1).

Corporations have different needs for video based on each corporation's primary business. This paper will discuss the use of corporate video in successfully communicating information for a corporation involved in design and systems engineering, production, system installation and test, and life-cycle support. That company is General Electric, whose Aerospace business operations compete globally for defense systems.

Commercial TV versus corporate video

Broadcast videos, such as "Nova" or the "National Geographic" specials, generally appeal to a much broader audience than do corporate videos. The scriptwriter, director, and producer literally have the universe from which to choose a topic, such as "how does DNA work" or "life on the Serengeti" or "the latest advances in medical imaging." The audience that watches science programs enjoys the encyclopedic selection of topics presented to them visually—which is why such programs are so successful and kept on the air (2).

Corporate videos designed to communicate technology have very different audiences and purposes than broadcast science programs. The prime audience is the customer the corporation wants to keep or the customer whose business the corporation wants to win. The producer/director/writer of these programs—and in corporations, these three jobs are sometimes handled by one person—is limited in subject matter to the technology about which the corporation wants to communicate information to the customer. The goal is to gain bookings and sales; to attract new potential customers; to maintain interest in a mature project; and to unveil test findings, new stages of invention, and new directions of that company's business.

Corporate video, by the very nature of a narrow subject, may appear to be restrictive to creative video approaches. In reality, the corporate producer has to be creative to achieve an interesting, polished effect, thereby offsetting topic limitations. If that corporate producer cannot communicate successfully using video, the high cost of video may drive the corporation to use another medium such as print.

The audience and the art of persuasion

The first step any corporate producer needs to take in order to produce a successful corporate video is to understand the corporate culture of that company and of the audience being addressed (3, 4). This step is important to determine the level of information being given to the audience and also to employ techniques of persuasion in the video with greatest effectiveness.

Every corporation can be characterized not only by its name and symbol, but also by its "corporate culture," which eventually becomes translated into the image the company projects. Each corporation has its own set of goals, its own language of shorthand conversation that the employees learn to interpret, and even its own dress code; in short, each company has a unique way of conducting business. Any employee who wants to be effective within that company learns the culture. According to Deal and Kennedy, "People who want to get ahead within their own companies also need to understand—at least intuitively—what makes their company tick . . . aside from considerations of personal success, managers must understand very clearly how the culture works if they want to accomplish what they set out to do" (5). With this in mind, a corporate producer, to successfully represent that company in a video, must understand the corporate culture.

The corporate producer working in the aerospace and defense industry must understand the corporate culture, the audience, and what I call the "customer/audience": members of the military branch that has contractually requested a video to show to that branch's own audience (figure 7.1).

For example, GE Government Electronic Systems Division in Moorestown, New Jersey, has for forty years designed, built, tested, and maintained radar systems, largely for U.S. defense purposes. For the past twenty years, this division has played a key role in developing the AEGIS Combat System for Ticonderoga-class ships of the U.S. Navy (6).

The corporate producer at GE/GESD might be assigned to produce a documentary on an engineering project for a manager of the corporation. In turn, this manager may be responding to a request by the U.S. Navy. The Navy needs the video to show to their audience: high-ranking Admirals, the

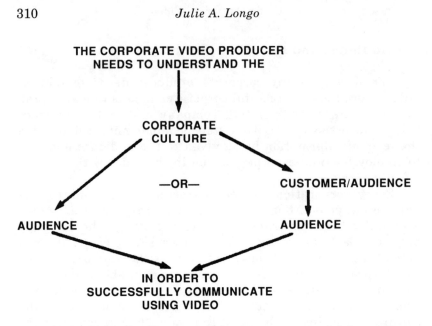

Figure 7.1 Understanding the audience for aerospace and defense video.

Joint Chiefs of Staff, or Congressional staffers. The producer must remember that to the corporation, the military is the audience of this video; the military is also the customer, with its own audience in mind.

The questions to ask concerning the customer/audience are "Who is the customer?" "What are their needs?" "What is the purpose of this video for the customer—to attract funds, to sell a new concept, to change perceptions, to address problems, or to convey any number of these messages simultaneously?" It is important to understand the culture of the "customer/audience." The end result of such a program needs to be a strong reflection of both the military branch that requested the video and the corporation requested to produce the program.

The video program can be enhanced by capturing the pride the customer feels about its own accomplishments besides a little quiet pride in the corporate culture of the producer. This approach suggests the teamwork involved in achieving success in the project that is the topic of the video. Another technique is to subtly highlight all the industries and military organizations that are part of the team in producing a defense system, yet keep the corporation which is producing the video quietly in the background. This is a mannerly approach that is elegant, appealing, and highly effective; the style of the video and the credits at the end of the program indicate the corporate origin of the tape.

High-tech minds live here

Videos produced for corporations involved with advanced technology have another requirement: that the video have solid technical content. Most defense industries have a sophisticated, high-technology base with a large number of the corporate managers, customers, and audience educated in engineering and science. Most personnel have an engineering, chemistry, physics, mathematics, or similar background, and thus are quick to spot technical substance. That technical content must be reflected in the writing as well as the look of the video program. Yet, the program must also have a sophisticated—almost broadcast quality—look for it to truly be successful for the corporation. Upper management of a high technology corporation is highly aware of the corporate image they need to project in the chosen medium.

Here, the corporate producer is skating on thin ice. First, many engineers, who in the course of their training rarely had time to study more than technical subjects of their field, have the idea that communication geared to promote the company's business necessarily has to be unsubstantive and even shallow. They don't want it to be that way, but they assume it has to be that way. Second, a corporate producer may hire a vendor whose video producers, directors, editors, and others involved in producing corporate videos have the idea that engineers are satisfied—even prefer—boring, uninspired video graphics; fussy charts; poor camera work; vague and shallow scripting; and so forth.

The first point is fairly easy to remedy—be certain the producer/writer has a thorough grasp of the technical topic, has conversational rapport with the engineers and scientists who are technical consultants on the projects, and is able to perform investigative research into the subject. Although thorough research may involve considerable amounts of time and effort, once the research is concluded, the script can be easily written. The understanding of the technical topic must be applied to creating video graphics that accurately represent the technical information needing to be conveyed.

Once the script has been written and graphics have been designed, the technical experts should review the material for content. With each carefully planned, researched, and written video program, the producer achieves greater confidence gained from the technical experts, including the managers who commissioned the program.

Although the producer/writer benefits from having a technical background, it is not essential if that producer is willing and able to assimilate technical information. However, a natural trap exists for the producer who is not knowledgeable about his or her program's basic subject. That is, the presentation can degenerate into a simplistic tutorial style. Such a presentation obviously may fall below the communication level of an expert audience, thereby rendering the presentation ineffective. A subtler trap can snare the unknowledgeable producer in that he or she can be side-tracked in his or her new-found knowledge by creating a program that addresses a topic parallel to the intended topic. For instance, radar systems engineers wanting to see a video concerning a technological breakthrough in sidelobe blanking techniques will not be satisfied with a tutorial presentation on signal processing.

Fortunately, in a video, every sentence or idea must be accompanied by a visual representation. This maxim is a godsend to technological corporations because it helps a greater number of people in the audience visualize quickly and accurately a technical concept such as the structure of DNA, or how a phased-array radar beam works. By using video, what is normally not visible to the eye can be illustrated and animated in a highly graphic manner. Conceptual information that normally could take weeks to understand now can take seconds with accurate and effective use of graphics and animation. In addition, when a corporation is trying to convey highly technical information to potential customers, the video visually gets across the exact same message and conveys the same technical content each time it is shown.

On no, not another industrial!

The second point—preventing hired writers, artists, cameramen, and editors from assuming that technical people like boring videos—is harder to correct and requires considerable effort by the producer. In my experience, engineers have settled for low quality in a video simply because they did not know they had access to better.

The successful corporate video producer, however, tries to ensure that, within the budget, the best cameramen, graphics designers, and editors are hired. The producer must spend time working with these people to get the video technically correct and also to encourage greatest use of creativity.

For instance, when I am confronted with a talented graphics designer who nevertheless assures me my video will have plenty of flowcharts and tables—something the graphics designer clearly thinks is what a technical audience wants—I start by explaining that although glitz is not credible in the eyes of most conservative companies, and most especially to engineers of military/industrial work, elegance, simplicity, sophistication, and understatedness are very credible and appreciated. My standing directive on programs I produce is "make it simple, but make it very, very good."

The camera work is the basis of any video program, so it is important to hire good cameramen, preferably with reputations for quality corporate work. If working with light—the liquid light of a chemical reaction in a test tube, the ephemeral light of a laser beam, the light of heated metal—get a cameraman who has a reputation for capturing that light on camera. In situations where camera work needs to be done while working around engineers who are anxiously trying to meet an important deadline on a project—a situation that commonly arises in a high technology corporation—hire a camera crew used to shooting in TV-reporter style, which means working fast and well. At other times, when the producer has more leisure and greater budget, hire a lighting director and, again, don't stint on the camera work. Good camera work doesn't have to be pretty or refined, just very clear, very steady, and very good.

Two other areas demanding attention are narration and music. Hire a narrator who can demonstrate competence and authority in handling a script with technical language, and coach that narrator as needed, not only for technical accuracy but for desired innuendoes in the voice that can help deliver a point effectively. If the producer is having music composed for the program, he or she must take the same care with the composer or music director as with the graphics artist. Music can be the most important persuasive element in a video program.

By taking the extra effort to encourage these people to do their creative best in what is commonly termed the video business "just an industrial tape," the producer achieves a quality of video programming that is noticed by the corporation and the customer (7). Again, the results include greater confidence in the producer to handle future projects. A sure sign of the producer's success may be the repeated use of the video program, often a clear indication that the video is a factor in increasing profit for the corporation.

The budget

A final thought in producing technical videos is that every producer appreciates being allocated an ample budget to accomplish the program. Frequently, however, the budget is small; sometimes, the corporate manager simply isn't aware of the cost of video, and sometimes the manager wants to get the most for the least.

On the other hand, first-time users of corporate video are astute in business and may be giving the producer a small project to see how well that producer handles the job in terms of technical accuracy, the quality of the video, and the financial handling of the project. If that producer can produce a dynamic program under such circumstances, there is a very good chance that the producer will be commissioned by the corporate managers to produce larger, more important programs. In this manner, the producer can build a solid reputation within the company.

Conclusion

In summary, all the best techniques used in producing high quality, non-broadcast video programs apply in producing a corporate video whose purpose is to communicate technological information. The producer needs to understand the corporate culture and the audience or audiences, and must thoroughly research the topic. All aspects of video—scriptwriting, graphics, camera work, music and narration, must be designed with the goal of maintaining the integrity of the topic. A producer representing a corporation must ensure that the video is well made to enhance that corporation's image. These are the points to keep in mind—because they work—in order to successfully use video to communicate technology.

References

1. Schindler, Steven. "Getting Down to Business," *Videography,* 14.1 (Jan. 1989): 41–44.

2. "Science On The Air." A fairly regular feature article in *Science News.*

3. Harrison, Roger. "Understanding Your Organization's Character," *Harvard Business Review* 50 (May-June 1972): 119–128.

4. Matrazzo, Donna. "The Key To The Script: Audience," *The Corporate Scriptwriting Book.* Media Concepts Press, c. 1980: 31–33.

5. Deal, Terrence E., and Allan A. Kennedy. *Corporate Cultures: The Rites and Rituals of Corporate Life.* Addison-Wesley Publications, c. 1982: 17.

6. Adams, F. G. "Putting AEGIS To Sea," *RCA Engineer* 26.7 (1981): 40.

7. See Ref. 1.

Using New Video Technology in External Organizational Communication: A Case Study of the Government Information Channel

❖

Ronnie Bankston and Laura Terlip

As the information age descends rapidly upon society, organizations are learning to use new video technologies as a means of communicating with their various publics. One innovative application of this new technology is the Government Information Channel (Channel 29) in Iowa City, Iowa. This service originated in 1986 and has grown from offering information in five areas during its test marketing phase to providing citizens with 75 different types of information in areas such as city government, police department data, and upcoming events. This paper describes the interactive video technology, its implementation and its current use. In addition, the authors evaluate the potential usefulness of the system in relation to local government's external and internal communication functions.

Introduction

There is little doubt that the information age has descended upon us. New technological developments have greatly expanded information storage and retrieval capabilities and provided greater access to information from a wide variety of sources. In addition, the ability to provide information in a wide variety of forms within short periods of time has increased dramatically. Private sector adoption of new technologies has had a significant impact on our life at work and at home.

Recent technological advances which have linked telephones and computers now allow us to accomplish everyday
activities such as paying bills, doing our banking or even en-
rolling in college classes without leaving our homes or actually speaking to another person (Veal, 1991). If we own a
personal computer, we can access information from data bases
around the world, carry on electronic conversations with others, shop, and make airline reservations (Taylor, 1990). As
technological developments continue we can expect that interactive systems which integrate a variety of media will have
an even greater impact on our activities (Cordell, 1991).

Specialists in corporate communication recognized early
on the value of using new technologies as a means of more
effectively reaching various organizational publics. The use of
video news releases (Shell, 1990) and computerized press kits
("Computerized press kits ...," 1989) have now become common place. Further, new technologies have been widely implemented to communicate with internal publics as well: E-mail
(Cordell, 1991), broadcast programming (" 'Channel 12' ...,"
1990) and interactive technologies for training (Wilson, 1991).

While private sector adoption and use of new technologies
is apparent, the use of new technologies to communicate with
various publics by local government is less visible. This is
problematic since all governmental organizations are currently
faced with a decrease in public confidence coupled with a
greater demand for information and accountability. At the
same time, budget cuts are resulting in a decrease in public
information officers across the country ("At city hall, ...,"
1992).

Approximately one hundred communities have attempted
to use new interactive computer technologies as a means of
communicating with the public. These efforts range from information kiosks at shopping malls to the establishment of
the Public Electronic Network (PEN) in Santa Monica, California. The latter service allows citizens to access information
such as city council agendas, staff reports, safety tips, and
the on line catalog at the public library from personal computers or municipal computer terminals. In addition, PEN allows for electronic conferencing among citizens and between
citizens and government officials (Varley, 1991).

This paper focuses on a unique use of new interactive
video technology by local government. Specifically, the paper

describes the Government Information Channel, an interactive video system currently in use in Iowa City, Iowa. An analysis of the system's function in local government's internal and external communication is also provided.

Government Information Channel 29

The City of Iowa City, the Iowa City Cable TV Office, and the Iowa City Broadband Telecommunications Commission are trying to marry television, telephone, and computer technologies. As a result, the residents of Iowa City and Coralville, Iowa have access to an interactive video system that provides a wide range of community information categories. Housing information, job opportunities, community calendars, and election information are only an interactive session away. (Refer to Appendix A for information on the Iowa City area.)

System development

In 1980 Drew Shaffer, a cable television specialist for the city, and several friends began to develop an interactive video system. The partnership, known as Response Television Corporation, pursued the project during the early and mid 1980s. In 1986 Shaffer met city officials to discuss the possibility of testing the system in Iowa City (Shaffer, personal communication, 1991). Later that year initial tests were conducted with a minimal number of categories and screens. The system continued to operate in this experimental mode until 1989 when an interactive specialist was hired and the number of information categories increased. Since 1989 the number of information categories, screens, interactive sessions, and project staff have increased significantly.

System design

Government Information Channel 29 is a single user system that does not require a home decoder or keyboard. The user only needs a touch tone telephone and a television set to interact with the system.

On the sender end, the system is tied to an Amiga 2000 computer and a software package developed by Response

Television Corporation. Information is distributed from the computer to the cable system via a genlock and modulator.

On the receiver end, the consumer uses a television and touch tone telephone to access system categories. Initially, the user turns his or her television set to cable channel 29. Users with cable ready sets tune in to channel 30. (Refer to Appendix B for a complete listing of the cable line up available to viewers in Iowa City and Coralville.) Once the Government Information Channel is displayed on the television set the user calls 356-5478. Hardware developed by Response Television decodes the phone signal and directs the user through the software. The user watches the television screen for directions throughout the session. Information is requested by pushing designated telephone buttons. When a category or screen has been requested the computer will locate and display the information, which is then distributed on the cable system to the user and anyone else that is viewing the channel. This interactive session, which is recorded by a computer, can last three minutes. Users keep track of time by monitoring a countdown that is displayed at the top of the television screen. If the session is not completed before the three minute time limit a computer generated voice is distributed to the user over the phone. The voice says, "Bye, and thanks for your interactive use." (Refer to Appendix C for information on interactive sessions.)

Information categories

The system started with only four or five information categories and approximately fifty screens. This limited menu allowed users to gain access to city council agendas, commission meeting agendas, and information about access programming (Shaffer, personal communication, 1991). By the fall of 1990 the system had expanded to over twenty five categories (City of Iowa City, 1991a). Users could not gain access to information about taxes, elections, missing children, jobs, recycling, bus routes, jokes, and cartoons.

As system awareness and usage increased new information categories emerged and existing categories were allocated more screens. In 1991 the system expanded at an unbelievable rate. Today there are over seventy categories available to users.

1. You Tell Us (Interactive Poll)
2. Directory of Information Categories
3. Instructions
4. Parks and Recreation
5. City News
6. City Council Agenda
7. Vote: Polling Places
8. Vote: Upcoming Elections
9. Vote: Election Results
10. Vote: Absentee Ballots
11. Vote: Who Can Vote?
12. Vote: How To Register?
13. Taxes
14. City Budget
15. Income Tax Information
16. School: Lunch Menus
17. School: Board of Directors Meeting Agenda
18. School: High School Sports Schedules
19. School: Mission Statements
20. Public Service Announcements
21. FBI Wanted Posters
22. Iowa City Police: APB
23. Iowa City Police: Crime Prevention
24. Iowa City Police: Radar Locations
25. Missing Children
26. Towlist
27. Parking Meters
28. Animal Shelter: Pet Regulations
29. Animal Shelter: Pet Care
30. Animal Shelter: How To Adopt A Pet
31. Animal Shelter: Lost And Found Files
32. Animal Shelter: Pet Health Information
33. GIC Program Schedule
34. Jobs: City of Iowa City
35. Jobs: JSI Iowa City
36. Jobs: JSI Cedar Rapids
37. Jobs: University of Iowa
38. Jobs: Volunteer Opportunities
39. Cable Subscriber Information
40. Bus: Routes & Schedules
41. Bus: Fares
42. Bus: How To Get There

43. Toll Free Numbers
44. About GIC
45. Jokes
46. Cartoon
47. Zodiac
48. Fun Facts
49. Maze
50. Electronic Art Gallery
51. Welcome: Health Services
52. Welcome: Libraries/Museums
53. Welcome: Area Events
54. Welcome: Trails In Eastern Iowa
55. Welcome: Kids Stuff
56. Senior Center: Activities
57. Senior Center: Movies
58. Senior Center: Family Album
59. Recycling: General Information
60. Recycling: Locations
61. Recycling: Household Waste
62. Housing: Temporary Housing
63. Housing: Rehabilitation
64. Housing: Help For Renters
65. Housing: Elderly And Handicapped
66. Housing: Legal Assistance
67. Housing: C.H.A.S.
68. Tours of Iowa City
69. Safe Sex: Aids
70. Safe Sex: Condoms
71. Safe Sex: Sexually Transmitted Diseases
72. Safe Sex: What Is Safe/Not Safe
73. Safe Sex: Phone Numbers For More Information
74. Sign Language Alphabet

Usage patterns

Government Information Channel 29 is expanding very quickly. However, the pattern of usage appears to be somewhat constant over time. Viewer usage data for the week of October 6–12, 1990, identifies the Directory, Cartoon, Zodiac, interactive poll (You Tell Us), Ivy, Fun Facts, Radar Locations, Jokes, Welcome to Iowa City, and Instructions as the top ten categories (City of Iowa City, 1991a). Viewer usage data for the first quarter of 1991 identifies the Directory, Jokes,

You Tell Us, Fun Facts, Cartoon, Zodiac, Interactive Maze, FBI Wanted Posters, Instructions, and Radar Locations as the top ten categories (City of Iowa City, 1991b).

These usage patterns might indicate that system users are going through an experimental stage and/or prefer the entertainment categories of the system. Thus, information obtained may not be as critical to some users as the interactive process itself. However, increased usage of the jobs, city news, and recycling categories indicates a demand for more "serious" information.

While the pattern of usage has remained somewhat constant the number of interactive sessions has grown significantly. Between January and March 1990 approximately 1500 calls were made to the system. During the same time period in 1991 the system received approximately 10,000 calls (City of Iowa City, 1991c). As of September 1991 the system was receiving between 800 and 1000 calls per week (Shaffer, 1991).

Future plans

At the present time the system is available whenever city government programs are not being broadcast. Thus, channel 29 is used primarily for the interactive video system. However, the rapid growth of the system warrants a separate channel. This option is under consideration at the present time.

As the system continues to expand, via a separate channel or in a shared channel capacity, Shaffer and his staff will add and delete information categories to meet community needs, examine ways to make the system more accessible to users, and maintain localism as a primary operating principle.

Channel 29 as organizational communication

Local government has an obligation to provide citizens with information about the services it provides. Citizens also have information needs that can be uniquely served by local government organizations. In addition, like their private sector counterparts, governmental organizations are interested in creating and maintaining a positive image in the community through the use of traditional public relations activities and functions.

In order to address the usefulness and the potential of
Channel 29, local government's ability to effectively communicate information to external and internal publics will be discussed. Further, the usefulness and the potential of the system
will also be addressed from the standpoint of the citizen/em-
ployee who interacts with the Government Information Channel.

External communication functions

From a local government perspective, interactive video
technology provides a cost effective way to accomplish several
goals within an external communication framework. First, the
Government Information Channel provides an effective means
of conveying information through multiple channels. Information provided on Channel 29 is also available through other
sources including print media, broadcast channels, and direct
contact with organizational members. Practitioners have long
recognized the need to use multiple modes and channels in
order to reach different audience segments or to reinforce certain messages. By providing Iowa City citizens with information in an interactive video format, local government may be
reaching individuals who do not or choose not to utilize other
media forms.

For example, school lunch menus are printed in the local
paper. However, individuals may not subscribe to the paper
or may misplace the particular issue containing the data.
Channel 29 fills a need in these instances. Similarly, frequent
users of the bus system may misplace their schedules and
infrequent users may not have a schedule and desire information in a timely fashion. Channel 29 fills this gap as well.
Finally, information used on an infrequent basis, such as location of polling places, can be accessed easily through the
system.

A second external communication role that is facilitated
by providing information on the Government Information
Channel is education. The potential to provide information on
sensitive public issues as well as more common topics is afforded by the interactive video technology.

Currently, several screens are devoted to safe sex. By fur-
nishing this type of information through the interactive system, individuals who might not feel comfortable discussing
the issue or even asking where to find information have access to the facts. In less sensitive areas such as recycling and

pet care, the system may serve to initially inform and/or reinforce knowledge about the local topics and issues.

A third external communication objective that is partially achieved through the new video technology is the facilitation of local government's mandate to make certain types of information public. Screens which provide information about city council and school board meeting agendas help the organizations meet open meeting law requirements. Similarly, the screen which provides city budget information helps in meeting legal requirements to make certain information public. Related to this, the "advertisement" of job openings provides another mechanism for attempting to attract candidates for jobs in compliance with affirmative action and EEOC guidelines. Not only does Channel 29 provide another mechanism that government can use to meet its obligation to the public, it also makes public access to the information easier.

Fourth, the Government Information Channel helps local government work to build an effective image. The presence of the technology itself works to send a metamessage about the municipality's concern for citizens and their access to information. In addition, several screens provide documents that are traditionally used in image building by organizations such as mission statements and city news.

Additional means of targeting specific publics is the sixth opportunity afforded by interactive video technology. Local government has an opportunity to direct specific messages to important constituents by providing categories and screens for them. This process not only provides information to the group but serves to underscore the community's concern and commitment to specific publics. Currently, Iowa City has special screens targeted to senior citizens, cable subscribers, and children. As the community changes, no doubt other groups will be targeted.

Related to targeting specific publics, Channel 29 also provides an opportunity to market the community itself. Tourists and visitors, new residents, and businesses all have access to information about Iowa City and what it has to offer via Welcome to Iowa City. These screens can provide access to information about health care, entertainment, and special events.

Finally, Channel 29 offers local government a new means of surveying citizens about local issues. The interactive poll, You Tell Us, has the potential to gather data about citizen attitudes to local issues, problems and proposed changes.

Internal communication functions

Iowa City depends heavily on several levels of government for its economic well being. A large part of the workforce in the community is employed in the public sector. Channel 29 therefore has the potential to provide information to citizens who also happen to be employees. Because the system offers information about several local governmental organizations, employees may use the system in order to find out about their own organization or other organizations they may be dependent upon. One example of this capability is the usage of screens on the city council or city news to check on actions that might affect one's own organization. From a more personal perspective, employees may discover job vacancies in other organizations that they may be eligible for through existing transfer processes.

Beyond helping to provide additional access to information about organizations, Channel 29 may impact on the actual work of certain individuals in local government. Provision of basic information on the system may help to reduce the number of calls and the subsequent commitment of manpower to that task. The speed of access may also reduce citizen frustration with employees and make "customer relations" easier.

In other instances, Channel 29 may help certain public employees' jobs easier. By providing information on missing children, road construction, and local all points bulletins, the work of the police force may be facilitated.

Finally, screens that describe information previously unavailable to citizens may help or hinder in certain circumstances. For example, access to radar locations may change the public's behavior in one of two ways: they may slow down or they may continue to speed but take a different route. The impact of the system in areas such as this is unclear at this time.

Citizens as receivers

By far the biggest advantage of Channel 29 to citizens in Iowa City is accessibility. Information that previously may have been difficult or time consuming to obtain is now readily available. Further, the system has the capability to aid citizens in obtaining an almost immediate response to problems related to towed vehicles or lost pets. Screens which contain information in areas such as parking violations may also help citizens avoid problems in the future. In the past, activities such as these required a phone call or visit to the appropriate office during working hours to obtain information. Now, Iowa City residents can access this data from the comfort of their homes almost 24 hours a day.

Channel 29, by providing information about what city government is doing, also makes it easier for citizens to engage in local activism. By opening access to information that was previously difficult to obtain, interactive video technology may make it easier to become involved in local and community affairs.

In summary, the use of interactive video technology provides a great many opportunities to local governments who wish to improve their internal and external communication. Systems such as this have the potential to lead to a more informed citizenry, an enhanced image of local government, and the effective use of a public access channel.

References

"At city hall, every day's a crisis" (1992, February). *Public Relations Journal*, 7.

" 'Channel 12' delivers company news into employee's living rooms" (1990, March). *Public Relations Journal*, 28–37.

City of Iowa City (1991a, 27 March). *Channel 29 Interactive Information Services Viewer Data Analysis*.

City of Iowa City (1991b, 30 May). Information Services Quarterly. *Report for the Third Quarter of FY91*.

City of Iowa City (1991c, 27 March). *Statistics Concerning Interactive Information Services Usage by Citizens*.

"Computerized press kits: Wave of the future?" (1989, October). *Public Relations Journal*, 13–14.

Cordell, Arthur J. (1991, March/April). "Preparing for the Challenge of the New Media." *The Futurist*, 21–24.

Cunningham, Scott, and Alan L. Porter. (1992, January/February). "Communication Networks." *The Futurist*, 19–22.

Shaffer, Drew. (1991, 1 October). Cable Television Specialist for the City of Iowa City. *Personal communication*.

Shell, Adam. (1990, November). "Corporate Video: Reaching Out to the TV Generation." *Public Relations Journal*, 28–37.

Taylor, Cathy. (1990, 1 October). "Other Media." *Adweek*, 42–46.

Varley, Pamela. (1991, November/December). "Electronic Democracy." *Technology Review*, 43–51.

Veal, Robert L. (1991, June). "The Integration of Telephone and Computer Technology." *Telecommunications, 25*, 6, 29–32.

Wilson, Bill. (1991, June). "Federal Express Delivers Pay for Knowledge." *Training*, 39–42.

Further Reading

Audiovisual Handbook. Santa Ana, CA: Toastmasters International, n.d.

Bittner, John R. *Broadcasting and Telecommunications.* Englewood Cliffs, NJ: Prentice-Hall, 1985.

Corporate and Organizational Video. Alan Richardson, ed. NY: McGraw-Hall, 1992.

Cowan, Robert A. *Teleconferencing.* Reston, VA: Reston, 1984.

Davenport, Thomas H., Robert Eccles, and Laurence Prusak. "Information Politics," *Sloan Management Review* (Fall 1992): 53–65.

Gross, Lynne S. *Telecommunications: An Introduction to Electronic Media.* Iowa: William C. Brown, 1989.

Marlow, Eugene. *Managing Corporate Media.* White Plains, NY: Knowledge Industries, 1989.

Meadow, Charles T., and Albert Tedesco. *Telecommunications for Management.* NY: McGraw Hill Publishing, 1985.

Morton, M. S. Scott. *The Corporation of the 1990s: Information Technology and Organizational Transformation.* NY: Oxford University Press, 1991.

Singleton, Lux A. Telecommunications in the Information Age. Cambridge, MA: Ballinger Publishing Company, 1986.

"Special Report: E-Mail—Pervasive and Persuasive," *IEEE Spectrum.* 29:10 (October 1992): 22–34.

Van Nostrand, William. *The Nonbroadcast Television Writer's Handbook.* White Plains, NY: Knowledge Industry Publications, 1983.

Van Nostrand, William. *The Scriptwriter's Handbook.* White Plains, NY: Knowledge Industry Publications, 1989.

8

Corporate Communications and Crisis

❖

Michael B. Goodman

Overview

It is 7:00 PM on a wintry Thursday. A light snow has fallen, not sticking to the sanded roadways which surround The GCOP (Giant Chemical, Oil, and Plastics) Company hydrocarbon chemical complex in Donnelsville, a quiet community of fifty thousand in southern New Jersey.

The plant, the largest hydrocarbon chemical complex in the world, produces forty percent of the world's supply of HEXO DEXOLENE—a new product which has revolutionized paints by increasing viscosity by one hundred percent. Hexo-dexolene, a petroleum derivative, is highly caustic in concentrated form; and turns to a highly toxic, colorless and odorless gas when it mixes with salt and water. It dissipates very slowly in gaseous state, but halogen can contain the gas. The product is harmless when mixed with other chemicals in a controlled manufacturing environment.

The forecast is for fair conditions through Sunday, highs in the 30s. A tank truck leased to GCOP Co. loaded with twelve thousand gallons (U.S.) of its GCOP HEXDEX Brand hexo-dexolene pulls out of the plant gate bound for a delivery in Eastern Connecticut. The sign over the gate reads: "1,793 Days Without a Fatality."

The driver, Al Benson, is thirty-eight years old and a professional driver with Ace Trucking for ten years. A Viet Nam Vet trained in the U.S. Army as a tank commander, he has been married to his second wife for five years. They have a four-year old son. Al has a safe driving record—no history of substance abuse, mental illness, or physical impairment.

He is driving a 1990 White/GM/Volvo Diesel Cab, last inspected in October 1991 and approved by all local, state, and federal highway safety standards. The cargo tank was manufactured in 1989 to GCOP standards for the transportation of HEXDEX. The corporation's specifications exceed all ICC, OSHA, ANSI, and other applicable standards.

Al pulls the rig onto the New Jersey Turnpike heading north. At the George Washington Bridge, he turns and stops at the toll for an inspection and waits until after midnight to cross.

He then passes over the Hudson River, through the maze of roadways under the residential towers on the Manhattan side, and onto the elevated roadway bridge over the East River, heading into the Bronx.

Suddenly, a van swerves in front of the truck from the left lane, cutting it off. The truck driver slams on the brakes and turns hard to the right, hitting the passenger car in the right lane.

Both vehicles slide solidly into the guard rail and concrete barrier. The cab and trailer jack-knife, severing the air-brake lines and locking all the tires. The truck shudders to a stop, overturning on the roadway.

Air hisses from the lines to the cab, fuel flows from a ruptured tank on the cab; the cargo tank has split along a welded seam—the contents flowing onto the roadway and into the storm drains which empty directly into the river.

Police arrive at the scene within minutes.

It is now 1:00 AM Friday. New York Police Department Officer Alvarez of Highway 1 calls GCOP to inform the company of the accident.

What do you do now? What steps do you take?

A panel of corporate officers and media representatives were faced with the situation just described, and the questions started a panel discussion titled "When Disaster Strikes" as part of the Schering-Plough Executive Lecture Series on Corporate Communication at Fairleigh Dickinson University in March 1990. (The script was written by Michael B. Goodman and Tom Garbett.)

Corporate representatives included: Moderator David E. Collins, Corporate Executive Vice President of Schering-Plough who handled the Tylenol scare as president of MacNeil; Robert Berzok, Director of Corporate Communications for Union

Carbide; S. C. "Duke" Watkins, Manager-Hazardous Material Transportation and Chemical Recovery for Allied-Signal; Gregory L. Johnson, Corporate Vice President and General Counsel of Warner-Lambert; Tom Garbett, Distinguished Visiting Professor at Fairleigh Dickinson University and corporate advertising consultant.

Media Representatives were the environmental reporter from the local newspaper, the business reporter from the state's largest daily, and news director from WWOR TV, regional independent station syndicated nationally on cable.

David Collins asked each panelist for observations and statements on the situation. And each panelist was asked to offer a summary on what to do when disaster strikes. Much of the discussion covered the points on planning, preparing for and handling a crisis which you will see below, and in the selected essays.

The panelists seemed to agree, which for a group of journalists and business representatives was unusual, since the relationship between the two is usually adversarial. But both agreed that the situation required cooperation among everyone involved.

Journalist and business executives, contrary to their normal adversarial roles, seemed to find common ground. It is in the best interest of everyone in a crisis situation for all parties to cooperate. Then the moderator David Collins was handed a note with the following information directed toward the press:

> At 7:00 AM you receive a call from THE GREEN GROUP, a small radical environmental organization that began in the late 1980s in Western Europe. The caller—William James— informs you of the incident saying it was no accident, that he personally drove the van, cut off the tanker to show the world how vulnerable all human beings are to industrial poisons in our water, air, and soil. Your story has hit the street. What do you do now?

The new complication, according to the newspaper reporter changed the character of the situation from "an accident to an incident." The TV news director said she would not go on the air with the news before she checked out the call. In the context of broadcast journalism's sensationalism, several people considered the comment to be somewhat at odds with the way stations have behaved in the past.

The hypothetical situation demonstrated the continued need for corporations to understand the nature of crisis, its impact on the health of the corporation and its employees, the strategic nature of communications in times of corporate stress, and methods for communicating during a crisis.

This chapter discusses understanding the stages of a crisis, planning and managing a crisis, and responding during the crisis and after.

Stages of a Crisis and the Corporate Response

Many people who write about crises and management use a medical analogy. The comparison is fitting. In the First World War, medics developed the triage technique for rendering aid on the battlefield—not seriously wounded could be treated and released with little effort and time, those near death for whom no amount of effort could make a difference, and those who would most likely recover if something were done immediately.

The triage model applies to communications and actions during the crisis itself, when time to contemplate and analyze is all but non-existent. The triage approach fits the management principle of applying limited resources for their greatest impact.

The other model borrowed from medicine is the development of disease through stages: prodromal, acute, chronic, and resolution to a normal state.

In practice you can refer to the precrisis stage, the clear signs of a crisis, the persistent reemergence of the crisis, and the resolution. Often companies do not see a potential for crisis in the normal course of business. For example, the W. R. Grace Company ignored for a long time the need to plan an orderly succession of its CEO until it became clear that nature would force such action. The public became aware of the problem when the nightly news reported the chairman's comment in 1992 that the governor of New York was "Mario the Homo."

Or the owner of the chicken processing plant who kept the fire exits of his plant bolted shut until a fire at the plant killed several workers. An analysis to develop a crisis plan would have spotted the gross violation of law as a potential crisis of major impact to the company and its people.

Airlines, utilities, computer operations, and hospitals plan for the unthinkable because they have learned from painful experience that the unthinkable has a nasty habit of happening.

Crisis Communication Plans

In the past what happened in a business was literally no one else's business. Corporations cut off questions with a curt, "No comment." Such closed door policies create an information vacuum. Investigative reporters of the 1990s and beyond, like their muckraker ancestors almost one hundred years before who spawned the practice of public relations, want to fill that vacuum. With the trend toward sensationalism, many reporters will do just that, often in ways damaging to the organization.

Employees also fill the information vacuum, fueling the rumor mill within an organization. Combine one disgruntled employee and one ruthless reporter and the result is at least a major headache for the company, at worst it can be the catalyst in a media feeding frenzy with an unpredictable outcome.

Cooperation with the media and employees is a much more prudent and mature policy for any organization to take in normal times and in times of crisis.

Planning for a crisis as a fact of corporate life is the first step in its resolution, and a subsequent return to normal operations. No one can predict when the event will occur, only that sometime in the life of an organization a product will fail, your market will evaporate because of a new invention, the stock will fall, an employee may be caught doing something illegal, the CEO will retire, the workforce will go on strike, a natural disaster will occur, a terrorist will plant a bomb.

It is perfectly normal for executives to avoid thinking about a crisis. Positive thinking is embedded in the way managers are taught to be effective. Problems are Opportunities; One man's misfortune is another's fortune, and so it goes. Admitting a crisis could occur is to entertain the worse of corporate sins: the notion of failure.

The tendency to ignore the worst also recognizes that people cannot control events. Being unable to control the forces of nature certainly does not mean weakness on the part of managers. It merely indicates that people must plan to deal with emergencies and their consequences. Weakness comes only when people do not prepare for events. Companies that get into trouble are often the ones which never considered that bad things would happen to them.

Emergencies, disasters, bomb threats, criminal charges, executive misconduct . . . none of these may happen, but a well run corporation develops plans in case the unthinkable occurs. Even the best run companies can and do have difficulties. Gerald Meyers in his book, *When It Hits the Fan,* identifies nine types of crises:

1. public perception,
2. sudden market shift,
3. product failure,
4. top management succession,
5. cash flow problems,
6. industrial relations,
7. hostile takeover,
8. adverse international events,
9. regulation and deregulation.

Planning for a crisis implies the people in the company can recognize a crisis when it occurs. People experience generally the same stages when faced with adversity or catastrophic loss:

- denial or isolation,
- anger,
- bargaining for time,
- depression and grief,
- and finally acceptance.

An organization is no different since it is made up of people. Organizations experience 1) shock, 2) a defensive retreat, 3) acknowledgment, 4) adaptation and change.

Responding to Pressure Groups

More and more interest groups make corporate life difficult for some companies either through public demonstrations staged to capture media attention, through announced boy-cotts of company products and services, through out and out harassment of company executives and employees, or through terrorist acts directed at the corporation.

Ask yourself what you would do in a similar situation the next time you see a Greenpeace boat being rammed by a Japanese fishing boat for trying to stop a shipment of nuclear retractor fuel at sea, or witness AIDS sufferers in ACT-UP in death costumes outside a drug company protesting the price of the experimental drugs for treatment, or Pro-life groups demonstrating in front of a multinational organization that makes RU-486 (the "morning after pill") available only in Europe.

Your answer is, of course, that if you look out your window and your first notion that there are folks out their who have ideas drastically different from your own, you are way behind in dealing with the immediate situation on your corporate doorstep. Planning for the inevitable can be good business.

The fast food industry provides an excellent illustration. People in New York's Long Island live in a fragile sea coast environment and are concerned about all types of pollution. Fast food restaurants began to hear calls for the ban on Styrofoam cups and other wrapping of hot food because its use was literally minutes, but it would take centuries for the material to breakdown in landfills.

Instead of considering these comments as those of radical environmentalists, the corporations decided to join the people and return to the use of paper products made from recyclable and recycled materials. The message: "We listen to you and we are all part of the community. As good citizens, we are doing our part." The fast food restaurant operators saw the protest as a message from their customers, as well as a comment on their products and services. Their response made good business sense. The decision resulted in prudent actions to turn a potential crisis into an opportunity for the organizations to work with the community and for them to get closer to their customers.

Selected Essays and Comment

The essay selected for this chapter is from the presentation at the annual Conference on Corporate Communication at Fairleigh Dickinson University. Each of the authors focuses on a part of corporate communications theory and practice that is associated with understanding crisis communication, planning for crises, and communicating in a crisis.

David Sturges, Bob Carrell, Douglas Newsom, and Marcus Barrera note that discussions of crisis communication focus attention on preparations, rather then the changing relationships between the corporation and the local and global audiences. Their discussion explores the difference between pre-crisis and post-crisis relationships with publics important to the organization.

ESSAY

Crisis Communication: Knowing How is Good; Knowing Why is Essential

❖

David L. Sturges, Bob Carrell, Jr., Douglas Newsom, and Marcus Barrera

When an organization is confronted with a crisis, it is concerned with three kinds of behavior: its own behavior as an organization, the behavior of the organization's members and the behavior of all its other publics. Publics, whether domestic or global, are those whose behavior may affect the organization or those who may be affected by the organization's behavior. Most writers on crisis communication focus on some or all of these behaviors, but most often as they are related to the need for preparations.

However, this paper raises a central question rarely treated in the literature, except by implication: What is the difference between pre-crisis and post-crisis environmental relationships with publics important to the organization?

Whether or not targeted publics are global, messages often go global and reach many unintended audiences. The effect on an organization may be direct or indirect because of our global interdependence in political and economic arenas. So every crisis communication plan must take into account the potential of global impact, even if the crisis is viewed as being only domestic.

Introduction

A string of crises, beginning with the Three-Mile Island nuclear leak in 1979 and extending through the San Francisco earthquake in late 1989, produced a period of change that is, perhaps, unparalleled in the history of business. This turbulence was further agitated by record levels of bankruptcies, hostile and friendly takeovers, mergers, inflation, stagflation, increased globalization of markets and record-breaking swings in stock prices. A crisis of some type seemed to lurk in the path of almost every business firm. It was only natural that during the 1980s the topic of crisis management often dominated professional management development seminars, conferences, and periodicals.

Early contributors to the concept of crisis management, such as Burson-Marsteller's Harold Burson, suggested that preparation to meet a crisis consisted of contingency planning for both organizational performance and communication policies and procedures to facilitate information flow to concerned audiences (1985). In addition to coping with a crisis, proper preparation was intended to feed the public opinion process as a way to influence groups of people significant to the organization.

Although much has been written about crisis communication, the focus has been on crisis management models that describe preparation for and performance during a specific time period associated with a crisis (Fink, 1986; Quarantelli, 1988; Mitroff, 1988). This paper suggests that crises do not occur in a vaccum. Timeliness and the focus of crisis management should extend far beyond operational timeframes and affected audiences included in most crisis communication models. Communication plans for any future crisis should begin today and must include both known and unknown audiences all around the world.

Current thoughts on crisis management

Organizations planning for crisis are concerned with (1) organizational performance, (2) organizational members' performances, (3) communication to all publics (audiences, groups, stakeholders) who may either (a) be affected by a crisis or (b) affect the organization by the groups' response to the crisis in the short-term or long-term (Newsom and Carrell, 1986). Organizations use two distinctly different planning processes: (1) preparing for a crisis and (2) managing a crisis (Quarantelli, 1988).

Crisis preparedness involves the process of creating a crisis plan, designating crisis management teams, training personnel to respond during a crisis, and amassing resources to address a crisis. This process is akin to "strategy" in the sense that it provides a framework of goals and objectives to be accomplished in the event of a crisis. Crisis management is implementing activities to achieve the plan's goals and objectives. This process equates to "tactics" where tactical goals and objectives are formulated using input from the plan subject to environmentally specific constraints inherent in each unique situation (Quarantelli, 1988). In this framework, crisis preparedness is an internal operational process where the organization produces what amounts to roadmaps to follow in the event of a crisis. This preparedness process results in no tangible activity except for developing and distributing crisis plan documents and holding training seminars and drills for employees. Crisis management is all "response" activity during a crisis.

A crisis for an organization passes through four distinct stages. The first is the "crisis build-up" or "prodromal period" (Fink, 1986).[1] This is a period during which clues or hints begin to appear about a potential crisis. Long before a triggering event happens, symptoms appear as precursors to a crisis. These precursors represent repeated messages and persistent sets of clues that, if they are recognized, may help an organization to implement activities intended to prevent a crisis or, at least, to lessen its potential effects on the organization. Organizations that remain sensitive to their environment, to important audiences and to relevant trends are positioned better to recognize and ward off the impact of a crisis.

The second stage is "crisis breakout" or "acute crisis." This is the period in which a triggering event causes a crisis to erupt into damaging reality. The physical, fiscal and emotional trauma to an organization and its relevant publics may be enormous. It is in this stage that the organization's management is put to its severest test.

"Abatement" is the third stage. In some situations, it may be called the "chronic crisis" stage because the effects of a crisis may linger for years. Charges, countercharges, demonstrations, inquiries, legal actions and continuing coverage by the mass media may serve to prolong the effects of a crisis. The last, or fourth, stage is the "termination" stage where a

---

[1]*Prodome* is a "set of symptoms leading to diagnosis of disease." *Prodromal* is an adjective describing the period of time the symptoms are detectable prior to outbreak of the disease itself.

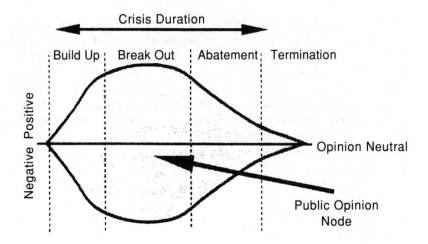

Figure 8.1. Public Opinion Node for crisis management as an isolated event.

final resolution signals that the crisis is no longer a threat to an organization's operational environment or to its constituent publics (Fink, 1986; Mitroff, 1988).

One potential weakness of this framework for crisis management is the assumption that crisis management is important and that it plays out its role of influencing opinions held by an organization's internal and external environmental constituents only during the time period described as the life cycle of a crisis (Fink, 1986; Mitroff, 1988). Figure 8.1 illustrates the "Public Opinion Node" for any constituent audience for an organization as this limited view of crisis management suggests it could be mapped. The Public Opinion Node contains all opinions, in various degrees of positive and negative direction, held by all members of any specific audience identified as important to the organization.

Rarely do crisis preparation of crisis management frameworks consider pre-existing attitudes and opinions and their impact on reaction of constituents to a crisis. A crisis does not occur in isolation. Rather, it occurs in the context of an operational environment which existed long before the onset of a crisis. As illustrated in Figure 8.2, the key question for organizations is, "What changes in relationships occur between pre-crisis, i.e., before-crisis build-up phase, environmental elements and post-crisis, i.e., after-crisis termination, environmental elements."

Figure 8.3 illustrates what may be the ultimate object of crisis management, although this objective is ignored or only

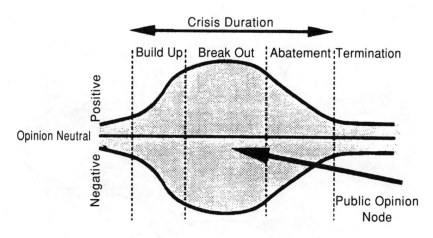

Figure 8.2. Public Opinion Node for crisis management
as continuing relationships.

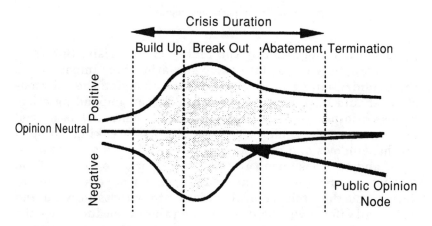

Figure 8.3. Public Opinion Node for crisis management's objective.

alluded to in most discussions of crisis management models.
The objective of crisis management beyond physically coping
with the aftermath of a crisis is to influence public opinion
development to the point that opinions held in the post-crisis
environment are at the same level or greater in positive
opinions and at the same level or less in negative opinions
among members in any constituent audience.

Crisis management proposes that damage control is one
objective (Burston, 1985). It tries to prevent drastic negative
changes in relationships with operational environmental

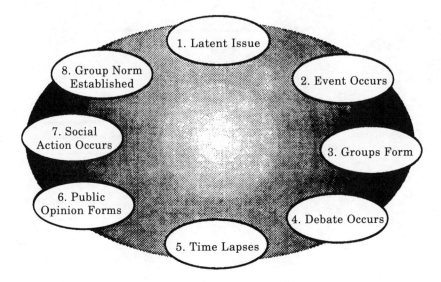

Figure 8.4. Group norm development process.

components brought on by the reality of the crisis. But damage control may be too late to save relationships important to the organization because the real work of saving the relationships should have been done long before an impending crisis looms. In other words, if a hurricane is coming, it is a good idea to tape the windows to prevent glass breaking, to open all the windows and doors to equalize inside and outside pressure, and to stack furniture on top of blocks to keep it from getting wet. However, if the house does not have a firm foundation and the architectural integrity to withstand wind and water, all efforts will be in vain when the hurricane blows the house off its foundation and crushes everything into rubble. In the case of crisis events, the foundation that may prevent an organization from collapsing is the foundation of positive opinion about the organization held by groups of people whose behavior potentially affects the organization's operation.

Why strive for the ultimate objective?

Although management theorists talk about organizational environment elements as if they are tangible, living entities, any environmental influence, except climatic conditions, results from behavior of people as a group. For example, government

1. Opinion is highly sensitive to important events.

2. Events of unusual magnitude are likely to swing public opinion from one extreme to another. Opinion does not become stabilized until the implications of events are seen with some perspective.

3. Opinion is generally determined more by events than by words—unless the words themselves are interpreted as an "event."

4. Verbal statements and outlines of courses of action have maximum importance when opinion is unstructured, when people are suggestible and seek some interpretation from a reliable source.

5. By and large, public opinion does not anticipate emergencies—it only reacts to them.

6. Psychologically, opinion is basically determined by self-interest. Events, or words, or any similar stimuli affect opinion only insofar as their relationship to self-interest is apparent.

7. Opinion does not remain aroused for any length of time unless people feel their self-interest is acutely involved or unless opinion—aroused by words—is sustained by events.

8. Once self-interest is involved, opinion is not easily changed.

9. When self-interest is involved, public opinion in a democracy is likely to be ahead of official policy.

10. When an opinion is held by a slight majority or when opinion is not solidly structured, an accomplished fact tends to shift opinion in the direction of acceptance.

11. At critical times, people become more sensitive to the adequacy of their leadership—if they have confidence in it, they are willing to assign more than usual responsibility to it; if they lack confidence in it, they are less tolerant than usual.

12. People are less reluctant to have critical decisions made by their leaders if they feel that somehow they, the people, are taking some part in the decision.

13. People have more opinions and are able to form opinions more easily about goals than they are to methods necessary to reach goals.

14. Public opinion, like individual opinion, is colored by desire. And when opinion is based chiefly on desire rather than on information, it is likely to show especially sharp shifts with events.

15. The important psychological dimensions of opinion are direction, intensity, breadth, and depth.

Figure 8.5. Cantril's Laws of Public Opinion

intervention is considered a tremendously important environmental influence in organization strategic and tactical planning. However, government is not a living entity whose actions create the influence. People acting as members of groups comprising the government exert the influence.

One of the most powerful determinants of group behavior is the expected behaviors established in the social norm development process based on the interactions of opinions held by group members. The interaction of opinions (outward expressions of attitudes, beliefs and emotions) results in a dominant opinion among the group's members which becomes the guide to behavior of all group members (Hart and Scott, 1977). Figure 8.4 illustrates the process, beginning with an issue, which potentially has relevance to individuals in a group throughout the cycle (Oskamp, 1977).

Opinion development for an individual shows consistent characteristics in relation to events perceived by the individual to affect self-interest. Cantril (1947) succinctly described some of these characteristics in what he called the "Laws of Public Opinion," (Figure 8.5) although they may more rightly be called "observations of public opinion." Among these characteristics are some having particular significance to crisis communication management.

Opinions are most malleable at the formation stage when the issue involved is salient to the individual but opinions about the issue are unstructured or only slightly structured in terms of direction, intensity, depth and breadth. Opinions are highly sensitive to events, especially those which the individual perceives to involve self-interest. Immediately following an event, opinion is firmly structured and is very difficult to alter. It is only with the passage of time, without events occurring to reinforce opinion in one direction or another, that public opinion of the group to which the individuals belongs begins to form sufficiently to influence the behavior of the group as a whole.

Comparing these characteristics to the process for developing the group's expected behaviors (social norms), the steps in the process where information has its greatest influence are during Step One when opinions are unstructured, and during Step Five when time allows information and actions to reinforce opinions in the desired direction while opposite opinions receive no reinforcement, thus allowing them to move toward neutral. The steps where information has its least influence are Step Two immediately following an event, and Step Four, while debate occurs. During these two steps, opinion is most structured and least likely to show significant shifts.

Crisis communication management tends to emphasize communicating to affected constituents during the breakout stage of crisis and continuing through abatement. Certainly, communication is necessary to ensure that constituents get important information about how to react to the emergency. However, communicating to constituents during these stages with an intent to influence the development of internalized opinions that will influence people's behavior toward the organization is least effective.

Crisis communication policy must recognize that communication to constituencies to prepare for crisis begins with program implementation the day the decision is made to establish such programs. At stake are opinions of people about the credibility and reliability of the organization involved in the crisis that will influence people's reaction in the event of crisis. Opinions are more readily influenced when they are unstructured, before some crisis event occurs to solidify them.

Communication during the crisis has two primary objectives. One is to appease third-party interveners (Ressler, 1982). The other is to keep employees informed. One third party, mass media, may have agendas for ferreting out information that have little or nothing to do with what the specifically affected publics' agendas are. If the information flowing through the media is inaccurate, inappropriate, counterproductive or downright hostile (either deservedly or undeservedly), it serves to reinforce negative opinions during the time lapse stage of norm development. Such reinforcement tends to influence the developing social norm into a direction not desired by the organization.

Mass media coverage can also negatively affect employees involved in the crisis. Employees should be an organization's most credible source, and their actual knowledge, as well as their perceptions of the crisis, and how it is being treated by the organization, are critical. If they aren't given timely, accurate and consistent information, they may lose faith in the organization's ability to overcome the crisis. This may cause them not to put forth their best efforts to resolve a crisis, just at the time when the organization needs them the most (Pincus and Acharya, 1987).

Crisis communication content objectives

Communication content as a component of crisis management must meet three needs. Each need must be addressed individually in crisis communication execution because of different objectives. First, instructing information tells audiences how they should behave in a crisis context (Quarantelli, 1988). For example, the audience's members might need to evacuate an area exposed to toxic fumes. Second, adjusting information

allows an audience to cope with the emotional aspects of a
crisis (Shrivastava and Mitroff, 1986; Kuklan, 1986). For example, the severity of damage to buildings, extent of casual-
ties, or what's being done to counteract danger represents
coping information. Third, internalizing information is ab-
sorbed by audience members and forms the basis for long-
term judgments (public opinion development about the image
of the organization) about the organization(s) involved in the
crisis (Newsom and Carrell, 1986).

Crisis communication policy must recognize that each of
these component needs must be addressed at each stage of
the crisis, although the need emphasized in communication
messages changes at each crisis stage. During a crisis build-
up, for example, messages probably emphasize internalizing
information to precondition the audience to the organization's
position related to the crisis situation. As build-up continues
and the crisis is determined to be unavoidable, the message
emphasis may shift to instruction to prepare audience members to respond to crisis with specific actions. At the crisis
breakout stage, the emphasis is oriented to instruction as the
need to induce immediate behavior among audience members
increases dramatically. As the immediate danger of the crisis
breakout subsides, emphasis shifts to adjusting information.
And, as the crisis enters abatement, internalizing information again assumes a primary emphasis. A crisis that trun-
cates the build-up stage puts considerable stress on an
organization to carefully plan and executive initial breakout
messages to take advantage of pre-existing public opinion of
constituent groups.

Environmental components of crisis communication policy

Management scholars tend to consider organizational operating environment elements to be included in crisis plans
as groups of people who, by their behavior, may affect the
organization (Donnelly, Gibson, Ivancevich, 1987). The operational environment is suggested to be comprised of internal
and external environments with the external environment divided into direct and indirect components (Donnelly, Gibson,
Ivancevich, 1987), as shown in Figure 8.6.

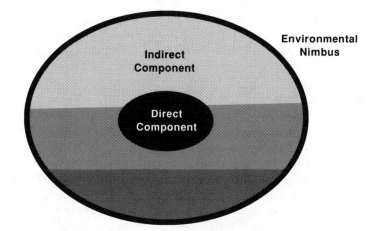

Figure 8.6. Operational Environmental Components

However, organizations should also consider other groups who are a part of the environmental nimbus, an ill-defined collection of groups whose potential influence may affect an organization or be affected by it, depending on circumstances (Newsom and Carrell, 1990). Any of these nimbus groups could slide into the indirect or direct categories as a situation develops. For example, Union Carbide identified environmental components when it built its chemical plant in Bhopal. What it didn't identify was a nimbus group in India consisting of poor, lower-class families who move in around major plant sites in hopes of getting jobs. As more and more squatters moved in, Union Carbide began to recognize a potential problem, but one based solely on the sheer numbers living around the plant. In one ghastly event, this group vaulted from the environmental nimbus to a direct component as more than two thousand died from toxic fumes and many thousands more were injured.

Although it may not have been the intent, communication technology has made the concept of environmental nimbus a reality for most organizations, even one that thinks of itself as "domestic-only." Even the slightest interaction with its operational environment can send shock waves into the nimbus that may result in serious operational concerns for the organization. Likewise, group activities in the nimbus, especially those in a global context that seem unrelated to the organization, may eventually cause resounding impact on an organization. For example, terrorist activity may not be perceived as a concern of an organization, but, terrorist's acts can affect an organization, ranging from disruption of the flow of resources to the deterioration of economic structures important to the organization's welfare.

The potential of nimbus groups to influence the organization is significant enough that communication policy of the organization must include concern for both the explicit messages (those the organization purposefully sets out to send) and implicit messages (those messages inferred by audiences from the actions of the organization). Exxon Corporation's explicit messages to the world following the tanker grounding in Prince William Sound were not supported by subsequent implicit messages sent as a result of Exxon's performance during the clean-up from the accident. The result has been worldwide opinion about Exxon that remains a considerable concern for Exxon's management today.

Conclusion

Organizations experience crisis not as isolated events, but as occurrences that develop in the milieu of public opinion in which the organization has been operating. Included in this milieu are some nimbus publics the organization had not recognized previously as being affected by the way it plans for and faces crisis.

Some of these nimbus publics are created by the crisis itself, such as Muslim reaction to U.S. bookstores that sold Salman Rushdie's *The Satanic Verses* after the Ayatollah condemned it. Some nimbus groups may be uncovered by a crisis, such as anti-American activism in Mexico in the aftermath of the U.S. invasion of Panama.

Most crisis communication models ignore the Public Opinion Node in the planning process. Furthermore, communication efforts are concentrated during the breakout and abatement periods of a crisis when the node is least responsive to messages that would have impact.

An adequate crisis communication model must provide for global environment, or nimbus, and be able to quickly identify nimbus audiences as well as constructing messages that focus on types of information when they can be most effective in contributing to an audience's behavior toward an organization.

References

Burson, H. 1985. Damage control in a crisis. *Management Review.* Dec. 1985, 44.

Cantril, H. 1947. *Gauging Public Opinion.* Princeton, N.J.: Princeton University Press.

Donnelly, J. H., Gibson, J. L. and Ivancevich, J. M. 1987. *Fundamentals of Management.* Plano, TX: Business Publications, Inc.

Dutton, J. E. 1986. The processing of crisis and non-crisis strategic issues. *Journal of Management Studies 25:4,* 373–385.

Fink, S. 1986. *Crisis Management: Planning for the Inevitable.* New York: American Management Association.

Hart, D., and W. Scott. 1977. The Organizational Imperative. *Administration and Society.*

Kuklan, H. 1986. Managing Crisis: Challenges and Complexities. *SAM Advanced Management Journal.* Autumn, 39–44.

Mitroff, I. I. 1988. Crisis Management: Cutting through the Confusion. *Sloam Management Review,* Winter, 15–20.

Newsom, D., and B. J. Carrell. 1990. Communication Campaigns and Cultural Awareness in the Global Village: The Spill-Over Factor. 7th Annual Intercultural and International Communications Conference. University of Miami. February 22–24, 1990.

Newsom, D., and B. J. Carrell. 1986. *Public Relations Writing: Form and Style.* Belmont, CA: Wadsworth Publishing Co.

Oskamp, S. 1977. *Attitudes and Opinions.* Englewood Cliffs, NJ: Prentice-Hall, Co.

Pincus, J. D., and L. Acharya. 1987. Employee communication during a crisis; The effects of stress in information processing. Paper presented to the Association for Education in Journalism and Mass Communication. San Antonio, TX. 1987.

Quarantelli, E. L. 1988. Disaster Crisis Management: A summary of research findings. *Journal of Management Studies, 25:4,* 373–385.

Ressler, J. 1982. Crisis Management. *Public Relations Quarterly,* Fall, 8–10.

352   *David L. Sturges, et al.*

Shaw, M. 1981. *Group Dynamics: The Psychology of Small Group Behavior.* New York, NY: McGraw-Hill Book Company.

Shrivastava, P., and I. I. Mitroff. 1987. Strategic Management of Corporate Crisis. *Columbia Journal of World Business,* Spring, 5–11.

Wisenblit, J. Z. 1989. Crisis management planning among U.S. corporations: empirical evidence and a proposed framework. *SAM Advanced Management Journal,* Spring, 34–41.

Zaltman, G., and R. Duncan. 1977. *Strategies for Planned Change.* New York, NY: John Wiley and Sons.

Further Reading

Barton, Laurence. *Crisis in Organizations: Managing and Communicating in the Heat of Chaos.* Cincinnati, Ohio: South-Western Publishing Co., 1993.

Burak, Patricia. *Crisis Management in a Cross-Cultural Setting.* Washington, D.C.: NAFSA Washington, 1986.

Fink, Steven. *Crisis Management: Planning for the Inevitable.* NY: AMACOM, 1986.

Huyler, Jean W. *Crisis Communications and Communicating About Negotiations.* NY: AMACOM, 1981.

Mazarr, Michael. *Improving International Crisis Communications: Final Report of the Study Group on Crisis Communication.* CSI Studies, 1991.

Meyers, Gerald D. *When It Hits the Fan: Managing the Nine Crises of Business.* Boston: Houghton Mifflin Company, 1986.

Wisenblit, Joseph Z. "Crisis Management Planning Among U.S. Corporations: Empirical Evidence and a Proposed Framework," *Advanced Management Journal* (Spring 1989): 31–41.

9

Corporate Communication in Global Markets

❖

Michael B. Goodman

Overview

"Act local, think global" has become the business mantra of the end of the century. The simplicity of the phase can lure the unsuspecting into a simpleminded interpretation.

Much has been said, written, and videotaped on the need to compete in global markets. And much of what has been said and written about globalization of business emphasizes the notion that even though we may want a quick and easy method for entering markets outside our own country, the reality is that doing business in another country can be complex and difficult.

The complexity is cultural and if we extend the discussion on corporate culture from chapter 5, we look at these determining forces for communications:

- Language
- Technology and the Environment
- Social Organization
- Contexts and Face-Saving
- Concepts of Authority
- Body Language and Non-verbal Communication
- Concepts of Time

Doing business successfully in an international, global, or transnational environment demands your attention to cultural, social, political, and religious practices, in addition to technical, business, legal, and financial practice.

Communication is key to each. Real communication—not just cookbook do's and don'ts such as not showing the soles of your shoes in Saudi Arabia, or not shaking hands with a Japanese after putting something in your back pocket, or always finishing the bottle when a Russian begins to toast you, or not discussing business with a Mexican on the first business meeting. Such advice may be very interesting to read and think about, but it rarely recognizes that after the do's and don'ts run out, what do you do next? That's where the "act local" part comes in. If you want to act local you must be local.

In other words, understand the country in which you are doing business. The first step is to make every effort you can to learn the language. Almost all nations, the French are a glaring exception, notice your effort to learn their language. This is more than just symbolic. Language encodes culture, and making an attempt to understand the words leads to an effort in trying to understand the way the people think.

These examples of simple language differences are by now classics, almost cliches for international communication: General Motor's efforts to sell its Chevy Nova in Mexico. Nova sounds like the Spanish *No va,* or no go! And Ford's Pinto is Portuguese slang for a small male appendage. The popular *Bich* are Bic pens in the English speaking world for obvious reasons.

The way people view technology and their environment are often culturally defined and can have an impact on international business communication. The way people view manmade work environments differ in perception of lighting, roominess, air temperature and humidity, access to electricity, telephones, and computers. People perceive their relationship to the physical environment differently. For some nature is to be controlled, for others it is neutral or negative, and for others it is something for man to be in harmony with. Even climate, topography, and population density have an impact on the way people perceive of themselves, and that has an impact on the way they communicate.

Social organization, or the influence of shared actions and institutions on the behavior of the individual, has a strong impact on business communication worldwide. Institutions and structures tend to reinforce social values; that is, the consensus of a group of people that a certain behavior has value.

For international business communication we might consider the following social structures which have influence in the workplace: kinship and family relationships; educational systems and ties to business; class and economic distinctions; religion; political and legal systems; professional organizations and unions; gender stereotypes and roles; emphasis on the group or the individual; attachment to the land; recreational activity. Each one of these areas should be the focus of background research before going overseas. Some familiarity with the major works of art and literature will give you some insight into the social organization of the country you plan to visit on business.

Contexts and face-saving refer to the way one communicates and the situation in which the communication occurs. We refer to cultures that are high-context, like the Japanese, and low-context like the German. A fuller explanation of this concept is given in the next section on the Pacific Rim.

Concept of authority and power, as well as how power is exercised in the workplace, differs from culture to culture. For instance, in Western cultures such as the United States and Europe, power is the ability to make and act on decisions. Power for such cultures is an abstract ideal discussed and debated by philosophers and theorists from John Stuart Mill to Karl Marx. For Asian cultures, power and authority are almost the opposite of the Western concepts. Power results from social order. Asians accept decision-making by consensus, and decide to be part of the group rather than the leader. Understanding the concept of power helps shape a business communication strategy. The direct approach to communication, so effective in the United States, may prove crude and offensive in France or Japan.

Body language and non-verbal communication are just as important in international and cross-cultural communications as they are in communications within a homogeneous culture. Watching movies and TV from a country you wish to visit before you go as well as when you arrive there will give you some cues to appropriate non-verbal behavior. Pay attention to kinesics or body movements, physical appearance and dress, eye contact, touching, proxemics or the space between people, and paralanguage or sounds and gestures used to communicate in place of words. Also colors, numbers and alphabets, symbols such as a national flag, and smell are important elements in international communication.

Concepts of time differ from culture to culture. In the twentieth century, physicists such as Albert Einstein, and more recently Steven Hawking, have demonstrated that time in the physical sense is relative. For purposes of communication across cultures, it helps to consider time as a social variable. In the Caribbean, for example, the American tourist is frustrated to distraction when asking for a cab and getting this response, "Come soon." Time is defined culturally and by shared social experience.

Communication in the New Europe

From the chaos and political instability that faced Europe at the end of the Second World War came a movement to unite the countries that had lead the world into global conflict twice in less than four decades. The concept was to link the countries economically in the hope that development of such ties would reduce the risk of going to war. Since 1950 numerous treaties, agreements, and acts have evolved into the European Community, which at the beginning of 1993 was made up of Germany, France, Italy, Britain, The Netherlands, Denmark, Ireland, Belgium, Luxembourg, Spain, Portugal, and Greece.

A main trading partner of the European Community is the European Free Trade Association (EFTA) which was formed in 1960 and includes Austria, Finland, Iceland, Liechtenstein, Norway, Sweden and Switzerland. The former communist block countries of central and Eastern Europe— Hungary, Poland, Romania, Slovakia, Czech Republic, Bulgaria, and the countries of the Commonwealth of Independent States and Russia—are developing new relationships with one another and with the European Community.

These enormous shifts in political and economic philosophy present a business communications challenge and opportunity. As barriers to trade are removed, the natural barriers of distance, culture, and language that have kept people apart for centuries begin to again play an important role in business transactions.

In the European Community, particularly since the fall of the Soviet Union, is a group of "Europeans." These are business professionals from all over Europe who tend to share a culture and belief system that has more in common with their international business counterparts in America or Asia. What they share with one another is often more than what they share with their own countrymen—taste in art, literature, music, recreational activities, cars, homes, attitudes toward work and money. What has emerged is a "global professional." For example, an advertising executive in France or England can function within the professional context almost anywhere in the world because of the commonality of activity. What has happened to almost all of the business professions is something that engineers have known and practiced for years— technical expertise translates well across many borders.

The business professional has emerged as a European class, often very well versed in the language and culture of the political nations he or she is working in and with. Other nations can hope to achieve this ideal of the international attitude and ability that Europeans have developed over centuries of trade.

Communication and the Pacific Rim

For Americans doing business with nations of the Pacific Rim we can add to the difficulties of language and culture the added differences in context and face-saving. The concept of communication context usually refers to the degree the situation influences the meaning for the participants in the communication.

Low-context cultures such as German and North American place a high emphasis on explicit communication, the law, and contracts. They rely on verbal communication, tolerate relatively little ambiguity, and place reduced emphasis on personal relationships and face-saving.

High-context cultures as Japanese and Latin American place high emphasis on personal relationships, present information indirectly and often ambiguously or through nuance, and act at all times to preserve one's prestige or outward dignity, to save face. The words, laws, and contracts are seen as less important than the bindings of personal relationships.

In the high context cultures of the Pacific Rim, business communicators from low-context cultures such as the U.S. will be confronted with controlled use of silence, or communication through intuition. The Japanese have elevated such meaningful silences to an art form and call it *haragei. Hara,* or literally belly, is the English equivalent of heart or center of one's being, the center of feelings, courage, and understanding, as well as the wisdom gained through one's experience. *Haragei* is the opposite of the argument or verbal confrontation so common to the business communication of Westerners.

Another concept in the high-context cultures of the Pacific Rim is the Korean *kibun* or moods or feelings. Koreans are very sensitive to maintaining harmony and go to what Westerners consider great lengths to maintain their own *kibun* as well as everyone else's. The concept plays a role in the aversion of most Asian Pacific Rim nations to bring bad or unpleasant news. It is also related to an unwillingness to say "no" directly as a way to save face.

In high-context cultures the differences between the surface truth and reality may be much more important than in low-context cultures which often make no such distinction. The Japanese use the terms *tatemae* and *honne*. *Tatemae* is the facade of a structure like a building, and *honne* is one's true voice, what one really thinks and feels. Every culture has such concepts to some degree. Even a quick scan of most European novels of the last century or the works of Henry James revels the richness that exists in the difference between the public expression and the private thoughts of individuals.

The status of the Pacific Rim as an economic and political force requires corporations of any size to develop a business and communication strategy that meets the business challenge effectively.

Communication with Developing Countries

For Americans doing business in developing countries, make every effort to understand the cultures, customs, and language of the people with whom you are communicating. Also, make no excuses about being from another culture. Chances are they know a lot more about you from movies, books, and mass media than you know of them. Many of the business professionals were educated in the U.S. and are more likely of a social class higher than most of their countrymen.

Developing countries may appear to have disadvantages compared to some of the advanced economies of the world. But remember they often have a rich artistic, religious, and cultural heritage that should be the focus on your building a business relationship with them. Since they may know English, you may show your interest in them by at least reading their literature in translation, being aware of their cultural and artistic accomplishments, and making an effort to learn their language.

But also be proud of who you are. Nothing seems less genuine than a foreigner who seems to "go native" at the expense of his or her own culture.

In communicating in a global environment, the understanding of contexts, situations, languages, cultures, motives, in short, making every effort to understand your audience's needs and expectations, should prove an appropriate and valuable approach to almost any new culture.

Communication Technologies Overcome Barriers of Time and Space

Chapter 7 described the importance of some communication media. Technologies such as satellites and E-mail have more and more replaced the telex and telephone in international business.

It is common in some companies that develop technologies to have groups all over the world work on projects around the clock. These professionals and technicians are connected to one another by computer networks. For example, a group in New York will work on a project. At the end of the work day, they will hand off the job to another group on the computer network in Los Angeles. In this way the work is passed around the world and around the clock, overcoming the communication barriers of time and space.

Technology advances in communication have created the global business environment that challenges us today.

Selected Essays and Comment

The essays selected for this chapter are from the presentations at the annual Conference on Corporate Communication at Fairleigh Dickinson University. Each of the authors focuses on a part of corporate communications theory and practice that is associated with understanding of communications and communicating in a global environment.

Dr. Nicholas D. J. Baldwin's essay, "They Speak English But . . . : The United Kingdom as a Foreign Country,"

demonstrates clearly the need to consider such important issues as culture, history, social class, education, politics, and
government. His essay is particularly important since for
Americans it is very easy to assume that people who speak
English also share the same social values. As Baldwin quotes
Churchill, the U.S. and Britain are "two nations separated by
a common language."

Mitch Baranowski's "The Politics of Broadcasting in the
European Community: The Television Without Frontiers Directive," demonstrates the efforts by the European Community to deregulate and internationalize television broadcasting.
The paper traces the history of media development in Europe,
and discusses the future for media policy in the European
Community.

'They Speak English But . . . ': The United Kingdom as a Foreign Country

❖

Nicholas D. J. Baldwin

For an English speaking visitor to the United Kingdom—
or indeed for the Brit travelling in the United States—language
is obviously not the problem that it can be in many other
countries. It can, however, cause difficulties, for, as has been
said, we are two nations separated by a common language.
For example, an English friend of mine while visiting his
American girlfriend asked her father, 'What time shall I knock
your daughter up in the morning?' and was promptly beaten
to a pulp by the father; he was completely unaware as to why
his enquiry—namely, what time he should wake his girlfriend
up by knocking on her bedroom door—should have so upset
her father. Similarly, a number of Brits have been brutally
injured in bar fights in the United States from asking burly
truck drivers they happened to be standing next to if they
would 'care for a fag'—a fag in Britain is a cigarette; apparently it has a completely different connotation in the United
States. It is therefore apparent that although they may speak
English, the United Kingdom is undoubtedly a foreign country. As a result, do not make the all-too-common mistake of
thinking that simply because the words employed are familiar, their meaning is the same. For example, the word 'subway' in Britain means 'a pedestrian walkway'—with not a
train in sight; an American looking for the British equivalent
to the U.S. subway must look for 'the Underground' or 'the
tube.' An 'elevator' is a 'lift,' a 'truck' is a 'lorry,' a 'liquor
store' is an 'off-licence,' a 'private school' is a 'Public School,'
'pantyhose' are 'tights,' 'the check' after a meal in Britain is

referred to as 'the bill.' A 'pencil eraser' is simply 'a rubber'—
a word which itself apparently has a very different meaning
in the United States. American men may use 'suspenders' to
hold up their 'pants' but the British equivalent would be
'braces'; 'suspenders' are what women use to hold up their
stockings—and, by the way, 'pants' are 'trousers,' for the word
'pants' in Britain means 'underwear.' In buildings in Britain
the 'first floor' is referred to as 'the ground floor'; what would
be called the 'second floor' in the United States would be the
'first floor' in Britain, and so on. 'Eggplants' are 'aubergines,'
'zucchini' are 'courgettes,' 'French fries' are 'chips,' 'chips' are
'crisps,' 'cookies' are 'biscuits,' the 'trunk' of an 'automobile' is
the 'boot' of a 'car,' its 'hood' is 'the bonnet,' its 'muffler' 'the
silencer,' 'gas' is 'petrol' (and by the way costs considerably
more in Britain!), and on it goes—the list could be almost
endless.

In addition to words that are different—indeed words that
can take on a whole new meaning—so also the real meaning
of phrases and sentences. For instance, when a Brit says 'Let's
meet up for a drink,' it means he will never contact you again,
the statement 'We must have lunch sometime' means 'Frankly
I do not mind very much if I ever see or hear from you again,'
while 'Well, we will have to see about that' means 'No, definitely not.' The phrase 'With the greatest respect' means 'I
am now going to humiliate you,' 'I beg your pardon' means
'drop dead' or, at the very least, 'get lost' and 'How are you?'
should, when used by a Brit, only ever be considered as a
rhetorical question.

Above all the British, and particularly, the English (as
against the Scot, the Irish and the Welsh) are different for
they have what can only be described as idiosyncratic ways of
doing things. For example, they wear a suit and tie even on
the hottest day of the year and never on any account wear
shorts. As with primitive tribesmen not wanting their photograph taken, so the British are frightened of letting strangers
know their names for fear of putting them in their power. The
British live in perpetual fear of body contact or even of proximity—it is perhaps for this reason that George Mikes was
able to observe, 'Continental people have a sex life, the English have hot water bottles.' Indeed, as soon as sex comes up
the British collectively tend to say 'Er . . .' instead of 'Ahh.'
The Anglo-Saxon conscience does not of course prevent the
Anglo-Saxon from sinning, it merely prevents him from enjoy-

ing his sin. Because of this an Englishman's idea of foreplay is marriage, whereas a love letter from an Englishman is likely to begin 'To Whom it May Concern.' It would seem that Englishmen have all the inherent sex appeal of a mug of cold tea or a plate of yesterday's fish and chips. Englishmen are feeble, ill-shaped, badly dressed, gauche, timid, destitute of style, dull, unadventurous and chauvinistic. In short, they lack fire. There is no passion, commitment or intensity about the English—as Michael Bywater observed 'he so clearly lacks joie de vivre that he doesn't have a word for it, having to borrow one from the French instead.' Clearly English women only mate with him for want of something better. English 'man' is fortunate to find himself inhabiting an island—alternatives for the women have not traditionally been readily at hand.

The British, and again more especially the English, are terrified of making fools of themselves in public. Embarrassment is the national disease—although it is one cured by drink, which goes some way to explain why on average one-fifth of their weekly shopping bill goes to alcohol. Indeed, the annual average consumption per person is approximately two hundred seventy pints of beer, twenty bottles of wine, nine litres of cider and ten litres of spirits. Drink has a strange effect on the English—after their fourth gin and tonic they are in danger of becoming sincere.

Heinrich Heine described 'silence' as 'a conversation with an Englishman,' and they are certainly backward in coming forward, for engaging in conversation means standing out from the crowd, the last thing anyone English wants to do. The one caviat to this rule is conversation concerning the weather, gardening, and possibly DIY (Do It Yourself—home maintenance). If you wish to strike up a conversation with a Brit, the first rule of thumb is to talk about the weather. The most noticeable difference to the position in the United States is the way the weather changes from day to day, even from hour to hour (as the British say, 'If you don't like the weather, wait a minute.'). Britain does not have such a wide range of temperatures as do many parts of the United States. Winters tend to be wet rather than freezing, summers tend to be warm rather than hot. The British may be a reserved people, but strike up a conversation about the weather (by way of a tip try 'Unusually mild for the time of year,' or 'Somewhat chilly for this month in comparison to last year') sit back and the Brit will hold forth. A word of warning however, should you strike up such a conversation on a train be careful not to miss your station or of course be so bored that you have to fight off the urge to hurl either yourself or the offending Brit from the train. You may be faced with the same problem if you ask about hardy perennials, or 101 uses for an orbital sander, but at least you'll get speech out of the British.

The British, and again particularly the English, have a strange, even perverse sense of humour. Their greatest pleasure is with the use of the double entendre, phrases capable of two meanings, especially if hinting at covert indecencies, and with making lavatorial jokes—the joint foundation stones of almost the entire British film industry. Actually for some quite unfathomable reason, the British have nigh on thirty words in their language for 'toilet,' including: toilet, loo, bathroom, ladies, gents, lavatory, little boys room, little girls room, latrine, water closet, WC, public convenience, lav, lavy, bog, john, head, can, privy, penny-house, powder-room and khasi. In addition, they have a whole variety of euphemisms for the tasks involved, including such classics as 'spending a penny,' 'doing finals,' 'communing with nature,' 'shedding a tear for Nelson' and 'shaking hands with the unemployed.'

The British have extraordinary habits. They sunburn under a fifty-watt bulb, central heating producing warm homes is still seen as something of a luxury and not really the British way. In Britain, if you are cold, then put on another sweater. Indeed, one can be led to the conclusion that the reason for their stiff upper lips is in fact because they are frozen. It would appear the British people are, above all else, allergic to novelty. It is for this reason that you enter a bathroom in Britain at your own risk. Nobody for example, can give a satisfactory explanation as to why in British handbasins there are two separate taps (faucets) on separate sides of the unit, one for scorchingly hot water and one for freezingly cold water—your choice when washing is which of the two alternatives to risk.

If you enter a British bathroom at your own risk, in sampling the product of a British kitchen you are certainly endangering if not your life, then at the very least, your taste buds. British 'cuisine' is a contradiction in terms, hell a place where the chefs are English. The British eat pizza with a knife and fork and, because they do not understand the recipe for ice, ration its use. They actually eat 'toad-in-the-hole,' 'jellied eels,' 'bubble and squeak' and 'spotted dick.' (Contrary to the view of some foreigners, these are not diseases, but are considered—by the British—to be traditional culinary delights.)

Joe Orton wrote in his diary that the English are the most tasteless nation on earth, which is why they set such store by good taste, while John Sessions observed that the English are always pretending they are full of finesse and charm but that this is only a mask behind which to hide the fact that they are in truth a vulgar people. If this is so, then perhaps it is a blend of this vulgarity with individuality, intractability, undauntedness, and their tendency to not be easily impressed which gives them their vitality. This mixture is the essence of the English. If you are what you drink the English are—in the words of Voltaire—like their own beer: froth on top, dregs at the bottom, excellent in the middle.

In Britain we drive on the left, which is right; whereas in the United States you drive on the right, which is wrong: one word of warning—in this instance when in Rome do as the Romans do.

However, if you are contemplating a visit to the United Kingdom don't panic. Some things are very much as you would expect: we sleep lying down, we walk upright, and we take a bath every year whether we need to or not.

The United Kingdom and the United States have arrived at where they are today from different origins and have encountered altogether different experiences in the interim, each being moulded and shaped by day-to-day events. This has led to a situation where although many people point to the close and strong links between the two countries, there are, in actual practice, considerable differences:

First, the United States owes its origins, its existence, to revolution; Great Britain does not—rather, its history, stretching back over a thousand years, has been shaped and moulded by evolution. This fact tends to underpin everything in British society; the guiding principle for the British is 'when it's not necessary to change, it is necessary not to change.'

Second, the United States has a formal, written, codified Constitution, Great Britain does not. Indeed, instead of attempting to tie together the numerous and varied strands of their constitution, to reduce their constitutional structure to a systematic codified form, to make them a consistent and coherent whole, the British have been content to leave the component parts of their constitution where the winds and waves of history have deposited them. The result of this is that the British constitution is a mixture of inter-related characteristics, a confusion of the true, the untrue and the obsolete, a welding of the written and the unwritten, an amalgam of practice and procedures, a weaving of the conventions, facts and fictions that have emerged and evolved through time.

Because of this, the powers, functions and responsibilities of many of the component parts are nebulous in the extreme, with the relative importance of each varying not only from time to time and in accordance to circumstances, but also occasionally even according to the views of observers and participants at any one time, each playing a constantly changing role as the substance of the constitution evolves. The result of this evolutionary development is that the system itself can often appear to be a blend of the vague with the indistinct, of the obscure with the turbid. As Viscount Bryce observed, the British constitution is:

> a mass of precedents carried in men's minds or recorded in writing, of dicta of lawyers or statesmen, of customs, usages, understandings, and beliefs bearing upon the methods of government, together with a certain number of statutes ... nearly all of them presupposing and mixed up with precedents and customs, and all of them covered with a parasitic growth of legal decisions and political habits, apart from which the statutes would be almost unworkable, or at any rate quite different in their working from what they really are.

Third, the United States has a Bill of Rights, Great Britain does not. In Britain there are no entrenched rights. Indeed, Parliament is supreme; Parliament can do anything and everything it wishes. Sir Ivor Jennings observed that Parliament could do anything except turn a man into a woman and a woman into a man. With all due respect to Sir Ivor, he was in fact wrong, because, constitutionally, Parliament can indeed pass a law stipulating that, henceforth, all men will be called women and all women will be called men. Unlike the position in the United States, the courts cannot strike down an act as unconstitutional. Quite simply the law in Britain is what Parliament says it is.

Fourth, the United States is a federal state with a formal separation of powers between the three branches of government—executive, legislative and judicial—and between the federal and state levels. Britain in contrast is a unitary state with all power ultimately centralized. For this reason, the British system of government would not accurately be symbolized by a neatly constructed layer cake with various distinct and separate planes. Instead, a far more realistic symbol would be that of a cake made from marble. For with a marble cake at whatever point it was sliced through, an inseparable mixture of differently colored ingredients would be revealed. There would be no clear horizontal stratification. On the contrary, vertical and diagonal lines would almost obliterate the horizontal ones, while in some places there would be unexpected whirls and an imperceptible merging of colors, to the extent that it would be difficult to tell where one ended and another began. This is how it is in the confused and chaotic marble cake that is the British structure of government.

Fifth, the United States elects its head of state—the President; Great Britain does not. Rather the British have a hereditary monarchy, the occupant there because they chose their parents wisely. The British do not even elect their head of government, the Prime Minister is not elected by the population at large but is the leader of the political party which commands the support of the majority in the House of Commons.

Sixth, the police in the United States are always armed; in Britain usually they are not. Indeed, only approximately ten percent of the police in Britain are trained in the use of firearms, and no police personnel permanently carry a weapon.

Seventh, there is no national health service in the United States; in Great Britain there is socialized medicine available (the National Health Service)—free to all at the point of treatment.

Eighth, in the United States nearly ninety percent of young people stay in education after the age of sixteen and something approaching sixty percent of people of college age go to college/university. By contrast in Great Britain only some sixty percent of young people stay on in full-time education after the age of sixteen and only approximately seventeen percent go on to full-time higher education.

Ninth, 'citizens' of the United States play incomprehensible games such as baseball and football. 'Subjects' in Britain play eminently sensible games such as cricket.

Tenth, in the United States there are an inordinate number of television channels; the British have basically four, and two of those have no advertising on them.

The question foreigners sometimes ask is 'What is the United Kingdom like?' It is a question which has been anticipated by the British Government, for each year they publish a wealth of statistical information about the country and its inhabitants. From this information one can ascertain the fact that, geographically, the mainland of the country is approximately six hundred miles in length from north to south and some three hundred miles in diameter at its widest point from west to east and that no place in the country is as much as seventy-five miles from tidal water. The UK's population is currently stable at about fifty-seven million. Since the turn of the century life expectancy at birth has risen from 49 years to 72.4 for a man and from 52 to 78.1 for a woman. At 234.1 people per square kilometre, the United Kingdom's population, is more than twice as dense as the population of China and denser than the European Community average (144.3). Despite its history of empire, non-European Community immigrants make up only 1.8% of the population. At an average of 43.6 hours per week, Britain's working hours are the longest in Europe. More inhabitants of the country get married than in any other European Community country, but the British get divorced more often also—12.6 out of every one thousand marriages end in divorce. Currently twenty-eight percent of children are born outside marriage. Average household incomes have increased by seventy-five percent over the past twenty years. Over the same period there have been improvements in the quality of the air in cities and in the condition of major rivers, although the figures show Britain to be one of the grubbiest countries in Western Europe, producing too much waste and having an unimpressive recycling record. Economically the statistics show a nation burdened with debt, which prefers to spend rather than invest, is poor in exporting, and has a bad record on inflation.

Putting all the information together, a picture can be gleaned of a country in which ownership of property and consumer items such as televisions and videos and of stocks and shares have grown considerably in recent years. Further, it is evident that the majority of the population have more free or leisure time than in previous generations. Television viewing is by far and away the most popular leisure activity be it scheduled programs or videos—video rentals in 1990 topped three hundred seventy-four million. Official statistics show that access to television is a percentage point above the figure for inside toilets; clearly a nation with priorities. Despite changes in recent years—fat intake having fallen by about twenty-five % over the past thirty years (although the British consumption of dairy produce is still twenty-eight % above the European Community average) and with the consumption of fruit increasing—the British diet nonetheless remains obstinately uncontinental: consumption of potatoes is higher than in any other Western European country except the Republic of Ireland and high-fat food such as fish and chips and the traditional British 'fry up' are still—according to survey data—the most popular meals.

What those who are not British may make of all this is hard to say. Perhaps they will conclude that Britain is a modest little country with much to be modest about, perhaps that Britain is a land of opportunity—at least for suppliers of television sets and videos, perhaps that the British must be a tolerant people, perhaps even that in matters of taste toleration can be taken too far.

On the global plane, it has been observed that Britain has lost an empire and not yet found a role. In the 1870s Britain possessed more battleships than the rest of the world combined and directly controlled about a fifth of the earth's surface. She had the world's largest economy, accounting for nearly a quarter of total manufacturing output and a similar proportion of world trade. In short, Britain was the greatest power the world had ever seen. Nonetheless, with the rise of other nations, the effects of two world wars and serious economic troubles, Britain has retreated from its global pre-eminence, given up its empire, cut its forces and military commitments and today stands as a medium-sized European power whose defense and security is entirely bound up with and dependent upon NATO.

The British have by now become accustomed to these facts, not least of all because they still find much in their nation to treasure. For example, ideas of friendship and loyalty genuinely run deep. There is very real joy taken in the use of language and, although they are poor in learning other people's languages, they often speak their own with considerable fluency, eloquence, and wit. Privacy and civility are both valued and rendered and there is little naked materialism and raw grasping of wealth. The National Health Service is, although often criticized, one of the few institutions over whose defense the British would man a barricade. Basic freedoms to think and write, to advocate and organize and to move about unhindered by officialdom are cherished and respected. Pride is taken in such things as their library service, their theatre, the BBC and indeed in the beauty of much of the nation itself, be it gardens, parks, or moorland. All of which—and more besides—may be hard to quantify—unlike gross domestic product, investment, exports and so on—but they help—along, it is true, with memories of past glories—to enable the British to accept their situation with stoicism and good humor.

Anglo-Saxon man and his society—the product of more than one thousand years of evolutionary development which included a succession of foreign occupants of the throne, invasion, civil war, and revolution—have survived and endured because of two key factors which became and remain the essential aspect of the British socio-political order. First was the emergence early on of the idea of limited kingship and an institutional framework for a constitutional monarchy, from which flowed power, order, and control. Second, made possible by the first, was a system of law that both preserved and protected the rights and liberties of the people and encouraged a respect for the autonomy of individual thought and action.

Nonetheless, the historical 'baggage' packed over these thousand years weigh heavily upon the shoulders of Anglo-Saxon man. A thousand years of fighting the cause of their small, cold, rain-swept islands built on coal off the north-west coast of continental Europe. Generation after generation learning to fit in, to conform, to follow rules, learning to avoid attracting attention, seeking to make sure that nothing unexpected ever happens. Generation after generation learning that language is a defense mechanism best used for concealing rather than revealing or explaining feelings. Generation after generation learning to stay hidden so that 'they can't see you coming until you can see the whites of their eyes.' Generation after generation of being subjects of a monarchy and its supporting aristocracy instilling into them the knowledge that, aspire as they may, there are some things one can only be born to. If Britain is a nation 'with class' it is because it is a nation of classes; there is a place for everyone provided everyone knows their place. Centuries of grey skies and rain, keeping his skin pale and pasty and instilling greyness into his character and into his soul. Two great wars draining his pockets and exhausting his energies, creating a society in which the object of government becomes the orderly management of decline, where uncompetitiveness and amateurism become the goals of nearly every endeavor and which is inventive only in thinking up reasons why something should not be done; for the British, when it is not necessary to change it is necessary not to change.

Having made these observations let us place Anglo-Saxon man under the microscope. If displayed, flayed, anatomized and dissected, what does one find? Anglo-Saxon man is nationalistic, with an automatic tendency to be both insular and parochial. To many he appears arrogant, pretentious and snobbish, coming across as aloof, distant and withdrawn, exuding smugness and self-righteousness. In actuality this is a defense mechanism, much as a grass snake emits an unpleasant odor with which to defend itself, for Anglo-Saxon man is essentially shy and reserved. As a result he does not make friends easily, but once he makes them he tends to keep them. He can be both witty and humorous, but usually with a large dose of cynicism—but then cynicism is the condom of the true romantic. Above all else he is—conservative, traditional and old-fashioned. He has a vision of the past rather than a plan for the future; for the British nostalgia isn't what it was. There is an all-pervading love of tradition; for the British all that 'was,' 'is.' The problem however is that love of what is ancient, tried and tested all too often manifests itself as fear of what is new, unknown, and different.

As a result, for many—not least of all Americans—the United Kingdom is a conundrum wrapped in an enigma inside a mystery. Its inhabitants possess the most complex of complex characters for, even more than is the case in most other countries, they live within the confines of their own myths and inherent contradictions—the home of Shakespeare, Milton, and Wordsworth is also home to the skinhead, *The Sun* 'newspaper' and the processed mushy pea. Perhaps it was for this reason that when Charles Lindbergh crossed the Atlantic all those years ago, looking down upon 'perfidious Albion'—the descendants of Caesar, Canute, Ethelred the Unready and William the Conqueror—he took the easy way out and landed in France.

The Politics of Broadcasting in the European Community: The Television without Frontiers Directive

❖

Mitch Baranowski

This paper takes the European media revolution as its starting point and traces the history of the European Community's first major legislation on audiovisual internationalization and deregulation—The Television without Frontiers Directive on Broadcasting. After considering theoretical models which help articulate European Community audiovisual policy, this paper discusses the decline of the "Old Order" of European electronic media and highlights key features of the "New Crisis" now facing the EC audiovisual sector. It also overviews specific policies embodied in the Directive which attempt to redress problems created by this new crisis. Finally, two specific programs—Media '95 and Audiovisual Eureka—are briefly discussed before the paper concludes with considerations on the future of EC audiovisual policy.

Introduction, the rationale for a common market communication policy

Within the last decade, developments in communication technologies, namely satellites and cable networks, have started what is commonly referred to as a "media revolution" in Europe. Improvements in satellite and cable transmissions have rapidly created a *de facto* abolition of national barriers to broadcasting and thus raised the stakes on the need for effective, consistent European regulation in the audiovisual

industry. Technological improvements have also rapidly multi-
plied the number of broadcasting outlets available to European
countries and thus made it imperative that Europe find some
way to collectively support production, promotion, and distribution of media programming. In addition, increasing competition
from abroad for European media services reaffirms the urgent
need for a stronger Common Market communication policy.

Reacting primarily to these three elements of the media
revolution—abolition of national borders, multiplication of
broadcasting channels, and competition from non-European
media powers like the United States—the European Community (EC) drafted the "Television without Frontiers" Directive
on Broadcasting. Effective October 3, 1991, the Directive os-
tensibly has two goals: to ensure the free circulation of broadcasts in the Community and protect the cultural objectives of
national programming.

The European media revolution

Matteo Maggiore has described the audiovisual (AV) sector of the European Community as an industry "that has culture for trade" (1990, 129). As a cultural industry, then, the
AV sector encompasses film and TV production, distribution
and financing, broadcasting, and the electronics industry. Both
public and, increasingly, private interests control its cultural
and industrial sectors.[1] In terms of revenue, people employed,
and budget allocation, the audiovisual sector of the EC is not
yet "impressive." In 1985, its turnover was estimated at ECU
15.4 billion, representing 0.4% of the EC's 1985 GNP. (Television alone accounted for more than half of this total.) About
120,000 people are currently employed in the whole of the
industry. Still, the audiovisual industry is growing quickly:
its turnover, for example, was estimated to exceed ECU 27
billion by the end of 1991. Also, because of its links to electronics, advertising, telecommunications and other information industries, the AV sector arguably should be considered
to be more economically vital to the Community than the figures indicate (Maggiore 1990, 11).[2] A brief look at the remarkable statistics surrounding the nature of the European
media revolution points to what kind of growth is expected
from the EC's audiovisual sector in the near future.

In 1988, for example, 50 television channels existed in
Europe, collectively broadcasting about 180,000 hours of pro-

gramming. By the end of 1992, a projected 100 television channels will exist with programming needs of about 500,000 hours
per year. Television channels are currently expanding at a
rate of 10 per year. This rapid expansion can be attributed
mostly to growth in the satellite and cable network industries. At this writing, each Member State of the European
Community has, on average, 3-4 broadcasting channels. By
1995, conservative estimates predict each Member State will
receive at least 30 television channels via terrestrial (i.e.,
Hertzian) frequencies, satellite broadcasts, or cable networks.
Currently, about 10 million European households (or 30 million people) subscribe to satellite television. As for cable penetration, about 16 million European households were linked
to cable by 1989, representing 18% of a total 130.1 million TV
households. By 1995, this number is expected to grow to 31
million (Maggiore 1990, 29; Lindheim 1989, 36; and Pragnell
1985, 3).

Before the advent of communication technologies such as
satellite and cable television, state control of broadcasting
was justified because it regulated what was perceived to be a
scarce resource-spectrum. With this obstacle now gone, however, Member States have been forced to rethink how to regulate the audiovisual industry in light of the "European
television explosion" (Berkowitz 1989, 63). The technological
innovation surrounding satellites and cable hurtles geographical barriers and national borders and realizes the "transborder
circulation" of programs and films. The reality of transfrontier
broadcasting prompted "supranational" regulation from the
European Community in keeping with its goals of ensuring
the free circulation of all goods, products, people and services
between Member States. To date, the European Community's
Television without Frontiers Directive has provided the best
legal framework for helping Member States think globally,
rather than nationally, about audiovisual communication.

In short, the relevant features of the "media revolution"
affecting European Community audiovisual policy can be described as follows:

> expanded air-time on satellites, cable networks, and deregu-
> lated terrestrial frequencies;
>
> a European software production sector pressed to keep pace
> with increasing programming demand;
>
> the transborder circulation of programs;

increasing investment in television and other media as well
as other closely related sectors (e.g., advertising, electronics
and telecommunications); and

a deeply-rooted mental habit of considering the media a public service that conflicts with deregulatory policymaking as it
is known in the United States.

Because of the dramatic expansion of television air-time, the
"media revolution" creates an enormous gap (between supply
and demand) in fiction production and forces the Community
to ask problematic questions that will duly affect the future
of the industry: Do the Member States have the resources to
fill all the new air-time? Is there a consumer demand that it
be expanded and/or filled? If it is to be filled, how, why, and
with what programming? Such questions make it imperative
that the European Community continue to create effective and
consistent broadcasting policy for the Member States. Divided,
the states fear further fragmentation, scattering and division
from non-European media powers like the United States. Together, they stand a chance at creating progressive ways to
help an audiovisual industry urgently in need of support.

The politics of mediating culture: theoretical underpinnings to internationalizing audiovisual production

In modernity, electronic technology has come to embody
progress, and this is especially true in the audiovisual industry. Symbolically linked to societal evolution, technology is
often presupposed to actively integrate the public into formation of a collective consciousness. The crux of McLuhan's ar-
guments, for example, is his faith in the redemptive potential
of new media technologies: each new electronic media technology is viewed as creating harmony, balance, community,
equality, and participation.[3] This normative theory of the electronic media, however, tends to view them as salvational and
transformative. It says, in effect, if only we had "better" media, we could transcend society's problems.

The term "media" here cannot be restricted solely to technological mediums, though this is often the case when regulatory bodies determine broadcasting policy. The term must be
expanded to include the plurality of local, regional, and

national agencies which disseminate ideas or information and thus organize culture. This broad definition acknowledges that the mass media are institutions which often "reflect, express and sometimes actively serve national interests as determined by more powerful actors and institutions" (McQuail 1987, 110).

Recognizing this broader definition, this essay defines communication policy as a body of operational laws, administrative regulations, and budgetary practices that allows a state government to regulate goods, services, and standards related to technical aspects of the broadcasting industry. Cultural policy is defined as that body of laws, regulations, and practices that allows a state government to ensure the cultural values, goals, and products it defines as important. These two policy areas are not mutually exclusive and, in the case of the European Community, they often overlap.

In terms of the European Community's reactions to changes in the audiovisual industry, its policies are often articulated using two common normative media theories. Specifically, the European Community's reactions to the international information marketplace can be better understood using development media theory and democratic-participant media theory.

Briefly, development media theory describes countries without a sound economic infrastructure and a history of colonialist exploitation. It attempts to counteract a perceived imbalance in the international flow of information and opposes foreign domination of the State, commerce, and the culture industry. Thus, media in developing countries should promote nationalism and established governmental policy. To foster solidarity, the media should also give priority to the national culture, the national language, and other developing countries in news and entertainment programming. Censorship of the media is justified as long as it is in the interest of the country's economic development.

Democratic-participant media theory originates partly as a reaction against the commercialization and monopolization of privately-owned media and partly as a response to the centralization and bureaucratization of public broadcasting institutions. In the bureaucratic state, market forces are perceived to subvert freedom of expression and undermine the social responsibility of media institutions. Thus, media organization and content should not be subject to the marketplace nor to state control. Democratic-participant media theory attempts to balance these concerns by focusing on the needs, interests and aspirations of the active "receiver" in society. In other words, the media should provide access to individual citizens and minority groups and be responsive to their needs. Small-scale, interactive and participative media forms are deemed more utilitarian than media conglomerates.[4]

Media imperialism and communication policymaking

Behind both the development and democratic-participant media theories lies the thesis of cultural or media imperialism. The danger inherent in media imperialism stems from the perception that industrialization of the mass media, especially in capitalist societies, can lead to the commodification of culture.[5]

For example, the United States has been criticized for organizing media monopolies and international news cartels with neo-colonialist zeal; it has also been accused of expanding its outlets for capital abroad to sustain its audiovisual industry's economic growth.[6] This sentiment is captured by the theory of economic dependence, which posits that the West (read, United States) deliberately perpetuates the dependency of smaller countries in the name of profitmaking.

Europe's typical reaction to any perceived economic dependency on capitalist America has been to adopt a culturally xenophobic, chauvinistic stance in the political arena, though economic ties usually cannot be severed cleanly by isolationist policies. European media scholars consistently point out the negative consequences of the commodification of culture: increased monopolization, manipulation, and homogenization of media content.[7] These negative aspects underlie the thesis of media imperialism, which rejects the imposition of "less worthy" external goods, services, or ideologies upon an indigenous culture.

In this respect, the thesis of media imperialism argues that although media can help in modernizing developing countries, they threaten to introduce "foreign" values at the expense of traditional ones. Foreign values are anathema to traditional cultures because they are perceived to legitimize capitalism and perpetuate commercialism. The process by which foreign values are introduced is also perceived to be imperialistic in that it deliberately subordinates smaller countries to the interests of dominant capitalist powers like the

United States. What makes the apparently simple thesis of media imperialism complex, however, is the fact that foreign media can penetrate traditional cultures in as many ways as receiving cultures can admit the products, practices, and values of Western media.[8]

European calls for measures against media imperialism began in the 1940s as a reaction to the United States' campaign to dismantle European news cartels in the name of the "free flow" of information and worldwide access to news. At a Unesco conference in 1945, the U.S. appealed to the United Nations to make the free flow of information a Unesco objective, and it has remained one ever since. Europeans and Third World nations resented the American rhetoric, especially since the actual flow of information favored the United States. By the 1960s, they had articulated a series of complaints about the imbalanced nature of information flow.[9]

These complaints received the empirical justification they needed when Unesco commissioned Tapio Varis in 1974 to perform a study of the international flow of television programs. Varis found that the global traffic in television was "a one-way street" (108). His report stressed America's dominance of the world media marketplace and raised questions in developing countries about the equity of cultural exchange between them and the United States. After the Varis report, Unesco began to seriously question the American principle of "free flow." This new vigorous inquiry indicated a definite shift in priorities for the developing countries—from national integration and socioeconomic modernization to cultural expression. The data from Varis's international flow studies (he conducted another study in 1983 that showed virtually no change in the balance of information flow) are often used to shore up claims about media imperialism and to rationalize protectionist media policies.[10]

Current data still support an imbalance in the export/import relations between Europe and the United States. Fictional programming accounts for about 37% of all programs transmitted in Europe. An average 27% of those fictional programs are domestically produced. Germany and the United Kingdom are the only two countries that produce more fiction than they buy, and in all countries the prime source of imported material is the U.S. In terms of business volume, the worldwide exchange of fiction programs accounts for more than USD 3 billion annually. Half of these exchanges takes place between Europe and the United States. In 1985, European exports amounted to 3.25% of European audiovisual turnover, while in 1986 American programs represented 44% of the imports in Europe. These American programs also garnered, on average, a 40% share of the audience (Maggiore 1990, 45).

Such a global commercialization of culture in favor of the United States has forced many European countries to restate modernization in the audiovisual industry in terms of preserving their cultural integrity.[11] In so far as media imperialism is perceived to occur, governments rely heavily upon the two-edged sword of communication and cultural policy to fend off its encroaching tentacles.

Most European countries have specific social, economic, or cultural ideals that the national media are expected to support, for example, national integration, socioeconomic modernization, and authentic self-expression. But policy decisions are based not only on ideals, but also on analyses of the dynamics of media institutionalization: who controls the media, how they are organized, what programs they broadcast, and what implications these factors have for the indigenous population.

How the European Community deals with such factors in the face of a "media revolution" provides a telling example of the conflict between American and European approaches to the audiovisual sector. Europeans are often characterized as fearing American imperialism and Americans as fearing European protectionism. It remains to be seen whether a European Europe can exist independently of its nation–states and assert this existence against media powers like the United States. Already its current media infrastructure struggles with the burden of competing against external commercial interests.

The "old order" and "new crisis" of European electronic media

During the reconstruction of post-World War II Europe, industrial monopolies were viewed generally as either benevolent or inevitable features of the consensus. When television replaced radio as the basic household amenity, its organizational and regulatory structure reflected the contemporary importance placed upon state control in the name of public service. Like monopolies in other industries, broadcasting monopolies assumed *de facto* control of the audiovisual industry. The traditional point of view thus promoted public service, linked to a concern for quality in programming, and actively spurned private interests.

The technological advances in the audiovisual industry described above have unquestionably changed the balance between commercial and non-commercial interests in the Member States. Prior to the impact of technological changes in the early 1980s, the "Old Order" of European electronic media had distinct characteristics, which Denis McQuail and the Euromedia Research Group effectively summarized. In short, said McQuail et al., the "Old Order" of European media:

> subordinated broadcasting to public service goals and public accountability, especially in the area of culture;
>
> dedicated national media to serving national interests, audiences and social institutions, especially to protect national language and culture;
>
> politicized broadcasting content, either by enforcing political neutralization or through balancing representation of diverse political opinions; and
>
> remained monopolistic in nature, non-commercial in principle, and resolute in thinking the purposes of broadcasting were not to be commercial or economic but cultural and political.
>
> (1990, 314–315)

In stressing the "public good" of broadcasting, traditional European media exemplified the good intentions characterized by normative media theory generally: cultural and informational quality, public accountability, fairness, diversity, independence, multiculturalism, nationalism. Despite good intentions, however, this kind of normative bias in European media bred conflicts between broadcasters, researchers, and political and cultural institutions over what direction the audiovisual industry should take.

As a result of such conflicts, an uneasy political climate existed long before the "media revolution," but this climate was doubtless affected by European governments' predictions about the impact of technological changes. (Technological changes are often anticipated in advance of their impact.) In any case, technological innovation, coupled with a change in the political climate, facilitated the breakdown of the "Old Order" of European media by pointing up the old media

systems' incapacity to handle increasing commercial interests
and demands in the audiovisual industry. Accompanying the
decline of the "Old Order" of European media were problems
which created a "New Crisis" in the AV sector.

The features of what developed into a crisis for the European audiovisual industry were summarized by McQuail et
al. as follows:

> loss of legitimacy for monopolistic public broadcasting systems;
>
> increased vogue for market solutions and deregulation in
> communication;
>
> European Community efforts to harmonize rules for broad-
> casting, reinforced by disappearance of national borders in
> face of satellite, cable, and foreign media intrusion;
>
> widespread desire to gain national and European profit from
> developing hardware and software industries associated with
> new technologies; and
>
> popular dissatisfaction with the old 'official' cultural regula-
> tion and establishment control.
>
> (1990, 316–317)

In light of the above features, new European media policies
need to be capable of accommodating a more liberal political
outlook, exploiting new economic opportunities in communication, and increasing cultural populism. Until now, the lack of
both a sound European media infrastructure and effective communication policy has created nothing short of a crisis in the
audiovisual industry, especially in the realm of fiction production.

The fiction gap

Europeans have good reason to fear "the death of an independent cultural production in Europe," as Matteo Maggiore
describes it (1990, 39). The problem is one of demand. Additional channel capacity creates a huge demand for programming content and stimulates competition for audiences and
advertising revenue between established European media
structures, emerging European structures, and foreign companies. A consideration of current production levels and estimated production needs points up the seriousness of the crisis
in fiction.

Given the expansion of air-time by satellites and cable networks mentioned earlier, it is estimated that by 1995, European broadcasting channels will need 1.5 million hours of programming per year. If fiction (dramas, serials, sitcoms, soaps, etc.), by a conservative estimate, accounts for a third of this total programming, the need for fictional programming is calculated at 500,000 hours per year. If half of all fictional programming is allowed to come from extra-European countries like the United States (and by all accounts this is again a conservative estimate), this still leaves a need for 250,000 hours of European fiction per year. Lastly, if half the need for European fiction is met by re-runs of previously produced programs and films, a demand still exists for *125,000* new fiction hours per year (Maggiore 1990, 41–42).

Admittedly, the upcoming fiction gap ought not to be filled solely by extra-European suppliers. But the fear is that by 1995, most programs broadcast in Western Europe could be non-European. This could easily become the reality for several reasons. First, original productions are expensive for Europeans. Europe lacks the audiovisual infrastructure to actively support preproduction (e.g., scriptwriting), financing, filming, distribution and promotion. Second, Europe has, in the past, naturally turned to the United States for cheap entertainment. American media companies are able to offer cheap entertainment because, by virtue of the size of their domestic market, they absorb production costs before marketing programs overseas. Programs are priced to effectively undercut the costs of original European productions. Third, in terms of production values, American programming generally appears more professional in terms of broadcasting quality, and thus offers a more appealing product. Of course, the cost per program increases according to a specific program's popularity. The popularity of American programs (mentioned above) only further compounds the problem for European commercial broadcasters, who increasingly must turn to advertising as a major revenue source. To attract advertisers, broadcasters typically feel compelled to use whatever programming necessary to reach a large audience and hold their attention.[12]

These tendencies leave the European audiovisual sector particularly open to be dominated by a few media giants who will control production as well as distribution. Thus, what appears initially to be diversification in the way of content (resulting from a plurality of broadcasting channels) may in fact lead to concentration and homogeneity on the European audiovisual scene. This concentration, of course, is not viewed favorably. It is horizontal rather than vertical in direction, as companies form conglomerations that encompass all aspects of audiovisual production. Bonds between broadcasters form frequently and are symptomatic of the conglomeratist attitude.[13]

The politics of broadcasting: internationalization and deregulation

Underlying European anxiety about media concentration is a reluctance to let go of the traditional public service model of communication. The switch from service to business means, to many Europeans, switching priorities from culture to capitalism. This, of course, does not necessarily have to be the case. There are benefits to competition, namely diversity (of choices of content) and lower prices (for products, services, etc.). Still, quantity does not always equal quality, and if concentration occurs unchecked it will likely lead to homogeneity of content and higher prices for media services.[14]

Deregulation ultimately amounts to dismantling the monopolies of public television. But deregulation is not "the absence of regulation," but an attempt to modify existing laws in an effort to open a previously restricted audiovisual "space" to private interests (Mattelart 1984, 27, 61). The European Community exists to unify the internal market and provide for the free circulation of goods. Its effort to establish "a legal framework for transborder broadcasting must be seen as the starting point for a European audiovisual policy" (Maggiore 1990, 33).

What EC policies for what form of deregulation?

A brief history of the first major EC legislation to address audiovisual internationalization will point up the difficulty Member States have in reaching accord on the apparently simple issue of broadcasting. I would argue this issue is made complex (and hence divisive) by the implicit cultural objectives maintained in most European broadcasting policies, especially those regarding quotas. This is readily apparent when one considers the delays that cultural objectives caused in approving the EC's first major directive on broadcasting.

In 1983, the Commission of the European Communities (CEC) gave a report to the European Council entitled, "Trends in broadcasting in Europe: Perspectives and options." This report marked the first major EC effort to comprehend changes in the audiovisual industry. It called attention to the projected increase in demand for audiovisual software in the near future. It also argued that there was a need for consistent action in support of program production.

In 1984, the Commission issued its Green Paper on "Television Without Frontiers" in recognition of the *de facto* abolition of barriers in the audiovisual space. The Green Paper served as the foundation for the EC's draft directive on broadcasting, issued in March 1986 and known as the "Television without Frontiers" Directive. The Directive had two main goals: to harmonize and coordinate Member States' legislation to ensure the free circulation of broadcasts and the cultural objectives of European programming.

On April 14, 1989, after swimming for more than three years through troubled waters in various Council committees, the draft Directive was approved by a "qualified majority" in the Internal Market Council. It was then submitted to the European Parliament for a second reading and further amendment. But in June 1989, after more committee delays, the European Council charged the Internal Market Council to approve the draft Directive within three months—no exceptions. Finally, on October 3, 1989, the Directive was approved by the General Affairs Council in Luxembourg by a majority vote, though Belgium and Denmark still opposed the measure. After a transition period of two years, the Directive took effect October 3, 1991, signaling Member States to comply with its provisions. These are set forth below.

The television without frontiers directive on broadcasting

Despite its shortcomings and limitations, the "Television without Frontiers" Directive is the most effective and consistent European legislation dealing with the audiovisual industry to date. As mentioned, two fundamental principles form the bedrock of the EC's Directive: free circulation and cultural objectives. Of the two, the former has been the easiest to articulate and approve, for free circulation of audiovisual software is consistent with the economistic approach of the EC.

Regarding free circulation, Article 2 imposes on all EC Member States the acceptance of broadcasts originating from another Member State. If a program complies with the laws of one Member State, then it must be accepted by all 12 Member States.[15] Article 20, however, does allow individual states to produce programs solely for national transmission. Otherwise, the only grounds for interrupting reception from other Member States is repeated violation of Article 22, which prohibits the transmission of programs "which might seriously impair the physical, mental or moral development of minors, in particular those that involve pornography or gratuitous violence" (CEC 1990, 21).

The Directive also places noteworthy restrictions on how often broadcasts may be interrupted for advertising. For feature films and television films, the limit is once every 45 minutes. For programs 30 minutes or less, advertising must fall between the programs, and then only if it does not endanger a program's integrity or value. Advertising should not, in the end, exceed a maximum volume of 15% of total daily broadcasting or 20% of any single hour of broadcasting.

Regarding cultural objectives, these are expressed in the quotas of broadcasts that should be reserved for European productions. Article 4 of Chapter III states:

> Member States shall ensure where practicable and by appropriate means, that broadcasters reserve for European works ... *a majority proportion of their transmission time,* excluding the time appointed to news, sports events, games, advertising and teletext services. This proportion, having regard to the broadcasters' informational, educational, cultural and entertainment responsibilities to its viewing public, should be achieved progressively, on the basis of suitable criteria (emphasis added).
>
> (CEC 1990, 18)

Thus, according to the EC Directive, TV stations must devote *most* of their programming time to European productions.[16] Member States are free to adopt strict quotas of their own but, for those Member States wishing to ignore the EC's quota recommendations, the Directive is only "politically binding," not juridically binding. What this means, of course, is that Member States can not yet be prosecuted for violating the EC's quota regulation regarding exports.

In trying to fulfill cultural objectives vis-à-vis quotas, the language of the EC's Directive remains vague, confusing and, ultimately, ineffective. In the end, the EC has trouble addressing cultural aspects because it remains an economistic institution that assumes cultural objectives can be treated like economic ones.

This is not to say the Commission of the European Communities has not made efforts to minimize purely economic thinking. Indeed, since January 1989, three CEC Directorates-General (DGs) have been closely involved in formulating audiovisual policy. DG III (Internal Market and Industrial Affairs) was responsible for drafting regulatory measures that ensure the free circulation of programs. DG X (Information, Communication and Culture) has been the EC leader regarding cultural objectives, while DG XIII (Telecommunications, Information Industries, and Innovations) has largely been concerned with technological hardware and broadcasting standards. Of the three DGs, DG III played the most significant role in drafting the "Television without Frontiers" Directive.

What EC programs for what form of internationalization?

As mentioned, the impact of any strength in the Directive is diluted by past and present discord over its cultural provisions. In the absence of more competent and effective European media policies, the market approach to audiovisual production has gained considerable power. Unless alternative media policies are formulated quickly, there will be no choices left in the audiovisual industry, only de facto winners and losers. To try and avoid such a situation, the EC supports two key programs in an effort to help the audiovisual industry in terms of production and financing.[17]

Media '95

Begun in 1986 by the Commission of the European Communities, Media '92 (as the plan was called then) was initiated with two assumptions in mind:

> first, that the professionals themselves must determine the form that aid to production must assume; and second, that the support has to result in the establishment of independent agencies and/or structures. Having set certain sectoral priorities, the programme limits itself to organizing consultations among the professionals on the problems of each sector and making elaborate proposals. The proposals assume the form of pilot projects financed up to 50%, in a proportion

that must decrease in time, by Media 92. The rest has to be provided by others: institutions, professionals, private sponsors, etc.

(Maggiore 1990, 63)

The Commission's initial funding of 50% acts as "seed-money." Pilot projects are supposed to become financially independent as quickly as possible. The first seven pilot structures were tagged for four audiovisual sectors—distribution, financing, production, and training. They are identified as follows:

European Film Distribution Office (EFDO)—loans up to half of distribution costs to low budget films and commits them to distribution in at least three EC countries;

Broadcasting across the barrier of European languages (Babel)—finances dubbing and subtitling of films;

Euro-AIM—supports independent producers in marketing and promotion as well as co-productions with other independents;

Media investment club—promotes use of advanced technology in audiovisual production;

European Script Fund—supports pre-production phase of scriptwriting;

Cartoon—finances European cartoon production; and

European audiovisual entrepreneurs (EAVE)—trains young producers in management skills.

(CEC 1991)

When it was proposed in 1986, the Commission restricted Media '92 to a relatively short life by agreeing to approve its funding on a year-by-year basis. Born a small action plan, Media '92's budget for 1987 amounted to ECU 1 million. In 1988, this figure increased to ECU 5 million; in 1989, the budget was ECU 7.5 million. The estimate for the 1990 budget is ECU 10 million. Such budget increases show the success of Media '92, and exemplify the confidence which the program has earned from the Commission.

Indeed, because each of the above pilot projects is now autonomous and seems to be doing well, the Council of Ministers approved financing Media '92 for an additional five years on December 21, 1990. Media '95, as the plan is now called, has been allotted a budget of ECU 200 million for 1991–1995

(CEC 1991, 7). Although it has been called "the most successful model for a European audiovisual policy as far as the support to softward (i.e. fiction) production is concerned" (Maggiore
1990, 65), Media '95 is far too small in budgetary terms to be
considered anything but an example of how to develop practical audiovisual policies.[18]

Audiovisual eureka

Another policy action, Audiovisual Eureka, was first proposed by the French government in December 1987. Its principles were first outlined in September 1989 at the Paris
conference "Assises de l'audiovisuel." In terms of scope and
size, Eureka dwarfs Media '95. Eureka's scope is technological as well as software-related. (Media '95 will likely serve as
the main model for action in the field of software.) As for
budget funds, in 1989, Jacques Delors, then-president of the
European Commission, asked the European Council at
Strasbourg to allocate ECU 250 million to support Eureka's
action in the audiovisual sector. Thus far, only the future
structure of Audiovisual Eureka has been concretely outlined.
Eureka's structure consists of three bodies: a Committee of
Coordinators (to oversee details of projects), a Secretariat (to
oversee administrative functions), and an Observatory (essentially a databank for necessary information). To this writer's
knowledge, Eureka's main function to date has been to serve
as a supranational coordinating committee for European audiovisual projects (e.g., coproductions). Thus, Eureka's performance is so far impossible to assess.

Conclusion: the future of EC audiovisual policy

One way of summarizing the material outlined above is
by recognizing the two key elements driving current audiovisual policy change: external pressure and internal conflict. As
described, external pressure on the AV sector comes from extra-European countries eager to exploit new markets. External pressure also comes from technological innovations (e.g.,
satellites and cable networks) that expand air-time. Internal
conflicts arise between old and new players over what kind of
new broadcasting order is going to emerge in reacting to external pressures.

The first element, externality, encompasses the major actors in European audiovisual industry: profitseeking broadcasting corporations, would-be broadcasters previously excluded by state monopoly arrangements, transnational corporations seeking to access foreign markets, and governments wanting to open up the audiovisual marketplace for economic-industrial goals.

The second element, conflict, highlights the value of the cultural goods at stake. Political conflicts arise mostly over who will have access to commercial rewards by exploiting audiovisual industry; up to now public service monopolies have controlled this access. Ideological conflicts then arise over cultural values: traditional elites, purists, pit themselves against "new commercialism" and/or "media imperialism."

In the end, one either defends the status quo or supports externally driven change. The "old order" has been defended primarily by public broadcasting bodies, established cultural institutions, consumer organizations and political parties of the left. By contrast, externally driven change has been promoted primarily by would-be hardware and software suppliers, political parties of the right, investors, advertisers and their agencies.

McQuail et al. have suggested a sequential model for understanding media policy change in Europe: first, diverse "old orders" of public monopoly are destabilized by technological and other changes (i.e., in political climate); second, supranational pressure in form of external commercial challenges elicits national resistance or adaptation. If new rules of entry and operation are adopted, then a provisional "new order" is created that is subject to modification depending on audience and market outcomes. Finally, a "new order" emerges that is actually a "mix" of both "old" and "new" systems. The variability of countries must be stressed as diluting general precise applicability of McQuail et al.'s model (1990, 327).

As for the European Community and its future role in the policymaking process, it must continue to push decision-making at the global level. It must focus on industrial and commercial matters with a supranational viewpoint. (But this is not to say that the EC's audiovisual proposals will be any less political than nationally-oriented cultural and ideological policymaking.) The four areas of audiovisual policy that require immediate regulation include multi-media groups (through anti-trust provisions), copyright, public subsidies to audiovisual production, and the free circulation of persons and equipment. Much remains to be accomplished, but the European Community has already proven to be the European leader in audiovisual policymaking.

Notes

1. When discussing the audiovisual industry, it should be recognized that culture, economics, and industrial production can be separated only in theoretical terms; in reality, cultural activity is determined by industrial and economic factors just as industrial activity depends upon a sense of its cultural mission.

2. Considering the stakes involved in High Definition Television, just one media service in the audiovisual industry, one would expect investment and interest to increase rapidly in the near future. Currently, HDTV has a predicted worldwide market value of USD 103 billion (Maggiore 1990, 114; Berkman 1990, 44).

3. McLuhan's positive outlook on technological determinism is apparent in his *Understanding Media: Extensions of Man,* 1964.

4. For a more thorough discussion of development media theory, democratic-participant media theory, and other normative media theories, the reader is referred to McQuail 1987, 126–132.

5. Bernard Miège (1989) attempts to clarify the link between culture and industry by recognizing that cultural production (e.g., of news or art) occurs as a specific aspect of the valorization of capital. That is, in capitalist cultural production, an investment of money is made into cultural labor, which in turn produces a "reproducible" material good that integrates the work of the artist/author/producer (e.g., a news article or compact disc). The cultural product has "use value" by virtue of the artist's work and the symbolic meanings associated with it. The cultural product also has "exchange value" in that it can be traded on the commercial marketplace as a commodity in exchange for money. Any cultural product, if it is to produced and consumed on a massive scale, must therefore be subject to economic constraints and specific modes of industrial reproduction. The "commoditization of culture" hinges on the symbiotic relationship between production and consumption and, of course, if the mass media profit from their cultural creations it is according to this dialectic.

6. Writers critical of America in this respect include Lee (1979), Mattelart (1984; 1985), Miège (1989), and Schiller (1990).

7. In this instance, see McQuail (1987), Miège (1989), or Mattelart (1984; 1985).

8. As Boyd-Barret defined it, media imperialism is:

the process whereby the ownership, structure, distribution or content of the media in any one country are singly or together subject to substantial pressure from the media interests of any other country or countries without proportionate reciprocation of influence by the country so affected.

(Quoted by Lee 1979, 37–38).

Of course, underlying this definition is the assumption that media have powerful influences; that is, the receiving culture is "innocent" until corrupted by the imperialistic culture. Another point of view might argue that a culture defines its identity, not solely from within, but by comparing itself to, and differentiating itself from, another culture. By encountering an "Other" culture, a people becomes conscious of its cultural practices and values. It projects onto the "Other" culture its understandings about what its own culture must be.

9. These complaints, as noted by Thomas Surprenant, included the following: a flagrant quantitative imbalance in information between North and South hemispheres; inequality in information resources—Americans with primary access to technological equipment and spectrum allocation; de facto hegemony and will to dominate—American indifference to developing countries; view of information as a commodity, and capitalistic use of information—extension of the colonial era—political, economic, and cultural neo-colonialism (1987, 49).

10. But it is important to note that Varis's findings are often pulled from context or misrepresented. Preben Sepstrup (1989) and Marit Bakke (1986, 136–137) both take issue with the implications of Varis's findings. For example, instead of looking at total imported television hours (as Varis did, coming up with 44% as the U.S. share of total imports for Western Europe), Sepstrup analyzes what he takes to be more relevant data—the percentage occupied by imports of total national supply. In this analysis, 73% of Western European programming is domestically produced, 13% originates from the United States, and 12% comes from other Western European countries. As Sepstrup notes,

It is a subjective judgment whether 13% is too much, but stressing the 44 percent instead of the 13 percent (the import share instead of the share of total supply) has, in my opinion, led to an exaggerated perception of the general role of U.S. television in Western Europe.

(1989, 40)

Given Sepstrup's comments, it would at least be fair to question the empirical basis for, say, the European Community's quota on imported TV programs and argue that the policy seems arbitrarily based on "hard" data.

11. France, Belgium, Denmark, and Germany have been the most vocal about preserving cultural heritage in the face of modernization.

12. The reader is referred to Collins et al. (1988) for a thorough treatment of the economics of television.

13. For example, in 1989, tenuous relationships were struck between Time, Inc. and Warner; News International (Murdoch) and Walt Disney; Havas, CLT, Bertelsmann, TVS, and Canal Plus; Maxwell, Fininvest, Bouygues, and Kirch-Pathe; W. H. Smith and Compagnie Générale des Eaux. Unfortunately, it is not within the scope of this report to provide detailed descriptions of the major TNCs in the AV sector, but the reader is referred to Maggiore, Pragnell, Sepstrup, and McQuail et al. for detailed discussions of the major corporate players.

14. Public broadcasting, in the face of the media revolution, is left in a particular quandary: how to compete with commercial television. It must do three things: 1) define its necessity as an quality-minded alternative to private broadcasting; 2) develop market strategies to increase its presence in the AV sector; 3) and create a public broadcasting service at the European level. This last point can be effected by 1) establishing a regulatory framework to ensure fair competition between national services; 2) encouraging European programme production and reserving a majority of air-time for its diffusion; and 3) defining its necessity as the preservation of cultural and linguistic diversity. The reader is referred to Strover (1989) and Negrine and Papathanassopoulos (1991) for further discussion of the current problems of the public service model of broadcasting.

15. Article 2.2 reads, in part, "Member States shall ensure freedom of reception and shall not restrict retransmission on their territory of television broadcasts from other Member States for reasons which fall within the fields coordinated by this directive" (Commission of the European Communities 1990, 18).

16. Article 5 sets a quota of ten percent of broadcasting time to be reserved for independent European productions (CEC 1990, 19).

17. Of course, the EC is not the only international institution involved in policymaking for the audiovisual industry. The Council of Europe has issued its own Convention on Broadcasting with the approval of the European Broadcasting Union. While similar in content to the EC's Directive, the Council of Europe's Convention does

not recommend quota limitations for extra-European imports, since the Council of Europe and EBU include extra-European countries in their memberships. Despite a wider geographical extension than the Twelve's Directive, however, the Convention is limited in power in that it is only a multilateral agreement between nations.

18. Interestingly, this fact is noted by the directors of Media '95, who write: "This figure [ECU 200 million] may seem small in view of the extent of the challenges to be met by our audiovisual industry, but its true value is clearer when it is known that during the pilot phase of the Programme, every ECU invested by MEDIA generated a turnover of 30 ECU!" (CEC 1991, 7)

References

Bakke, Marit. "Culture at Stake." In: *New Media Politics: Comparative Perspectives in Western Europe.* McQuail, D., and Siune, K., eds., New York: Sage, 1986.

Berkman, Barbara. "Europe's 1995 HDTV goal: A standard of its own." *Electronic Business.* August 20, 1990: 44–45.

Berkowitz, Seth. "European TV Explosion." *Video Times.* Summer/Fall 1989: 63–67.

Collins, Richard, Nicholas Garnham, and Gareth Locksley. *The Economics of Television: The UK Case.* London: Sage, 1988.

Commission of the European Communities. *The European Community Policy in the Audiovisual Field.* Luxembourg: Office for Official Publications of the European Communities, 1990.

Commission of the European Communities. *MEDIA: Guide for the Audiovisual Industry.* Luxembourg: Official Publications of the European Communities, 1991.

Lee, Chin-Chuan. *Media Imperialism Reconsidered: The Homogenizing of Television Culture.* Beverly Hills: Sage, 1979.

Lindheim, James B. "1992: Meeting the Communication Challenge." *Communication World.* July/August 1989: 35–39.

Maggiore, Matteo. *Audiovisual Production in the Single Market.* Luxembourg: Office for Official Publications of the European Communities, 1990.

Mattelart, Armand, Michele Mattelart, and Xavier Delcourt. *International Image Markets: In Search of an Alternative Perspective.* London: Comedia Publishing Group, 1984.

Mattelart, Armand, and Yves Stourdze. *Technology, Culture and Communication: A Report to the French Minister of Research and Industry.* North-Holland: Amsterdam, New York, Oxford, 1985.

McLuhan, Marshall. *Understanding Media: Extensions of Man.* New York: McGraw-Hill, 1964.

McQuail, Denis. *Mass Communication Theory.* New York: Sage, 1987.

McQuail, Denis, and Euromedia Research Group. "Caging the Beast: Constructing a Framework for the Analysis of Media Change in Western Europe." *European Journal of Communication.* 5:313–331, 1990.

Miège, Bernard. *The Capitalization of Cultural Production.* New York: International General, 1989.

Negrine, R., and S. Papathanassopoulos. "The Internationalization of Television." *European Journal of Communication.* 6:9–32, 1991.

Pragnell, Anthony. *Television in Europe: Quality and Values in a Time of Change.* Manchester: The European Institute of Mass Media, Media Monograph No. 5, 1985.

Schiller, Herbert. "The Global Commercialization of Culture." *Directions PCDS.* 4(1):1–4, 1990.

Sepstrup, Preben. "Implications of current developments in West European broadcasting." *Media, Culture and Society.* Vol. 11:29–54, 1989.

———. "Transnationalization of Television in Western Europe." Paper presented to the Seventh Annual Intercultural and International Communication Conference, University of Miami, Florida, February 1990.

Strover, Sharon. "European Communication Policy and Integration." Paper prepared for the Commission on European Communities, December 1989.

Surprenant, Thomas T. "Problems and Trends in International Information and Communication Policies." *Information Processing and Management.* Vol. 23(1):47–64, 1987.

Varis, Tapio. "Global Traffic in Television." *Journal of Communication.* 102–109, Winter 1974.

———. *International Flow of TV Programs.* Unesco Report. Unesco Publications, 1985.

Further Reading

Barnlund, Dean C. *Communicative Styles of Japan and America: Images and Realities.* Belmont, CA: Wadsworth, 1989.

Business America: The Magazine of International Trade. Washington, D.C.: U.S. Department of Commerce (published biweekly).

Copeland, Lennie, and Lewis Griggs. *Going International: How to Make Friends and Deal Effectively in the Global Marketplace.* New York: Random House, 1985.

Europe: The Magazine of the European Community. Washington, D.C.: EC Delegation to the United States (ten times per year).

Europe: World Partner—The External Relations of the European Community. Luxembourg: Office for Official Publications of the European Communities, 1991.

The European Community 1992 and Beyond. Luxembourg: Office for Official Publications of the European Communities, 1991.

The European Community in the Nineties. Washington, D.C.: EC Delegation to the United States, 1992.

Frederick, Howard. *Global Communication and International Relations.* Belmont, CA: Wadsworth Publishing Company, 1993.

Hall, Edward F. *Hidden Differences: Doing Business with Japan.* Garden City, NY: Anchor/Doubleday, 1987.

Haglund, E. "Japan: Cultural Considerations," *International Journal of Intercultural Relations* 8 (1984): 61–76.

Hodgson, Kent. "Adapting Ethical Decisions to a Global Marketplace," *Management Review* (May 1992): 53–57.

Rowland, D. *Japanese Business Etiquette: A Practical Guide to Success in the Global Market Place.* New York: Praeger, 1986.

Terpstra, V., and K. David. *The Cultural Environment of International Business.* Cincinnati: South Western, 1985.

Victor, David. *International Business Communication.* New York: Harper Collins Publishers, 1992.

Contributors

NICHOLAS D. J. BALDWIN is the director of Wroxton College of Fairleigh Dickinson University in Wroxton, England. He has lectured and written widely on political structures and on the European Community. He has stood for Parliament from his native Devon.

RONNIE BANKSTON is professor in the Department of Communication and Theater Arts at the University of Northern Iowa. His Ph.D. is from the University of Iowa.

MITCH BARANOWSKI has served in Brussels, Belgium as a public relations representative for Up With People Europe. He is has an M.A. in international communication from the University of Texas at Austin.

NANCY BLETHEN, APR, is president of her own public relations agency, Blethen Associates. She holds an M.Ed. from Rutgers University.

ANN BOHARA AND PATRICK MCLAURIN, The Wharton School, University of Pennsylvania (1990). Dr. Bohara and Mr. McLaurin's article (Perceptions of Communicative Competence in Organizational Settings) was presented at the *Third Conference on Corporate Communication,* May 1990 as "Styles and Stereotypes: The Relationships Between Corporate and Ethnic Communication." They have revised and updated their text for this book. The article appears here with their permission.

WILLIAM BUCHHOLZ is director of business communications programs at Bentley College. He has published widely including Communication Consulting and Training in Business, Industry and Government. He received his Ph.D. from the University of Illinois, Urbana.

RANDALL CAPPS is head of the Department of Communication and Broadcasting at Western Kentucky University. He has an Ed.D. from the University of Virginia, and has consulted various corporations including General Motors and IBM.

DONALD P. CUSHMAN is professor of communication at SUNY at Albany. He is the co-author of five books on management and high-speed management. He is an active consultant to business.

RICHARD DOETKOTT is professor of communications at Chapman University in Orange, California. He has won awards for TV production and for cultural arts center design.

TIL DALLAVALLE has an M.S. in telecommunications from Polytechnic.

ALICIA ESPOSITO is a Total Quality Management consultant with Bellcore. She has an M.S. in technical communication from Rensselaer Polytechnic Institute.

MICHAEL B. GOODMAN is professor and the director of the M.A. Program in Corporate and Organizational Communication in the Department of English/Communications at Fairleigh Dickinson University.

Before coming to Fairleigh Dickinson University in 1986, he directed the graduate and undergraduate business communications programs at Northeastern University in Boston (1982–86), and he taught business communications and literature courses at New York University, New York Institute of Technology, SUNY/College at Old Westbury, and SUNY at Stony Brook. He is the founder and director of the annual Conference on Corporate Communication sponsored by Fairleigh Dickinson University.

He has published widely. He is also associate editor for Corporate and Organizational Communication of the *IEEE Transactions on Professional Communication,* and guest editor of the June 1989 Special Issue on Corporate Communication. He has presented papers on managerial communication and the proposal writing process at the

International Professional Communication Conference of the IEEE-Professional Communication Society, The Association for Business Communication International Convention, and at the International Technical Communication Conference. In June 1992, he lectured in Moscow.

Goodman is also a consultant to several aerospace companies, medical institutions, manufacturers, and corporations on corporate communication, effective written communication, problem-solving, and new business proposals. He began his consulting practice in 1981.

LORETTA HARPER is vice chancellor for human resources at North Carolina State University. She has a Ph.D. from Georgia State University.

STEVE LANG has an M.S. from Polytechnic University and was director of Corporate Telecommunications Information Systems for Bellcore before becoming an independent consultant.

JULIE LONGO is a senior engineering staff member at Martin Marietta where she manages technical video. She is a Rutgers university graduate.

JAY MORRIS teaches at Ohio University and is the coordinator of Athens Community Television.

LAWRENCE RIFKIND is assistant dean at Georgia State university. He received his Ph.D. in communication from Florida State University.

LAURA TERLIP teaches classes in organizational communication and corporate culture at University of Northern Iowa. She has a Ph.D. from the University of Oklahoma and an M.Sc. in industrial relations from the London School of Economics.

TERRI TOLES-PATKIN teaches organizational communication and telecom policy. Her publications include articles on the theory and technology of video. She has a Ph.D. from Cornell University.

JEANNE STEELE has been a newspaper reporter and public relations professional and has won awards for her videoscriptwriting. She is a doctoral candidate at The University of North Carolina at Chapel Hill.

DULCIE MURDOCK STRAUGHAN is professor of communication at The University of North Carolina at Chapel Hill. She has published widely on communication law and public relations. She holds a Ph.D. from the University of North Carolina.

DAVID L. STURGES is professor at the University of Texas Pan-American. He received his Ph.D. from the University of North Texas.

NANCY VANARSDALE teaches at East Stroudsburg University, and is a consultant to *Time* magazine. She earned her Ph.D. from New York University.

MARGARET WHITNEY earned her Ph.D. at Rensselaer Polytechnic Institute, and works at Albany International Corporation.

KRISTIN WOOLEVER directs the graduate program in technical and professional writing at Northeastern University. She is the author of several books including *Writing for the Computer Industry*. She has a Ph.D. from the University of Pittsburgh.

Name Index

Subject Index

405

HOUGHTON COLLEGE LIBRARY - Houghton, NY

1000216801